P9-DBO-345

TECHNOLOGICAL INNOVATION: GENERATING ECONOMIC RESULTS

ADVANCES IN THE STUDY OF ENTREPRENEURSHIP, INNOVATION AND ECONOMIC GROWTH

Series Editor: Gary D. Libecap

Recent Volumes:

ADVANCES IN THE STUDY OF ENTREPRENEURSHIP,
INNOVATION AND ECONOMIC GROWTH   VOLUME 18

TECHNOLOGICAL INNOVATION: GENERATING ECONOMIC RESULTS

EDITED BY

GARY D. LIBECAP

The University of Arizona, USA

MARIE C. THURSBY

Georgia Institute of Technology, Atlanta, GA, USA

Emerald

United Kingdom – North America – Japan –
India – Malaysia – China

Emerald Group Publishing Limited
Howard House, Wagon Lane, Bingley BD16 1WA, UK

First edition 2008

Copyright © 2008 Emerald Group Publishing Limited

Reprints and permission service
Contact: books@emeraldinsight.com

British Library Cataloguing in Publication Data
A catalogue record for this book is available from the British Library

ISBN: 978-0-7623-1481-2

Awarded in recognition of
Emerald's production
department's adherence to
quality systems and processes
when preparing scholarly
journals for print

INVESTOR IN PEOPLE

CONTENTS

LIST OF CONTRIBUTORS

Margo A. Bagley	University of Virginia School of Law, Charlottesville, VA, USA
William J. Carney	Emory University School of Law, Atlanta, GA, USA
Marco Ceccagnoli	College of Management, Georgia Institute of Technology, Atlanta, GA, USA
Meadow Clendenin	Emory University School of Law, Atlanta, GA, USA
Anne W. Fuller	College of Management, Georgia Institute of Technology, Atlanta, GA, USA
Stuart J.H. Graham	Boalt Hall School of Law, University of California, Berkeley, CA, USA; College of Management, Georgia Institute of Technology, Atlanta, GA, USA
Louise Hallenborg	Lund, Sweden, Malmö, Sweden
Matthew J. Higgins	College of Management, Georgia Institute of Technology, Atlanta, GA, USA
Jill Perry-Smith	Goizueta Business School, Emory University, Atlanta, GA, USA
Anne M. Rector	Emory University School of Law, Atlanta, GA, USA
Frank T. Rothaermel	College of Management, Georgia Institute of Technology, Atlanta, GA, USA
Marie C. Thursby	College of Management, Georgia Institute of Technology, Atlanta, GA, USA
Leslie H. Vincent	University of Kentucky, Gatton College of Business & Economics, Lexington, KY, USA

INTRODUCTION

Marie C. Thursby

Technological innovation is not simply invention, but rather is a process that includes all the steps from the decision to conduct research to the identification of opportunities and paths for that research to contribute to society through diffusion and commercial application. While scientific discovery is central, it is a single (albeit critical) piece of a complex process involving navigation of the business, legal, regulatory, and economic issues that define the innovation landscape.

Understanding the interplay of these issues is difficult at best. A yearly survey by the Industrial Research Institute routinely lists "managing research and development (R&D) for business growth," "integration of R&D and business strategy," and "making innovation happen" among the top five problems in R&D. Moreover, in areas with the most radical advances in science and technology, such as biotechnology and nanotechnology, inventions increasingly emanate from university labs so that commercialization depends on a more complicated web or coordination of university and industry actions – most notably the engagement of entrepreneurial enterprises.

Whether innovation involves coordination within or between institutions, it clearly involves professionals with training from a variety of disciplines. Successful innovation involves inventors who typically are scientists and engineers; corporate or technology transfer professionals who evaluate inventions in terms of commercial potential and develop business models for commercialization; and attorneys involved in various aspects of intellectual property protection. The problem is that each of the professionals involved

Technological Innovation: Generating Economic Results
Advances in the Study of Entrepreneurship, Innovation and
Economic Growth, Volume 18, 1–8
Copyright © 2008 by Elsevier Ltd.
ISSN: 1048-4736/doi:10.1016/S1048-4736(07)00012-4

needs to understand aspects of the others' expertise in order to effectively facilitate both invention and commercialization.

This problem calls for an educational approach that integrates the technological, business, and legal issues involved in innovation. Chapter 8 in this series discussed the design and challenges involved with developing such programs, focusing on a program underway at Georgia Institute of Technology and Emory University (Thursby, 2005). This program, Technological Innovation: Generating Economic Results (TI:GER®), teams PhD students in science and engineering with MBA and JD students to examine issues related to the commercial application of the PhD students' research. Students participate in this two-year program while continuing their respective degree studies. TI:GER® core classes cover topics related to business opportunity recognition, intellectual property protection, multi-disciplinary team functioning, industry analysis, market and financial analysis, strategies for technology commercialization, as well as regulatory and public policy issues.

One of the challenges of integrative programs, particularly at the graduate level, is a lack of curricular materials appropriate for use in this multidisciplinary setting. With students from such disparate backgrounds in the same program, many students will not have sufficient backgrounds in fundamental principles of "the other disciplines." Science and engineering students are unlikely to have taken elementary courses in law, economics, or business. Similarly, the law students may not have studied business or economics, and business students are unlikely to have taken law courses. Thus, there is a need for materials that cover topics at a level that is understandable to all, but not boring to the students who are well versed in their own area of interest.

This volume is a response to that need. Using funds from the Ewing Marion Kauffman Foundation, we engaged TI:GER® faculty to write the eleven chapters that follow. The Kauffman funds are part of a larger grant from the Foundation to support a series of faculty development workshops on the integrative approach to graduation education in technology commercialization and entrepreneurship taken by the TI:GER® program. The authors were asked not only to describe basic principles and/or laws, but also to ground their arguments in rigorous empirical research to the extent possible and to point out where there are disagreements or controversies surrounding these principles. Most of the chapters provide extensive references to academic journals and law reviews for those students who want to pursue topics in more detail. The chapters provide the background for topics covered in the first year of the program and, as such, can be used as a text for a year-long, team-based technology entrepreneurship program. The chapters can also serve as stand alone articles for use in other entrepreneurship programs.

Chapter 1, "Appropriating the Returns from Innovation," by Marco Ceccagnoli and Frank T. Rothaermel, examines why technological invention, which underlies process and product innovations, is often insufficient for the original inventor to reap the rewards from the invention. The authors begin by citing well-known cases, such as the CAT scanner, diet cola, and commercial jets, in which the companies introducing the innovation failed to capture the lion's share of the profits, or Schumpeterian rents, from it. Thus, the authors point to the fact that appropriating the returns to innovation is a key strategic challenge in technology-intensive industries and one that ultimately determines high-tech firms' performance and survival. Using a framework originally developed by Teece (1986), the authors discuss how the *appropriability regime*, which is largely a function of technological and legal factors, and ownership of *specialized complementary assets* interact to determine whether an innovator or imitator is more likely to extract innovation rents, and they consider the strategic options of an innovator attempting to commercialize its innovations. The chapter then reviews empirical evidence from the biotech and pharmaceutical industries in support of the framework. They also highlight the differences across industries in the effectiveness of various legal appropriability mechanisms, such as patents or secrecy, as well as complementary assets.

Chapter 2, "The Benefits and Liabilities of Multidisciplinary Commercialization Teams: How Professional Composition and Social Networks Influence Team Processes," by Jill Perry-Smith and Leslie H. Vincent, focuses on multidisciplinary teams' unique nature, benefits, and challenges when operating in the arena of technology commercialization. The aim of this chapter is to provide students insights into potential problems as they begin working in their TI:GER® teams. The authors first establish that, while multiple experts may benefit a team by enabling creative problem solving and superior performance outcomes, they also bring with them differences (e.g., cultural norms and learning styles) that may undermine team processes. The chapter discusses the impact of team members' external social networks and identifies potential impediments to effective team functioning stemming from the unique composition of multidisciplinary teams. The authors examine task conflict, process conflict, relationship conflict, team versus individual professional identification, and team cohesion.

Chapter 3, "Intellectual Property Protection in the Global Economy," by Louise Hallenborg, Marco Ceccagnoli, and Meadow Clendenin, is the first of three chapters that deals with legal mechanisms for appropriating returns from innovation. The chapter provides an overview of five modes of intellectual property protection – patents, designs, copyrights, trademarks, and trade secrets – available in the United States, the European Union, and Japan. After describing the purposes of and principal differences among the five types of IP protection and outlining the advantages of each form, the chapter provides country- and region-specific information. The authors highlight the aspects of IP law in which international harmonization has, or has not yet, occurred, and offer insights into the relative advantages of various national and regional IP protection systems.

The next two chapters explore patents and other legal mechanisms in more depth. Chapter 4, "Patents and Technology Commercialization: Issues and Opportunities," by Margo A. Bagley, discusses current issues raised by the monopoly power granted to patent holders. After reviewing the way in which patent laws operate in the global marketplace and providing an overview of the US law of patents, the chapter describes the benefits and costs to academia of the impact of the Bayh-Dole Act, which allows universities to capture returns from federally funded inventions. The unintended side effects of Bayh-Dole are illustrated by examining the "publish or profit" predicament facing a hypothetical PhD student who discovers interesting properties of a class of chemical compounds. The chapter also discusses the challenges created by the fact that at the same time Bayh-Dole was passed, the Supreme Court decision in *Diamond v. Chakrabarty* extended patentability to genetically engineered micro-organisms, which opened up patenting to early-stage inventions that are essentially research tools. The chapter concludes by discussing issues of patent licensing and enforcement in university and industry settings and by noting the high degree of flux in the US patent system today.

Chapter 5, "Beyond Patents: The Role of Copyrights, Trademarks, and Trade Secrets in Technology Commercialization," by Stuart J.H. Graham, posits that, while researchers and teachers of university technology transfer often think exclusively in terms of patents and the Bayh-Dole Act, we ought to adopt a more nuanced view of IP rights. The author discusses the primary non-patent types of IP protection, copyright, trademark, and trade secret. He picks up the theme introduced by Ceccagnoli and Rothaermel that while patents are normally the "default" position when we think about protecting technologies and profiting from them, empirical evidence suggests that patents are among the *least* important means of capturing value from innovation. Graham argues that while many consider that IP protections act as substitutes for one another, thinking about IP rights as complements is a more relevant way of approaching this issue. Adopting this more nuanced view better reflects reality and does a superior job of alerting our audiences to the opportunities available in the technology commercialization process. Finally, this chapter discusses the role of copyright and patenting of software, both as enablers and as obstacles, in a model of innovation called "open or community innovation," in which a community of individuals collaboratively creates some technological advance and cedes some portion of their ownership rights in the intellectual capital to the community.

Chapter 6 is the first of three chapters on issues of strategy. In "Marketing Strategy Considerations in the Commercialization of New Technologies: An Overview and Framework for Strategy Development," Leslie H. Vincent, provides an overview of the role of marketing strategy in the commercialization of breakthrough technologies. Identifying market opportunities and developing strategies to take advantage of them are critical for commercialization. While this may seem intuitive, it is often ignored by technology entrepreneurs who tend to focus more on the technology than on markets. This point is particularly salient in the case of university inventions, many of which are nothing more than a proof of concept or lab scale prototype (Jensen & Thursby, 2001). Defining market opportunities for early-stage inventions can be difficult, so much so that many university inventions end up with applications that are not anticipated at the time of license (Shane, 2000; Thursby & Thursby, 2002). This chapter discusses the important concepts and elements that must be considered when developing market applications for breakthrough technologies. The chapter begins by providing an overview of marketing strategy in general, as well as the performance implications associated with effective strategy development and implementation. The discussion then focuses on three critical decisions that must be made early on in the strategy development process: target market selection, segmentation, and positioning. These strategic decisions are then related to the more tactical considerations related to the specific elements, or marketing mix, of a product's marketing strategy.

Chapter 7, "Competitive Advantage in Technology Intensive Industries," by Frank T. Rothaermel, turns to a more general view of strategy. The chapter introduces the reader to the meaning of competitive advantage and posits that a firm's strategy is defined as the managers' theory about how to gain and sustain competitive advantage. The author demonstrates how a firm creates its competitive advantage by creating more economic value than its rivals, and explains that profitability depends upon value, price, and costs. The relationship among these factors is explored in the context of high-technology consumer goods – laptop computers and cars. Next, the chapter explains the SWOT [s(trengths) w(eaknesses) o(pportunities) t(hreats)] analysis. Examining the interplay of firm resources, capabilities, and competencies, the chapter emphasizes that both must be present to possess core competencies essential to gaining and sustaining competitive advantage through strategy. Next, the chapter describes the value chain by which a firm transforms inputs into outputs, adding value at each stage through the primary activities of research, development, production, marketing and sales, and customer service, which in turn rely upon essential support activities that add value indirectly. After describing the PEST [p(olitical) e(conomic) s(ocial) t(echnological)] Model for assessing a firm's general external environment, the chapter explains Porter's Five Forces Model. The chapter then describes the strategic group model and illustrates that model by reference to the pharmaceutical industry. The author notes that opportunities and threats to a company differ based upon the strategic group to which that firm belongs within an industry. Finally, the chapter explores the importance of strategy in technology-intensive industries and emphasizes that sustained competitive advantage can be accomplished only through continued innovation.

Chapter 8, "Technology Commercialization: Cooperative versus Competitive Strategies," by Anne W. Fuller and Marie C. Thursby, presents a framework for evaluating commercialization strategies available to start-up innovators operating in high technology industries. The authors draw on a stream of research by Gans, Hsu, and Stern, which shows that whether firms commercialize their inventions by entering existing product markets in competition with incumbent firms or take what is called a cooperative approach, forming some type of alliance varies significantly across industries and inventions (Gans, Hsu, & Stern, 2002; Gans & Stern, 2003). The chapter first describes the options available to an innovator and explains how the attractiveness of alliances versus competition is affected by three factors: intellectual property rights' strength, requisite complementary assets, and licensing/alliance transaction costs. As explained, the attractiveness of alliances as compared to product market competition increases both with the strength of the innovator's IP rights and the cost of acquiring the needed complementary assets. The four distinct commercialization environments defined by these factors then are related to the likelihood an innovator will commercialize an invention through cooperation or competition. The chapter then applies the framework to five case studies of start-up innovators in a major research university's business incubator.

The final three chapters focus on financial issues in commercialization. Chapter 9, "Introduction to Finance and Valuing Early Stage Technology," by Matthew J. Higgins, is a basic guide to introduce students to different techniques utilized to value new technologies. Estimating a value for early-stage technologies or ventures is, in general, challenging in large part because of uncertainty. Many types of uncertainty are involved, including uncertainty with respect to a technology's probability of success, uncertainty with respect to the actual market that will be served, uncertainty that the market will be there when a product based on the technology arrives, and uncertainty with respect to projects costs and revenues. While all these challenges exist in the valuation of new technologies, it does not suggest that one should just simply throw their hands in the air and not attempt a rigorous valuation exercise. Completing a valuation cannot be done within a black box, and this chapter provides an introduction to various techniques. The chapter begins with a review of sources for funding, which range from friends/family/bootstrap investors and "angel" investors to government grants, strategic alliance partners, venture capitalists, and public debt or equity markets or internal funds. The chapter then turns to a review of the foundation of corporate finance – the time value of money – and moves through brief discussions on discounted cash flow, decision tree analysis, Monte-Carlo analysis, and real option analysis. The chapter ends with a discussion emphasizing the need to place valuation into a larger context of firm control rights and ownership.

Chapter 10, "Venture Capital Financing and Documentation," by William J. Carney, outlines the steps involved in obtaining venture capital funding for a start-up business. The chapter first discusses access to VCs and provides the reasons behind VCs' preference for investing in a traditional C corporation rather than a limited liability company or other pass-through entity. The author then describes both the due diligence performed by VC's counsel and the documentation a start-up must provide to satisfy that diligence need. Next, the chapter addresses typical terms of financing deals with VCs, including the types of securities issued and the rights, preferences, and pricing of those securities. Finally, the chapter concludes with a chart identifying the VC financing terms available before and after a significant market downturn, as well as a sample term sheet summarizing the terms of preferred stock to be issued to a hypothetical VC or VC group investing in a start-up business.

Chapter 11, "The Anatomy of Contracts in Licensing: The Context of Bayh-Dole," by Anne M. Rector and Marie C. Thursby, explains the structure of two contracts commonly involved in university licensing: the license granting a company (or companies) outside the university rights to make, sell, or lease products or processes based on a university invention, and the nondisclosure agreement (NDA) that plays a role in the license negotiation process. The chapter explains that license contracts often contain a complex combination of payment terms intended to provide sufficient incentives for licensees to undertake the (often risky) development of embryonic research. The chapter discusses these incentives in the context of the Bayh-Dole Act discussed in Chapter 4. While that chapter discussed broad issues, this chapter relates the intent of the Act to contract terms as due diligence to address the concerns of university licensing professionals (which are framed by the Act) who often negotiate licensing agreements. The chapter then examines the same incentive issues (and the universal contract issues of money, risk, control, standards, and endgame) in the context of nondisclosure agreements, used by potential licensing partners to protect their respective interests while sharing information about a licensable technology. The chapter concludes with an assignment that provides students with an opportunity to evaluate both a license and a nondisclosure agreement, not from the university's perspective but from that of a client interested in licensing an invention.

REFERENCES

Gans, J. S., Hsu, D. H., & Stern, S. (2002). When does start-up innovation spur the gale of creative destruction? *RAND Journal of Economics*, *33*(4), 571–586.

Gans, J. S., & Stern, S. (2003). The product market and the market for "ideas": Commercialization strategies for technology entrepreneurs. *Research Policy*, *32*, 333–350.

Jensen, R., & Thursby, M. C. (2001). Proofs and prototypes for sale: The licensing of university inventions. *The American Economic Review*, *91*(1), 240–259.

Shane, S. (2000). Prior knowledge and the discovery of entrepreneurial opportunities. *Organization Science*, *11*, 448–469.

Teece, D. J. (1986). Profiting from technological innovation: Implications for integration, collaboration, licensing and public policy. *Research Policy*, *15*, 285–305.

Thursby, J., & Thursby, M. C. (2002). Who is selling the ivory tower? Sources of growth in university licensing. *Management Science*, *48*, 90–104.

Thursby, M. C. (2005). Introducing technology entrepreneurship to graduate education: An integrative approach. In: G. B. Libecap (Ed.), University entrepreneurship and technology transfer. *Advances in the study of entrepreneurship, innovation, and economic growth* (Vol. 16, pp. 211–240). London: Elsevier.

PART I:
THE INNOVATION PROCESS:
A MULTIDISCIPLINARY
APPROACH

CHAPTER 1

APPROPRIATING THE RETURNS FROM INNOVATION

Marco Ceccagnoli and Frank T. Rothaermel

ABSTRACT

This chapter explores the extent to which an innovator is able to capture innovation rents. After examining the two main drivers of such rents, the strength of the appropriability regime and the ownership of specialized complementary assets, the chapter examines how their interaction is so critical in affecting imitation, commercialization options, and firm performance. After reviewing the underlying conceptual framework and empirical evidence, and using a perspective that cuts across both time and industries, the authors then discuss the implications of innovation profits for the resources to be devoted to the discovery of new or improved product and processes.

1. INTRODUCTION

Although significant science and engineering competencies are needed to invent new processes and products, technological prowess that underlies process and product innovations is simply not enough to benefit from innovation. While invention is a necessary first step to innovation, it is not

Technological Innovation: Generating Economic Results
Advances in the Study of Entrepreneurship, Innovation and
Economic Growth, Volume 18, 11–34
ISSN: 1048-4736/doi:10.1016/S1048-4736(07)00001-X

sufficient for commercial success (Teece, 1986). Innovators frequently fail to appropriate the returns to their innovations. This implies that protecting the returns to innovation is a key strategic challenge in technology-intensive industries. Commercially successful innovations create temporary monopolies, which in turn enable firms to extract transitory Schumpeterian rents. In high-technology industries, competitive advantage can be sustained only through a string of continuous innovations.[1] Thus, a firm's ability to appropriate rents from innovation determines its performance and continued survival.

Table 1 depicts several high-profile examples in which innovators lost to imitators, because the innovators were unable to appropriate the returns to their own innovation(s). Why does this happen so frequently? To answer this question, we focus on two factors highlighted by Teece's seminal treatise on profiting from technological innovation: the appropriability regime and the complementary assets (Teece, 1986; Abernathy & Utterback, 1978; Anderson & Tushman, 1990). Today, it is widely accepted that innovators seeking to profit from their inventions must understand the strength of the appropriability regime and the nature of the complementary assets required to commercialize their inventions.

The commercialization of the CAT scanner provides a well-known example in which the innovator, Electrical Musical Instruments (EMI), lost to the imitator, GE Medical Systems.[2] In the 1970s, EMI was a widely diversified British multinational corporation holding, for example, the rights to The Beatles records and competing in phonographic records, movies, and advanced electronics. Based on breakthrough research conducted in the 1960s by Godfrey Hounsfield, a senior research engineer at EMI (and 1976 Nobel Laureate in Medicine), EMI developed the CAT scanner, originally

Table 1.   Innovators Failing to Appropriate the Returns to Innovation.

Innovator	Innovation	Lost to Imitator
EMI	CAT scanner	GE Medical Systems
RC Cola	Diet cola	Coca-Cola and Pepsi
Bowmar	Pocket calculator	TI, HP
DeHavilland	Commercial jet	Boeing
Ampex	Video recorder	Matsushita
MITS	PC	Apple, IBM
Xerox	GUI interface	Apple, Microsoft
Prodigy	Online service	AOL, EarthLink, other ISPs

designed to take three-dimensional pictures of the brain, and later of the entire human body. This invention is hailed as the most significant technological breakthrough in radiology since William Conrad Röntgen (Nobel Laureate in Physics, 1901) discovered the use of X-rays for imaging in 1895. Moreover, the invention of the CAT scanner paved the way for follow-up innovations like nuclear magnetic resonance tomography.

In spring 1972, EMI launched the CAT scanner. Despite being aware that it lacked some of the requisite manufacturing and distribution assets, EMI decided to go it alone rather than to license its technology to a strong incumbent in medical devices like GE Medical Systems. Prior to market entry, the EMI management had little understanding of how effectively their patents would protect their innovation, and of the importance of complementary assets such as large-scale manufacturing and a distribution and marketing network. Still, EMI was able to create enormous excitement about its breakthrough innovation, which was first demonstrated at a medical conference.

Based on its technological lead, EMI became the market leader worldwide early on, with a strong position in the United States. Yet EMI was unable to sustain this lead because it could not satisfy the surge in demand, given its limited production capabilities, or solve the technological problems it encountered when setting up a production facility in the United States. By the mid-1970s, entrants into the CAT scanner business, like GE Medical Systems and others with strong technological and complementary assets, began to capture significant market share from EMI. It is important to recall that GE did not invent the CAT scanner, but GE soon became the market leader because it possessed the requisite complementary assets necessary to succeed in this new market – especially large-scale manufacturing and a distribution network combined with a strong technical maintenance force. On the other hand, the innovator, EMI, was unable to acquire or develop the needed complementary assets to sustain its initial lead. This deficiency eventually led EMI to exit the market. To add insult to injury, the poor-performing unit EMI Medical was acquired by GE Medical Systems.

The CAT scanner example clearly highlights the competitive race between innovators and imitators. The innovator (EMI) races to acquire complementary assets, and the imitator (GE Medical Systems) races to build the technological assets necessary to create the innovation, frequently through reverse engineering, and without infringing on the innovator's patents.

2. APPROPRIABILITY REGIME AND COMPLEMENTARY ASSETS: THE TEECE FRAMEWORK

EMI's strategy neglected the two most important determinants of innovation profits: the *appropriability regime* and the *specialized complementary assets.*

The *appropriability regime* mainly depends on legal and technological factors. On one hand, the realization of rents from innovation depends on strong, or effective, intellectual property rights (IPR) protection by the legal system. On the other hand, characteristics of technology, such as degree of codification, complexity, and ease of reverse engineering, determine the height of barriers to imitation, which in turn affect the ease with which rivals can imitate the innovation. In the EMI case, while the CAT scanner was a remarkable advance in medical technology, it only re-combined simple and well-known computing, X-ray, and imaging technologies in a new, albeit revolutionary, way. Once the idea of re-combining the different elements became widely known, it was difficult to protect because it was easy to replicate through reverse engineering. Moreover, patents were not effectively enforced by both companies and courts, partly due to fears of their anti-competitive effects and partly due to the view that patents were a cost- rather than profit-generating activity. As a result, the appropriability regime that EMI faced when commercializing the CAT scanner was weak.

The second fundamental component of appropriability is the ownership of *specialized complementary assets.* Teece (1986) highlighted the importance of complementary assets in understanding the performance implications of a new technology when he examined the reason many innovators were unable to capture the economic rents flowing from their innovations. He argued that the commercialization of an innovation 'requires that the know-how in question be utilized in conjunction with other capabilities or assets. Services such as marketing, competitive manufacturing, and after-sales support are almost always needed. These services are obtained from complementary assets, which are specialized' (Teece, 1986, p. 288). The commercialization of the CAT scanner provides a compelling example: the innovator, EMI, lost to the follower, GE Medical Systems, because EMI lacked specialized complementary assets.

In his conceptual framework, Teece (1986) differentiated among three different types of complementary assets: generic, specialized, and cospecialized. *Complementary assets* that are *generic* need not be adjusted to the innovation, because they can frequently be contracted for in the market on competitive terms. General purpose manufacturing equipment falls into this category. *Specialized complementary assets* exhibit unilateral dependence between the innovation and the complementary assets, and *cospecialized complementary assets* are characterized by a bilateral dependence. GE Medical System's stellar reputation for quality and service in hospital equipment is considered a specialized complementary asset, whereas specialized repair facilities for Mazda's rotary engine would be a cospecialized complementary asset. Because the distinction between unilateral and bilateral dependence of the complementary assets and the innovation in question is not critical to our analysis, we use the term specialized complementary assets here to denote both specialized and cospecialized complementary assets.

Why are complementary assets so critical in commercializing innovation? When large-scale and high-quality manufacturing capabilities are necessary complementary assets, the owner of such assets is in a position to satisfy a large surge in customer demand, while maintaining product quality. A lack of large-scale manufacturing capabilities was the reason, for example, that innovator Immunex, a biotechnology firm, lost out to second-mover Johnson & Johnson, a healthcare conglomerate, in commercializing a biotechnology-based drug for rheumatoid arthritis. Immunex was the innovator in this market through its breakthrough development of the drug Enbrel in 1998, and its sales reached quickly $750 million in 2001. Surprised by the large demand for its highly successful new drug, Immunex had not created the necessary large-scale manufacturing capabilities to satisfy such an exponential surge in demand. This strategic oversight provided Johnson & Johnson an opportunity to enter the market for biotechnology-based rheumatoid arthritis drugs with its own product (Remicade), developed by its fully owned subsidiary Centocor, which by 2002 had closed the lead held by Immunex's Enbrel. Immunex's innovative advantage dissipated due to a lack of the necessary complementary assets in manufacturing (Hill & Jones, 2007).

Moreover, a large-scale manufacturing capability allows the company to ride down the experience curve faster due to learning effects and scale economies, and thus reach a low-cost position that is not attainable by competitors lacking such manufacturing capabilities. This was precisely one of the problems EMI faced. While it built a manufacturing plant in the United States to supply the largest market for medical devices in the world, EMI was unable to create a manufacturing capability necessary to produce the quantity and quality that would satisfy demand in the United States.

This problem exacerbated another problem faced by EMI: its lack of knowledge of the U.S. market for medical equipment and the way hospitals purchase and maintain such high-ticket items. As a case in point, in the U.K., due to the nature of its socialized healthcare system, only a few regional hospitals are equipped with expensive medical devices like CAT scanners or MRI systems; thus, the market for such high-ticket items is relatively thin. This was the mental mindset of EMI's managers when entering the U.S. market. They did not realize that in the United States, competition among hospitals is decentralized, and hospitals compete with one another precisely by providing the latest advances in medical devices. Thus, most hospitals in the United States are equipped with a set of high-ticket items such as CAT scanners. Overall, the delivery of healthcare in the United States is much more capital-intensive than in Europe, where it tends to be more labor-intensive. This difference has significant implications for the demand for medical devices and explains the surge in U.S. demand for CAT scanners, which EMI had not anticipated.

In summary, strategy scholars have highlighted the importance of ownership of specialized complementary assets in profiting from innovation. These assets are frequently built over long periods of time and thus are path dependent and idiosyncratic (Teece, Pisano, & Shuen, 1997). Their market availability is limited because firms tend to gain control over them to avoid potential bargaining problems. Overall, specialized complementary assets constitute the bulk of a firm's resources and capabilities that are valuable and difficult to imitate, and they can therefore be a source of sustainable competitive advantage (Barney, 1991).

2.1. Interaction between Appropriability Regime and Complementary Assets

In this section, we discuss who – the innovator or imitator – is more likely to extract innovation rents. In Section 2.2, we discuss in more detail the strategic options on which an innovator can draw when attempting to commercialize its innovations.

The interaction between the strength of the appropriability regime and the ownership of specialized complementary assets determines the degree to which firms profit from their innovations. A strong appropriability regime is typically sufficient to capture at least a positive fraction of the innovation rents. But even in such a case, a greater degree of specialization in complementary assets corresponds to greater rents for its owner. When the innovator owns such assets, it can capture almost all of the value associated with its innovation. When assets are specialized and owned by a different firm, rents have to be shared through an alliance, which in high-tech industries typically takes the form of technology licensing agreements (discussed in Chapter 8), such as in the pharmaceutical industry after the emergence of biotechnology (Rothaermel, 2001a, 2001b; Rothaermel & Hill, 2005). Teece's (1986) conceptual framework depicting the interaction between the appropriability regime and the complementary assets is summarized in Fig. 1.

The case of weak appropriability is analyzed by Teece in greater detail, most likely because during the decades preceding his work, courts typically provided weak protection to patent holders. Weak appropriability and generic complementary assets seem to be the unfortunate case of many entrepreneurial ventures seeking to 'build a better mousetrap.' Think about simple toys, for example, where entrepreneurial inventors often introduce tiny improvements from which they hope to generate quick revenues. Such simple inventions, however, are easily imitated and complementary assets are easily acquired, with customers appropriating most of the value created by the innovations.

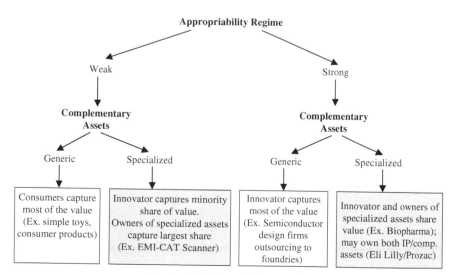

Fig. 1. The Teece Framework.

The combination of a weak appropriability regime and specialized complementary assets typically allows the owners of such assets to capture the lion's share of the value created by the innovation. This is the case exemplified by the EMI/GE race.

With stronger appropriability, the innovator usually captures a greater share of the profits. It may be able to capture most of the profits if it is able to easily acquire the necessary complementary assets. When specialized assets are required, an alliance should allow the parties to earn a return commensurate with the assets they bring to the table and with their respective bargaining power. A strong appropriability regime typically safeguards the innovator, which can disclose and protect its inventions to its potential alliance partners without fear of imitation. A strong appropriability regime does not simply happen by coincidence, but can be strategically enacted by the innovator not only through patenting, but also through following up with aggressive patent litigation. The U.S. semiconductor firm Intel is said to follow such a legal strategy (Somaya, 2003).

2.2. Appropriability Regime, Complementary Assets, and Commercialization Strategies

Innovations create opportunities for companies to capture first-mover advantages and thus temporary monopolies (Hill & Jones, 2007). But how should the innovator leverage its innovation towards commercial success and sustained competitive advantage? While we have focused more on theoretical descriptions by highlighting who captures the rents to innovation above, in this section we focus on the strategies available to the innovator in a more normative fashion: answering the question what an innovator *should do* given certain scenarios.

An innovator basically has three strategic options at its disposal: (1) develop and commercialize the innovation itself, if necessary, through forward vertical integration; (2) develop and commercialize the innovation jointly with a partner through strategic alliances or a joint venture; and (3) license the innovation to another company or companies, and let them develop and market the innovation in exchange for royalties. The optimal strategy to be pursued depends upon (1) the availability and the type of complementary assets; (2) the height of imitation barriers, addressing the degree of difficulty of imitating the innovation by competitors (which is determined by the appropriability regime); and (3) the number of capable competitors, which interact with the strength of the appropriability regime in determining the likelihood of imitation.

The first question the innovator must answer is whether it possesses the necessary complementary assets to commercialize the new technology. We discussed different types of complementary assets above. Assuming the innovator possesses specialized complementary assets to commercialize the innovation, the next question to consider is the height of barriers to imitation. These barriers define the degree of difficulty competitors face when attempting to imitate the innovation. Assuming the barriers to imitation are high, due to a strong appropriability regime, and the number of capable competitors is low, the inventor should go it alone – i.e., pursue a forward vertical integration strategy. The innovator will then be in a position to leverage its complementary assets to extract monopoly rents from the innovation, and barriers to imitation will delay entry. If the number of capable competitors remains low, the innovator might be able to build a sustained competitive advantage.

More often than not, however, the innovator does not possess the required complementary assets to commercialize the innovation. If the barriers to imitation remain high (due to a strong appropriability regime) and the number of capable competitors is not too large, the innovator may profit from the innovation through developing it jointly with the holder of complementary assets through an alliance or joint venture. While an alliance is a contractual agreement between two independent parties to share knowledge and resources and to co-develop product and processes, joint ventures are newly established third entities generally created by two parent companies to accomplish certain tasks, such as developing a new product or process. Alliances tend to be non-equity, contract-based cooperative agreements, whereas joint ventures are equity-based through setting up a third organization. As a consequence, non-equity alliances are much more frequent, although joint ventures are considered to establish stronger ties between firms. Intensive inter-firm cooperation based on alliances and joint ventures is a scenario that has played out in the pharmaceutical industry after the emergence of biotechnology; thus, one can now observe a (temporary) cooperative equilibrium between the innovating biotechnology firms and the large incumbent pharmaceutical companies (Teece, 1992; Gans & Stern, 2000; Rothaermel, 2000). In this industry, thousands of alliances and joint ventures have been documented in which the returns to innovation are shared by biotechnology and pharmaceutical companies (Rothaermel & Deeds, 2004). The distribution of rents, in turn, depends on the relative bargaining power of each party.

If the innovator lacks the necessary complementary assets and the barriers to imitation are low due to a weak appropriability regime combined with a large number of capable competitors, then the innovator should license the innovation to at least capture some of the innovation rents. Not only does imitation generally cost only 40–60% of the innovation, but imitation of an innovation through reverse engineering, for example, also is frequently possible within a few short years. While EMI held patents on its CAT scanner, the barriers to imitation were low, because GE Medical Systems (one of the first customers to purchase a CAT scanner from EMI) was able to quickly imitate the CAT scanner through reverse engineering and thus invent around EMI's thicket of patents. Thus, the barriers to imitation for the CAT scanner were low. Moreover, EMI faced a very capable and aggressive competitor in GE Medical Systems. Given this situation, EMI probably would have been better off either to enter into an alliance or joint venture or to license the commercialization of the CAT scanner directly to GE Medical Systems.

The decision between these two remaining strategic options depends on the appropriability regime, which appeared to be weak initially when the CAT scanner was first commercialized. This implies that EMI probably would have done best to license its innovation to GE Medical Systems. This is exactly the strategy Microsoft followed when faced with the question of how to commercialize its MS-DOS operation system. It opted for a non-exclusive license to IBM, which (involuntarily) aided Microsoft in making MS-DOS the first and only industry standard for operating systems in the PC industry. Microsoft was able to defend this lead for over 25 years, through continuing innovations that leveraged the standard created through widespread adoption of MS-DOS. Microsoft's innovation strategy thus resulted in a sustainable competitive advantage.

Finding an appropriate partner to leverage the partner's complementary assets to commercialize an innovation may not always be this straightforward, because alliances often enable one partner to learn more than the other, and thus capabilities are frequently transferred. Here, the holder of complementary assets would be interested in obtaining the R&D capabilities of the innovator, while protecting its complementary assets. The innovator has the opposite motivation. The result is that learning races frequently ensue in alliances, especially in alliances initiated to commercialize innovations (Hamel, 1991). Note that often the holder of specialized complementary assets is more advantageously positioned to learn, and thus to appropriate innovation capabilities, because these firms tend to be larger and thus have more resources at their proposal, combined with an existing

R&D capability. In contrast, innovators frequently lack any competence in complementary assets, especially if those assets are downstream value chain activities like large-scale manufacturing, distribution, and after-sales service. Innovative firms tend to be small research-intensive outfits that exclusively focus on discovery and early-stage development of new products and processes.

Going it alone through vertical integration may have to be achieved, absent any appropriate partners. Not infrequently, major innovations require complementary assets that are unavailable in the market, yet their nature is specialized and requires significant sunk investments to be successfully commercialized. Downstream integration frequently takes substantial time if the capabilities are to be built from scratch. In such a case, both the demand for licensing and the potential rents to be realized are very low or absent, whereas the potential commercial success could be high. The key challenge, here, is to find a partner willing to share the financial risks of developing the cospecialized assets. With weak appropriability, however, partners may well be unwilling to share such risks, which are exacerbated by the high likelihood of imitation. Downstream integration remains the only alternative left. This option should be pursued only if the investment is expected to yield positive net returns to the innovator, a principle that should always guide rational investment decisions.

3. PROFITING FROM INNOVATION: EMPIRICAL EVIDENCE

While we discussed theoretical decision points on how to commercialize an innovation, what does the empirical literature tell us about how well these theoretical conjectures hold up? Overall, the theoretical model presented holds up pretty well. Rothaermel and Hill (2005), for example, found support for the notion that the type of complementary assets (generic versus specialized) needed to commercialize a new technology is critical in determining the industry- and firm-level performance implications of a competence-destroying technological discontinuity. Competence-destroying technological discontinuities are radical innovations that emerge exogenous to incumbent industries, and to which established firms must respond to ensure continued survival.

At the industry level, Rothaermel and Hill (2005) hypothesized, incumbent industry performance declines if the new technology can be commercialized through generic complementary assets, whereas incumbent industry performance improves if the new technology can be commercialized through specialized complementary assets. At the firm level, they posited, an incumbent firm's financial strength has a stronger positive impact on firm performance in the post-discontinuity time period if the new technology can be commercialized through generic complementary assets. They further hypothesized, however, that an incumbent firm's R&D capability has a stronger positive impact on firm performance in the post-discontinuity time period if the new technology has to be commercialized through specialized complementary assets. Drawing on multi-industry, time series, and panel data over a 26-year period to analyze pre- and post-discontinuity industry and firm performance, they found broad support for their theoretical model. Their findings are summarized in Table 2.

Further, several empirical studies find evidence for the innovation framework described on the right-hand side of Fig. 1 (Rothaermel, 2001a; Rothaermel, 2001b). Most of these studies have focused on the pharmaceutical industry after the emergence of biotechnology. Here, the appropriability regime is relatively strong, especially after the Supreme Court decision in 1980 that new life forms can be patented (*Diamond v. Chakrabarty*, 447 U.S. 303 (1980)). Moreover, specialized complementary assets (in the form of large-scale manufacturing, clinical trial, and regulatory management) as well as large sales forces are critical in commercializing new biotechnology drugs. Since the scientific breakthrough of genetic engineering in the mid-1970s, numerous new biotechnology entrants demand access to the market for pharmaceuticals, which is controlled by a few incumbent pharmaceutical firms. These incumbent pharmaceutical firms have developed path-dependent, firm-specific competencies with respect to certain drug and disease areas that are valuable, rare, and difficult to imitate; thus, these competencies may, according to the resource-based view of the firm, form a basis of a competitive advantage (Barney, 1991). For example, Eli Lilly enjoys a dominant position in human insulin and growth hormones, while Hoffman-La Roche has developed a strong hold in anti-anxiety drugs. This degree of specialization reduces the number of potential strategic alliance partners for new biotechnology firms and further accentuates the value of the incumbents' downstream, market-related value chain activities – i.e., specialization enhances the value of their complementary assets.

Hence, these incumbents can benefit from the technological breakthrough in biotechnology to the extent it enables them to create and extract innovation rents based on their specialized complementary assets, through strategic alliances, joint ventures, and licensing agreements with new

Table 2. Technological Discontinuities, Complementary Assets, and Incumbent Industry and Firm Performance (Rothaermel & Hill, 2005).

Technological Discontinuity	Industry Examples	Impact on Incumbent Upstream Technological Competencies	Type of Complementary Assets Needed to Commercialize New Technology	Impact on Downstream Complementary Assets	Effect on Incumbent Industry Performance	Stronger Effect on Incumbent Firm Performance
PC, Electric arc furnace	Computer, steel	Destroying	Generic	Destroying	Decline	Financial strength
Biotechnology, wireless telephony	Pharmaceutical, telecommunications	Destroying	Specialized	Enhancing	Improvement	R&D capability

Table 3.   Top-Ten Biotechnology Drugs, 2001.

Product	Indication	2001 Sales (millions)	Developer	Marketer
Procrit	Red blood cell enhancement	3,430	Amgen	Johnson & Johnson
Epogen	Red blood cell enhancement	2,109	Amgen	Amgen
Intron A	Hepatitis C, certain cancers	1,447	Biogen	Schering-Plough
Neupogen	Restoration of white blood cells	1,346	Amgen	Amgen
Humulin	Diabetes	1,061	Genentech	Lilly
Avonex	Multiple sclerosis	972	Biogen	Biogen
Rituxan	B-cell non-Hodgkin's lymphoma	819	IDEC	Genentech, IDEC
Enbrel	Rheumatoid arthritis	762	Immunex	AHP, Immunex
Remicade	Rheumatoid arthritis, Chron's disease	721	MedImmune	Johnson & Johnson
Cerezyme	Enzyme replacement therapy	570	Genzyme	Genzyme

Source: Standard and Poor's Biotechnology Industry Report, May 2002.

biotechnology firms. The emergence of a cooperative equilibrium in the biopharmaceutical industry has also been highlighted by other researchers and is exemplified in Table 3, which depicts the top-ten selling biotechnology drugs in 2001.

What is interesting to note is that none of the top-ten selling drugs was developed by the incumbent pharmaceutical companies. Thus, all new biotechnology drugs were discovered and developed by new biotechnology firms leveraging their R&D competencies in the new biotechnology paradigm. About half of these drugs were commercialized by incumbent pharmaceutical companies. This empirical outcome is in line with Teece's theoretical predictions (Teece, 1986, 1992).

It is important to note, however, that more recently several more biotechnology companies were able to integrate downstream, as there are now fewer cooperative arrangements between biotechnology ventures and large pharmaceutical companies to commercialize new drugs. Rothaermel and Deeds (2004) document a new product development process based on an alliance system orchestrated by biotechnology companies, by which the biotechnology firms reach upstream to universities for basic knowledge, and then downstream to pharmaceutical companies to commercialize their innovations. While this integrated new product development process resonates with Teece's framework, Rothaermel and Deeds also demonstrate that the new biotechnology companies withdraw from this integrated product development process in a discriminate fashion, as the new venture accrues more resources to discover, develop, and commercialize promising projects through vertical integration. They empirically tested their model on a sample of 325 biotechnology firms that entered into 2,565 alliances over a 25-year period; they found broad support for the hypothesized product development system and the negative moderating effect of firm size. Thus, the effect of complementary assets on firm performance is likely to change over time.

This finding also resonates with the recent study of Rothaermel and Boeker (2008), who found, through studying over 32,000 dyads (i.e., pairs) between pharmaceutical and biotechnology companies over time, that a pharmaceutical company and a biotechnology firm are more likely to enter into an alliance based on complementarities when the biotechnology firm is younger. This finding echoes the theoretical conjecture above that the holder of complementary assets (e.g., a large pharmaceutical firm) is more likely to acquire the R&D skills necessary to create the innovation from the innovator (e.g., a biotech start-up) than the other way around. Evidence from litigation provides further support for this notion. For example, the first biotechnology drug to be commercialized was Humulin, a human insulin, which was discovered and developed by the biotechnology firm Genentech and commercialized by the pharmaceutical company Eli Lilly in 1982. Later, however, Genentech sued Lilly, accusing it of misusing materials provided by Genentech to commercialize recombinant human insulin. In other words, Lilly was concerned that Genentech had appropriated relevant R&D skills through their alliance to commercialize Humulin.

Differences in the strength of complementary assets have also been documented across different industries. Both changes in appropriability over time and across industries are analyzed in Section 3.1.

3.1. Degree of Appropriability and Inter-Industry Differences: Empirical Evidence

Systematic empirical evidence on the effectiveness of different appropriability strategies for the U.S. manufacturing sector is available from the 1983

Yale University survey and the 1994 Carnegie Mellon University (CMU) survey, summarized for selected industries in Table 4 (Levin, Klevorick, Nelson, & Winter, 1987; Cohen, Nelson, & Walsh, 2000).

Focusing on the more recent CMU survey first, Table 4 suggests that the most effective mechanisms to protect product innovations across a wide number of industries is secrecy, closely followed by being first to market, which captures the effectiveness of first mover advantages (Lieberman & Montgomery, 1988). The ownership of specialized complementary assets represents the third most effective mechanism, whereas patent protection is rated as the least effective relative to these other mechanisms.

Several policy and management changes lead us to expect that the relative strength of different appropriability strategies has changed since the early 1980s, about the time during which the earlier Yale survey was conducted. In particular, belief in the importance of patents and intellectual property (IP) protection in stimulating innovation is the main economic rationale underpinning the trend towards a strengthening of IP protection that has characterized the last two decades, particularly in the United States. In 1982, the Court of Appeals for the Federal Circuit was established to make patent protection more uniform. Indirectly, this also strengthened patent protection. Plaintiff success rates, as well as damages in infringement, have also risen. In the early 1980s, we also witnessed an expansion of what can be patented, when the courts decided that life forms and software were both patentable. Patent coverage has been extended recently to business methods as well. Patents have also become a growing preoccupation of management.

The comparison between the earlier 1983 Yale survey and the 1994 CMU survey, shown in Table 4, confirms that substantial changes in appropriability conditions have taken place in the United States over time and across industries, as perceived by survey respondents.[3] The data highlight that patents are more recently perceived as significantly more important, with almost a 30% increase in the percentage of firms within industries ranking patents as the first or second most important mechanism of appropriation. Being first to market is also slightly more important, whereas ownership of complementary assets is slightly less important to protect the competitive advantage from an innovation. The sharper difference is related to the effectiveness of secrecy, with a change in the perceived effectiveness of over 90%.

Sharper differences across time characterize some industries, such as computers, machinery, and controlling devices. Such variations reflect the fact that the strength of appropriability has an important endogenous component: exogenous changes in the appropriability regime may have a

Table 4. Comparing the 1983 Yale and 1994 CMU Appropriability Surveys: Selected High-Tech Industries[a].

	Number of Observations		% Firms within Industries Ranking Appropriability Strategy as First or Second Most Important											
			Patent Protection			Secrecy			Being First to Market			Complementary Assets		
	Yale	CMU	Yale	CMU	% Change	Yale	CMU	% Change	Yale	CMU	% Change	Yale	CMU	% Change
Industrial chemicals	73	52	0.75	0.78	4%	0.59	0.98	66%	0.80	0.68	-15%	0.79	0.78	-1%
Drugs and medicines	17	47	0.94	0.80	-15%	0.53	0.91	72%	0.71	0.71	1%	0.71	0.51	-28%
General industrial machinery	32	18	0.47	0.78	66%	0.41	0.94	132%	0.78	0.89	14%	0.81	0.83	3%
Computers	21	28	0.29	0.64	125%	0.43	0.79	83%	0.86	0.89	4%	0.62	0.61	-2%
Communication equipment	17	22	0.41	0.62	50%	0.53	0.81	53%	0.88	1.00	13%	0.94	0.81	-14%
Semiconductors	10	17	0.50	0.63	25%	0.20	0.94	369%	0.90	0.94	4%	0.70	0.75	7%
Motor vehicles	24	27	0.63	0.76	22%	0.33	0.76	128%	0.71	0.92	30%	0.79	0.60	-24%
Aircraft and missiles	21	41	0.38	0.54	41%	0.48	0.95	99%	1.00	0.92	-8%	0.71	0.62	-14%
Search and navigation equipment	9	29	0.44	0.66	47%	0.67	0.97	45%	1.00	0.86	-14%	0.89	0.83	-7%
Measuring and controlling device	18	25	0.33	0.65	96%	0.28	0.87	213%	0.94	0.96	1%	0.78	0.74	-5%
Medical instruments	12	60	0.58	0.73	26%	0.50	0.83	67%	1.00	0.90	-10%	0.83	0.72	-14%
Total manufacturing	650	852	0.53	0.67	28%	0.47	0.89	91%	0.84	0.87	4%	0.80	0.73	-8%

[a]Based on own computation using original *respondent-level* Yale and CMU surveys data.

different effect on firms' use of different strategies in different industries within the same country (Hall & Ziedonis, 2001). In particular, the increase in firms' propensity to patent, as a consequence of a stronger appropriability regime in industries such as electronics and semiconductors, has spawned patent portfolio races whose main objectives are both to discourage infringement suits and to strengthen incumbents' bargaining positions in cross-licensing negotiations.

Overall, considering that both patent protection and trade secrecy are knowledge-related proprietary strategies, the strength of the appropriability regime seems to have increased over time in the United States. Teece's (1986) framework implies that we increasingly observe cases falling on the right-hand side of the tree represented in Fig. 1, where innovators capture a greater share of innovation rents due to a strengthened appropriability regime. This is consistent with the widespread belief that innovation is increasingly the key source of competitiveness and economic growth.

Interestingly enough, changes in the appropriability regime that have taken place since the early 1980s likely have affected the evolution of the degree to which EMI has profited from its CAT scanner itself. Indeed, EMI started to enforce its patents between the end of the 1970s and the beginning of the 1980s. Legal documents and company interviews suggest that the company, despite suffering imitation and bankruptcy of its medical device operation, was able to succeed against infringers and extract a substantial fraction of rents through 'stick' licensing.[4] In a recent interview, IP managers familiar with these matters estimated that EMI realized over $100 million in 'stick' licensing revenues related to the CAT scanner.[5]

The strengthening of patent protection is expected to have a profound impact on the way a firm profits from innovation as well. Consistent with Teece's framework, Arora and Ceccagnoli (2006) provide systematic empirical evidence suggesting that firms lacking the specialized complementary assets required to commercialize innovation typically license more when patent protection is strong, in contrast to firms that have specialized complementary assets, which license less. Their work also suggests that in a world of strong IPR, although technology buyers enjoy lower transactions costs and gain from trading technology, they also lose some bargaining power in technology alliances in favor of IP owners and therefore realize lower returns on the ownership of specialized complementary assets. This may in part explain the increasing downward pressure on the profitability of 'big Pharma,' which seems to suffer in a world placing increasing rewards on the owners of upstream proprietary knowledge.[6]

3.2. Quantifying the Returns Provided by Patent Strategies

Assuming firms apply for patents if net benefits of doing so are positive, Arora, Ceccagnoli, and Cohen (2007) have used survey-based responses on a firm's propensity to patent (% of innovations for which a firm applies for patent protection) to compute an unobservable concept, the *patent premium* – i.e., the proportional increment to the value of an innovation realized by patenting. Results indicate that patents provide a positive expected premium only for a small fraction of innovations. In fact, on average, the relative magnitude of benefits and costs suggests that firms expect to lose about 50% of an innovation's value by patenting it in a broad set of manufacturing industries. Put differently, patenting the typical invention is not profitable in most industries because the opportunity costs of patenting (including the cost of information disclosure, the likelihood of inventing around, and the cost of enforcement) are substantial. The patent premium is around unity for the typical patent portfolio of the average firm in biotechnology and pharmaceuticals, meaning that a firm expects no difference, on average, between payoffs realized by patenting or not. In medical instruments, instead, patenting the typical innovation is worthwhile. Only innovations for which there is a premium greater than unity are eventually patented. Indeed, the average expected premium for the innovations that firms choose to patent is about 1.5, suggesting that firms expect to earn, on average, a 50% premium over the no-patenting case. Such a premium, conditional on patenting, is about 1.6 in the health-related industries and 1.4 in electronics and semiconductors (see Fig. 2). Overall, these results suggest that even in

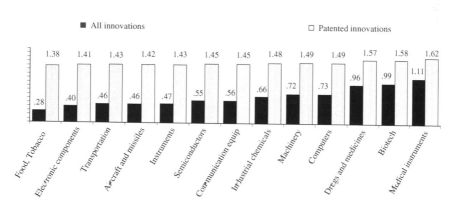

Fig. 2.   The Patent Premium (Arora et al., 2007).

those industries where patenting is not profitable on average, some inventions are profitable to patent and may actually provide large payoffs from doing so. This, however, does not mean that patenting is a sufficient condition to profit from innovation. Indeed, in most cases, patent strategies must be integrated with appropriate strategies to leverage or acquire complementary assets, exploit lead times, or maintain secrecy over other aspects of an innovation.

In a recent study, Ceccagnoli (2008) directly links the degree of appropriability achieved through different strategies and the way firms enforce their patents to firm performance. He finds that among the various appropriability strategies considered in the previous section (see Table 4), the strength of a firm's patent protection strategy and the ownership of specialized complementary assets are associated with a substantial increase in the stock market valuation of a firm's R&D assets relative to tangible assets. He also finds that among the patent strategies that are increasingly and purposefully used by technology-intensive companies, *patent preemption* – defined as the patenting of substitute or complements of other innovations owned by the firm – tends to remarkably improve the rate of return to R&D investments, as valued by the stock market. Consistent with existing theories, his empirical findings also indicate that patent preemption tends to improve the profits due to a firm's R&D and firm performance, and this effect is higher for innovating incumbents with higher market power and those facing the threat of entry and it is lower when R&D competition is characterized by the discovery of drastic innovations.

4. THE TWO FACES OF APPROPRIABILITY: PROTECTION VERSUS INCENTIVES

The degree to which a firm captures the value created through the introduction of its innovations has a dual function. It increases an innovating firm's profits and market power, which has been the focus of much of the previous discussion, but it also affects its inventive efforts. Previous empirical studies on the impact of appropriability have mostly focused on the first effect. Theoretical work, in particular economic analysis of the impact of patent protection, has instead focused on the incentive effect. The main rationale of patent protection is indeed to stimulate innovative investments, while at the same time promoting the diffusion of technological knowledge. By providing restrictions to the use of patented inventions, patent law provides the ability to recover the investment needed to introduce technological innovations, in exchange for disclosure of the technical details of the patented inventions to the public. The main social cost is the restriction in use, and thus the inefficiencies associated with monopoly protection.

The empirical work presented above, and in particular the results of Table 4, have been interpreted as suggesting that the inducement provided by patents for innovation is small in most industries. However, these results do not imply that patents provide little incentives to invest in R&D. Indeed, the estimates of the patent premium suggest that patents could be effective for a small fraction of innovations and still provide substantial average returns. Moreover, incentive effects depend on the impact of appropriability on the marginal benefits of R&D investments. Indeed, there is still no clear empirical consensus on the idea that greater appropriability of profits due to innovation, conferred by patents or any other mechanism, actually stimulates investments in innovation. To address this point, recent economic studies have attempted to quantify the incentive effect of patents.

In particular, Arora et al. (2003) provided robust evidence of a positive incentive effect of the strength of patent protection, using firm-level data from the CMU survey. They estimate an economic model in which firms' R&D decisions depend on expected returns, which are conditioned by the effectiveness of patent protection. The study further recognizes that if one firm benefits from stronger patent protection in a specific area, its competitors will also benefit from it. Their quantitative estimates suggest that a 10% increase in the strength of appropriability provided by patent protection would increase R&D investments by 7%, the firm's propensity to patent by 17%, and the number of patents applied for by each firm by 15%. Moreover, their results indicate that the incentive effect of patents varies substantially across industries, with the largest effect in pharmaceuticals, biotechnology, medical instruments, and computers. In semiconductors and communications equipment, the incentive effect of patent protection is much lower, although still positive and not negligible.

5. CONCLUSION

Strategies used to capture the value created by innovative investment are a fundamental source of a firm's competitive advantage. The degree to which firms profit from innovation is critically affected by the interplay of imitation-related factors, such as ownership and strength of IP and the

number of capable innovators, and the ownership of specialized complementary assets required for successful product and process market
introduction.

During the last two decades we have witnessed economic and legal
changes, as well as evolving managerial practices, related to the strength
of available appropriation strategies. These changes have affected the
propensity to use different appropriation strategies, firm performance, and
the division of labor and profits from the value created by innovation, in
a world that places increasing importance on innovation for firms'
competitiveness, productivity, and economic growth.

Within this evolving competitive environment, the understanding of the
relationship between appropriability and innovation investments is particularly important, not only for policy, but also for strategy and entrepreneurship.
Appropriability conditions and the effective management of IP should indeed
guide entrepreneurs and companies alike in their choices about allocating
resources for the creation of value through technological innovations.

NOTES

1. See discussion in Chapter 7.
2. See EMI and CT Scanner (A) and (B), Harvard Business Cases 9-383-194 and
383-195.
3. A sample of comparable firms was built using original *respondent-level* Yale
and CMU surveys data, i.e., only using public firms operating in comparable
industries. Each firm's responses on both product and process appropriability
mechanisms were used to compute a dummy equal to one if any mechanism was
rated as the first or second most effective in protecting the competitive advantage
from its innovations. Table 2 shows the percentage of firms rating each mechanism as
first or second most effective.
4. In a 1983 legal document we find clear and official evidence of the 'stick'
licensing activities: 'The CT manufacturing industry is a decade old. EMI, a
corporation organized under the laws of England, started production of the CT
scanners in the United States, in Chicago, Illinois, and made delivery of its first
orders in 1973. Several years ago, it discontinued making the machines and closed its
Chicago plant. It licenses others to manufacture under these patents; in all, there are
approximately ten licensees in the United States, including General Electric
Company, Johnson & Johnson, and Pfizer, Inc. The latter three, in contested
litigation, challenged the validity of plaintiff's patents; however, those separate
litigations, which extended over a two-year period, were settled before trial in return
for licenses issued by EMI to the contestants.' (*EMI Limited, Plaintiff, v. Picker
International, Inc., Defendant*; No. 83,Civ. 0759, U.S. District Court for the Southern
District of New York; 565 F. Supp. 905, 1983).

5. Interview by Marco Ceccagnoli with Dr Stephen Potter, Commercial Director of QED (patent licensing division of EMI, subject of a management buy-out in 1996: http://www.qed-ip.com), June 1st, 2003, INSEAD (Fontainebleau, France).

6. An increasing fraction of R&D expenses of large pharmaceutical companies includes the cost of developing drugs that are in-licensed from smaller biopharmaceutical firms, which in turn aggressively safeguard their proprietary knowledge and are able to extract a significant fraction of rents associated with their innovations.

ACKNOWLEDGMENTS

Rothaermel gratefully acknowledges financial support from National Science Foundation Grant SES 0545544 (CAREER Award). Any opinions, findings, conclusions, or recommendations expressed in this material are those of the authors and do not necessarily reflect the views of the National Science Foundation.

REFERENCES

Abernathy, W. I., & Utterback, J. M. (1978). Patterns of industrial innovation. *Technology Review, 80*, 40–47.

Anderson, P., & Tushman, M. L. (1990). Technological discontinuities and dominant design: A cyclical model of technological change. *Administrative Science Quarterly, 35*, 604–633.

Arora, A., & Ceccagnoli, M. (2006). Patent protection, complementary assets, and firms' incentives for technology licensing. *Management Science, 52*, 292–308.

Arora, A., Ceccagnoli, M., & Cohen, W. M. (2007). R&D and the patent premium. *International Journal of Industrial Organization* (forthcoming).

Barney, J. (1991). Firm resources and sustained competitive advantage. *Journal of Management, 17*, 99–120.

Ceccagnoli, M. (2008). Appropriability, preemption, and firm performance. *Strategic Management Journal* (forthcoming).

Cohen, W. M., Nelson, R. R., & Walsh, J. P. (2000). *Protecting their intellectual assets: Appropriability conditions and why U.S. manufacturing firms patent or not.* NBER Working Paper 7552. Retrieved March 31, 2007, from http://www.nber.org/papers/w7552

Diamond v. Chakrabarty, 447 U.S. 303 (1980).

EMI Ltd. v. Picker International, Inc., 565 F. Supp. 905 (S.D.N.Y. 1983).

Gans, J. S., & Stern, S. (2000). Incumbency and R&D incentives: Licensing the gale of creative destruction. *Journal of Economics and Management Strategy, 9*, 485–511.

Hall, B., & Ziedonis, R. H. (2001). The patent paradox revisited: An empirical study of patenting in the U.S. semiconductor industry, 1979–1995. *RAND Journal of Economics, 32*, 101–128.

Hamel, G. (1991). Competition for competence and inter-partner learning within international strategic alliances [summer special issue]. *Strategic Management Journal, 12*, 83–103.

Hill, C. W. L., & Jones, G. R. (2007). *Strategic management theory: An integrated approach* (7th ed.). Boston: Houghton Mifflin.

Levin, R. C., Klevorick, A. K., Nelson, R. R., & Winter, S. G. (1987). Appropriating the returns from industrial R&D. *Brookings Papers on Economic Activity, 1987*(3), 783–820.

Lieberman, M. B., & Montgomery, D. B. (1988). First-mover advantages [summer special issue]. *Strategic Management Journal, 9*, 41–58.

Rothaermel, F. T. (2000). Technological discontinuities and the nature of competition. *Technology Analysis & Strategic Management, 12*(2), 149–160.

Rothaermel, F. T. (2001a). Incumbent's advantage through exploiting complementary assets via interfirm cooperation. *Strategic Management Journal, 22*(6–7), 687–699.

Rothaermel, F. T. (2001b). Complementary assets, strategic alliances, and the incumbent's advantage: An empirical study of industry and firm effects in the biopharmaceutical industry. *Research Policy, 30*(8), 1235–1251.

Rothaermel, F. T., & Boeker, W. (2008). Old technology meets new technology: Complementarities, similarities, and alliance formation. *Strategic Management Journal, 29*(1), 47–77.

Rothaermel, F. T., & Deeds, D. L. (2004). Exploration and exploitation alliances in biotechnology: A system of new product development. *Strategic Management Journal, 25*, 201–221.

Rothaermel, F. T., & Hill, C. W. L. (2005). Technological discontinuities and complementary assets: A longitudinal study of industry and firm performance. *Organization Science, 16*, 52–70.

Somaya, D. (2003). Strategic determinants of decisions not to settle patent litigation. *Strategic Management Journal, 24*, 17–38.

Teece, D. J. (1986). Profiting from technological innovation: Implications for integration, collaboration, licensing and public policy. *Research Policy, 15*, 285–305.

Teece, D. J. (1992). Competition, cooperation, and innovation: Organizational arrangements for regimes of rapid technological progress. *Journal of Economic Behavior & Organization, 18*, 1–25.

Teece, D. J., Pisano, G., & Shuen, A. (1997). Dynamic capabilities and strategic management. *Strategic Management Journal, 18*, 509–533.

CHAPTER 2

THE BENEFITS AND LIABILITIES OF MULTIDISCIPLINARY COMMERCIALIZATION TEAMS: HOW PROFESSIONAL COMPOSITION AND SOCIAL NETWORKS INFLUENCE TEAM PROCESSES

Jill Perry-Smith and Leslie H. Vincent

ABSTRACT

In this chapter, we focus on the people component of the technology commercialization process. We review how the need for a variety of skills and knowledge sets creates unique challenges and opportunities for the team, particularly given the complexities associated with commercialization and the need for creativity throughout the process. We suggest that simply having a multidisciplinary team in place does not ensure success and highlight the potential benefits and liabilities. In particular, we highlight the relevancy of team composition in terms of professional orientation and

Technological Innovation: Generating Economic Results
Advances in the Study of Entrepreneurship, Innovation and
Economic Growth, Volume 18, 35–60
ISSN: 1048-4736/doi:10.1016/S1048-4736(07)00002-1

social network ties. We then review how team composition influences
internal team processes.

INTRODUCTION

The nature of innovation is changing. Innovation is becoming multidisciplinary and technologically complex and occurs at the intersection of
different fields. Many high-tech start-up firms are emerging, as firms that use
or invest in rapidly emerging or evolving technology as the critical part of
their market offering (Park, 2005). By their very nature, start-up firms differ
from well-established organizations. Past research has highlighted several key
differences between established organizations and emerging firms. Start-ups
(in comparison to established firms) typically have limited resources (in terms
of physical, human, informational, and financial resources), lack established
routines and processes, and face greater uncertainty and complexity in decision making (Busenitz & Barney, 1997; Katz & Gartner, 1988). Furthermore,
high-tech start-ups are considered to operate in the extremes of these
differences, where they face not only the challenges associated with other
types of start-ups but also technology challenges that stem from the novelty
and uncertainty associated with the technology itself (Julien, 1995).

Given this unique environment, a great deal of research has focused on
different attributes of the start-up team or founders to compensate for the
challenges associated with this dynamic environment. These high-tech start-
ups must not only focus on the cutting edge technology but also develop new
markets for that technology, as well as manage the entrepreneurial team
(Park, 2005). Therefore, one can think of these firms as comprising three
things: people; technology; and the environment. This chapter focuses on the
people component. High-tech start-ups generally consist of more than just a
single individual serving as the entrepreneur; usually they involve the
formation of teams of individuals with the necessary skill base to transform
the technology into a viable business venture (Bygrave & Hofer, 1991;
Cohen & Levinthal, 1990). Therefore, teams require a mixture of different
skills (including technical, legal, and business) to acquire the necessary
resources to push the technology into the market. While the combination of
these different skills is critical to the success of high-tech start-ups, it also
creates some unique challenges and opportunities for the team.

The path to technology commercialization requires the combination of
many different knowledge sets. As mentioned earlier, technology commercialization is an uncertain and unpredictable undertaking. Past research has

outlined four stages of the technology commercialization process (Veryzer, Jr., 1998). The first phase deals primarily with concept generation and exploration and then progresses into the second phase, or technical development and design. The third phase involves prototype construction. The process concludes with commercialization. Within each stage of this process, the knowledge requirements differ. For example, early on in the process when the technology concept is still fuzzy, teams need information relating not only to the technology, but also to customers, competition, and regulatory considerations (Zahay, Griffin, & Fredericks, 2004). As teams progress into the development phase, information relating to the technology and to customer wants and needs becomes of even greater importance. Finally, as teams test and validate their technology in preparation for commercialization, the focus shifts again to include even more different types of information needed to complete the task. In other words, the successful commercialization of a technology requires integrated information from multiple disciplines. Therefore, it is no surprise that multidisciplinary teams are critical to the successful development and launch of a new technology.

Creative thinking is critical for multidisciplinary teams and can be defined as a general approach to work that involves the generation of novel and useful ideas and solutions to difficult problems (Amabile, 1996; Shalley, 1991). Given the complexities associated with going from idea to commercialization, creative thinking is required to get the team over a variety of obstacles and challenges. Thus, not only is creativity required at the early stage of concept generation, but it may also be a key ingredient that moves the idea toward successful commercialization and adoption (Ford, 1996). In other words, throughout the commercialization process, many challenges and obstacles must be addressed. When this occurs, creative thinking is often required to move the project forward. Throughout this chapter, we will refer to creativity in this sense, as opposed to considering only the creativity of an idea or product. We begin by highlighting the relevancy of team composition, in terms of professional orientation and social network ties, for multidisciplinary commercialization teams. We then review how team composition influences internal team processes.

TEAM COMPOSITION

One of the great strengths of multidisciplinary teams is bringing together individuals from diverse professional backgrounds to work through the challenges associated with commercialization early on. The TI:GER® team program is one important application of this idea (Thursby, 2005). One of the primary benefits of working in teams is that, as a unit, the team is more likely to have access to the necessary information and expertise to solve problems (Williams & O'Reilly, 1998). For example, information and decision-making theories propose that diversity in groups will enhance available knowledge and information; thus enhancing the performance of groups (Kanter, 1988; Tziner & Eden, 1985). While an individual working alone can consult with others, individuals working together on a team with a common objective are more likely to have ownership over the problem (Robbins, 2003). As team members versus individuals working alone, these individuals are simultaneously immersed in the nuances of the problem (in this case, commercialization of a scientific idea) that include a multitude of issues that may change over time, but they also are able to directly apply relevant expertise. As such, the team has the capacity to work in concert, almost in real time, sharing ideas and working through issues. As a result, new product development time may be shorter for cross-functional groups (Brown & Eisenhardt, 1995; Keller, 2001). Further, if all goes well, individuals can fulfill affiliative needs and receive other personal and social benefits of being part of a team. For example, individuals in high-functioning teams may experience their time on the team as less painful and more enjoyable and report higher levels of satisfaction and interest in remaining on the team.

In addition, collections of individuals with diverse information and ideas hold great promise for creativity. Teams of this sort provide opportunities for surfacing a greater variety of potential solutions, including more experimentation and learning behaviors (Gibson & Vermeulen, 2003; O'Reilly, Williams, & Barsade, 1998). To be creative, teams must first have the capacity (via input from individual members) to come up with unusual solutions, make connections between seemingly unrelated pieces of information, and consider a variety of approaches (Mumford & Gustafson, 1988; Torrance, 1974). As a result, teams composed of individuals representing diverse professional backgrounds have extraordinary potential to achieve superior results and very high performance.

While this type of team has great potential, it simultaneously is one of the more difficult types of teams to manage successfully. For example, individuals may not always share unique information in groups (Paulus & Yang, 2000). In addition, individuals in diverse groups may experience more conflict, and group communication may be more difficult (Bettenhausen, 1991; Williams & O'Reilly, 1998), undermining the individual's commitment to the group beyond basic requirements. In addition, cross-functional groups have been noted both as having difficulty in reconciling diverse ideas and as moving from wildly different perspectives towards consensus and convergent thinking (Bettenhausen, 1991; Dougherty, 1992). However, particularly relevant to multidisciplinary teams is how the team's unique composition contributes to these group processes and creates teams that simultaneously have great potential yet at the same time can experience complex inter-workings that undermine this potential.

While there are many ways to think of team composition, such as demographic characteristics, tenure on the team, and personality (Williams & O'Reilly, 1998), we focus on two types of compositions particularly relevant to multidisciplinary teams in a commercialization context: professional composition and social composition. We view multidisciplinary teams comprising individuals who bring to the team their unique views and experi-ences. For commercialization teams, we argue that a team member's profes-sion of origin plays a strong role in their views and experiences. In addition, we suggest that a team member's social ties outside the team are relevant. Essentially, we are suggesting that team members bring these outside experiences into the team. In the sections that follow, we review how and why this occurs.

We recognize that diversity of information is not the only facet of teams that can lead to creativity. For example, team members should be open to new experiences (Tagger, 2002), feel free to express ideas that may go against the group (DeDreu & West, 2001), or act in environments that encourage creative processes (Drazin, Glynn, & Kazanjian, 1999; Gilson, Mathieu, Shalley, & Ruddy, 2005). However, we focus on the team's composition in terms of professions and social networks as a relevant first-order feature of multidisciplinary teams focused on commercialization.

Professional Composition

One way of thinking about professions is in terms of what a person does or their area of expertise. Broadly speaking, professions have been defined as an organized group of individuals with highly specialized, somewhat esoteric knowledge (Johnson, Morgeson, Ilgen, Meyer, & Lloyd, 2006; Pratt, Rockmann, & Kaufmann, 2006; MacDonald, 1995). On TI:GER teams, for example, law school students are distinct from others in the group because of their growing knowledge of and interest in the law. The business school students are knowledgeable about marketing and strategy formulation, and, of course, the scientists/engineers bring technical knowledge about the idea. However, more than this, professions represent ways of thinking, behaving, and approaching problems, characterized by "occupational" cultures (Van Maanen & Barley, 1984). Consistent with a cultural view of professions, membership within the profession is often marked by a variety of rituals and intense socialization processes (Pratt et al., 2006) and other characteristics of "occupational" cultures, such as newcomers struggling to understand not only the specialized knowledge but also profession-specific jargon, dress, procedures, and ways of approaching problems. For those within the profession, the norms of behavior are taken for granted, but outsiders have some trouble understanding these norms.

As a result, if we consider the TI:GER team as one type of multi-disciplinary team, the JD students, the MBA students, and the PhD students not only bring different areas of expertise but also bring with them unique views on how to approach problems, unique jargon, and preferences for interacting within teams. All of this manifests itself within the team, creating a situation ripe for difficulty. Dougherty (1992) describes the different styles used to organize thinking as "interpretive schemes" that help individuals make sense of problems and issues that may arise in new product innovation teams. A critical component of interpretive schemes for innovation is how people learn (Fleck, 1979), and this component becomes particularly important in teams where members learn in different ways. In the technology commercialization context, teams not only must provide diverse and content specific expertise, but also must connect, integrate, and come to consensus around this information.

More specifically, team members may differ in their goal orientations, in that individual members can hold either a learning orientation or a performance orientation towards a task. With a learning orientation, the individual has an intrinsic interest in acquiring new skills and master new situations. On the other hand, a performance orientation reflects an extrinsic interest to demonstrate competence, thus leading to positive evaluation by others (Bell & Kozlowski, 2002). These goal orientations impact how individual team members will respond to the task (e.g., Dweck, Hong, & Chiu, 1993). Individuals with a learning orientation enjoy challenging tasks that require the use of complex learning strategies, while individuals with a performance orientation tend to avoid difficult tasks and seek less challenging tasks where the chance of a successful outcome is more likely (Bell & Kozlowski, 2002). Continuing with our discussion of TI:GER teams as one example of multidisciplinary teams, the MBA student may exhibit more of a performance orientation, while the PhD student may exhibit more of a learning orientation.

In addition, team members may have different preferences and experiences related to learning autonomously or learning with others. For example, the

MBA students on TI:GER teams tend to have worked on substantially more teams in the past in comparison to the PhD students (Vincent, 2005). Furthermore, the MBA students report stronger preferences toward working in teams and overall positive evaluations of the team experiences than do JD or PhD students (Vincent, 2005). As a result, individuals in multidisciplinary teams may differ not only in working on teams but also on what it means to work as a team. Overall, these differences may result in team members' having different goals for the task (Dougherty, 1992; Lovelace, Shapiro, & Weingart, 2001) and ignoring important information, making collective learning less likely.

The impact of these differences is magnified by the possibility that individuals on multi-professional teams may identify more with their professional groups and less with their work groups. For example, TI:GER teams are work groups comprising individuals who are brought together to interdependently complete a particular task. However, some individuals may identify more strongly either with psychological groups or with individuals who may not be working together on a particular task but who share a common identity (Turner, 1985). According to social identity and social categorization theories, individuals may classify themselves according to membership in psychological (or social) groups (Tajfel & Turner, 1979; Turner, 1985). The social group can involve any salient classification such as sex, nationality, or race, but the relevant classification for social categorization is context dependent and can be thought of as any characteristic that is salient in a particular situation (Turner, 1985).

Here, we focus on professional groups as the salient group within a multidisciplinary team context. Each member of the TI:GER team is brought in to fill their particular role as "research scientist," "lawyer," or "business professional" in training, all of which heighten the salience of these differences. Li and Hambrick (2005) refer to these as "factional groups," when members are brought in to represent a particular organization or profession and are aware that they are representing a particular viewpoint. In addition, research suggests that professionals in organizations or groups that are not filled with similar members of a profession tend to be more committed to the profession than to the focal organization or group (Johnson et al., 2006; Wallace, 1995). This may be true even for those in the early stages of immersion in the respective professions, because professional identification is a process that commences at the beginning of a program and continues beyond graduation (Becker & Carper, 1956; Johnson et al., 2006). Thus, group members may psychologically classify themselves according to their respective professional target (their psychological group) versus the work group (their multidisciplinary team).

Social categorizations, such as by profession, can undermine the performance of the work group, as individuals compare themselves with others in the work group (the out group) in ways to build their self-esteem (Turner, 1985). As a result, differences become magnified and individuals become more entrenched in their particular psychological group instead of embracing different perspectives, seeking understanding, or forming attachments with work group members. As a result, the sharing of diverse perspectives and embracing of new ideas that are critical for creative thinking may be less likely to emerge.

Social Composition: Informal Ties Outside the Team

While the professional composition of multidisciplinary teams is simultaneously beneficial and complex, the social composition of these teams provides similar opportunities for success. We can think about social composition as reflecting relationships among team members (relationship within the team) as well as relationships individuals have with people outside the team (external ties). In contrast to human capital, these relationships represent the team's social capital (Oh, Chung, & Labianca, 2004) or the configuration of social relationships that have the potential to be transferred into meaningful outputs. Consistent with our view that each member of the team brings with them relevant experiences and perspectives, in this section, we will focus primarily on social relationships outside the team.

Teams do not exist in isolation and are part of a broader social system that extends beyond the team. Just as each individual brings to the team a unique perspective and background represented by functional area, tenure in an organization, personality, and (as we are suggesting here) professional identification, each team member also brings to the team that person's collection of social interactions and social experiences outside the team. Several seminal research projects have suggested that connections outside the team are important (Ancona & Caldwell, 1992; Tushman, 1977; Allen, 1984). For example, in a study of new-product teams in high-technology companies, Ancona and Caldwell (1992) found that the most innovative teams had external connections with peers that involved providing feedback, coordination, and support. In contrast, teams working in isolation, with minimal engagement about their project with others outside their team, or those engaged in purely technical kinds of exchanges with outsiders (e.g., adding to information exchange regarding technologies or markets) were among the lowest performing teams.

In addition, informal social ties outside the team are an important source for information that can help the team work through problems and be more efficient. For example, teams benefit from both highly codified knowledge as well as less tangible, non-codified types of knowledge. In one study of new product development units (Hansen, 1999), teams with strong connections to other teams providing non-codified types of knowledge were able to complete their projects more quickly. In contrast, teams with weaker connections to other teams providing codified knowledge were able to complete their projects faster (Hansen, 1999). While knowledge sharing with groups or individuals outside the team is generally helpful, in a field study of 182 work groups, Cummings (2004) found that external knowledge sharing helped teams perform better when team members reflected diverse organizational affiliations or roles. This suggests that multidisciplinary teams may in particular be able to benefit from sharing ideas with and seeking feedback from parties outside the team.

Furthermore, the team's composition can influence the kind of external ties a team has. Studying 1,518 project teams, Reagans, Zuckerman, and McEvily (2004) found that teams with diverse functions tended to have connections that reached a broader range of constituencies outside the team. This type of range may facilitate the implementation of new ideas, suggested by the authors' finding that groups with this type of range were able to complete their projects faster. In a setting of entrepreneurial firms, Murray (2004) explored how academic scientists contribute social capital to new entrepreneurial teams. Her research suggests that academic scientists contribute resources, support, and expertise from others outside the team, such as individuals in their local laboratory networks and individuals in their cosmopolitan network of colleagues and co-authors. Taken together, this series of studies suggests how team members, as representatives of their respective professional areas, serve as conduits to the profession for the team. These ties may represent similar perspectives of the focal individual but may help facilitate the transfer of perspectives and information relevant to the task. In this way, diverse professional teams, in addition to providing relevant knowledge and expertise, provide important social resources from their respective social networks, and research suggests that this type of external communication, associated with diverse knowledge areas, is related to higher technical quality and innovation (Ancona & Caldwell, 1992; Keller, 2001).

A complementary view is that individuals transfer ways of behaving across team boundaries. Team members' external ties can provide the team with the type of cognitive diversity needed for both creative thinking and getting over the many humps and challenges associated with commercialization.

Individuals transfer ways of behaving across team boundaries, such that individuals' social reality outside the team may influence the way they approach problems and interact with their teammates (Beckman, 2006; Pettigrew, 1986). For example, certain types of external ties may provide individuals with more experience with being flexible with ideas, reconciling differing views and making unusual connections. In contrast to strong friendship connections, weaker connections are expected to facilitate creative thinking (Perry-Smith, 2006; Perry-Smith & Shalley, 2003). Individuals with weaker ties tend to be exposed to differing, and potentially contradictory, perspectives from their contacts who are less likely either to know one another or to think similarly compared to close friends. In the team setting, these types of connections outside the team may be helpful because they may facilitate flexible and heterogeneous views that individuals can bring to the team. Thus, these team members may be important sources for creative ideas as well as for helping the team reconcile diverse views (Perry-Smith & Shalley, 2006).

The idea that complicates the social composition perspective is that teams must achieve an appropriate balance between internal informal social ties and external social ties. For example, in one study (Oh et al., 2004), the most effective teams had the appropriate combination of outside ties and internal cohesion. However, as noted earlier, the team's professional composition may influence the kinds of external ties that the team has. Given the scope of commercialization teams, certain types of social compositions within the team may facilitate performance on some tasks (e.g., more standard, implementation kinds of activities) but undermine performance on others (e.g., more challenging, creative kinds of activities). As a result, the internal team process that a team employs becomes critical for effectively managing what has the potential to contribute to, and helps teams achieve, exceptional performance, but that same process can have the tendency to undermine performance and make life on the team both difficult and unpleasant.

TEAM PROCESSES

In the previous section, the discussion focused on the composition of multifunctional teams, in terms of professions and social ties outside the team, which influences the mix of different perspectives within the team. Bringing together these different resources and perspectives has the potential to ultimately lead to superior performance in new technologies commercialization, but it can also create challenges to effective team functioning that may dampen their potential. Overall, the professional and social composition of these multidisciplinary teams, while beneficial in terms of creating novel solutions and approaches to complex problems, also creates greater complexity in terms of fostering effective team processes. The next section of this chapter focuses on the team process challenges created by the professional and social composition among team members that are especially pertinent for multidisciplinary teams. We focus on the most pertinent problems encountered by multidisciplinary teams, including team conflict, identification, cohesion, and team cooperation, and we discuss the implications associated with each process.

Conflict

Conflict can be thought of as the process resulting from the tension between team members due to either real or perceived differences; conflict is one of the many challenges teams face when working together (DeDreu & Weingart, 2003). It can manifest both in the social relationships between team members and in the task itself. While different perspectives and sources of background information can facilitate creative processes, diversity in terms of profession, due to the associated differences in identification, may lead to types of conflict – such as emotional and behavioral – that can undermine group functioning. Three different types of conflict can be present within teams: (1) task conflict, (2) process conflict, and (3) relationship conflict.

While on the surface the notion of conflict seems counterproductive to effective team functioning, it need not always be the case. Conflict can force team members to confront issues and acknowledge perspectives that may differ from their own, which can ultimately lead to creative problem-solving; thus enhancing team effectiveness (DeDreu & Weingart, 2003; Tjosvold, 1997). *Task conflict* is constructive in nature and refers to the differences in perspectives and opinions among team members relating to the task itself (Jehn & Mannix, 2001). Task conflict includes disagreements and debates regarding task content that revolve around what actions are necessary to complete the task. Task conflict is somewhat inevitable for multidisciplinary teams. In this case, team members have different vocabularies and languages that they bring with them due to their divergent professional experiences. Furthermore, they may even have different goals for the task at hand (Lovelace et al., 2001). Individuals from different backgrounds also have different perceptions of the environment (Amason, 1996); therefore, the approach taken to accomplish the task at hand will be different for each individual comprising the team.

A great deal of research has examined the impact of task conflict on team decision-making effectiveness, and research supports the notion that teams make better decisions when some disagreement relating to the task forces teams to consider multiple alternatives (Schulz-Hardt, Jochims, & Frey, 2002; Hollenbeck, Colquit, Ilgen, LePine, & Hedlund, 1998; Hollenbeck et al., 1995). This is particularly the case for multidisciplinary teams, because the discussion that emerges from contesting these differing ideas will ultimately lead to a higher quality decision outcome based on the synergizing of these different perspectives (e.g., Jehn, Northcraft, & Neale, 1999; Schwenk, 1990). In addition, the decision-quality-benefits-associated-with-task-conflict research has demonstrated that team consensus and commitment are also enhanced by the challenging of ideas within the team (e.g., Amason, 1996; Folger, 1977). The positive effect of task conflict is even more pronounced for teams facing a complex task (Jehn, 1995). Team members engaged in debating their perspectives with others will feel more involved in the decision process and therefore are more likely to become committed to and satisfied with the decision reached by the team.

While task conflict is associated with creative problem-solving, team commitment, and satisfaction, there is a point at which too much conflict can lead to negative outcomes for the team, suggesting that a moderate level of task conflict is optimal for team functioning. Too much task conflict can interfere with team consensus and distract team members from achieving their task-related goals (e.g., Amason, 1996; Jehn & Mannix, 2001). For example, a study by Amason and Schweiger (1997) found teams need some amount of task conflict in order to make good quality decisions in the completion of the task, but they also need to reach consensus relating to their decisions in order for the quality of the decision not to be effected. As a follow-up to this, a study by Jehn and Mannix (2001) addressed the issue of the timing of the task conflict on the team outcomes. Their results suggest that task conflict is most beneficial during the middle of the task as opposed to early on or in the later stages of completion. Task conflict early on has the potential to interfere with the team's focus on its specified purpose, and task conflict late in the project can interfere with team consensus and implementation activities.

Process conflict involves disagreements among team members about the process required to complete the task, or how to do the task. Teams comprising individuals with diverse backgrounds, and thus having access to a diverse set of information, often experience more difficulty in defining how to proceed ahead with the task (i.e., process conflict) than groups with similar backgrounds (Jehn et al., 1999). Process conflict involves delegating tasks among team members, as well as deciding who is responsible for key activities and how much responsibility individual team members should receive. Unlike task conflict, process conflict does not necessarily benefit team performance outcomes. Jehn (1995) found that process conflict hindered both group morale as well as the productivity of the team. Jehn explains this finding: process conflict can lead to dissatisfaction, lack of commitment, and uncertainty among team members. Furthermore, process conflict can spill over into the task itself and impede the quality of task-related discussions by focusing on irrelevant discussions that will not aid in the completion of the task (Jehn, 1995; Jehn et al., 1999). In a follow-up study by Jehn and Mannix (2001), results suggest that high-performing teams differ in terms of the amount of process conflict compared to that of low-performing teams. High-performing teams have low levels of process conflict throughout the early and middle stages of a project's completion compared to their low-performing counterparts. As the task nears completion, however, process conflict is significantly higher for high-performing teams. The increase in process conflict is potentially due to debates that occur, as teams get close to the deadline, over which team members are responsible for what tasks in order to complete the project.

The third type of conflict that teams can experience is relationship conflict. *Relationship conflict* can be thought of as conflict based more on emotion; it primarily focuses on personal characteristics (Amason, 1996). Relationship conflict includes disagreements regarding personal issues that have no bearing on the task to be completed, and it has a negative impact on team functioning and task performance (e.g., DeDreu & Weingart, 2003). Increasing relationship conflict takes resources away from the task; as a result, information processing and creative thinking are likely to suffer (Carnevale & Probst, 1998). In other words, group members become focused on each other instead of on the task at hand, and this focus can ultimately lead to increased tension among team members as well as feelings of frustration (DeDreu & Weingart, 2003; Jehn & Mannix, 2001). For example, teams experiencing relational conflict may be more frustrated and dissatisfied with their group experience (Jehn et al., 1999). Individuals in these groups prefer to work alone, get less personal development, and may experience the conflict as a distraction from their group and other activities. Further, these groups may experience more behavioral disintegration, which involves less information sharing, less collaborative behavior, and more individual versus joint decision making within the group (Li & Hambrick, 2005). While groups certainly can survive without these types of behaviors, these represent the more subtle behaviors that may be needed to go beyond acceptable solutions to extraordinary ones. In addition, these processes are generally thought to undermine implementation of ideas, going beyond developing an idea, which requires creative thinking related to flexibility, working closely together, and divergent thinking (Ancona & Caldwell, 1992). Lastly, while divergent thoughts, ideas, and perspectives are important, groups can stall if they cannot achieve cognitive consensus, or consistencies in how key issues should be addressed (Mohammed & Ringseis, 2001).

Conflict is inevitable within multidisciplinary teams. The key, however, is for team members to be aware of the different types of conflict that can occur and to be prepared to respond to the nature of the conflict before it gets out of hand and interferes with effective team functioning. Managing conflict is not an easy task for teams, but teams with more success in managing conflict are characterized as having high levels of trust, collaborative communication, and an environment open to diverse viewpoints (DeDreu & Weingart, 2003). Thus, teams that use collaborative communication, as opposed to contentious communication, when expressing divergent viewpoints are likely to have more effective team functioning (Lovelace et al., 2001). Furthermore, trust has been posited to play a critical role in managing team conflict. Development of trust within teams can be facilitated through several different factors, including shared social norms, repeated interactions, face-to-face communication, shared experiences, and the anticipation of future association (Powell, 1990; Jarvenpaa & Leidner, 1999).

Identification

One of the challenges facing multifunctional teams is overcoming disciplinary biases and stereotypes. Strong identification with one's professional area can hinder effective functioning between members of multidisciplinary teams (Sethi, 2000a). Identities are extensions of an individual's self-concept and motivate individuals to behave in ways that will enhance their own perception about their identity. Therefore, team members who believe that their own professional area is superior to that of another team member will make downward comparisons regarding that other team member. To overcome one's identity with functional or professional area while working in multidisciplinary teams, these members must create an identity with the team and perceive a personal interest in the outcome of the team. This creation of a team identity is referred to as a superordinate identity. For teams comprising individuals from very different backgrounds, the creation of a superordinate identity can be critical for effective team functioning and the integration of diverse ideas (Sethi, Smith, & Park, 2001).

Past research has demonstrated that teams with high superordinate identification have higher levels of performance than those teams whose team members identify with their functional areas over that of the team (Sethi, 2000a). This increased performance comes about through a shifting of members' viewpoints, from an initial focus on the different backgrounds, to a focus on the success and the task facing the team. Individuals with a high superordinate identity come to view themselves in light of the common team rather than merely as an individual with unique qualities associated with their professional area (Mackie & Goethals, 1987). This shift in perception generates acceptance from other team members and a willingness to understand their unique approach to completing the task (Ashforth & Mael, 1989; Wilder, 1986). From this, the communication within the team is more effective, including increased knowledge sharing, listening to others' perspectives in order to make effective decisions, and constructive challenging of ideas (Deshpande & Zaltman, 1982; Maltz & Kohli, 1996).

When individuals identify with the team, they also perceive a personal stake in the team's ultimate success. This increased motivation has been shown to increase the likelihood of creative solutions to the team's task within a new product development context (Sethi, 2000a). Past research has highlighted that when a high superordinate identity is present, teams are more likely to make novel connections between market needs and technology capabilities (Sethi, 2000b). In other words, the creation of a superordinate identity also creates a mechanism for the integration of team members that will lead to more effective team outcomes in terms of both team functioning and the task itself (Sethi, 2000b).

Furthermore, for teams engaged in technology commercialization outside of traditional organizational boundaries, the creation of this superordinate identity can be an even greater challenge. Most of the research focused on the role of identification within team functioning has occurred within the organizational setting, where team members from different functional areas become part of cross-functional teams. However, while team members do come from different areas within the organization, they are all still members of the organization itself and thus already have some identification in place with regards to the organization. For teams comprising individuals with different professional backgrounds that come together outside of this organizational setting, there is no overarching common identity for them to build upon. Rather, the team must create a brand new identity in order to facilitate effective team functioning.

Cohesion: Informal Network Ties within the Team

While identity is focused on one's identification with their functional department, professional affiliation, or group, and deals with an individual's self-concept, cohesion involves the interpersonal attraction or liking between team members (Beal, Cohen, Burke, & McLendon, 2003). Interactions that occur among team members are considered to be a vital part of intrateam process. These interactions can be of two distinct types: (1) socioemotional and (2) task (Gladstein, 1984; McGrath, 1984). Socioemotional interaction focuses on who in the team is talking to whom. In particular, we focus on informal social interactions that are not required as part of the job or task, in contrast to task-focused interaction, which refers specifically to the interaction that occurs within the team as it relates directly to the team's task (Hackman, 1987). In doing so, we integrate network views of relationships with cohesion.

Cohesion involves the affective component of the individual's relationship with the team and focuses on the strength of ties among team members (Ashforth & Mael, 1989; Sethi et al., 2001). Similarly, relationships are often described in terms of their strength. Relationships exist along a continuum from very strong friendship ties to acquaintance ties with less emotional intensity and closeness (Granovetter, 1973). As a result, cohesion can be thought of in terms of the average closeness amongst all team members or the density of informal friendship relationships within the team (Oh et al., 2004; Reagans et al., 2004). In very dense groups, each member of the team is a friend of every other member of the team.

These types of cohesive friendship groups have many advantages. Social cohesion among team members is generally viewed as a desirable quality of high-performing teams. For example, densely connected teams tend to have higher performance, have more satisfied group members, and have increased levels of consensus among team members (Beal et al., 2003; Balkundi & Harrison, 2006; Sethi et al., 2001). In addition, friendship groups have the benefit of high cooperation and commitment, which should help groups perform better (Jehn & Shah, 1997). Further, teams are more willing to share unique information with friends, particularly when friends possess distinct information (Gruenfeld, Mannix, Williams, & Neale, 1996).

Yet, strong friendship ties are more likely between people who are similar (Ibarra, 1992; Lincoln & Miller, 1979). Thus, diverse groups in terms of professional orientation may be less likely to experience the close ties thought to help group functioning (Lau & Murningham, 1988; Milliken & Martins, 1996; Reagans et al., 2004). Research has shown that individuals are more likely to communicate with those who are similar to themselves (e.g., Pfeffer, 1981, 1983; Zenger & Lawrence, 1989). Therefore, the diversity present within multidisciplinary teams can make communication between team members a challenge. This increased difficulty in internal team communication stems from different professional goals, education, and viewpoints (Keller, 2001).

For creative tasks, less is known about the relationship between the closeness among team members and performance, but there is some suggestion that too much cohesion may undermine creative and innovative outcomes. In a study of 141 cross-functional new product development teams, Sethi et al. (2001) found that teams with a high level of social cohesion had lower levels of new product innovativeness. This was in part due to the presence of groupthink among the team members, leading to less creative decisions and solutions relating to the task at hand. Furthermore, high levels of social cohesion can ultimately impact the amount of search behavior in which teams engage while completing the task (i.e., number of alternatives considered, information search, and selective consideration of information and alternatives). However, there is reason to believe that cohesion may help teams to be more creative in some cases. The results of a recent study (Perry-Smith & Shalley, 2006) suggest that the relationship between the closeness among team members and creativity has a U-shaped form, such that low levels of closeness and high levels of closeness are associated with high creativity.

Communication: Task-Focused Interaction

Task-focused interaction provides an assessment of whether a group is using its resources and time efficiently and effectively and enhances the performance potential of the team (Stewart & Barrick, 2000). Task-focused interaction is a synergistic process teams must develop to enhance performance (e.g., Barry & Stewart, 1997; Campion, Medsker, & Higgs, 1993). This interaction is the process by which ideas and information are transferred among team members (Mintzberg, 1973). In this section, we will focus on the role of task-focused interaction in terms of effective team functioning.

The role of communication and collaboration in multidisciplinary teams is paramount to the ultimate success of the team. Teams with higher levels of communication and cooperation have higher success rates than do teams with low levels of communication across the different disciplines (Pinto & Pinto, 1990). Teams that are able to acquire and disseminate information (either from internal or external sources) effectively are better positioned to make critical decisions regarding their task. In addition, communication and collaboration among team members is also related to team identification and cohesion, discussed in the previous sections (Keller, 2001).

Communication within multidisciplinary teams focused on technology commercialization or new product development can be an even greater challenge, given the unique nature of the task at hand. Multidisciplinary teams engaged in highly complex tasks require high levels of interdependence among team members in order for the task to be successfully completed. Interdependence is the extent to which team members cooperate and work together interactively to complete tasks. High interdependence must occur when team members' dependence on others for information or other resources is critical to the successful completion of the task (Campion et al., 1993; Emery & Trist, 1965). Without effective communication and collaboration, the team will not be able to complete its task. Therefore, in this section we will focus on certain characteristics of communication and the impact of these characteristics on successful completion of the task: the types of task communication; the frequency of communication necessary; and, finally, the different media of communication available to teams.

Four distinct categories of task-related communication can occur within teams (McGrath, 1984). The first of these is generating ideas and planning team activities. The second category is selecting appropriate alternatives in order to complete the task. The next task category is negotiating and, in particular, negotiating conflicts of interest. Finally, the last category is executing the work itself. Teams perform all four of these different tasks, but with different frequency depending on the type of team. In the case of multidisciplinary teams, where the task itself is complex and uncertain, teams spend more time on conceptual tasks (generating ideas and plans, and choosing between alternatives) than on tasks that are more behavioral in nature (negotiation and work execution) (Stewart & Barrick, 2000).

In addition to the type of communication, teams must also consider the frequency with which communication occurs. For example, March and Simon (1958) postulated that increased communication frequency fosters efficiency and ease of communication between team members. This ultimately leads to a shared language among team members and can help them to value and assimilate information in a more efficient manner (e.g., Tushman, 1978; Zenger & Lawrence, 1989). The development of this shared language is critical for multidisciplinary teams, especially those focused on complex tasks where the development of a shared language is critical in achieving desired performance goals. Without this shared language, individuals within the team are likely to misinterpret information necessary to complete the task (Rogers & Bhowmik, 1971).

Related to the frequency of communication is the nature of the communication occurrence. In other words, communication can be either formal or informal, where formal communication is that which occurs during scheduled meetings or appointments or through written communication (Kahn, 1996). Informal communication, on the other hand, is unplanned communication. Both types of communication are important to the completion of a team's task. However, research has shown that the more successful multidisciplinary teams engage in higher levels of informal communication while working on the project (Pinto & Pinto, 1990). One of the difficulties in promoting frequent communication between team members of multidisciplinary teams is that they are not always located within the same physical area, thereby making informal communication somewhat of a challenge.

Finally, communication can differ according to the medium through which the information is transferred among individuals (i.e., face-to-face versus written). Face-to-face communication is thought to be a richer method of communication because it can provide instant feedback (i.e., two-way communication), transmit both verbal and non-verbal cues, use natural language, and convey emotions (Fulk, 1993). Written communication is considered less rich than face-to-face interactions because the communication is one-way with fewer cues for the recipient of the information (Dennis & Kinney, 1998). The impact of the medium on communication can have significant performance implications. Daft and Lengel (1986) highlighted the need for matching the communication medium with the nature of the task itself. In other words, for tasks that are highly complex, where there could be multiple interpretations of the information, teams must engage in those communication mediums that are rich in nature. Therefore, face-to-face communication should lead to better performance for tasks that are equivocal in nature. On the other hand, for tasks that are less uncertain and can be executed by obtaining and sharing needed information, less rich medium (such as email or written communication) will suffice.

CONCLUSION

The purpose of this chapter was to focus on the unique nature of multi-disciplinary teams and, in particular, teams engaged in the highly uncertain and complex task of technology commercialization. As mentioned earlier, the benefits associated with using these diverse teams stem from many sources, including the bringing together of the necessary skills and knowledge required for technology commercialization, as well as the diverse set of ideas and perspectives that will foster creative problem-solving and ultimately lead to superior performance outcomes. However, simply having a multidisciplinary team in place does not ensure success.

We have suggested that multidisciplinary teams are more complex than having team members with diverse bases of knowledge. Our basic point is that, in addition to their areas of expertise, these individuals bring with them other differences that can undermine a variety of intrateam processes. We have attempted to capture these "other" differences in terms of professions and outside social ties. Multidisciplinary teams are composed of individuals reflecting different professions, which reflect different cultural norms. As such, these multidisciplinary teams are composed of individuals with different ways of thinking, behaving, and approaching problems. For example, individuals may have different learning styles and preferences for working with others. In addition, we view each person as bringing into the team their social networks outside of the team. For example, outside ties provide the team with sources of unique information and social capital that can provide a context for optimal performance. These ties are also influenced by the social composition of the team, by tapping into potentially helpful resources and expertise.

With these diverse perspectives come hurdles that the team must overcome in order to function effectively. This chapter highlighted potential impediments to effective team functioning (conflict, identification, cohesion, and communication) that relate to the unique composition of multidisciplinary teams. Conflict can have both positive and negative implications for the team, depending on the amount and nature of the conflict in which the team engages. For example, task conflict can lead to more creative outcomes in multidisciplinary teams, which then can lead to desirable performance outcomes. However, process and relationship conflict are more problematic for teams, and steps should be taken as soon as possible to alleviate these sources of conflict within the team. Team identification and cohesion are also critical processes that must occur in order for multidisciplinary teams to function effectively. Due to the inherent nature of these diverse teams, teams must be aware of the different orientations that are represented on a single team; instead of focusing on their differences, they must rather focus on the task at hand and build identification toward the team itself, rather than the individual professional backgrounds. In addition to strong team identification, team cohesion, which fosters team communication and collaboration, should also be considered, although the relationship between closeness and creativity is complex.

We have highlighted the benefits and liabilities of commercialization teams in hopes of providing some insight for these multidisciplinary teams. Our goal is to make team members aware of potential problems or pitfalls that can hinder effective team functioning and ultimately impact the performance of the team.

REFERENCES

Allen, T. J. (1984). *Managing the flow of technology: Technology transfer and the dissemination of technological information within the R&D organization.* Cambridge, MA: MIT Press.

Amabile, T. M. (1996). *Creativity in context.* Boulder: Westview Press.

Amason, A. (1996). Distinguishing the effects of functional and dysfunctional conflict on strategic decision making: Resolving a paradox for top management groups. *Academy of Management Journal, 39,* 123–148.

Amason, A., & Schweiger, D. (1997). The effect of conflict on strategic decision making effectiveness and organizational performance. In: C. K. W. DeDreu & E. Van de Vliert (Eds), *Using conflict in organizations* (pp. 101–115). London: Sage.

Ancona, D. G., & Caldwell, D. F. (1992). Demography and design: Predictors of new product team performance. *Organization Science, 3,* 321–341.

Ashforth, B. E., & Mael, F. (1989). Social identity theory and the organization. *Academy of Management Review, 14*(1), 20–39.

Balkundi, P., & Harrison, D. A. (2006). Ties, leaders, and time in teams: Strong inference about network structure's effects on team viability and performance. *Academy of Management Journal, 49,* 49–68.

Barry, B., & Stewart, G. L. (1997). Composition, process, and performance in self-managed groups: The role of personality. *Journal of Applied Psychology, 82*(1), 62–78.

Beal, D. J., Cohen, R. R., Burke, M. J., & McLendon, C. L. (2003). Cohesion and performance in groups: A meta-analytic clarification of construct relations. *Journal of Applied Psychology, 88,* 989–1004.

Becker, H. S., & Carper, J. W. (1956). The development of identification with an occupation. *American Journal of Sociology, 61,* 289–298.

Beckman, C. M. (2006). The influence of founding team company affiliations on firm behavior. *Academy of Management Journal, 49,* 741–758.

Bell, B. S., & Kozlowski, S. W. (2002). Goal orientation and ability: Interactive effects on self-efficacy, performance, and knowledge. *Journal of Applied Psychology, 87*(3), 497–505.

Bettenhausen, K. L. (1991). Five years of groups research: What we have learned and what needs to be addressed. *Journal of Management, 17,* 345–381.

Brown, S. L., & Eisenhardt, K. M. (1995). Product development: Past research, present findings, and future directions. *Academy of Management Review, 20,* 343–378.

Busenitz, L. W., & Barney, J. B. (1997). Differences between entrepreneurs and managers in large organizations: Biases and heuristics in strategic decision-making. *Journal of Business Venturing, 12,* 9–30.

Bygrave, W. D., & Hofer, C. W. (1991). Theorizing about entrepreneurship. *Entrepreneurship Theory and Practice, 16*(2), 13–22.

Campion, M. A., Medsker, G. J., & Higgs, A. C. (1993). Relations between work group characteristics and effectiveness: Implications for designing effective work groups. *Personnel Psychology, 46*, 823–850.

Carnevale, P. J., & Probst, T. M. (1998). Social values and social conflict in creative problem solving and categorization. *Journal of Personality and Social Psychology, 74*, 1300–1309.

Cohen, W., & Levinthal, D. (1990). Absorptive capacity: A new perspective on learning and innovation. *Administrative Science Quarterly, 35*, 128–152.

Cummings, J. (2004). Work groups, structural diversity, and knowledge sharing in a global organization. *Management Science, 50*(3), 352–364.

Daft, R. L., & Lengel, R. H. (1986). Organizational information requirements, media richness, and structural design. *Management Science, 32*(5), 554–571.

DeDreu, C., & Weingart, L. R. (2003). Task versus relationship conflict, team performance, and team member satisfaction: A meta-analysis. *Journal of Applied Psychology, 88*(4), 741–749.

DeDreu, C. K., & West, M. A. (2001). Minority dissent and team innovation. *Journal of Applied Psychology, 86*, 1191–1201.

Dennis, A. R., & Kinney, S. T. (1998). Testing media richness theory in the new media: The effects of cues, feedback, and task equivocality. *Information Systems Research, 9*(3), 256–274.

Deshpande, R., & Zaltman, G. (1982). Factors affecting the use of market research information: A path analysis. *Journal of Marketing Research, 19*(1), 14–31.

Dougherty, D. (1992). Interpretive barriers to successful product innovation in large firms. *Organization Science, 3*, 179–202.

Drazin, R., Glynn, M. A., & Kazanjian, R. (1999). Multilevel theorizing about creativity in organizations: A sensemaking perspective. *Academy of Management Review, 24*(2), 286–307.

Dweck, C. S., Hong, Y., & Chiu, C. (1993). Implicit theories: Individual differences in the likelihood and meaning of dispositional inference. *Personality and Social Psychology Bulletin, 19*, 644–656.

Emery, F. E., & Trist, E. L. (1965). The causal texture of organizational environments. *Human Relations, 18*, 21–31.

Fleck, L. (1979). In: T. Trenn & R. K. Merton (Eds), *Genesis and development of a scientific fact* (F. Bradley and T. Trenn, Trans.). Chicago: University of Chicago Press (Original work published in 1935).

Folger, R. (1977). Distributive and procedural justice: Combined impact of voice and improvement of experienced inequality. *Journal of Personality and Social Psychology, 35*, 108–119.

Ford, C. M. (1996). A theory of individual creative action in multiple social domain. *Academy of Management Review, 21*, 215–239.

Fulk, J. (1993). Social construction of communication technology. *Academy of Management Journal, 36*(5), 921–950.

Gibson, C., & Vermeulen, F. (2003). A healthy divide: Subgroups as a stimulus for team learning behavior. *Administrative Science Quarterly, 48*, 202–239.

Gilson, L., Mathieu, J., Shalley, C., & Ruddy, T. (2005). Creativity and standardization: Complementary or conflicting drivers of team effectiveness? *Academy of Management Journal, 48*(3), 521–531.

Gladstein, D. L. (1984). Groups in context: A model of task group effectiveness. *Administrative Science Quarterly, 29*, 499–517.

Granovetter, M. S. (1973). The strength of weak ties. *American Journal of Sociology, 6,* 1360–1380.

Gruenfeld, D., Mannix, E., Williams, K., & Neale, M. (1996). Group composition and decision making: How member familiarity and information distribution affect process and performance. *Organizational Behavior and Human Decision Processes, 67*(1), 1–15.

Hackman, R. (1987). The design of work teams. In: J. Lorsch (Ed.), *Handbook of organizational behavior* (pp. 315–342). Englewood Cliffs, NJ: Prentice Hall.

Hansen, M. T. (1999). The search-transfer problem: The role of weak ties in sharing knowledge across organizational subunits. *Administrative Science Quarterly, 37,* 422–447.

Hollenbeck, J. R., Colquit, J. A., Ilgen, D. R., LePine, J. A., & Hedlund, J. (1998). Accuracy decomposition and team decision making: Testing theoretical boundary conditions. *Journal of Applied Psychology, 83,* 494–500.

Hollenbeck, J. R., Ilgen, D. R., Sego, D. J., Hedlund, J., Major, D. A., & Phillips, J. (1995). Multilevel theory of team decision making: Decision performance in teams incorporating distributed expertise. *Journal of Applied Psychology, 80,* 292–316.

Ibarra, H. (1992). Homopholy and differential returns: Sex differences in network structure and access in an advertising firm. *Administrative Science Quarterly, 37,* 422–447.

Jarvenpaa, S. L., & Leidner, D. E. (1999). Communication and trust in global virtual teams. *Organization Science, 10*(6), 791–815.

Jehn, K. A. (1995). A multimethod examination of the benefits and detriments of intragroup conflict. *Administrative Science Quarterly, 40,* 256–282.

Jehn, K. A., & Mannix, E. A. (2001). The dynamic nature of conflict: A longitudinal study of intragroup conflict and group performance. *Academy of Management Journal, 44*(2), 238–251.

Jehn, K. A., Northcraft, G. B., & Neale, M. A. (1999). Why differences make a difference: A field study of diversity, conflict, and performance in workgroups. *Administrative Science Quarterly, 44,* 741–763.

Jehn, K. A., & Shah, P. P. (1997). Interpersonal relationships and task performance: An examination of mediating processes in friendship and acquaintance groups. *Journal of Personality and Social Psychology, 72,* 775–791.

Johnson, M. D., Morgeson, F. P., Ilgen, D. R., Meyer, C. J., & Lloyd, J. W. (2006). Multiple professional identities: Examining differences in identification across work-related targets. *Journal of Applied Psychology, 91,* 498–506.

Julien, P. (1995). New technologies and technological information in small businesses. *Journal of Business Venturing, 10*(6), 459–475.

Kahn, K. B. (1996). Interdepartmental integration: A definition with implications for product development performance. *Journal of Product Innovation Management, 13,* 137–151.

Kanter, R. M. (1988). When a thousand flowers bloom: Structural, collective, and social conditions for innovation in organization. In: B. M. Staw & L. L. Cummings (Eds), *Research in organizational behavior* (Vol. 10, pp. 169–211). Greenwich, CT: JAI Press.

Katz, J., & Gartner, W. B. (1988). Properties of emerging organizations. *Academy of Management Review, 13*(3), 429–441.

Keller, R. T. (2001). Cross-functional project groups in research and new product development: Diversity, communications, job stress, and outcomes. *Academy of Management Journal, 44,* 547–555.

Lau, D. C., & Murningham, J. K. (1988). Demographic diversity and faultlines: The compositional dynamics of organizational groups. *Academy of Management Review*, *23*, 325–340.

Li, J., & Hambrick, D. C. (2005). Factional groups: A new vantage in demographic faultlines, conflict, and disintegration in work teams. *Academy of Management Journal*, *48*(5), 794–813.

Lincoln, J. R., & Miller, J. (1979). Work and friendship ties in organizations: A comparative analysis of relational networks. *Administrative Science Quarterly*, *24*, 181–199.

Lovelace, K., Shapiro, D. L., & Weingart, L. R. (2001). Maximizing cross-functional new product teams' innovativeness and constraint adherence: A conflict communications perspective. *Academy of Management Journal*, *44*(4), 779–793.

MacDonald, K. M. (1995). *The sociology of the professions*. London: Sage.

Mackie, D. M., & Goethals, G. R. (1987). Individual and group goals. In: C. Hendrick (Ed.), *Review of personality and social psychology* (Vol. 8, pp. 144–166). Newbury Park, CA: Sage.

Maltz, E., & Kohli, A. K. (1996). Market intelligence dissemination across functional boundaries. *Journal of Marketing Research*, *33*(1), 47–61.

March, J. G., & Simon, H. A. (1958). *Organizations*. New York: Wiley.

McGrath, J. E. (1984). *Groups: Interaction and performance*. Englewood Cliffs, NJ: Prentice-Hall.

Milliken, F. J., & Martins, L. L. (1996). Searching for common threads: Understanding the multiple effects of diversity in organizational groups. *Academy of Management Review*, *21*, 402–434.

Mintzberg, H. (1973). *The Nature of Managerial Work*. New York, NY: Harper & Row.

Mohammed, S., & Ringseis, E. (2001). Cognitive diversity and consensus in group decision making: The role of inputs, processes and outcomes. *Organizational Behavior and Group Decision Processes*, *85*(2), 310–335.

Murray, F. (2004). The role of academic inventors in entrepreneurial firms: Sharing the laboratory life. *Research Policy*, *33*, 643–659.

Oh, H., Chung, M., & Labianca, G. (2004). Group social capital and group effectiveness: The role of informal socializing ties. *Academy of Management Journal*, *47*, 860–875.

O'Reilly, C., Williams, K., & Barsade, S. (1998). Group democracy and innovation: Does diversity help? *Research on Managing Teams*, *1*, 183–207.

Park, J. S. (2005). Opportunity recognition and product innovation in entrepreneurial hi-tech start-ups: A new perspective and supporting case study. *Technovation*, *25*, 739–752.

Paulus, P. B., & Yang, H. (2000). Idea generation in groups: A basis for creativity in organizations. *Organizational Behavior and Human Decision Processes*, *82*, 76–87.

Perry-Smith, J. E. (2006). Social yet creative: The role of social relationships in facilitating individual creativity. *Academy of Management Journal*, *49*, 85–101.

Perry-Smith, J. E., & Shalley, C. E. (2003). The social side of creativity: A static and dynamic social network perspective. *Academy of Management Review*, *28*, 89–106.

Perry-Smith, J. E. & Shalley, C. E. (2006). *Team creativity: The role of team member informal interactions*. Paper presented at the annual academy of management meetings, Atlanta, Georgia.

Pettigrew, T. F. (1986). Intergroup contact theory. *Annual Review of Psychology*, *49*, 65–85.

Pfeffer, J. (1981). *Power in Organizations*. Marshfield, MA: Pitman.

Pfeffer, J. (1983). Organizational demography. *Research in Organizational Behavior*, *5*, 295–357.

Pinto, M. B., & Pinto, J. K. (1990). Project team communication and cross-functional cooperation in new product development. *Journal of Product Innovation Management*, *7*, 200–212.

Powell, W. W. (1990). Neither market nor hierarchy: Network forms of organization. *Research in Organizational Behavior, 12,* 295–336.

Pratt, M. G., Rockmann, K. W., & Kaufmann, J. B. (2006). Constructing professional identity: The role of work and identity learning cycles in the customization of identity among medical residents. *Academy of Management Journal, 49,* 235–262.

Reagans, R., Zuckerman, E., & McEvily, B. (2004). How to make the team: Social networks vs. demography as criteria for designing effective teams. *Administrative Science Quarterly, 49,* 101–133.

Robbins, S. P. (2003). *Essentials of organizational behavior.* Upper Saddle River, NJ: Prentice Hall.

Rogers, E., & Bhowmik, D. (1971). Homophily-heterophily: Relational concepts for communication research. *Public Opinion Quarterly, 34,* 523–538.

Schulz-Hardt, S., Jochims, M., & Frey, D. (2002). Productive conflict in group decision making: Genuine and contrived dissent as strategies to counteract biased information seeking. *Organizational Behavior and Human Decision Processes, 88,* 563–586.

Schwenk, C. R. (1990). Effects of devil's advocacy and dialectical inquiry on decision making: A meta-analysis. *Organizational Behavior and Human Decision Processes, 47,* 161–176.

Sethi, R. (2000a). Superordinate identity in cross-functional product development teams: Its antecedents and effect on new product performance. *Journal of the Academy of Marketing Science, 28*(3), 330–344.

Sethi, R. (2000b). New product quality and product development teams. *Journal of Marketing, 64*(2), 1–14.

Sethi, R., Smith, D. C., & Park, C. W. (2001). Cross-functional product development teams, creativity, and the innovativeness of consumer products. *Journal of Marketing Research, 38*(1), 73–85.

Shalley, C. E. (1991). Effects of productivity goals, creativity goals, and personal discretion on individual creativity. *Journal of Applied Psychology, 76,* 179–185.

Stewart, G. L., & Barrick, M. R. (2000). Team structure and performance: Assessing the mediating role of intrateam process and the moderating role of task type. *Academy of Management Journal, 43*(2), 135–148.

Tagger, S. (2002). Individual creativity and group ability to utilize individual creative resources: A multilevel model. *Academy of Management Journal, 45,* 315–330.

Tajfel, H., & Turner, J. C. (1979). An integrative theory of intergroup conflict. In: W. G. Austin & S. Worchel (Eds), *The social psychology of intergroup relations* (pp. 7–24). Monterrey, CA: Brooks/Cole.

Thursby, M. (2005). Introducing technology entrepreneurship to graduate education: An integrative approach. In: G. Libecap (Ed.), *University entrepreneurship and technology transfer; process, design, and intellectual property (Advances in the study of entrepreneurship, innovation and economic growth)* (Vol. 16, pp. 211–240). London: Elsevier.

Tjosvold, D. (1997). Conflict within Interdependence: It's value for productivity and individuality. In: C. K. W. DeDreu & E. Van de Vliert (Eds), *Using conflict in organizations* (pp. 23–37). London: Sage.

Turner, J. C. (1985). Social categorization and the self concept: A social cognitive theory of group behavior. In: E. J. Lawler (Ed.), *Advances in group processes: Theory and research* (Vol. 2, pp. 77–122). Greenwich, CT: JAI Press.

Tushman, M. L. (1977). Special boundary roles in the innovation process. *Administrative Science Quarterly, 22*, 587–605.

Tushman, M. L. (1978). Technical communication in R&D laboratories: The impact of project work characteristics. *Academy of Management Journal, 21*(4), 624–645.

Tziner, A., & Eden, D. (1985). Effects of crew composition on crew performance: Does the whole equal the sum of its parts? *Journal of Applied Psychology, 70*, 85–93.

Van Maanen, J., & Barley, S. R. (1984). Occupational communities: Culture and control in organizations. In: B. M. Staw & L. L. Cummings (Eds), *Research in organizational behavior* (Vol. 6, pp. 287–365). Greenwich, CT: JAI Press.

Veryzer, R. W., Jr. (1998). Discontinuous innovation and the new product development process. *Journal of Product Innovation Management, 15*(4), 304–321.

Vincent, L. (2005). *Marketing strategy formulation in the commercialization of new technologies.* Unpublished doctoral dissertation. Georgia Institute of Technology, Atlanta, GA.

Wallace, J. E. (1995). Organizational and professional commitment in professional and nonprofessional organizations. *Administrative Science Quarterly, 40*, 228–255.

Wilder, D. A. (1986). Social categorization: Implications for creation and reduction of intergroup bias. *Advances in Experimental Psychology, 19*, 291–355.

Williams, K. Y., & O'Reilly, C. A. (1998). Demography and diversity in organizations: A review of 40 years of research. In: B. M. Staw & L. L. Cummings (Eds), *Research in organizational behavior* (Vol. 20, pp. 77–140). Greenwich, CT: JAI Press.

Zahay, D., Griffin, A., & Fredericks, E. (2004). Sources, uses, and forms of data in the new product development process. *Industrial Marketing Management, 33*, 657–666.

Zenger, T. R., & Lawrence, B. S. (1989). Organizational demography: The differential effects of age and tenure distributions on technical communication. *Academy of Management Journal, 32*(2), 353–376.

PART II:
INTELLECTUAL PROPERTY

CHAPTER 3

INTELLECTUAL PROPERTY PROTECTION IN THE GLOBAL ECONOMY

Louise Hallenborg, Marco Ceccagnoli and Meadow Clendenin

ABSTRACT

This chapter provides an overview of five modes of intellectual property (IP) protection – patents, designs, copyrights, trademarks, and trade secrets – available in the United States, the European Union, and Japan. After describing the purposes of and principal differences among the five types of IP protection and outlining the advantages of each form, the chapter provides country- and region-specific information. The authors highlight the aspects of IP law in which international harmonization has, or has not yet, occurred, and offer insights into the relative advantages of various national and regional IP protection systems.

INTRODUCTION

Intellectual property rights – patents, designs, copyright, trademarks, and trade secrets – can be extremely valuable assets in today's global economy and have become increasingly important over the years.[1] In the high-tech

Technological Innovation: Generating Economic Results
Advances in the Study of Entrepreneurship, Innovation and
Economic Growth, Volume 18, 63–116
ISSN: 1048-4736/doi:10.1016/S1048-4736(07)00003-3

world, which is characterized by high development costs and opportunities for others to exploit what has been created, ownership of intellectual property is a key to success. Expensive research and development projects might never be undertaken if results could easily be duplicated by competitors.[2]

This chapter describes the patent, design, copyright, trademark, and trade secret laws protecting intellectual property within the United States (US), the European Union (EU), some specific European countries, and Japan. It sets out the criteria used for granting protection, the scope of the rights, and the remedies available when a violation occurs. It does not attempt to treat the entire set of issues, nor to cover the full set of countries comprising the global economy; instead, it should be viewed as an introduction to basic intellectual property protection in today's advanced countries.

What is Intellectual Property?

"Intellectual property very broadly means the legal rights which result from intellectual activity in the industrial, scientific, literary, and artistic fields."[3] Generally speaking, there are five major types of intellectual property: (i) patents, (ii) designs, (iii) copyrights, (iv) trademarks, and (v) trade secrets.[4] Each type of right has its own criteria for protection, scope, and duration.[5] Some intellectual properties can be subject to simultaneous protection under several systems; at the same time, some achievements are not protected at all. Countries have laws to protect intellectual property for two main reasons. One is to give statutory expression to the moral and economic rights of creators in their creations and the right of the public in access to those creations. The second is to provide an incentive to participate in the creative and innovative processes, to promote the dissemination and use of their results, and to encourage fair trade that contributes to economic and social development.[6]

Overview of Differences among Patents, Designs, Copyrights, Trademarks, and Trade Secrets

The different intellectual property rights have a common trait: each is exclusionary in nature.[7] The rights are mostly "negative," in the sense that they are intended to prevent others from copying, adapting, selling, and making certain other uses of the protected product, process, or work without authorization. The exclusionary rights, however, are mostly time-limited, and once protection has expired the invention or work can be used and exploited by anyone.[8]

Patents

Patents commonly are used to protect commercial and industrial products. They are granted on a country-by-country basis by the national patent offices of most countries around the world.[9] Patents are territorial by definition – for example, a US patent is enforceable only in the US and its territories.[10] There is no such thing as a global patent.[11] In most cases, to obtain a patent in a given country, an inventor must file a patent application before the relevant patent office. The systems and criteria for granting patents differ by country, but most countries require the invention to be novel, non-obvious (inventive step), capable of industrial applicability (utility), and properly disclosed in the application.[12] Countries' definitions of patents vary slightly. In general, a patent can be described as a time-limited right in a new invention – a machine, a manufacture, a useful process or composition of matter, or any new and useful improvement thereof – granted by a government authority upon application. During the term of the patent, usually 20 years,[13] the owner is granted the right to exclude others from producing, using, distributing, or selling the invention without the patent owner's prior consent.[14] However, in many countries, mathematical methods, physical phenomena, discoveries of natural substances, methods for medical treatment (as opposed to medical products), and abstract ideas are not patentable.[15]

Designs. The system for protection of industrial design is different around the world,[16] and national protection of designs requires application and registration in most countries.[17] As with patent registrations, the effects of a national design registration are limited to the country in which the design is registered.[18] In some countries, the design and appearance of a product is protected through a special form of patent.[19] In other countries, patents do not protect the appearance of a product; instead, these countries provide a registration process for designs.[20] A design can typically be protected if it gives a new overall impression in relation to previous designs.[21] The right holder can prevent others from using, selling, importing, or exporting products with a design not different in an overall impression to the holder's.[22] The term of the design protection varies from country to country, between a maximum of 14 and 25 years.[23]

Copyrights

Copyrights protect creative works – that is, a literary, musical, scientific, or artistic work.[24] A copyright can be described as an exclusive right regulating the use of a particular expression of an idea. Almost any expression is copyrightable – apart from words, very short phrases, and facts.[25] Ideas of works are not protected; instead, copyright protects the specific expression of that idea.[26] Hence, so long as a person does not copy the wording or significant parts of the wording ("expression") of J.K. Rowling's books on Harry Potter, the idea of a book about a little boy with glasses going to witchcraft and wizard school is open to anyone.

Unlike the industrial rights – patent, design, and trademark – copyright is obtained immediately upon fixation, without any formal measures.[27] Copyright can generally be said to include two sets of rights: moral rights and economic rights.[28] Moral rights are the creator's right to prevent distortion, mutilation, or modification of his/her work that may be prejudicial to his/her honor or reputation.[29] The economic rights include rights of reproduction, broadcasting, public performance, modification, translation, derivation, public recitation, public display, distribution, and other ways of making the work available to the public.[30] As the name discloses, copyright is construed as protection against *copying*.[31] It does not prevent others from later independently creating something similar or identical. The duration of copyright protection is different in different countries; however, in principle, the work is protected during the creator's lifetime and 50–70 years after his death or, for works made for hire, 95 years from fixation in a tangible medium of expression.[32]

Trademarks

A trademark can be a word, name, symbol, device, or combinations thereof used to identify goods or services of a company and to distinguish those from goods provided by others.[33] A service mark is the same as a trademark, except that it identifies and distinguishes the source of a service rather than a product.[34] The terms "trademark" and "mark" are commonly used to refer to both trademarks and service marks. Generally, to be eligible for trademark protection, the trademark must be distinct and not confusingly similar to another trademark registered for the same or similar goods or services.[35] In most countries, generic trademarks – commonly used names or descriptions such as "clear water" for bottled water – cannot be protected.[36] A trademark owner can prevent others from using a similar mark for the same goods or services.[37] However, goods or services provided by the parties do not have to be the same if the prior mark is famous enough that dilution of the mark's distinctiveness might occur from the other parties' use.[38]

Although some countries afford protection for unregistered trademarks, in most countries trademark protection requires application and registration before a national or regional office.[39] The effects of a registration are limited to the country or, in the case of regional registration, countries concerned.[40] Trademark protection is in reality not limited in time; a registration can be renewed indefinitely by payment of renewal fees.[41]

Trade Secrets

The definition of trade secret varies from country to country. In most countries it can be defined as commercially valuable information that is not in the public domain and is the subject of reasonable efforts to maintain its secrecy.[42] An example is the Coca-Cola recipe, which has been protected as a trade secret for over a century.[43] As opposed to patents, whose purpose is for the invention to be public and well known, the value of a trade secret lies in its secrecy.[44] As soon as the secret is disclosed, protection is lost.[45] Therefore, trade secrets are difficult to maintain. Unlike most intellectual properties, trade secrets protect only against misappropriation and not against duplication or reverse engineering.[46] This means that the same "trade secret" may be used by more than one business on condition that each made the discovery independently and that they all maintain its secrecy. Trade secrets have several advantages over other forms of intellectual property, including that no public disclosure is required and that there is no time limit on protection.

INTERNATIONAL PROTECTION OF INTELLECTUAL PROPERTY

Patents

Filing patent applications in foreign countries is expensive, mainly because the text of the application has to be translated into the local language. However, a number of systems (due to international cooperation) allow applicants to lower the cost of filing foreign patent applications. The Paris Convention for the Protection of Industrial Property, adhered to by 171 countries,[47] provides that each country guarantees the citizens of the other countries the same rights in patent and trademark matters that it gives to its own citizens; it also sets a minimum level for protection in the contracting countries. By virtue of the Paris Convention, most foreign patent applications can effectively be backdated to the filing date of a national patent application for up to six months, if the national patent application is that of a Paris Convention state.[48] This is called claiming "priority" from the national patent application, and the first year after a patent application is filed is often called the "priority year."[49] Another treaty, called the Patent Cooperation Treaty (PCT) and administered by the World Intellectual Property Organization, allows filing of an international patent application, covering virtually all industrialized countries in the world, instead of filing separate foreign patent applications.[50] PCT is presently adhered to by more than 130 member countries, including all important industrial countries within and outside Europe and also China.[51] An international patent application does not lead to grant of an international patent; instead, it is a bundle of national or regional patent applications that remain as a single application for up to 18 months.[52] At the end of that time, the international patent application must be divided and progressed as individual patent applications in the desired countries or regions.[53] A PCT application is usually the best alternative if a patent is sought in 11 or more countries, because the PCT system caps payments at 10 designations. The PCT system also allows the applicant to avoid paying follow-up fees until 30 months after the filing date or priority date and then only if he/she wishes to proceed further with the application.[54]

The European Patent Office handles European patent applications for the member states of the European Patent Convention (EPC).[55] The EPC is not exclusively for EU member states; not all the EU member states have joined, and it is also open to other states than those within the EU.[56] Upon grant, a European patent is validated in the desired European countries, and only then must translations be prepared. Obtaining patents in several European countries through one application procedure significantly simplifies the application process.

Designs

As within the patent field, systems simplify the process of obtaining national protection in several countries for the same design. The Hague Agreement (1925) is an international system that confers national protection by filing of a single application with the WIPO.[57] This application must designate the states in which protection is sought. This system applies only in certain EU member states (Belgium, Bulgaria, Estonia, France, Germany, Greece, Hungary, Italy, Luxembourg, the Netherlands, Romania, Slovenia, and Spain with limited effect) plus other non-EU countries.[58] As The Hague

Agreement confers a bundle of national registrations and not a unitary registration, if protection is not available in one of the designated countries, the application will be rejected only in that country, and rejection in one country will not exclude protection in the other designated countries.

Within the EU, under the Community Design (unitary system), a single application confers protection throughout the whole EU.[59] This is not a set of national registrations, but instead a single registration with equal value in all member states.[60]

Copyrights

As with many other areas of intellectual property, copyright has been subject to extensive international cooperation. Copyrights are territorial, meaning that no "international copyright" automatically protects an author's writing or a composer's song throughout the entire world. Protection against unauthorized use in a specific country depends upon the national laws of that country. Many countries do, however, offer protection to foreign works through adherence to The Berne Convention for the Protection of Literary and Artistic Works, established in 1886 in Berne, Switzerland.[61] Under the Berne Convention, an author's rights are respected in another country as if the author were a citizen of that country.[62] For example, works by US authors are protected by French copyright in France, and vice versa, because both the US and France are signatories to the Berne Convention. The Berne Convention also precludes formalities for copyright protection, meaning that copyright in the signatory states cannot be dependent on formalities such as registration or copyright notice.[63] This provision does not, however, prevent a member nation from taking adherence to formalities into account when determining what remedies apply.[64] Furthermore, under the Berne Convention, the minimum duration for copyright protection is the life of the author plus 50 years,[65] and the signatory states must provide for protection of six rights: translation, reproduction, public performance, adaptation, paternity, and integrity.[66]

Trademarks

WIPO administers the Madrid Protocol, which provides a system for filing for an international registration (IR) that avoids the need to register separately the same trademark with each national or regional office.[67]

The IR is a single registration with one registration number covering several countries, as chosen in the applicant's designation.[68] The system is available only to the individuals or legal entities that are nationals of, domiciled in, or have a real and effective commercial or industrial establishment in, a country that is a member of the Madrid Protocol.[69] Before filing an application for an IR, the applicant must own a trademark registration or application in its country of origin for which international protection is sought.[70] This application or registration is referred to as the basis for the IR.[71] Once a basis registration of application is secured, the applicant files an international application with the trademark office in its country of origin.[72] The national office transmits the application to WIPO, which then sends the application for examination by the local trademark offices in the countries in which the applicant has requested protection.[73] If the application is granted, the owner of the IR will have secured the same degree of protection given to holders of national registrations in those countries.[74] The protection's term is 20 years, but it can be renewed for an unlimited number of additional 20-year periods.[75] Advantages of the IR are that only one application need be filed, in one language, and with one fee; no translation is necessary. Furthermore, filing fees for an IR are generally lower than fees involved in national filings.

Also, the EU provides a system for a Community Trademark (CTM), through which an applicant can obtain trademark protection within all of the EU member states upon a single application.[76] This application does not require designation – the application is filed and, if protection is possible, it is granted in all member states.[77] A CTM is not a bundle of national trademarks, but a unitary mark protection.[78] If protection is not possible in one member state, the whole application is rejected.[79]

Trade Secrets

The protection of trade secrets varies from country to country.[80] The nature of a trade secret is that it remains secret; therefore no registration is required or possible. The disclosure of a trade secret means complete loss of protection. In most countries, a court ruling is the only certain way to discover that information is a trade secret. From an international perspective, trade secrets have been subject to some cooperation and harmonization through vehicles such as the WTO's Agreement on Trade-Related Aspects of Intellectual Property Rights (TRIPS), which entered into force in January 1995.[81]

ADVANTAGES OF THE DIFFERENT INTELLECTUAL PROPERTY RIGHTS

The laws governing patents, designs, copyrights, trade secrets, and trademarks provide legal protection to an individual's or a company's intellectual property. Patents are, however, often considered the most powerful right because they, unlike trade secrets, protect against both deliberate misuse and good-faith origination of the same or similar inventions. Patents can also serve as legal barriers and allow firms to capture above-normal returns from their innovations. The mere existence of a patent can scare off competitors, and the threat of patent litigation may be a powerful deterrent to would-be imitators. Patent registrations also often make financing, mergers, acquisitions, or partnering proposals more attractive. They generally enhance a business's professional reputation, contribute to inventors' prestige, and protect shareholder value. Although expensive, patent protection is available under several systems that make protecting the same invention in several countries easier and cheaper (e.g., the EPC and PCT).

Unlike patents, copyrights are immediate and, compared to most intellectual property rights, inexpensive and long-term. However, copyrights do not protect against other identical or similar works that have been created independently. They protect only against "copying," where the original copyright holder's work has been used as a model.

The right holder of a registered design can prevent others from making, offering, putting on the market, importing, exporting, or using products incorporating the design. Design rights include protection against both deliberate copying and independent development of a similar design, which provides the design right holder with an advantage compared to copyright and unregistered designs.

A trademark holder also is protected against deliberate misuse as well as good-faith infringements of his trademark. Strength of the trademark rights, in comparison to other intellectual property rights, lies in the fact that trademark rights can be upheld for an infinite period of time upon payment of renewal fees.[82] A trademark holder whose trademark registration expires due to failure to pay a renewal fee also can apply for a new registration of the trademark.[83] This is an obvious difference from patents: if a patent expires because the inventor fails to pay renewal fees, the inventor cannot obtain a new patent registration.[84]

Trade secrets, similarly, are not limited in time.[85] Although they can be maintained forever, trade secret protection is far from the legal strengths of a patent, but may be very powerful if the secret is maintained. One important limitation of the rights conferred is that a trade secret protects only against misappropriation. Therefore, the same trade secret may well exist in two different businesses at the same time.

COUNTRY- AND REGION-SPECIFIC INFORMATION

United States

Patents
In the US, patents are issued by the United States Patent and Trademark Office (USPTO), an agency of the US Department of Commerce.[86]
  US patent law creates three types of patents:[87]

1. *Utility patent*, which may be granted to anyone who invents or discovers any new and useful process, machine, article of manufacture or compositions of matters, or any new useful improvement thereof;
2. *Design patent*, which may be granted to anyone who invents a new, original, and ornamental design for an article of manufacture; and
3. *Plant patent*, which may be granted to anyone who invents or discovers and asexually (from cuttings and grafts, not seeds) reproduces any distinct and new variety of plants.

  Of these three types of patents, utility patents are the most common. In this chapter's discussion of patents, utility patents will be meant unless otherwise specifically stated. The maximum term of a new patent is 20 years for utility patents[88] (extended through change in law in 1999 from a maximum of 17 years from the date of issuance), calculated from the date of filing the application in the US or, in special cases, from the date an earlier, related application was filed.[89] In 1999, a guarantee was introduced pledging US inventors of utility and plant patents a 17-year patent term if their applications are delayed by the USPTO process.[90] In general, patents will continue to last 20 years from the filing date, which should generally give a bit more than 17 years validity from issue date. The patent term for utility is subject to the payment of maintenance fees, and will expire earlier if fees are not paid.[91] Maintenance fees must be paid to keep in force a patent based on an application filed on or after December 12, 1980.[92] Prior to this date, no maintenance fees were required.[93]
  Unlike many other countries in which a "first-to-file" system prevails, the US system protects the "first-to-invent."[94] This means that in the US, if two

inventors independently of one another develop similar inventions, a patent will be awarded to the first to invent (with some restrictions), while in most countries outside the US, the inventor first to apply for a patent application will be awarded the patent   without regard to who first invented.

In either type of system, timely filing of the patent application is crucial. A utility patent is granted for a "new" and "useful" invention.[95] These requirements imply that if the invention has been described in a printed publication anywhere in the world or if it has been in public use or on sale in the US *more than one year* prior to the filing of a patent application, a patent cannot be obtained in the US.[96] The use or publication of an invention before the filing of the application does not, as in many other countries, invalidate US patentability; rather, it may be useful evidence of being the first inventor. Pre-filing publication also permits an inventor to test the potential market before committing to the high cost of filing a patent application.

If the subject matter sought to be patented is not shown with precision by the prior art, and if the subject matter involves one or several differences compared to the most similar invention known, a patent still may be refused if the differences are obvious. Generally, substituting one material for another or changes in size do not create patentability.[97] The "useful" criterion of patent law refers to the condition that the subject matter has a useful purpose and operativeness.[98] Thus, a machine that will not perform its intended purpose would not be called useful and therefore will be denied a patent.

In 1995, several changes were made to US patent law. One change was the creation of a provisional patent application process.[99] Provisional filings require only modest fees, are not examined, and do not start the 20-year term clock.[100] However, they expire after one year unless followed by a non-provisional application.[101] The advantage of a provisional filing is to establish an earlier date of priority without requiring filing of specific claims.

In 1998, a federal appeals court ruled that useful, novel, and non-obvious business methods may be patented.[102] This opened the door to an increasing number of patent applications. As the name suggests, business method patents protect ways of doing business, as opposed to specific articles or manufacturing methods.[103] Business method applications are examined on the same criteria as are other patent categories.[104] The business method patents include investment systems, insurance schemes, Internet commerce systems, information systems, and training methods.[105] However, they are most often encountered in computer and Internet-related applications. Probably one of the most famous business method patents was granted to Amazon.com founder Jeff Bezos in September 1999 for a one-click method of processing customer orders over the Internet.[106] Clicking on an item places an order and adds the customer's details automatically without the need for further customer input.[107] In February 2000, Bezos was granted a patent for an Internet-based customer referral and commission payment system.[108] In Europe, business methods can be patented only if they involve a technical effect.[109] The fact that non-technological business methods are not patentable in Europe does not prevent European companies from filing a patent application for non-technological business methods in the US, valid of course only in US territory.

In the words of the statute, a US patent includes "the right to exclude others from making, using, offering for sale or selling" the invention in the US or "importing" the invention to the US.[110] Note that the right conferred is the right to *exclude* others from making, using, offering for sale, selling, or importing, not necessarily the right for the patent owner *to do* so himself/herself, since the patent owner's right might be subject to the patent rights of others.[111] Patents are always issued to individuals.[112] However, commercial rights are usually assigned to the organization for which the individual works.[113] A patent owner who produces or sells patented products, or a person who does so for or under the patent owner, is required to mark the products with the word "Patent" and the patent number.[114] Otherwise, the patentee may not recover damages from an infringer, unless the infringer was duly notified of the infringement and continued to infringe after the notice.[115] Statements such as "Patent applied for" or "Patent pending" have no legal effect.[116] The protection granted through a patent does not start until the application has been approved and the patent granted.[117]

The Patent Process.   In 2005, 390,733 patent applications were filed with the USPTO.[118] The USPTO granted 143,806 applications, out of which 73,279 were from US residents.[119] The application and patent protection process before the USPTO can be not only very time-consuming but also costly, as Table 1 shows.

The preparation of applications and management of negotiations with the USPTO by specialized patent attorneys and agents may take one to two years, and sometimes even more.[120] US patent applications are secret until 18 months after the filing date, sometimes even until the date the patent is granted.[121] As a result, a patent search to determine whether a business can make or use an invention is limited in utility. In many cases, the business owner may not know that he/she has infringed a patent until the patentee sends a letter demanding a license fee. Although marking an invention as "patent pending" or "patent applied for" while the application is in process has no legal effect, it sometimes provides greater protection than the patent

Table 1. USPTO Fees (USD)[a].

Type of Right	Description	Fee	Small Entity Fee[b] (If Applicable)
Patent	Basic application fee	300.00	150.00
Patent	Maintenance fee due at 3.5 years	900.00	450.00
Patent	Maintenance fee due at 7.5 years	2,300.00	1,150.00
Patent	Maintenance fee due at 11.5 years	3,800.00	1,900.00
Patent	Surcharge if payment of maintenance fee is 6 months late	130.00	65.00
Trademark	Basic application for registration fee	325.00	n/a
Trademark	Application for renewal fee due every 10 years	400.00	n/a

[a]Fees as of December 2004, http://www.uspto.gov/web/offices/ac/qs/ope/fee2007february01.htm
[b]Small entity means an independent inventor, a small business concern, or a non-profit organization eligible for reduced patent fees. In order to establish small entity status for the purpose of paying a maintenance fee, a written assertion of entitlement to small entity status must be filed prior to or with the maintenance fee paid as a small entity. A written assertion is only required to be filed once and will remain effective until changed. For more information see http://www.uspto.gov/web/offices/pac/mpep/documents/0500_509_02.htm#sect509.02

itself, because competitors are not sure of the scope of the patent. US patent applications are, since a change in US patent legislation in 1999, published 18 months after the earliest effective filing date or priority date claimed by an application.[122] Also, applications filed abroad will be published by the USPTO after 18 months.[123] A publication fee of US $300 is payable with the issue fee when the application is allowed.[124] An inventor may request that his patent application should not be published;[125] however, such a request must be made at the time of filing the application, and then only if the invention has not been and will not be the subject of an application filed in a foreign country that requires publication 18 months after filing (or earlier claimed priority date) or under the PCT.[126] Following publication, the application for patent is no longer held in confidence by USPTO, and any member of the public may request access to the entire file history of the application.[127]

The application must include a detailed description of how to make and use the invention.[128] It must also include one or more "patent claims," which are sentences that define the scope of the invention for which the inventor feels he/she is entitled to patent protection.[129] A patent is granted not upon the idea or suggestion of, for example, a new machine, but upon the new machine itself. The application must include an enabling description of the actual machine or other subject matter for which a patent is sought.[130]

Each patent application is assigned to one of nearly 150,000 patent sub-classes.[131] The patent claims stated in the application are later used by an examining group within this sub-classification at the Patent Office to determine whether the criteria for a patent, such as "novelty" and "non-obviousness," are fulfilled.[132] If the application seems to fulfill the standards for patentability, an examiner will further investigate whether the claimed innovation conflicts with any pending applications or recently granted patents.[133]

Dispute Resolution. Disputes arising during the patenting process are handled by the USPTO's Board of Patent Appeals and Interferences (the Board).[134] The parties involved in dispute are given opportunity to review the other's application and a hearing is held to determine who invented first.[135] Most cases, however, are resolved between the parties before a final hearing by the Board, often by cross-licensing agreements.

The validity of issued patents is challenged in federal district court.[136] The federal courts have exclusive jurisdiction over disputes involving infringement of patents.[137]

An infringement of a patent consists of the unauthorized making, using, offering for sale, or selling any patented invention within the US or US territories, or importing into the US any patented invention, during the term of the patent.[138] A patent owner who believes his/her patent is being infringed may sue for relief in the appropriate federal court.[139] The patent owner may ask the court for injunctive relief (a judgment ordering the defendant to cease the patent infringement) and/or sue for damages.[140] In such an infringement suit, the defendant may raise the question of the patent's validity, a question that is then decided by the court.[141] Also, the alleged infringing party may sue for declaratory relief – a judgment that the plaintiff is not infringing any patent held by the defendant and may continue its operations as before.[142] Furthermore, the defendant may claim that its actions do not constitute infringement.[143] Whether infringement exists is determined mainly by evaluating the wording of the patent claims.[144] If the defendant's action does not fall within the wording of any of the patent claims, there is no infringement.[145] The decision of the district court may be appealed to the Court of Appeals for the Federal Circuit, whose decision may be appealed to the US Supreme Court.[146] Disputes may be resolved by the parties at any point in the process.

In November 1999, a new first inventor defense (sometimes referred to as "prior user defense") became effective.[147] The defense applies to actions for infringement of claims that may be infringed by any method of doing or conducting an entity's business.[148] The provision applies only if the defendant, acting in good faith, had reduced the subject matter in question to practice at least one year before the effective filing date of the patent sought to be enforced.[149] If those requirements are met, the defendant is protected where it made good faith use before the effective filing date of the patent and that use is either commercial or, in the case of a non-profit research lab or a non-profit entity such as university, research center, or hospital, a use for which the public is the intended beneficiary.[150] The defense does not render the patent invalid.[151]

Copyrights
The purpose of copyright law is to protect the original expression of an idea, whether it is literary, artistic, commercial, or other, including screenplays, sculpture, music, computer programs, choreography, videogames, and architectural works.[152] The two minimum qualifications for obtaining copyright, according to US legislation are "originality in expression" and "fixation."[153] "Originality" does not imply novelty in the sense that the work has never been created; it only means that the creator did not copy the work from elsewhere. "Fixation" means that a copyrighted work must be fixed on copies (as defined in 17 U.S.C. § 101) or phonograms.[154]

Although almost any expression is copyrightable, some things cannot be subject to copyright protection. According to American copyright law, ornamentation, lettering, or coloring; mere listing of ingredients or contents; titles, names, short phrases, and slogans; familiar symbols or designs; and variations of typography are not copyrightable.[155] This also is true for ideas, methods, systems, processes, procedures, concepts, principles, discoveries, and devices, unless they are descriptions, explanations, or illustrations of such.[156]

A copyright need not be applied for or registered to be obtained; the rights are afforded to the creator as soon as the originality and fixation requirements are fulfilled.[157] However, registration of a copyright in the US Copyright Office before an infringement gives the copyright owner additional remedies under the US Copyright Act.[158] Registration provides evidence of validity of the claim, but most importantly it enables the right holder to file an infringement suit in court and to file for statutory damages, which are a minimum fine the court can assess, particularly if actual damages are difficult to calculate.[159] This remedy is unavailable without registration.[160] A registration is also a requirement for, and will make it more likely that the copyright holder may recover, attorneys' fees if claims are litigated.[161] In comparison to the patent application process, copyright registration is fast and inexpensive. It requires only simple forms and the deposit of one or more copies of the work, together with a payment of a registration fee of US $45.[162] The registration may be made at any time within the term of the copyright.[163]

The copyright owner is afforded the following exclusive rights under the US Copyright Act. (i) *The reproduction right* establishes that only the copyright owner may reproduce or copy the work.[164] Examples of prohibited unauthorized acts are photocopying a book, copying a computer program, and using parts of a song in a new song. An infringement does not necessarily require that the entire original be copied; it is sufficient that a substantial and material portion has been copied. (ii) *The right to prepare derivative works* means that the copyright owner has the exclusive right to transform his original work, such as making a motion picture out of a book, or translating it, or creating a second updated version of a software program.[165] (iii) *The distribution right* affords the copyright owner the sole right to lease, sell, rent, or lend copies or phonorecords of the work to the public and the right to prohibit distribution of unauthorized copies.[166] However, after the first sale or distribution of a copy, the copyright owner can no longer control what happens to that copy. An exception to this "first sale doctrine" is the renting, leasing, or selling software and phonorecords, which cannot then be rented or loaned for commercial purposes. (iv) *The right to perform the work publicly* in the case of literary, musical, dramatic, and choreographic works, pantomimes, and motion pictures and other audiovisual works.[167] (v) *The right to display the copyrighted work publicly* in the case of literary, musical, dramatic, and choreographic works, pantomimes, and pictorial, graphic, or sculptural works, including the individual images of picture or other audiovisual work, and in the case of sound recordings, by means of digital audio transmission.[168]

These copyright holder's rights are subject to some limitations designed to protect the public interest. American courts have developed a doctrine of fair use, now incorporated in the US Copyright Act, meaning that fair use may be made of a copyright protected work in some limited circumstances, such as criticism, news reports, education, and research.[169] Courts have sometimes held that the fair use doctrine allows making copies of software programs needed for reverse engineering purposes.[170]

In the US, for works created on or after January 1, 1978, copyright protection lasts for the life of the creator plus 70 years.[171] If the work was made for hire, the term is 95 years from the date of publication or 120 years from the date of creation – whichever expires first.[172]

Mere ownership of a book, manuscript, painting, or other copy or phonorecord does not give the possessor copyright.[173] The rights entailed with copyright protection are vested in the author – that is, the creator of the work.[174] Any or all of the copyright owner's exclusive rights may be transferred.[175] Such a transfer is not valid unless it is made in writing and signed by the copyright owner or by the owner's duly authorized agent.[176] In contrast, a transfer of non-exclusive rights does not require written agreement.[177]

The Copyright Act does not require the use of a copyright notice.[178] However, if a proper copyright note is included (such as "©," "Copyright," or "Copr." and the owner's name and year of first publication) on the work as published, certain legal benefits may follow.[179] The copyright holder is responsible for applying the copyright notice,[180] which does not require any advance permission or registration.[181]

Software and Database Protection. Computer software is eligible for copyright protection under US law as it is considered a type of literary work.[182] Since copyright protects not the idea of the program but the source code/algorithm, an infringement occurs only if source code is identical.[183] As programming has become less linear, it has also become easier to write code that performs the same functions as another program, without copying the first code. Many software corporations therefore find the protection provided by copyright for software inadequate. Lately, creators of software have circumvented the problem of protecting the idea behind the software by applying for patents on the algorithm or process of software. If the functional aspects of software are *novel* and *non-obvious*, they can also be subject to patent protection in the US.[184] Although patent protection is more expensive and time-consuming than copyright, it is broader because the source code does not have to be identical if both software products follow the same process. Protection by patent includes not only the algorithms but also the interfaces where these represent technological inventions.

In the US, databases can be protected only by copyright, as compilations.[185] Section 101, Title 17 of the US Code defines a compilation as "a collection and assembling of pre-existing materials or of data that are selected in such a way that the resulting work as a whole constitutes an original work of authorship."[186] Thus, copyright protection is afforded only when the work as a whole constitutes an original work of authorship. Although certain court rulings have found a protectable element in the so-called "sweat of the brow" or "industrious collection" tests, the prevailing US Supreme Court doctrine does not allow copyright protection unless an original selection, co-ordination, and arrangement of data can be proven.[187]

If there is no original/creative selection involved, the database is not protected.[188] There is no protection against extraction of data; however, it would be a violation to copy the entire database if the originality test were satisfied. Databases must contain a minimum level of creativity to receive protection,[189] due to the strength of free speech as guaranteed in the US Constitution. For example, a top-ten list of famous persons could be copyrighted because of the subjective (and thus original) nature of the selection criterion. The individual names are not protected, and so anyone may copy a particular name from the list. However, copying the list as a whole (or a substantial portion) is not permitted under copyright law.

Trademarks
Single words, titles, and short phrases may not be copyrightable under US law; however, if they meet the appropriate qualifications they may be protected as trademarks. A trademark is "any word, name, symbol, or device or any combination thereof" adopted and used by a merchant to identify his goods and distinguish them from those manufactured or sold by others.[190] Trademarks are relatively easy to obtain, provided that no one else has prior rights to the same or similar mark for goods or services of the same general type in the same geographic territory and that the mark is not otherwise unprotectable (i.e., due to being generic, immoral, descriptive, and deceptive or merely a surname). The US Supreme Court has ruled that under very special circumstances even a mere color can be a trademark.[191]

Trademark rights in the US can be established through legitimate use of the trademark or through registration.[192] A federal trademark registration, obtained upon application before the USPTO, provides the owner substantial legal benefits.[193] One benefit of a registered trademark is the owner's exclusive right to use the mark nationwide on or in connection with the goods and/or services listed in the registration.[194] The owner of an unregistered mark is limited to using the mark only in the geographic area in which the unregistered mark is actually being used. Furthermore, registration gives the trademark owner the ability to bring an action concerning the mark in federal court.[195] The US registration can be used as a basis to obtain registration in foreign countries (e.g., through the Madrid Protocol, of which the US became a member in November 2003).[196] The Madrid Protocol allows businesses and individuals in the US to file for trademark protection in multiple countries using one application, in a single language, through a single national trademark office, and for a single filing fee.[197] Finally, a registration affords the ability to file the US registration with the US Customs Service to prevent importation of infringing foreign goods.[198] The goods and/or services for which registration is sought must be specified in the application.[199] The cost for application, registration, and maintenance is dependent on the number of classes in which protection is sought.[200] Currently, the price is US $400 per class (see Table 1).[201]

US trademark rights are based on the use of the mark in commerce.[202] Usually, the first to use a mark has priority over subsequent users, except where an individual has filed an "intent-to-use" application, which functions as a nationwide name reservation that eventually becomes a registered mark.[203]

A trademark owner can prevent others from using a confusingly similar mark.[204] Such use can be prevented even if the similarity was unintended, whether the use would confuse or deceive the public.[205] The test for confusing similarity has been defined by courts as if an ordinary prospective purchaser, exercising due care under the circumstances, is likely to regard the alternative product as coming from the same source as the trademarked product.[206] The goods or services sold by the parties need not even be the same if the prior mark is sufficiently famous.[207] For example, McDonald's managed to stop a motel owner from calling its motel chain "McSleep."[208]

Trademarks must continuously be protected by the owner to prevent them from falling into the public domain. Protection may be lost if an owner fails to protect its mark and allows it to be used in unauthorized ways or in ways that may cause it to cease being identified with only the goods and services of the owner. Also, a mark may be lost if it becomes "generic." A classic example of such a loss of a mark is "cellophane,"[209] which initially identified a brand of thin plastic wrapping paper.[210] However, the mark became so widely used to identify all forms of that type of wrapping paper that the courts ruled that it had become generic and ceased to be a valid mark.[211] The public no longer associated "cellophane" with a particular company.[212] Another example in the danger zone is "Rollerblade," which runs the risk of becoming a generic mark for inline skates.

Unlike copyrights or patents, which have finite terms of duration, trademarks can last indefinitely if the owner continues to use the mark on or in connection with the goods and/or services in the registration and files all necessary documentation in the USPTO at the appropriate times.[213]

Any time a merchant claims rights in a mark, he/she may use the "TM" (trademark) or "SM" (service mark) as an alert to the public, regardless of whether the merchant has filed an application with the USPTO.[214] However, the federal registration symbol "®" may be used only after the USPTO actually registers a mark and not while an application is pending.[215] Also, the registration symbol may be used only with the mark on or in connection with the goods and/or services listed in the federal trademark registration.[216] Several foreign countries use the "®" to indicate that a mark is registered in that country. Use of the symbol by the holder of a foreign registration may be proper.[217]

Domain names are becoming increasingly important. Although domain names are not always trademarks, they may be used as such when used to identify a product, service, or business entity.[218] In 1999, the US enacted the Anticybersquatting Consumer Protection Act, which creates a cause of action for certain misuses of marks and personal names and imposes particularly rigorous rules on damages.[219]

Trade Secrets

As of April 2006, the fundamentals of trade secret law were implemented in 47 US states via their adoption of the Uniform Trade Secrets Act.[220] The act defines trade secrets as "[i]nformation, including a formula, pattern, compilation, program, device, method, technique or process that both (i) derives independent economic value, actual or potential, from not being generally known to, and not being readily ascertainable by proper means by, other persons who can obtain economic value from its disclosure or use; and (ii) is the subject of efforts that are reasonable under the circumstances to maintain its secrecy."[221]

Contrary to patents, copyrights, and trademarks, trade secret involves no registration or certificate telling third parties that a business is claiming information as a trade secret. The only way to determine whether information is a trade secret is by a court ruling. The standard for trade secret protection is also lower for other forms of intellectual property, which depend on novelty or originality. To be subject to trade secret protection, the owner must use "reasonable efforts" to maintain the secrecy, for instance by marking materials as "secret" or "confidential," by limiting access to those who need to know, by demanding non-disclosure agreements with employees and business associates, and by taking action if unauthorized disclosure occurs.

The protection of trade secrets is not limited to a set term. Despite its unlimited time, however, trade secret protection is more limited compared to other intellectual property rights. Trade secrets are protected only against misappropriation, not against duplication or reverse engineering. This means that, in reality, a trade secret may be used by more than one business on condition that each made the discovery independently and that they all maintain its secrecy. According to the US Economic Espionage Act, theft of trade secrets is a crime.[222]

Ownership Issues within the Workplace

Copyrights. The general rule under US copyright law is that the person who creates a work is the author and copyright owner of that work.[223] There is, however, an exception to that principle. If a work is "made for hire," all the rights will be vested in the employer (firm, organization, or individual), not in the employee.[224] If the work is created by an employee within the scope of his/her employment, the work is considered to be made for hire and all the rights vest in the employer (unless there is a written agreement stating otherwise).[225] An example is a newspaper article written by a staff journalist for publication in the newspaper that employs the journalist. If a work is created by an independent contractor (i.e., someone not considered an employee) and the work is a specially ordered or commissioned work, then it can be a work made for hire if there is a written agreement between the parties stating that the work is made for hire and if it is for use as a contribution to a collective work, a part of a motion picture or other audiovisual work, a translation, a supplementary work, a compilation, an instructional text, a test, an answer material for a test, or an atlas. This means that if a company uses an independent contractor, rather than an employee, to design its web site, the company must ensure that it gets an assignment of copyright in the web site design. The copyright in any letterheads, brochures, logos, and packaging designed by non-employees must be assigned and transferred to the company. Many companies had an unpleasant surprise when they wanted to update tailor-made software and discovered that they do not own the source code of software created by independent contractors.

The copyright for a work made for hire is 95 years from the date of publication or 120 years from the date of creation – whichever expires first.[226] A work not made for hire is protected by copyright for the life of the creator plus 70 years.[227]

Patents. The US Patent Act requires the human inventor, not the corporate employer, to apply for a patent.[228] The inventor is the presumptive patent owner, unless there is an assignment to a third party.[229] A company wishing to own an employee's or a contractor's patentable invention must obtain a written assignment to be recorded promptly at the USPTO.[230] Employment contracts generally determine who has the right to exploit a patent. Unless a written contract stipulates otherwise, if the employee was hired to invent, it is presumed that the invention belongs to the employer; if the employee was not hired to invent, the employer acquires only a non-exclusive, non-transferable, royalty-free right to use the invention in its business. This calls for non-disclosure agreements, proprietary right transfer agreements, assignment instruments, and non-competition clauses.

European Union

Patents
There is extensive cooperation within the EU in the field of intellectual property, including the patent area. The national patent laws in the member states have been harmonized. National patents are granted upon application before the appropriate national Patent Office in each member state. In order to be patentable, an invention must be new, involve an inventive step, and be capable of industrial application.[231] In the EU countries, it is possible to patent computer software only if, when run on a computer, it produces a "technical effect."[232] Business methods are excluded from patent protection in most EU states.[233] However, under European Patent Organisation (EPO) case law, a business method can benefit from patent protection if its technical implementation (generally by way of software) is itself an invention.[234] An invention is not considered to be new if it has been disclosed publicly in any way, anywhere in the world. This means that the EU countries do not provide any grace period for national patent applications. Once granted, the national patent is kept in force by annual renewal fees for a maximum of 20 years after the filing date of the application. The afforded rights with the national patents differ among the member states.[235] In all the EU states, a holder of a national patent in an EU country can prevent others from using his/her invention and can seek an injunction or damages for infringement though the courts.

The EU has also made efforts to harmonize the biotech field through the adoption in 1998 of the Biotech Directive (98/44/EC).[236] The directive was intended to promote and enable the development of the biotech industry in the EU at a time when there were inconsistencies of legislation among the member states.[237] These discrepancies led to a competitive disadvantage to US and Japanese businesses, which were able to protect such inventions in their own markets. Most of the member states have yet to implement the directive, although the due date for implementation (July 30, 2000) is long since past.[238]

Through the creation of the European Patent Convention (EPC) in 1973, the issuance of patents within the EU has been centralized and economized.[239] Although created upon EU-initiative, the EPC is not exclusive to the EU member states, nor are all EU states members of the convention.[240] The EPC is a treaty signed by 27 European countries.[241]

Through the EPC, patent protection can be obtained through a single application and a single examination process, in as many of the joined countries as the applicant desires.[242] A body has been created to administer the so-called European patent applications: the European Patent Organisation (EPO) in Munich, Germany.[243] A European patent granted under the EPC confers on its owner the same right as a national patent in those EPC countries he/she designated in the application.[244] Thus, essentially, a European patent is not one patent but a "bundle" of national patents with a coordinated application and examination process. In every such country, the patent has the same status as if it were issued by the national patent organization with the same legal effects.[245] Once granted, a European patent can be annulled only by separate proceedings in each elected country.[246] However, during the first nine months after the grant of the patent, anyone can start an opposition procedure at the EPO to annul the patent in all these countries at once.[247]

A European patent may be filed before the EPO directly or before the national patent offices in a member state, on condition that the national authority has undertaken to mediate such applications to the EPO.[248] The costs for filing a European patent application depend on the number of claims, the size of the application, and whether the European application is based on a prior PCT application.[249] As a general rule, for an applicant seeking protection in more than three or four EPC states, it is cheaper to file a single EPC application than to file separate national patent applications. An application before the EPO will be published 18 months after the priority date.[250] In 2005, the EPO received 128,713 patent applications.[251] Only 53,258 were granted, out of which 13,681 were to non-residents.[252]

Inventions that are susceptible of industrial application, are new, and involve an inventive step are patentable according to the EPC.[253] An invention is considered as susceptible of industrial application "if it can be made or used in any kind of industry, including agriculture."[254] "An invention shall be considered as involving an inventive step if, having regard to the state of the art, it is not obvious to a person skilled in the art."[255] Novel means the invention is not a part of the prior art on the date of the European patent application filing or its priority date.[256] Note that, unlike the rule in the US, the EPC has no grace period for a European patent application. This means that any invention used, sold, or otherwise disclosed anywhere in the world will prevent a European patent from issuance.[257] The contents of prior unpublished European patent applications are considered to be prior art for the purpose of determining novelty.[258] Discoveries; scientific theories and mathematical methods; esthetic creations; schemes, rules, and methods for performing mental acts, playing games, or doing business; and programs for computers are mere presentations of information and not inventions.[259]

When a patent has been granted, the patent must be translated and fees must be paid for the various national patent offices if the applicant wishes to obtain protection.[260] Because all of the member states of the EPC require translation, the costs for the European patent have increased.

Upon approval, the European patent is granted for 20 years from the date of filing the application, in the countries for which the application was designated.[261] The rights conferred with the granted patent are determined by the various national laws.[262] The national rules on scope of protection, infringement, and enforcement are to be used; however, the EPC contains provisions on the term of protection and grounds for invalidity.[263]

If a European patent is denied, a patent cannot be obtained via the EPO or via the national authorities regardless of whether the specific EPC countries were designated in the application ("all eggs in one basket" effect).[264] If an application is rejected, the applicant may appeal the decision to the EPO Board of Appeals as the last resort with regards to the European patent claims.[265] However, before filing an appeal, applicants often request proceedings in the form of an oral hearing.

There is an ongoing process within the EU to create a Community Patent (CP) – a common patent providing automatic protection within all of the EU member states upon a single application.[266] The underlying thought is to create a CP with the same effects in all EU member states, a CP not in any aspect ruled by national law.[267] The applicant would not have to designate the countries in which patent protection is sought, and the resulting patent would not be a bundle of national patents.[268] The CP would not replace the existing option of protecting inventions in Europe using the European patent or national patents.[269] The aim of the proposed CP is to offer European inventors and companies a quicker and cheaper system than the EPC and thereby increase European competitiveness in the patent field in relation to other countries, most notably the US and Japan.[270] Indeed, one reason that the European patent (EPC) system is not used to the same extent as the American and Japanese systems is the high cost for application. Application cost is substantially higher due to translation and renewal fees, which are proportional to the number of European countries to which protection is actually extended. The costs for the translation of the average European application are 25% of the procedure costs.[271] The cost of the current European patent has been recently estimated as three to five times higher than the cost of patenting in Japan and the US. The preparation of a CP in EC legislation is well under way. In March 2003, the EU reached an agreement on a common political approach regarding the outlines of the jurisdiction system, language regime, costs, role of the national patent offices, and distribution fees.[272] The next important steps will be drafting a regulation, a diplomatic conference to revise the EPC and the accession to the convention of the EU, ratification of a revised EPC, and the establishment of the CP courts and procedures.

Designs. Unlike in the US, the EU does not allow patent registration for designs or the appearance of a product.[273] While a patent covers the function, operation, or construction of an invention, a special design protection available within the EU covers only the appearance of a product and cannot protect its function.[274] Design protection does not exclude that the work is also protected by copyright as an artistic work.[275]

Design protection arises under three systems in Europe: an international design application, national design protection, and two forms of community-wide protection.

The first type of design protection is the international design application, which can be filed according to the Hague Agreement and will be valid for all member states of the Agreement.[276] However, not all EU states belong to this Agreement.[277]

A second way of protecting design within the EU is through the filing of a national design application in an EU state. The national laws on protection of design have been harmonized in the EU member states. In most EU states, designs are awarded double nationwide protection via copyright (awarded upon creation) and by registration of the designs before the national offices. In order to be registered, a design must be new and have an individual character (i.e., characteristics that differ from other designs produced before).[278] The design must also have a visible external shape and be exclusively adopted for its esthetic quality and not its functional purpose.[279] In some countries,[280] disclosure of the design outside that country does not constitute a bar to registration. Other countries[281] provide a grace period, meaning that expositions of the protected object by the applicant within a period of time prior to registration do not prevent registration. The registration and examination process is different in each country.[282] A registered design can, upon payment of maintenance fees, last up to a maximum of 25 years.[283] Once registered, the design right holder is protected not only against an identical, but also against a divergent imitation, if it gives a similar esthetical general impression. Some countries, such as the UK, also provide for nationwide protection of a unregistered design, arising without any formalities if it fulfils the criteria for protection.[284] This unregistered right lasts for a shorter period than for registered designs.

Thirdly, as of 2003, the EU provides community-wide design protection – through the Unregistered Community Designs (UCDs) and through the Registered Community Designs (RCDs).[285] The two forms of community-wide design protection have equal effect throughout the EU; the definitions are the same as are the protection requirements (novelty and individual character).[286] The requirements for protection are that no identical design has been made available to the public before the UDC has first been made available to the public, or before the filing or priority date of the RCD.[287] Designs are considered to be identical if their features differ only in immaterial details.[288] They are also protectable if the overall impression produced on the informed user differs from the overall impression of designs made available to the public earlier.[289] The design right includes any design that does not produce on the informed user a different overall impression.[290] Both UCD and RCD exclude protection for non-visible parts, technical function, interconnections, and things against public policy or morality.[291] The UCD is obtained automatically from the first disclosure in the EU. A design is deemed to have been made available to the public if it was published, exhibited, used in trade, or otherwise disclosed (with some exceptions).[292] If the first disclosure takes place in a non-EU country, the UCD is not available because there is no grace period. The RCD requires application and registration at the Office for Harmonization in the Internal Market, in Alicante, Spain.[293] It is an easy, fast, and inexpensive filing and registration process, in a one-language, one-application, and one-fee system providing protection within the whole EU. As for RCDs, disclosure during the 12-month period preceding the date for filing the application is not taken into account to assess novelty or individual character of the design.[294]

The main difference between the RCD and the UCD, apart from the process to obtain protection, is the term of protection. While the RCD initially lasts for five years, with four renewal options each for a five-year period (in total a maximum 25-year term), the UCD lasts three years after disclosure, without any possibility for renewal.[295] Another major difference is the rights conferred. The RCD gives the holder the exclusive right to use and prevent others from making, offering, putting on the market, importing, exporting, using, or stocking for such purposes products incorporating the design.[296] It protects against both deliberate copying and independent development of a similar design.[297] The UCD affords the right holder the right to prevent only if the use results from deliberate copying.[298]

Copyrights

Unlike in the design and trademark field, the EU has no unitary system for copyright. This may be explained by the fact that registration is not required for obtaining copyright protection within the EU.[299] Instead, the national legislations in the different member states are decisive on the rights conferred, the requirements for protection, infringements, and so forth.[300] The member states are obligated to give foreigners and their works the same protection afforded to nationals and their works.[301] Due to extensive harmonization through a vast number of directives and Green papers,[302] the national laws within the EU correspond greatly to one another. Copyrights are obtained immediately without registration or other formalities.[303] The national copyright laws protect literary works or works of language, computer programs (in general algorithms, source code, data flow diagrams, programming flow charts, and object code), musical works, pantomime, choreographic works, artistic works (including works of applied art such as fashion creations and furniture), photographic, and cinematographic works.[304] The EU countries do not protect the idea but rather the form or esthetical content of work. Protection will be afforded in individual "original" works, which calls for a minimal level of creativity by the author's own intellectual creation.[305] Most countries exclude works created by accident, by nature, or by machines.

The exclusive rights conferred with copyright protection in EU member states comprise moral and economic rights, enforced by both civil and criminal remedies.[306] The economic rights involve the right to publish the work, to reproduce it, to distribute, lend and rent it, to transcribe the work (i.e., oral to written), to perform the work in public, to transmit it (by radio, TV, telephone, broadcast), and the right to translate, modify, or otherwise transform it. The moral rights are the right to be identified as an author, the right to object to distortion, the right to prevent it from being published, and so forth.[307] Moral rights are, unlike economic rights, non-transferable.[308] The author's rights have some limitations, among others in favor of sciences and art, private use, freedom of information, and administration for justice and public. If the name of the author and source are indicated, then analyses, quotes, press reviews, parodies, sketches, and caricatures are permitted, as are broadcastings of speeches and public meetings. The EU copyright expires 70 years after the author's death.[309]

The national laws also offer vast remedies and sanctions in the event of infringement, such as demanding preliminary and regular injunctions before court and claiming damages. In some countries, such as Germany, a plaintiff should send a warning letter before filing a lawsuit in order to avoid the risk of bearing all costs of the action if the defendant immediately accepts the claims before the court. Copyright infringement is also a criminal offense. Currently, efforts are underway to harmonize the enforcement of intellectual property rights, including copyrights, within the EU.

Ownership issues within the workplace are handled differently in the EU states. Most EU states presume that the author (employee) is the owner of copyright works and not the employer.[310] As regards software and databases, however, in the absence of an agreement stating otherwise, if the author is an employee and the work is created in the course of his employment, the economic rights in the work will be vested in the employer. The legal rights in copyright can be assigned and transferred, usually only through written agreement.[311]

The so-called "InfoSoc directive"[312] is the latest step in the EU harmonization in the copyright field. It is the first time that the European Union has explicitly regulated copyright law for digital media. The purpose and aim of the directive is to harmonize and strengthen the national laws of the member states, basically adjusting imbalances regarding the exclusive rights of distribution, reproduction, and publication of the copyright holder. The emphasis lies upon granting the copyright holder rights to interdict. In essence, the new provisions allow copyright holders to prohibit any kind of temporary or permanent copy and display of their works on the Internet. The directive also addresses caching, a computer-science process that is technically necessary for data transfer on the Internet. Under certain circumstances, which are expressly regulated by the law, caching is not infringing and therefore need not be authorized by the copyright holder. However, if the transmission of data at large is infringing copyright law (e.g., because there was no authorization given for downloading music), the copyright owner can prohibit the caching. The directive allows private copies of music, texts, or other works so long as the private Internet user is not using them for commercial purposes. In addition, it must be guaranteed that the copyright owner gets just compensation. The realization of this compensation is left for every member state of the EU to manage. Besides the regulations concerning the online use of the Internet, the directive deals with the off-line trade of digital media (i.e., the admissibility of devices for protection against unauthorized copying). The copyright law directive explicitly approves the use of these systems. Furthermore, it grants copyright holders the entire control for production and distribution of devices that circumvent protection against unauthorized copying. The member states are obligated to give adequate remedies against production, import, distribution, sale, and advertisement in relation to the circumvention devices. This provision will also enact criminal law provisions by the member states. The directive was to be implemented in all the member states at the latest by December 22, 2002, a deadline most member states failed to meet.

Software and Database Protection. In the EU, software, or more specifically its source code, has traditionally been protected by copyright rather than patent law.[313] The EPO has a restrictive approach to computer software-related inventions, in comparison to less conservative approaches found elsewhere, such as in the US. The EPO has taken the position that only business methods and computer software-related inventions that are of "technical character" may be patented.[314] The Board of Appeals has established that a computer program is not of "technical character" simply because it is a computer program.[315] Such character requires further effects that can be derived from the hardware's execution of the instructions provided by the software or the software's solving of a technical problem.[316]

The EU has far-reaching plans to harmonize the Community rules on the patentability of computer-related software. In September 2003, the EU parliament adopted a directive on the patentability of computer-implemented inventions.[317] The directive defines computer-implemented inventions as any invention under the EPC involving the use of a computer, network, or other programmable apparatus with non-technical features realized by a computer program in its implementation.[318] In addition to technical features, the invention must contribute to the state of the art.[319] The directive excludes data and information processing, handling, and presentation from patentability. The directive is believed to completely prevent most software patents in Europe. The directive proposal has been severely criticized because it is seen as substantially weakening the measure of patent harmonization and adding to legal confusion on patentability of computer inventions. The Irish Presidency of the Council of the European Union facilitated in reaching of a common position by the EU Competition Council at its May 2004 meeting, by drafting a Patentability of Computer-Implemented Inventions Directive. The directive was approved on May 18, 2004.

Protection of databases also has been harmonized within the EU through the EU Database Protection Directive 96/9/EC of March 11, 1996.[320] In generic terms, a database is nothing more than a collection of data. The database directive defines it as "a collection of independent works, data, or other materials arranged in a systematic or methodical way and individually accessible by electronic or other means."[321] This definition includes a broad range of material such as texts, sound recordings, images, numbers, facts, and data. The directive ascertains that a database, whether or not it is accessed electronically, may be protected by copyright on the condition that the selection or arrangement of its contents meets the minimum originality threshold required to be eligible for copyright protection (i.e., it is the author's own intellectual creation).[322] Copyright protection of the database is distinct from copyright protection for the contents of the database. The rights afforded for the copyright holder are the rights to prevent extraction and/or re-utilization, of the whole or of a substantial part evaluated qualitatively and/or quantitatively, of the contents of that database.[323] Even the extraction and/or re-utilization of insubstantial parts of its contents can amount to an infringement, if done repeatedly and systematically.[324] The rights conferred are granted for a period of 15 years from the date the database had been published or manufactured.[325] The directive does not apply to the computer programs used in making or operating the database, but some materials necessary for operation of the database, such as indexation and thesaurus systems, may be eligible for protection.[326] The database directive also introduced a unique *sui generis* right that is independent from any copyright existing on the database.[327] It was designed to protect makers of a database who have spent considerable time and great effort in compiling data that fails the test of creativity.

Copyright owners of databases will qualify for protection under conventional copyright treaties, either if they are nationals of an EU state or if the copyrightable database has been published, for the first time, within the EU. Copyright owners from third countries will receive minimum protection under the Berne Convention and the TRIPS agreement for creative databases. Sui generis protection is available to both natural and legal persons.[328] Natural persons who are nationals of an EU country or legal persons having their main administrative center within the EU will qualify.[329] Third party nationals, such as US citizens and legal personalities, will therefore not be able to acquire protection. Whether such protection will be granted depends on whether the EU enters into international agreements concerning database investment protection. At present, such an instrument does not exist, despite unproductive attempts by WIPO to establish a world database treaty.

Trademarks
In 1989, a harmonization directive[330] on the member states' trademark legislation, once implemented, brought into line the member states' national legislation about the criteria for, and the rights conferred with, a national trademark registration.

All signs capable of distinguishing goods or services of one business from those of another undertaking are eligible for national trademark protection in the EU member states.[331] This includes three-dimensional, sound, and color marks.[332] Protection can be acquired through registration before a national Trademark Office.[333] Trademark protection through registration in EU countries is awarded for 10 years after the application date[334] and is renewable for an unlimited number of 10-year periods. To be eligible for registration, a trademark must be distinctive for the goods or services for which the application regards, not be deceptive or contrary to law or morality, and not similar or identical to any earlier marks for the same or similar goods or services. Descriptive marks are not registrable. A registered trademark can be canceled for non-use for five years or if the trademark becomes generic.

Some EU countries also recognize trademark rights derived by use.[335] In some countries, such as the UK, the remedies are different for registered and unregistered trademarks.

The right conferred with a trademark is the right of exclusive use of the trademark for products and/or services designated as regards registered marks, from the date of registration. A trademark owner in the EU states can seek several civil sanctions against infringements. A deliberate use of another's registered mark on goods by another person, without the trademark holder's knowledge, may be a criminal offense in some countries.

Many EU countries are members of the Madrid Protocol allowing businesses and individuals in those countries to file for trademark protection in multiple countries using one application, filed in a single language, through a single national trademark office, and for a single filing fee.[336]

In 1994, the Community Trademark Regulation[337] entered into force, providing for the grant of a single trademark – the Community Trademark (CTM). The regulation became practically effective in 1996, when the Office of Harmonization for the Internal Market [Trade Marks and Designs] (OHIM) was opened in Alicante, Spain. The system was an immediate success, with 40,000 applications in 1996 – a trend that since then has been maintained.[338] The CTM regulation introduced a common system for trademarks within the EU.[339] Through registration, and only through registration, under a single application, a CTM grants uniform protection to a trademark in all member states of the EU.[340] The application is not to be designated only for certain countries.[341] The CTM is not a bundle of national trademark registrations but is unitary in nature and will extend automatically to all EU member states.[342] The CTM exists as a parallel to the national systems of registration of trademarks.

A CTM can be applied for either directly before the OHIM or through a national registration office (i.e., one of the EU member states).[343] The application can be drafted in any of the EU languages.[344] Hence, a Swedish applicant can write the application in Swedish. In the EC trademark regulation, there are five official languages: English, French, Italian, Spanish, and German.[345] An application not written in one of the five official languages must indicate one of the official languages as a second language, which will be used for correspondence with OHIM and in opposition, revocation, and invalidity proceedings.[346]

To be eligible for CTM registration, the mark must consist of graphical signs that are capable of distinguishing goods or services.[347] Such signs can be words, personal names, designs, letters, shapes of goods or packaging, sounds, smells, three-dimensional objects, logotypes, slogans, or numerals.[348] In general, the marks cannot consist solely of the characteristics of, or designate the nature, quality, or geographical origin of, the goods or services for which the mark was applied.[349] It is also not possible to register trademarks that are generic or deceive the public as to the nature, quality, or geographical origin of the goods or services.[350] An application will be refused if the trademark is identical or confusingly similar to an earlier trademark for the same goods or services in any of the member states.[351] Confusion includes the likelihood of association with the earlier mark.[352] An application may also be refused if the mark is identical or confusingly similar to an earlier mark for different goods or services if the earlier mark has a reputation in a member state and the use of the mark will take unfair advantage of or be detrimental to the distinctiveness or reputation of the earlier mark.[353] If there is an obstacle or disqualification for registration of the trademark applied for in simply one of the EU member states, the trademark cannot be registered as a CTM and the application will be rejected as a whole.[354] Decisions by OHIM are appealed to the Board of Appeals.[355] Appeals must be filed in writing at the OHIM within two months after the date of notification of the decision.[356] Within four months after the date of notification of the decision, a written statement setting out the grounds for appeal must be filed.[357] The notice of appeal must be filed in the language of the proceedings in which the decision was taken.[358]

If there are no obstacles, the CTM will be registered on condition of the payment of a registration fee (the application fee is €900 plus €150 for each class of goods or services exceeding three; the registration fee is €850 plus €150 for each class of goods or services exceeding three).[359] A registered CTM is valid for 10 years after the filing of the application and may be renewed 10 years at a time upon the payment of renewal fees.

After registration, a CTM may be declared invalid upon request, either before OHIM or upon objection to validity and counterclaim in infringement proceedings.[360] Once canceled, the mark will cease to have effect in all member states of the EU.[361] A CTM must also be used in order to be maintained.[362] The requirement of use is fulfilled if the trademark has been used for the registered goods or services within the EU.[363] Since use in a single member state can satisfy the use requirement, a CTM is rather easy to maintain. A CTM registration is inexpensive compared with the overall costs of national registration in all the countries of the EU. Although it may seem attractive to obtain protection over the whole EU territory, however, the costs may be excessive unless a mark actually needs protection in several member states. A number of national trademark rights may be sufficient. Another reason to register nationally may be the existence of an obstacle in one or more countries. An application for a CTM may, in general, be converted to a national right while maintaining the date of priority from the CTM application, national priority, or previous seniority.

A CTM can be used as security, be assigned, and be licensed. However, assignment and licensing must be registered to be valid in relation to a third party. National legislation determines the remedies for infringement of a CTM. Infringement suits are brought in the different countries, before national courts.

Due to amendments,[364] the CTM can now be owned by any natural or legal person, including authorities established under public law. The CTM is an open system, meaning that applicants from countries outside the EU territory can apply for and be registered as holders of a CTM. Such applicants must either be nationals of an EU member state, be a national of a country which has enacted the Paris Convention or is a WTO member, be domiciled or have an establishment in an EU member state or a Paris Convention State, or be a national of a state that gives reciprocal protection to the member states and recognizes CTM registration as proof of country or origin. The US is the single largest applicant country (27% in 2001).

On May 1, 2004, ten countries (Czech Republic, Estonia, Cyprus, Latvia, Lithuania, Hungary, Malta, Poland, Slovenia, and Slovakia) entered as new members of the EU. The EU and the accession states agreed that all CTMs and Community Designs registered or applied for before the date of accession would automatically be extended to the territory of the new EU member states. This extension would take place without the imposition of any additional fees. The EU has granted trademark owners in the EU candidate countries opposition rights for all trademark applications filed six months before the accession date. The enlargement inevitably increases the breadth of trademark clearance searches. All applications applied for after May 1, 2004, have to qualify also in the accession states. Thus, for example, if a mark applied for is a descriptive term in Slovenia, but distinctive in all other territories of the EU, it will be refused after May 1, 2004.

Recently the Council of Ministers approved the creation of a link between the CTM and the Madrid Protocol.[365] The linkage has reduced the costs of international protection and makes administration easier.[366] The link between the CTM and Madrid Protocol makes it possible for those who hold Madrid Protocol IRs to request extensions of protection into all EU member states via the CTM system.[367] In the same way, CTM holders in the EU are able to use their CTM registration as the basis for a Madrid Protocol IR and request extension of protection into any of 72 member countries.[368]

In April 2004, the European Parliament passed a controversial Directive[369] on measures and procedures to ensure the enforcement of intellectual property rights. The directive is designed to harmonize intellectual property enforcement laws across the EU in order to fight counterfeiting and other infringements of intellectual and industrial property rights. The differences between the national enforcement systems regarding intellectual property infringement are considered by the Commission not only to be harmful to the inner market but also to make it difficult to fight counterfeit and pirated goods. Non-commercial activity and consumers acting in good faith would not be covered. The directive's scope ranges from simple factual changes to strengthening rights holders' positions through more powerful enforcement measures. Common rules on injunctions, civil searches, provisional and precautionary measures to allow early and fast action, calculation of damages, and civil sanctions are to be introduced. The directive is expected to have a significant impact on online piracy and the online sale of counterfeit goods, giving rights holders and authorities stronger weapons in their battle against counterfeiting. It is also likely to play a role in future campaigns against rights infringements, such as that against private users of music and film download sites by the entertainment industry. However, the directive must be implemented in order to have effect. Implementation was due by April 2006, but several countries had failed to complete the necessary steps as of 2007.

Defenses against abuse of domain name registration system are waged differently in the different EU member states than in the US. Generally, if the domain name is identical or similar to another's protected trademark, and that the use can cause consumer confusion, it can be successfully battled through trademark legislation. In some countries, trademark rules may also be used against a person who registers a valuable mark, not with the intent to use it himself/herself but instead to extort money from the business holding the trademark rights.[370] However, as solely private use of a trademark is not prohibited under EU trademark law, that approach requires the cybersquatting to have a commercial side.[371] In some countries,[372] it is considered unfair competition and in conflict with public policy for a competitor to register a domain name simply to sell it to the rightful trademark owners.[373] In some EU states, the registering of a domain name of a trademark or another sign without being the holder of rights to it, in order to sell it to the lawful holder of the right, constitutes fraud, and acts taken to make a lawful holder of a trademark buy a domain name may qualify as extortion.[374]

Most EU countries' registration bodies for domain names have not adopted the Internet Corporation for Assigned Names and Numbers (ICANN) Uniform Domain-Name Dispute-Resolution Policy (UDRP). However, several countries have not provided alternative resolution systems for domain name disputes.[375]

Trade Secrets

The EU does not have any specific legal provisions to protect trade secrets or undisclosed information. Instead, this is governed by national rules in the member states. The definitions of trade secrets vary among the EU countries, but generally trade secrets are commercially valuable information, not in the public domain and intended to be maintained as secret. Most of the EU countries provide strong protection against misappropriation and afford private litigants remedies such as injunctive relief and damages. Several countries also provide criminal penalties.

Japan

Patents

In Japan, patents are governed by the Japanese Patent Act of 1959. The first section of the Patent Act reads, "The purpose of this Act is through promoting the protection and the utilization of inventions, to encourage inventions, and thereby to contribute to the development of industry."[376] Hence, the aim of the patent legislation is to promote industry and technology development. This may also explain why the Japanese Patent Office (JPO) is placed under the Ministry of Trade. Japan is the most patent active country in the world, with more than 400,000 patent applications filed every year.[377] In 2005, 427,078 patent applications were filed before the JPO (359,382 for residents and 22,120 for non-residents). In total 122,944 patents were granted, out of which 109,641 were for residents.[378] In terms of applications per capita or population per unit, Japan reigned this category with 31 applications per 10,000 nationals.[379] However, Japan's higher number of patent applications is partly related to the relatively narrow scope of the claims of the typical patent.

Patents are granted upon application before the JPO. Applications may also be filed in English.[380] Furthermore, as Japan is a member to the PCT, a foreign language application may be made within that system, although a translation will have to be furnished at a later point within the PCT. Decisions by the JPO can be appealed to an internal Patent Appeal Board, and a further appeal can be made to the Tokyo High Court.[381] All applications for Japanese patents are disclosed by the JPO in its Official Patent Gazette 18 months after the date of the application, or earlier if requested by the applicant.[382]

Patents can be obtained for inventions that are "highly advanced creation of technical ideas utilizing the laws of nature."[383] The limitation of subject matter is that which is in contravention of public order or morality.[384] Like the EU, the Japanese patent system features a first-to-file system.[385] The requirements for patentability are novelty, inventive step, and industrial application. Furthermore, an invention must relate to a product or process and contain a "technical" idea.[386] Novel means novel at the time of filing the patent application. Publications, public knowledge, or public use of an invention anywhere in the world will jeopardize the novelty requirement.[387] In cases where the invention was published against the inventor's will or by the inventor himself, a grace period of six months is provided.[388] Industrial applicability requires that the invention must be utilized and exploited in industrial activities.[389] Inventions that may be utilized or exploited only in experimental or scientific activities are not patentable.[390] An invention of a computer program may, since September 1, 2002, be patentable, and so are business methods, if they meet certain criteria.[391]

Patents are granted for 20 years from the date of filing the application.[392] The rights conferred are the exclusive rights of use, being defined as manufacture, use, assignment, lease, importation, offering for sale, and so forth.[393] Any use of the patented invention without prior permission is an infringement.[394] There are some limitations of the patentee's exclusive rights for instance by statutory or contractual licenses, by experimental research, or by exhaustion (first act of commercial exploitation).[395] The patent owner may grant licenses to a third party, both exclusive and non-exclusive licenses.[396] Exclusive licenses become effective upon their registration before the JPO.[397]

The rights to an employee's inventions are vested in the employee unless the employer requests a transfer of the invention in exchange for an equitable remuneration.[398] If no such transfer is requested, the employer automatically receives a non-exclusive license without any obligation to remunerate the employee.[399] Historically, it was standard practice that employers requested transfer of an invention against remuneration commonly fixed by internal company guidelines, usually fairly low. The law, however, requires adequate compensation in accordance with the invention's commercial success.[400] In 1999, the Tokyo District Court established that this provision overruled internal company rules and set the remuneration in the range of an ordinary licensing fee.[401] The decision also held that an employee's claim for adequate compensation is barred 10 years after the date the employee could reasonably estimate the invention's commercial success, and not after the date of the transfer. This court decision has led to a number of lawsuits by former employees requesting proper compensation for their inventions. The most well-known suit is that of Shuji Nakamura, the inventor of the blue light emitting diode paving the way to commercial use of full color displays on cell phones and electronic devices.[402] He received 2,000 yen (approximately US $180) for his invention from his employer Nichia Chemical Industries, which by Japanese standards was considered generous (!).[403] The original patent on Nakamura's work is believed to have earned US $1.4 billion in sales for Nichia.[404] In August 2001, he filed a lawsuit and claimed an initial fee of 2 billion yen, later increased to 20 billion yen, from his now former employer; he has become a hero among Japanese inventors.[405] On January 30, 2004, The Tokyo District Court ordered Nichia to pay an unprecedented 20 billion yen (approximately US $180 million) to Nakamura for his transfer of patent rights to the company.[406]

New rules on damage calculation in patent infringement cases were recently introduced in Japan, making courts more assertive in awarding damages.

Designs. Designs are governed by Japan's Design Act of 1959, extensively revised in 1999. The "shape, pattern, or color or any combination thereof in an article which produces an esthetic impression on the sense of sight" are protectable designs.[407] Other criteria are that designs must be capable of being used in industrial manufacture and require world wide novelty and a creative step.[408] Designs in Japan are protected only to the extent that they are embodied in an article, that is, a movable three-dimensional object.[409] Two-dimensional designs are not protected.[410] Designs that give rise to confusion with someone else's business or are "indispensable to secure the functions of an article" are not protectable under design registration.[411] Designs are afforded upon application before the JPO. A six-month grace period is provided if the design was published by the inventor or against his will.[412] Similar designs by the same owner must be filed on the same day.[413] Because they will be treated as independent designs, similar designs may not be filed later, as in such a case a previously filed design will be invoked to protect the later application, even if by the same applicant.[414] If the same applicant is filing similar designs on the same day, he/she must indicate an associated design. Design rights are granted for 15 years from the date of registration.[415] The owner of a design right has an exclusive right to commercially exploit the design in Japan.[416] The owner may prohibit others from using the registered design as well as any design similar to it with regard to the subject article. Japan is not a contracting party to the Hague Agreement.[417]

Copyrights

Copyrights in Japan are governed by the Copyright Act of May 6, 1970.[418] Copyrights are defined as "the rights of authors, etc. and the rights neighboring thereto with respect [copyrightable] works as well as performances, phonograms, broadcasts and wire-broadcasts."[419] There is no fixation requirement for a copyright to arise. To be subject to protection, the work must show a certain amount of creativity, excluding compilations that do not show any creativity of selection.[420] Works of applied art can be protected only if they are non-utilitarian and produced in small numbers. Japanese case law, however, reveals that copyright protection mostly is determined in terms of the degree of originality rather than the production method or number of items produced. Book titles, type faces, and advertising slogans have been held insufficient as to the level of creativity and therefore not protected.

The rights to a work protected by copyright are vested in the author, normally the creator, unless the work is made during the course of employment and published under the name of the employer.[421] This rule does not apply to computer programs.[422] The right holder has both moral and economic rights.[423] The moral rights are mainly the right to preserve the work's integrity against distortion or mutilation.[424] Unlike many other countries, the Japanese Copyright Act protects not only the expression of a work but also any idea inherent in the work and provides the copyright holder the right to prevent parodies. The economic rights (which, unlike the moral rights, can be transferred) include the right of reproduction, performance, presentation, public transmission, exhibition, recitation, distribution, transfer, and translation.[425] There are some limitations to the exclusive rights for private use, for libraries, quotations, educational purposes, and so forth.[426] Japanese copyrights are valid for a shorter term than copyrights in most industrial countries, as they extend for a period of 50 years after the death of the author.[427]

In Japan, software can be protected by copyright law as a work of authorship. However, the protection granted does not extend to "any computer programming language, rule, or algorithm used for creating such work."[428] Compilation works can be subject to copyright protection to the extent they are creative in selection or arrangement.[429] The protection of compilation work does not prejudice the rights of authors of component works or parts of works brought together in the compilation.[430] A database, which is "a collection of information, such as dissertations, numerical values, or diagrams, which is systematically organized so that such information can be searched by use of a computer," can also be protected as a work of authorship if it possesses creativity in the selection or systematic organization of those pieces of information.[431]

Trademarks

Trademarks are governed by the Trademark Act of 1959.[432] Registration before JPO is required for protection of trademarks under Japanese law, and no rights arise from the mere use of a trademark. Trademarks are defined as "characters, figures, signs, three-dimensional shapes, or any combination thereof, or any combination thereof with colors."[433] Marks that are generic or descriptive or merely indicate a geographical name are unregistrable, as are those marks that contravene public order, represent another person's surname, are similar to another's unregistered well-known mark, or conflict with someone else's previously registered mark.[434] Since Japan is a signatory of the Paris Convention, a six-month priority period is available for applicants who have filed trademark applications in a signatory country.[435] Japan is also a member of the Madrid Protocol and requires English as a working language in the international applications.[436] The JPO will register a trademark within 18 months from the date of application. Once a trademark is registered, it is published by the JPO in its Official Trademark Gazette.[437] There is a post-grant opposition period of two months.[438] Trademarks are initially granted for a period of 10 years and can be renewed indefinitely.[439] The rights conferred with the trademark are the exclusive rights of use (applying the mark on goods, assigning the mark, proving services under the mark, advertising and displaying trademarked goods or services).[440] The exclusive rights also extend to the same or similar marks used on the same or similar goods or services. All foreign users of the Japanese system should be aware that pronunciation rules in Japanese tend to differ from those in other languages, leading to the fact that otherwise dissimilar marks become similar and vice versa. Regarding foreign marks, the Japanese courts will generally assume English pronunciation unless consumers pronounce the mark differently. Trademarks can be subject to licensing, both exclusive and non-exclusive. Registration of exclusive licenses is required for them to take effect.

Japan is one of the few countries where abuse of the domain name registration system is explicitly regulated by law. The Japanese Unfair Competition Prevention Act, revised in June 2001, declares that to "acquir[e] or hold[] a right to use a domain name(s) that is identical or similar to another person's specific indication of goods or services (which means a name, trade name, trademark, mark, or any other indication of a person's goods or services), or the acts of using any such domain name(s), for the purpose of acquiring an illicit gain or causing injury to another person" is an act of unfair competition.[441]

Trade Secrets
In Japan, trade secrets are protected under the Unfair Competition Prevention Law and the Civil Code.[442] The law defines a trade secret as any technical or business information that is useful in commercial activities such as manufacturing or marketing, which is kept secret and not publicly known.[443] An infringement occurs when a person procures a trade secret by theft, fraud, or extortion, or when someone who has lawfully acquired a trade secret then uses or discloses it without authorization for unfair competition.[444] Injunctive relief and damages are among the remedies available.[445] The amount of damages is generally determined on the basis of the greater of either the profit that the misappropriating person has obtained from the misappropriation or the ordinary license fee for the use of these trade secrets.[446] The trade secret holder may also request destruction of articles produced as a result of the illegally obtained trade secret.[447] No criminal penalties are available.

CONCLUSIONS REGARDING INTERNATIONAL DIFFERENCES

While quite a few aspects of patent law have been harmonized internationally (not in the least due to treaties like the PCT or TRIPS), there are still many differences among the US, European, and Japanese systems. One major difference is the first-to-file versus first-to-invent principle. In the EU and Japan – where the first-to-file principle prevails – when two people apply for a patent on the same invention, the first person to have filed his application gets the patent (assuming the invention is patentable). This is true even if the second person did in fact create the invention first; all that counts is the filing date of the application. In the US, the first-to-invent principle governs. In the event of two applications for the same invention (a so-called interference), a determination is made of who invented first. If the person who filed later is found to have invented earlier, he/she may be awarded the patent.[448]

Another important difference is the European non-recognition of a grace period for patent applications: if the invention has become publicly available (including selling the invention, giving a lecture about it, showing it to an investor without a non-disclosure agreement, publishing it in a magazine, and so on) in any way before the patent application was filed, the application will be rejected. While in most jurisdictions an "absolute novelty" principle is upheld for patent protection, an inventor in the US has a one-year grace period to file a patent application after the invention has first been publicly disclosed. This means that the inventor can freely publish his/her invention without losing patent rights. However, this applies only for the US. An inventor who does so automatically loses all potential patent rights in EU as well as many other countries in the world. Under certain conditions, a Japanese inventor can benefit from a six-month grace period. Some countries, for instance, Germany and the EU (for the RCD), provide grace periods for design registration, but not for patent registration. If protecting a product with both a patent and a design registration, the timing of the applications will be crucial: it must be ensured that publishing one or the other of the rights does not destroy the novelty and bar the registration of the other application.

A third major difference is the fact that the US provides patent protection to business methods and software, while the EU countries hold a restrictive policy and afford patent protection only to the extent business methods and software involve technical effect or characters. Japan holds a similar position as the EU.

The two most important requirements in European patent law are that, to be patentable, an invention must be novel and must involve an inventive step. This is comparable to the US requirement that the invention must be novel and must not be obvious. In fact, the PCT, which streamlines the filing process in its member countries, also requires that an invention be novel and involve an inventive step, but the PCT states that being non-obvious is sufficient to involve an inventive step.

Despite vast international harmonization of copyright protection, many differences still exist. Most countries, including the EU member states, the US, and Japan, afford copyright protection without undertaking formalities. In some countries, such as the US, registration of copyright is possible and even a prerequisite for enforcement through lawsuit. Rules on ownership and transfer of a copyright and other related employment issues also greatly differ across the world, as does the scope of protection. In comparison to other countries, the Japanese copyright legislation is far-reaching, in the sense that it protects ideas and permits the holder to prevent parodies of the work.

The ways to obtain trademark rights also vary across the world. In France and Japan, trademark rights can be obtained only through registration, while US, Germany, and UK also provide protection through use of unregistered marks. These variations indicate that anyone involved in the creative process who wants international protection of intellectual property would be well-advised to get expert assistance.

NOTES

1. See, for example, discussion in Chapter 1.
2. *Ibid.*
3. *WIPO Intellectual Property Handbook: Policy, Law and Use*, available at http://www.wipo.int/export/sites/www/about-ip/en/iprm/pdf/ch1.pdf [hereinafter WIPO Handbook].
4. http://www.wipo.int/about-ip/en/index.html
5. See, e.g., 17 U.S.C. § 102 (2006) (discussing scope of copyrights in general); Japanese Patent Act, article 67 (Act. No. 121 of 1959) (discussing 20-year duration of patents).
6. WIPO Handbook, § 3.8, 164, available at http://www.wipo.int/export/sites/www/about-ip/en/iprm/pdf/ch3.pdf
7. See, e.g., *Image Tech. Servs. v. Eastman Kodak Co.*, 125 F.3d 1195, 1214 (9th Cir. 1997) (discussing the exclusionary nature of patent rights).
8. See, e.g., 35 U.S.C. § 154(a) (2006) (right to exclude others from exploiting the patented invention expires 20 years after the date of filing the patent application).
9. John Gladstone Mills III, *A Transnational Patent Convention For the Acquisition and Enforcement of International Patent Rights*, 88 J. Pat. & Trademark Off. Soc'y 958, 961 (2006).
10. *Ibid.* at 958.
11. *Ibid.* at 961.
12. WIPO Handbook § 2.6, 17.

13. This relates to utility patents and excludes plant and design patents.

14. WIPO Handbook, § 2.5, 17.

15. WIPO, *Understanding Intellectual Property* (p. 6), available at http://www.wipo.int/freepublications/en/intproperty/895/wipo_pub_895.pdf [hereinafter WIPO *Understanding IP*].

16. *Ibid.* at 9.

17. *Ibid.*

18. WIPO Handbook, § 2.638, 112.

19. See, e.g., 35 U.S.C. 171 (2006).

20. WIPO Handbook, § 2.649, 114.

21. http://www.artslaw.com.au/LegalInformation/ProtectingYourDesigns.asp

22. http://www.artslaw.com.au/LegalInformation/ProtectingYourDesigns.asp

23. See, e.g., 35 U.S.C. 173 (2006) (design patent term is 14 years from date of grant); U.K. Registered Designs Act 1949 (c.88) § 8 (initial registration of design right is for 5 years, but can be renewed up to four times).

24. See, e.g., 17 U.S.C. 102 (2006).

25. See *Feist Publications, Inc. v. Rural Telephone Service Co.*, 499 U.S. 340 (1991).

26. WIPO Handbook, § 2.164, 40.

27. The US is a rare example of where registration of copyright is possible and a prerequisite for some additional remedies against infringements. However, note that the copyright is not dependent on any formality.

28. WIPO Handbook, § 2.200, 46.

29. *Ibid.*

30. *Ibid.* at § 2.182, 43.

31. *Ibid.*

32. See, e.g., 17 U.S.C. § 302(1) (duration of copyright is the life of author and 70 years after author's death).

33. WIPO Handbook, § 2.334, 70, http://www.wipo.int/export/sites/www/about-ip/en/iprm/pdf/ch2.pdf

34. *Ibid.* at § 2.322, 68.

35. *Ibid.* at § 2.452, 85.

36. *Ibid.* at § 2.632.

37. *Ibid.* at § 2.452, 85.

38. WIPO Handbook, § 2.485, 89, http://www.wipo.int/export/sites/www/about-ip/en/iprm/pdf/ch2.pdf

39. *Ibid.* at § 2.405, 79.

40. *Ibid.*

41. *Ibid.* at § 2.430, 82.

42. *Ibid.* at § 2.834, 150.

43. http://en.wikipedia.org/wiki/Trade_secret

44. WIPO Handbook, § 2.833, 150.

45. *Ibid.* at § 2.837, 151.

46. *Ibid.* at § 2.851, 155.

47. http://www.wipo.int/treaties/en/ShowResults.jsp?lang=en&treaty_id=2

48. WIPO Handbook at § 2.427.

49. *Ibid.* at § 2.59, 24.

50. http://www.wipo.int/pct/en/texts/articles/atoc.htm

51. http://www.wipo.int/treaties/en/ShowResults.jsp?lang = en&treaty_id = 6

52. http://www.wipo.int/pct/en/treaty/about.htm

53. *Ibid.*

54. Patent Cooperation Treaty, article 39(1)(a), June 19, 1970.

55. http://www.epo.org/about-us/office.html

56. http://annual-report.european-patent-office.org/facts_figures/_pdf/facts_figures_05.pdf

57. http://www.wipo.int/hague/en/

58. For a list of member states see http://www.wipo.int/treaties/en/ShowResults.jsp?lang = en&treaty_id = 9

59. http://oami.europa.eu/en/design/default.htm

60. *Ibid.*

61. For a list of member states see http://www.wipo.int/treaties/en/ip/berne/index.html

62. Berne Convention, article 5(1), September 9, 1986, available at http://www.wipo.int/treaties/en/ip/berne/trtdocs_wo001.html#P109_16834

63. *Ibid.* article 5(2).

64. *Ibid.*

65. *Ibid.* article 7(1).

66. *Ibid.*

67. Madrid Agreement, article 1(2), April 14, 1891, available at http://www.wipo.int/madrid/en/legal_texts/trtdocs_wo015.html#a1

68. *Ibid.*

69. For a list of member states see http://www.wipo.int/treaties/en/ShowResults.jsp?lang = en&treaty_id = 8. For a version of the online text of the Madrid Protocol see http://www.wipo.int/madrid/en/legal_texts/trtdocs_ wo016.html

70. Madrid Agreement, supra note 7, article 3.

71. *Ibid.* article 3ter(2).

72. *Ibid.* article 1(2).

73. *Ibid.* article 3.

74. *Ibid.* article 4.

75. Madrid Agreement, supra note 7, articles 6 and 7.

76. http://oami.europa.eu/en/mark/

77. *Ibid.*

78. *Ibid.*

79. *Ibid.*

80. MacLaren, T. (1993). *Worldwide trade secrets law.* Deerfield, IL: Clark Boardman Callaghan.

81. http://www.wto.int/english/thewto_e/whatis_e/tif_e/agrm7_e.htm

82. Madrid Agreement, supra note 7, articles 6 and 7.

83. WIPO Handbook, § 2.428, 82.

84. *Ibid.* § 2.136, 35.

85. http://en.wikipedia.org/wiki/Trade_secret

86. http://www.uspto.gov/web/menu/intro.html

87. http://www.uspto.gov/web/offices/pac/doc/general/index.html#patent

88. Plant patents also last a maximum of 20 years, while design patents a maximum of 14 years.

89. Under certain circumstances, patent term extensions or adjustments may be available, for instance, due to delays in governmental processing, i.e., obtaining approval for regulated foods, drugs, and cosmetics.

90. http://www.uspto.gov/web/offices/dcom/olia/aipa/index.htm

91. http://www.uspto.gov/web/offices/pac/maintfee/. Plant patents also need to be maintained by payment of fees in order to last 20 years. However, design patents have a term of 14 years from grant, and no fees are necessary to maintain a design patent in force.

92. http://www.uspto.gov/web/offices/pac/doc/general/index.html#faqs

93. *Ibid.*

94. *Ibid.*

95. 35 U.S.C. 101 (2006).

96. 35 U.S.C. 102(a) (2006).

97. http://www.uspto.gov/web/offices/pac/doc/general/index.html#novelty

98. http://www.uspto.gov/web/offices/pac/doc/general/index.html#whatpat

99. http://www.uspto.gov/web/offices/pac/provapp.htm

100. *Ibid.*

101. *Ibid.*

102. *State St. Bank & Trust Co. v. Signature Financial Group, Inc.*, 149 F.3d 1368 (Fed. Cir. 1998).

103. http://www.uspto.gov/web/menu/busmethp/index.html

104. *Ibid.*

105. http://www.uspto.gov/web/menu/busmethp/busmethpat.htm

106. Patent No. 5,960,411.

107. *Ibid.*

108. Patent No. 6,029,141.

109. http://www.european-patent-office.org/news/pressrel/2000_08_18_e.htm

110. 35 U.S.C. 154 (2006).

111. *Ibid.*

112. http://www.uspto.gov/web/offices/pac/doc/general/index.html#who

113. http://www.uspto.gov/web/offices/pac/doc/general/index.html#assignments

114. http://www.uspto.gov/web/offices/pac/doc/general/index.html#marking

115. *Ibid.*

116. *Ibid.*

117. *Ibid.*

118. http://www.wipo.int/ipstats/en/statistics/patents/

119. http://www.wipo.int/ipstats/en/statistics/patents/grantedbyoffice/index.html

120. http://www.uspto.gov/main/faq/p220026.htm

121. http://www.uspto.gov/web/offices/pac/doc/general/index.html#pub

122. Note that the 18 months are calculated from the earliest filing date in the history of the application, so if you file a provisional application first, the utility application will be published 18 months after your provisional filing date.

123. http://www.uspto.gov/web/offices/pac/doc/general/index.html#pub

124. http://www.uspto.gov/web/offices/ac/qs/ope/fee2007february01.htm

125. http://www.uspto.gov/web/offices/pac/doc/general/index.html#pub

126. *Ibid.*

127. *Ibid.*

128. 35 U.S.C. 111(a)(2)(A) (2006).
129. 35 U.S.C. 112 (2006).
130. *Ibid.*
131. http://www.uspto.gov/go/classification/help.htm#3
132. *Ibid.*
133. *Ibid.*
134. 35 U.S.C. 134 (2006).
135. 35 U.S.C. 135 (2006).
136. 35 U.S.C. 141 (2006).
137. http://www.uspto.gov/web/offices/pac/doc/general/index.html#infringement
138. 35 U.S.C. 271 (2006).
139. http://www.uspto.gov/web/offices/pac/doc/general/index.html#infringement
140. 35 U.S.C. 283 (2006).
141. 35 U.S.C. 282 (2006).
142. 35 U.S.C. 271(e)(5) (2006).
143. 35 U.S.C. 282 (2006).
144. http://www.uspto.gov/web/offices/pac/doc/general/index.html#spec
145. *Ibid.*
146. http://www.uspto.gov/web/offices/pac/doc/general/index.html#infringement
147. http://www.uspto.gov/web/offices/dcom/olia/aipa/summary.htm
148. *Ibid.*
149. http://www.uspto.gov/web/offices/ac/ahrpa/opa/bulletin/hr1907ih.htm
150. *Ibid.*
151. *Ibid.*
152. http://www.copyright.gov/circs/circ1.html#wwp
153. http://www.copyright.gov/circs/circ1.html#hsc
154. See 17 U.S.C. 114 (2006).
155. http://www.copyright.gov/circs/circ1.html#hsc
156. *Ibid.*
157. *Ibid.*
158. http://www.copyright.gov/circs/circ1.html#cr
159. As an example, the minimum for statutory damages under Federal law is $750. 17 U.S.C. 504(c) (2006).
160. http://www.copyright.gov/circs/circ1.html#cr
161. *Ibid.*
162. http://www.copyright.gov/docs/fees.html
163. http://www.copyright.gov/circs/circ1.html#cr
164. 17 U.S.C. 106 (2006).
165. *Ibid.*
166. *Ibid.*
167. *Ibid.*
168. *Ibid.*
169. 17 U.S.C. 107.
170. See, e.g., *Sega Enters. v. Accolade, Inc.*, 1993 U.S. App. LEXIS 78 (1993).
171. 17 U.S.C. 302(a).
172. 17 U.S.C. 302(c).
173. http://www.copyright.gov/circs/circ1.html#cr

174. 17 U.S.C. 201(a).
175. 17 U.S.C. 201(d).
176. http://www.copyright.gov/circs/circl.html#toc
177. *Ibid.*
178. http://www.copyright.gov/circs/circl.html#noc
179. *Ibid.*
180. *Ibid.*
181. *Ibid.*
182. http://www.copyright.gov/circs/circl.html#wwp
183. 17 U.S.C. 117 (2006).
184. See 35 U.S.C. 101 (2006).
185. http://www.copyright.gov/circs/circl.html#wwp
186. 17 U.S.C. 101.
187. See *Feist Publications, Inc. v. Rural Telephone Service Co.*, 499 U.S. 340 (1991).
188. *Ibid.*
189. See *Feist*, 499 U.S. 340.
190. 15 U.S.C. 1127 (2006).
191. *Qualitex Co. v. Jacobson Prods. Co., Inc.*, 514 U.S. 159 (1995).
192. http://www.uspto.gov/web/offices/tac/doc/basic/appcontent.htm#basis
193. http://www.uspto.gov/web/offices/tac/doc/basic/register.htm
194. *Ibid.*
195. *Ibid.*
196. *Ibid.*
197. http://www.wipo.int/madrid/en/
198. http://www.uspto.gov/web/offices/tac/doc/basic/register.htm
199. http://www.uspto.gov/web/offices/tac/doc/basic/appcontent.htm#goods
200. http://www.uspto.gov/web/offices/ac/qs/ope/fee2004apr01.htm#tm
201. *Ibid.*
202. 15 U.S.C. 1051(a).
203. 15 U.S.C. 1051(b).
204. 15 U.S.C. 1125.
205. *Ibid.*
206. See, e.g., *AutoZone, Inc. v. Tandy Corp.*, 373 F.3d 786 (6th Cir. 2004).
207. See *ibid.* at 797.
208. *Quality Inns Int'l v. McDonald's Corp.*, 695 F. Supp. 198 (D. Md. 1998).
209. *DuPont Cellophane Co. v. Waxed Products Co.*, 85 F.2d 75 (2nd Cir. 1936).
210. *Ibid.*
211. *Ibid.*
212. *Ibid.*
213. http://www.uspto.gov/web/offices/tac/doc/basic/maintain.htm
214. http://www.uspto.gov/web/offices/tac/tmfaq.htm#Basic007
215. *Ibid.*
216. http://www.uspto.gov/web/offices/tac/tmfaq.htm#Basic008
217. *Ibid.*
218. http://www.uspto.gov/web/offices/tac/notices/guide299.htm
219. Anticybersquatting Consumer Protection Act, November 29, 1999, P.L. 106–113, § 1000(a)(9).

220. See http://www.nccusl.org/Update/uniformact_factsheets/uniformacts-fs-utsa.asp

221. *Ibid.*

222. Economic Espionage Act of 1996, October 11, 1996, 104 P.L. 294, 101.

223. 17 U.S.C. 201.

224. http://www.copyright.gov/circs/circ1.html#wccc

225. 17 U.S.C. 201(b).

226. Sonny Bono Copyright Term Extension Act, October 27, 1998, P.L. 105–298, 102.

227. 17 U.S.C. 302.

228. http://www.uspto.gov/web/offices/pac/doc/general/index.html#who

229. 35 U.S.C. 152.

230. http://www.uspto.gov/web/offices/pac/doc/general/index.html#who

231. http://www.epo.org/patents/Grant-procedure/About-patents.html

232. http://www.european-patent-office.org/news/pressrel/2000_08_18_e.htm

233. *Ibid.*

234. *Ibid.*

235. For instance, the rights afforded with a German patent are far reaching, compared to many other countries. According to German case law, for an infringement to have been committed it is enough that an unauthorized third party provided material means that can be used to realize the purpose of the patent – an actual direct infringement is not necessary.

236. http://eur-lex.europa.eu/smartapi/cgi/sga_doc?smartapi!celexplus!prod! DocNumber&lg = en&type_doc = Directive&an_doc = 1998&nu_doc = 44

237. *Ibid.*

238. http://en.wikipedia.org/wiki/Directive_on_the_patentability_of_biotechnological_ inventions#External_links

239. http://www.european-patent-office.org/legal/epc/e/ma1.html

240. http://en.wikipedia.org/wiki/European_Patent_Convention#External_links

241. For a list of Member states see http://www.european-patent-office.org/epo/ facts_figures/facts2002/pdf/facts_figures_02.pdf

242. http://www.european-patent-office.org/legal/epc/index.html

243. http://www.epo.org/about-us/epo.html

244. European Patent Convention, article 64(1), 78, October 5, 1973, available at http:// webserv.epo.org/projects/babylon/eponet.nsf/0/b8be2484d06e90dec1257258003c8a3c/ $FILE/epc_2006_e-bookmarks.pdf

245. *Ibid.* article 64(1).

246. *Ibid.* article 138(1).

247. *Ibid.* article 99.

248. *Ibid.* article 75.

249. European Patent Convention, Rules Relating to Fees article 2, 414.

250. European Patent Convention, article 93.

251. http://www.wipo.int/ipstats/en/statistics/patents/filed/index.html

252. *Ibid.*

253. *Ibid.* article 52.

254. *Ibid.* article 57.

255. *Ibid.* article 56.

256. European Patent Convention, article 54.

257. *Ibid.*

258. *Ibid.*
259. *Ibid.* article 52.
260. *Ibid.* article 137.
261. European Patent Convention, article 63.
262. *Ibid.* article 64.
263. *Ibid.*
264. *Ibid.* article 97.
265. *Ibid.* article 110.
266. http://ec.europa.eu/internal_market/indprop/patent/index_en.htm
267. Press release, EUROPA, *Patents: Commission sets out vision for improving patent system in Europe*, April 3, 2007, http://europa.eu/rapid/pressReleasesAction.do? reference = IP/07/463&type = HTML&aged = 0&language = EN&guiLanguage = fr
268. *Ibid.*
269. *Ibid.*
270. *Ibid.*
271. http://ec.europa.eu/internal_market/indprop/docs/patent/compat_costs_en.pdf
272. *Ibid.*
273. European Patent Convention, article 52.
274. Council Regulation (EC) No. 6/2002, December 12, 2001, article 7, available at http://eur-lex.europa.eu/LexUriServ/LexUriServ.do?uri = CELEX:31998L0071:EN: NOT [hereinafter Reg. 6/2002.]
275. http://www.wipo.int/about-ip/en/about_id.html#how
276. http://www.wipo.int/treaties/en/registration/hague/
277. http://www.wipo.int/treaties/en/ShowResults.jsp?lang = en&treaty_id = 9
278. WIPO Handbook § 2.655, 115.
279. *Ibid.* § 2.652, 115.
280. Such as the UK.
281. Such as Germany.
282. Please note that, for instance, the German Patent Office does not examine the criteria of protection in the application procedure. Hence, initially the design registration only has formal character. Before a legal dispute, an owner of a design should therefore definitely make sure by searches that his design is capable of being protected.
283. In Germany, however, the maximum term is 20 years.
284. In the UK, the unregistered design right lasts for the shorter of 15 years from design or 10 years from first marketing. Also note that the UK unregistered design right only is available to EU nationals or those of a few other countries (for example, New Zealand), or to those who market a product in the EU first.
285. http://europa.eu/scadplus/leg/en/lvb/l26033.htm
286. *Ibid.*
287. *Ibid.*
288. Reg. 6/2002, article 5.
289. *Ibid.* article 6.
290. *Ibid.*
291. *Ibid.* articles 8 and 9.
292. *Ibid.* article 7.
293. Reg. 6/2002.
294. *Ibid.*

295. *Ibid.* articles 11 and 12.

296. *Ibid.* article 19.

297. Reg. 6/2002, article 19.

298. *Ibid.*

299. http://www.wipo.int/copyright/en/faq/faqs.htm#rights

300. *Ibid.*

301. Berne Convention, article 5.

302. "In Britain, the Republic of Ireland, and other similar Commonwealth jurisdictions (i.e., Australia), a green paper is a tentative government report of a proposal without any commitment to action; the first step in changing the law." http://en.wikipedia.org/wiki/Green_Paper

303. However, in Italy works can be registered through an optional registration process before the Office of Literary, Artistic, and Scientific Property. Registration does not confer any additional rights; it is merely useful as evidence in enforcing copyright. http://www.wipo.int/copyright/en/faq/faqs.htm#P81_9657

304. WIPO Handbook, § 2.176, 42.

305. In the UK, the criteria of originality, unlike most continental laws, does not call for minimal creativity. The UK, however, has a second requirement for protection for literary, dramatic, or musical works that it is "recorded, in writing or otherwise."

306. WIPO Handbook, § 2.200, 46.

307. *Ibid.*

308. *Ibid.*

309. However, computer-generated works (without human author) last 50 years from the making in the UK.

310. In the UK, however, it is a presumption that an employer is the first owner of copyright in works made by an employee.

311. Germany, however, has a different perspective. In Germany, only the person creating a work can be regarded as the author. This means that according to German copyright law, publishers, producers, or companies cannot be considered authors of copyrightable works created by employees etc. This also means that foreign companies cannot allege copyright protection in Germany, even if such protection is afforded legal entities in their home countries. However, there is an exception to the rule: software created under an employment; the economic rights of the creator (employee) are transferred to the employer. According to German law, author's moral and exploitation rights cannot be separated. Therefore, the copyright as such can only be transferred by inheritance. No other conveyance is possible and any such agreements are invalid. However, copyright can be licensed. The content and scope of the granted utilization rights must be explicitly enumerated. A license of unknown means of utilization is invalid.

312. Directive 2001/29/EC of the European Parliament and of the Council of May 22, 2001, on the harmonization of certain aspects of copyright and related rights in the information society of the European Union.

313. http://www.wipo.int/copyright/en/faq/faqs.htm#rights

314. http://www.european-patent-office.org/news/pressrel/2000_08_18_e.htm

315. *Ibid.*

316. *Ibid.*

317. Directive on the patentability of computer-implemented inventions (2002/0047/COD) available at http://en.wikipedia.org/wiki/Directive_on_the_patentability_of_computer-implemented_inventions

318. Proposal for a Directive of the European Parliament and of the Council on the patentability of computer-implemented inventions, definitions available at http://eur-lex.europa.eu/LexUriServ/LexUriServ.do?uri = CELEX:52002PC0092:EN: NOT

319. *Ibid.*

320. Directive 96/9/EC on the Legal Protection of Databases, March 11, 1996, available at http://europa.eu.int/ISPO/infosoc/legreg/docs/969ec.html [hereinafter Directive 96/9/EC].

321. *Ibid.* Ch. 1, article 1.

322. *Ibid.* Ch. 2, article 3.

323. *Ibid.* Ch. 3, article 7.

324. *Ibid.* Ch. 3, article 7(5).

325. Directive 96/9/EC Ch. 3, article 10.

326. *Ibid.* Preamble 20.

327. See Directive 96/9/EC.

328. Directive 96/9/EC, Ch. 3, article 4.

329. *Ibid.* Preamble 56.

330. 89/104/EEG.

331. http://oami.europa.eu/en/mark/marque/faq/faq01.htm#200

332. *Ibid.*

333. http://www.wipo.int/about-ip/en/about_trademarks.html#how_extensive

334. In Germany, the 10-year period is calculated from the end of the month in which the application was filed.

335. For instance, the UK, Germany, and Sweden.

336. For a list of member states see http://www.wipo.int/treaties/en/ShowResults.jsp?lang = en&treaty_id = 8

337. EEG 40/94.

338. http://www.ladas.com/Trademarks/EuropeanCommunity/CTMProgress Report2000.html

339. http://oami.europa.eu/en/mark/marque/faq/faq01.htm#400

340. *Ibid.*

341. *Ibid.*

342. *Ibid.*

343. http://oami.europa.eu/en/mark/marque/faq/faq02.htm

344. http://oami.europa.eu/en/mark/marque/faq/faq02.htm#300

345. *Ibid.*

346. *Ibid.*

347. http://oami.europa.eu/en/mark/marque/faq/faq01.htm

348. *Ibid.*

349. *Ibid.*

350. *Ibid.*

351. *Ibid.*

352. *Ibid.*

353. http://oami.europa.eu/en/mark/marque/faq/faq01.htm

354. *Ibid.*

355. *Ibid.*

356. http://oami.europa.eu/en/mark/marque/faq/faq10.htm#100

357. *Ibid.*

358. *Ibid.*

359. http://oami.europa.eu/en/mark/marque/faq/faq03.htm

360. http://oami.europa.eu/en/mark/marque/faq/faq09.htm#300

361. *Ibid.*

362. *Ibid.*

363. http://oami.europa.eu/en/mark/marque/faq/faq01.htm#1000

364. Through the EU Council Regulation 422/2004.

365. http://oami.europa.eu/en/mark/marque/faq/faq12.htm#200

366. *Ibid.*

367. *Ibid.*

368. *Ibid.*

369. 2004/48/EC.

370. Such as "passing off" in UK.

371. Germany, for instance, has an approach that domains with the ending .com are assumed to be used commercially.

372. For instance Germany.

373. In Germany, such conduct is in conflict with public policy and considered unfair competition if the parties are competitors in the market. However, as long as the rights of third parties are not violated the trade with domain names is considered lawful.

374. This is, for instance, the case in France.

375. For instance, the French ANFI (ccTLDs, .re, .fr) and the UK domain registry, Nominet (.uk, .co.uk, .me.uk). In Germany, domain name disputes are referred to general courts. Anyone who feels that "his" or "her" domain is registered for someone else can file for a DISPUTE entry before DENIC (Deutschen Network Information Center), the German office for domain name registrations. For a DISPUTE entry to be approved, the claimant must show in a credible manner that it is possible that he/she might have a right to the domain. A domain that bears a DISPUTE entry can still be used by its holder, but cannot be transferred to anyone else. Any holder of a DISPUTE entry automatically becomes the domain holder as soon as the domain is released.

376. Japan Patent Act, Ch. 1, article 1, available at http://www.cas.go.jp/jp/seisaku/hourei/data/PA.pdf

377. www.jpo.go.jp; IPL Newsletter vol. 21, no. 2, Winter 2003.

378. http://www.wipo.int/ipstats/en/statistics/patents/filed/index.html

379. This should be compared to Germany, the US, and UK second to fourth on the list with 10, 7, and 6 patent applications filed per 10,000 nationals, respectively.

380. Japan Patent Act, article 36-2.

381. *Ibid.* article 178.

382. http://www.jpo.go.jp/tetuzuki_e/index.htm

383. Japan Patent Act, article 2.

384. *Ibid.* article 32.

385. *Ibid.* article 41.

386. *Ibid.* article 2.

387. *Ibid.* article 29.
388. Japan Patent Act, article 30.
389. *Ibid.* article 29.
390. *Ibid.* article 69.
391. *Ibid.* article 2.
392. *Ibid.* article 67.
393. Japan Patent Act, article 101.
394. *Ibid.*
395. *Ibid.* article 69.
396. *Ibid.* article 27.
397. *Ibid.*
398. Japan Patent Act, article 35.
399. *Ibid.*
400. *Ibid.*
401. Tokyo District Court April 16, 1999.
402. Todd Zaun, Japanese company to pay ex-employee $8.1 million for invention, *New York Times*, January 12, 2005, available at http://www.nytimes.com/2005/01/12/business/worldbusiness/12light.html?ei = 5070&en = 9e02b15eeb8d3d0b&ex = 1177473600&adxnn 1 = 1&adxnnlx = 1177346662-GM3ZSkHRq9nNdZq7/VfOow
403. *Ibid.*
404. *Ibid.*
405. *Ibid.*
406. *Ibid.*
407. Japan Design Act, article 2, available at http://www.wipo.int/clea/docs_new/pdf/en/jp/jp037en.pdf
408. *Ibid.* article 3.
409. *Ibid.* article 2.
410. *Ibid.* article 5.
411. *Ibid.*
412. Japan Design Act, article 4.
413. *Ibid.* article 3bis.
414. *Ibid.*
415. *Ibid.* article 15.
416. *Ibid.* article 23.
417. http://www.wipo.int/treaties/en/documents/pdf/hague.pdf
418. Japan Copyright Act, available at http://www.cas.go.jp/jp/seisaku/hourei/data/CA.pdf
419. *Ibid.* article 1.
420. *Ibid.* article 2.
421. *Ibid.* article 15.
422. *Ibid.* article 15.
423. Japan Copyright Act, article 17.
424. *Ibid.* article 20.
425. *Ibid.* articles 21–28.
426. See, e.g., Japan Copyright Act, article 31.
427. Japan Copyright Act, article 101.
428. *Ibid.* article 10.

429. *Ibid.* article 12.

430. *Ibid.* article 12.

431. *Ibid.* article 2(x-3).

432. Japan Trademark Act, available at http://www.wipo.int/clea/docs_new/pdf/en/jp/jp038en.pdf

433. *Ibid.* § 2.

434. *Ibid.* § 4.

435. *Ibid.* § 9.

436. *Ibid.* § 68bis.

437. Japan Trademark Act, § 12bis.

438. *Ibid.* § 43bis.

439. *Ibid.* § 19.

440. *Ibid.* § 2.

441. http://www.cas.go.jp/jp/seisaku/hourei/data/ucpa.pdf

442. *Ibid.*

443. Japan Unfair Competition Prevention Act, article 2(6), available at http://www.cas.go.jp/jp/seisaku/hourei/data/ucpa.pdf

444. *Ibid.* article 2(1)(iv).

445. *Ibid.* articles 3 and 4.

446. *Ibid.* article 4.

447. *Ibid.* article 3.

448. Notice, however, that there is a legislative effort underway in the US to revise the current patent system so that the first to file receives the patent (see The Patent Reform Act of 2007, under examination in both the US Senate and House of Representatives: http://www.publicknowledge.org/bill/110-hr1908).

CHAPTER 4

PATENTS AND TECHNOLOGY COMMERCIALIZATION: ISSUES AND OPPORTUNITIES

Margo A. Bagley

ABSTRACT

This chapter discusses current issues raised by the use of patents in university-industry technology commercialization. After introducing how patent laws operate in the global marketplace, this chapter provides an overview of the U.S. patent system, describing aspects of the process by which patents are obtained and enforced. The focus of the chapter then turns to some of the benefits and costs to academia of the impact of the Bayh-Dole Act, which allows universities to capture returns from federally funded research. The chapter identifies some of the challenges created by the expanding scope of subject matter eligible for patent protection and concludes with a discussion of some of the issues and opportunities associated with the strategic licensing and enforcement of patents that may impact invention and innovation in the academy and beyond.

INTRODUCTION

In June 2006, Research in Motion, Inc., maker of the Blackberry handheld device, agreed to pay NTP, Inc. $600 million to settle a patent infringement

Technological Innovation: Generating Economic Results
Advances in the Study of Entrepreneurship, Innovation and
Economic Growth, Volume 18, 117–147
ISSN: 1048-4736/doi:10.1016/S1048-4736(07)00004-5

suit that threatened to shut down the Blackberry service. In 2004, Microsoft Corp. was ordered to pay Eolas Technologies over $500 million in patent infringement damages. After the U.S. Court of Appeals for the Federal Circuit's (CAFC) decision in 2000 that Eli Lilly's patent on Prozac was invalid, shareholders dumped $36 billion in Lilly stock, roughly a third of the pharmaceutical giant's market capitalization. These are just a few examples of the power of patent protection to create issues and opportunities in the marketplace by "rewarding some innovators while potentially inhibiting the activities of others."[1]

Even in the university context, patents can have tremendous power. In fiscal year 2004 alone, approximately 154 U.S. universities reaped over $1 billion in net patent licensing income, and executed 3,928 new licenses, largely as a result of university–industry technology transfer initiatives.[2] In 2005, Emory University announced its $540 million sale of intellectual property, considered to be the largest such deal in the history of American higher education.[3]

Patents on university-generated research allow for the creation of revenue for university coffers, stimulate economic growth in surrounding munici-palities,[4] and provide beneficial products to consumers around the world.[5] For example, the Wisconsin Alumni Research Foundation (WARF), which handles technology transfer for the University of Wisconsin-Madison, has contributed approximately $750 million to fund basic research at the university over the past 80 years.[6]

Not surprisingly, a tool with such power is both very popular and very controversial in the university context and in the larger society. Recent studies of the patent system by the National Academy of Sciences and the Federal Trade Commission, as well as testimony by the head of the U.S. Patent and Trademark Office (USPTO) in congressional hearings, highlight significant flaws in a system that some say is in crisis.[7] This chapter provides a brief overview of the global and U.S. patent systems and considers some of the current issues relating to the promise and peril of patents, with a particular focus on their use in commercializing university-generated research.

THE GLOBAL PATENT SYSTEM

Patent law historically has been territorial in nature, with sovereign states granting patents and providing means for patentees to enforce their rights only within their borders. Treaties pertaining to patents have generally taken one of two forms: procedural or substantive. Procedural treaties are designed to make it easier for applicants to obtain patent protection in other countries by, for example, limiting protectionist actions by members. Substantive treaties generally require member countries to provide minimum levels and types of protection for patent holders, thus increasing the value of patents internationally.

The two most important procedural treaties are the Paris Convention for the Protection of Industrial Property and the Patent Cooperation Treaty, both administered by the World Intellectual Property Organization (WIPO), a United Nations agency.[8] The Paris Convention, first signed in 1886, is the oldest intellectual property treaty and provides the key benefits of national treatment and a right of priority. "National treatment" means that if a member has a patent system, it must provide patent rights to foreign applicants on the same terms as it provides them to domestic applicants. The "right of priority" gives an applicant in a first member country the right to file a patent application in other member countries within one year after her initial filing date and have those later filings treated as if they were filed on the date of the first application, essentially giving applicants more time to determine where they would like to seek patent protection. The Patent Cooperation Treaty extends the Paris Convention right of priority out to 30 months, giving applicants even more time to evaluate the commercial potential and likely markets for their inventions and to generate capital that can be used to pay the often expensive costs of prosecuting patent applications in multiple countries.

The most important substantive intellectual property treaty is the Agreement on Trade-Related Aspects of Intellectual Property Rights (the TRIPS agreement), an annex to the World Trade Organization (WTO) agreement negotiated during the Uruguay Round of the General Agreement on Tariffs and Trade (GATT) in 1994.[9] The patent provisions of the TRIPS agreement require member countries to provide, among other things, a minimum 20-year patent term from filing, patent protection for inventions in all areas of technology (with limited exceptions), and a variety of remedies and enforcement protections for patent owners.

The TRIPS agreement is controversial, in part because 75% of the member countries of the WTO are developing or least developed countries, most of which do not have highly developed R&D infrastructures. As a result, most patents in such countries would be obtained by foreigners, increasing prices for domestic consumers and resulting in a flow of money out of the country to those foreign patent holders. Even more troubling, many of the developing country members are plagued by a variety of public health challenges such as HIV/AIDS and other infectious and chronic diseases. TRIPS limitations on the ability of countries to engage in compulsory licensing – authorizing third parties to practice the invention and pay a royalty without the consent of the patent holder – raised fears that countries might not be able to provide their citizens with affordable drugs to meet such public health issues. While a recent amendment to the TRIPS agreement was designed to address this concern, a variety of criticisms of the agreement remain.

In addition to these broad international treaties, several regional treaties allow an applicant to file one application with a central office and obtain patent protection in multiple countries, although the patent must be enforced, in cases of infringement, in each individual country. The most significant regional treaty is the Convention on the Grant of European Patents (EPC), signed in 1973 by a group of countries seeking to create a uniform European patent system.[10] The EPC established the European Patent Office (EPO) and contains substantive and procedural requirements for obtaining a European patent, valid in all member countries with only a single application. However, the European patent that results is in actuality a bundle of national patents that still must be enforced in each country where infringement is taking place.

Having to enforce patents in multiple jurisdictions creates considerable uncertainty for patentees because the decisions of a court in one country are not binding on a court in another country. Thus, the same patent could be found valid and infringed in one country and invalid and not infringed in a neighboring country. As a result, many patentees would prefer a global patent that could be obtained by filing a single application in one patent office, would cover all countries, and could be asserted in a single court proceeding against infringing activity in multiple countries. While there have been and will continue to be efforts to harmonize patent law, such as the ongoing negotiations at the WIPO on the Substantive Patent Law Treaty, the many obstacles to such a system are too numerous to consider here.[11] Suffice it to say that such a system, if it can be achieved at all, is likely a very long way off in the future.

PATENT LAW BASICS

The substantial power a patent can allow its owner to wield cause patents to be considered the "gold standard of intellectual property protection."[12] Patents give their owners the right to exclude others from making, using, selling, offering to sell, or importing the patented invention for a term of about 20 years.[13] The U.S. patent statute provides for both injunctive relief, at the discretion of the court, and money damages[14] for patent infringement. In addition, damages may be trebled for willful infringement.[15]

Because patent rights can be extremely lucrative, they provide significant incentives both for inventors to create innovations that can be patented and for investors to fund research that may result in a patent. For example, it is estimated that WARF, which owns broad patents covering embryonic stem cells and methods for producing them, could reap royalties of $200 million/year just from research performed under California's Proposition 71.[16]

U.S. patent law actually provides for three different types of patents: *utility patents*, for useful, novel, and non-obvious machines, compositions of matter, articles of manufacture, and processes; *design patents*, covering novel and non-obvious ornamental designs for articles of manufacture; and *plant patents*, covering new and distinct asexually reproducible (i.e., non-seed reproduction such as by budding or grafting) plants. Utility patents are the most common, with the USPTO having issued over 7 million of them, compared to roughly 500,000 design patents and approximately 16,000 plant patents.[17] As such, the word "patent" in the remainder of this chapter will refer to utility patents unless otherwise noted.

More generally, the word "patent" is used to denote both the public document in which an invention is disclosed and the bundle of intangible rights granted by the federal government to an inventor in exchange for the disclosure of his/her invention to the public. This federal system of invention promotion and disclosure has been in place since the 1790 Patent Act, created by the first Congress pursuant to Article I, § 8, cl. 8 of the U.S. Constitution, which authorizes Congress "to promote the progress of science and useful arts, by securing for limited times to authors and inventors the exclusive right to their respective writings and discoveries."

Although the exclusionary power of patents is anticompetitive, patents co-exist quite peaceably with antitrust laws. In fact, guidelines promulgated by the U.S. Department of Justice (DOJ), which polices antitrust violations, articulate some of the perceived benefits of patents and other types of intellectual property:

The intellectual property laws and the antitrust laws share the common purpose of promoting innovation and enhancing consumer welfare. The intellectual property laws provide incentives for innovation and its dissemination and commercialization by establishing enforceable property rights for the creators of new and useful products, more efficient processes, and original works of expression. In the absence of intellectual property rights, imitators could more rapidly exploit the efforts of innovators and investors without compensation. Rapid imitation would reduce the commercial value of innovation and erode incentives to invest, ultimately to the detriment of consumers.[18]

As this quote suggests, patents are important for innovation and technology commercialization. They provide incentives for parties to undertake expensive and risky research.[19] Patents induce upfront funding of projects with the expectation that monopoly profits can be generated over the longer term.[20] They also encourage the disclosure of information that others can build upon in developing even more innovations. Patent licensing income can be an important component of a company's bottom line: reported revenue from patent licensing topped $100 billion in 1998.[21] It is no surprise that more and more applicants are filing patent applications on their discoveries than ever before, with over 400,000 applications being filed in the USPTO in 2006 alone.

To obtain a patent on an invention, an inventor must prepare and file an application disclosing and claiming the invention in the USPTO and participate in the prosecution of the application. Prosecution is the process by which the USPTO determines whether a patent should issue on an invention. While an inventor can choose to prepare, file, and prosecute the application pro se, many inventors choose to hire a patent attorney or patent agent to handle the process.

Both patent attorneys and patent agents have science or engineering backgrounds and are registered to represent clients before the USPTO; the difference between the two is that patent attorneys are also lawyers. While the patent application must be filed in the inventor's name, in the case of university and corporate researchers, the inventors generally will have assigned the ownership rights to their inventions to their employer as a condition of employment, and the employer will prosecute the application and enforce any resulting patent.

In the U.S., patents may be granted only for claims directed to new and useful processes, machines, articles of manufacture, and compositions of matter. These four subject matter categories are not mutually exclusive; an invention can be classifiable in more than one category. Likewise, an inventor need not specify in which category his/her invention is properly classified, so long as it can be encompassed within one of the four.

Abstract ideas, natural phenomena, and laws of nature historically have been considered ineligible for patent protection. However, over the past 25 plus years, these categories have been construed narrowly in the face of an unprecedented judicial expansion in the scope of patent-eligible subject matter that has been deemed, by the U.S. Supreme Court, to include "anything under the sun that is made by man."[22] Thus, living organisms such as bacteria, transgenic animals, and plants, some of which could be considered natural phenomena, as well as computer software and business methods, some of which could be considered abstract ideas, now are all eligible for patent protection.[23]

In addition to being of the right type, an invention must be novel and non-obvious to be patentable. To determine whether the requirements of novelty and non-obviousness are met, the claimed invention must be compared with the prior art.[24] Prior art is defined in the U.S. patent statute and can be described as "knowledge that is available, including what would be obvious from it, at a given time, to a person of ordinary skill in an art."[25] While applicants are not required to conduct a search of the prior art before filing a patent application, they do have a duty, throughout the pendency of the application, to inform the USPTO of information material to the patentability of the invention of which they are aware. Failure to comply with this duty can result in the unenforceability of later patents issuing from an application in which inequitable conduct (i.e., violation of the duty) took place.

In the U.S., patent-defeating prior art can include patents and printed publications from anywhere in the world, public knowledge or use of the invention before the applicant's date of invention in the U.S., or public use or sale in the U.S. more than one year before the patent application filing date.[26] Thus, an inventor can lose the right to obtain a potentially lucrative patent on an invention by publicly disclosing her invention, such as through presentation or publication, before filing a patent application.

The definition of a "printed publication" is very broad, and has been interpreted by courts to include microfilm, microfiche, Internet postings, videotapes, and, most recently, slides affixed to poster boards, as long as they are publicly accessible.[27] That latest expansion of the phrase was enunciated in the CAFC's 2004 *In Re Klopfenstein* decision.[28] For the first time, the court held that university researchers who presented study results at a scientific conference more than two years before filing a patent application covering the advance were barred from patenting the disclosed invention, even though no copies of any enabling document were distributed.[29] The rejection was based on the fact that slides disclosing the later-claimed invention were displayed on posters at the conference for two and a half days without any notice that note-taking was prohibited.[30] Thus, researchers who engage in early public data-sharing of their results may jeopardize their ability to later patent their findings if they do not track and control the timing, nature, and circumstances of their disclosures.

In most countries, an inventor creates prior art that will prevent her from later obtaining a patent on her invention if she discloses the invention to the public before filing a patent application.[31] In the U.S., inventors have a one-year grace period in which they can disclose the invention to the public and still retain the right to obtain a patent on the invention.[32] The grace period is an important policy tool that recognizes an inventor's need to assess the commercial potential of an invention or engage in public academic discourse before making the decision to seek patent protection.

However, the current grace period presents academic researchers with two problems. First, the lack of a one-year grace period in major foreign patent systems virtually eliminates the benefit of the U.S. grace period for inventors whose discoveries will require patent protection abroad to fulfill their commercial potential.[33] Second, even a one-year grace period often is not long enough to accommodate the needs of many researchers, due to the realities of academic research and technology transfer office (TTO) practices. It is not uncommon for more than a year to transpire before academic research progresses to the point at which its commercial potential can be assessed effectively. University inventions tend to be at a very early stage when they are first disclosed to TTO personnel, who generally have limited resources and data for making decisions about which inventions to attempt to patent.[34] This situation is complicated by the propensity of TTOs to use provisional patent applications to save money while securing a priority filing date for university-generated inventions.

Introduced into U.S. law in 1995, provisional applications offer applicants a lower filing fee and an additional 12 months beyond the one-year grace period in which to determine whether to file a regular non-provisional application for a patent.[35] Provisional applications also protect an applicant's right to file in other countries as long as the provisional application is filed before the invention is disclosed to the public.[36] The provisional application is not examined by the USPTO, and will simply lapse after 12 months and have no further effect unless a regular non-provisional application is filed by that time.

Provisional applications are attractive to TTOs precisely because of the embryonic nature of most university inventions. Funding and staffing are perpetual problems for most university TTOs, and provisional applications provide benefits in both areas. As of this writing, for a university, the filing fee for a provisional application is $75.00 versus $500.00 for a non-provisional (regular) utility application.[37] Moreover, since the provisional application will not be examined, TTOs may choose to spend less time and money on the drafting of the provisional application, based on an understanding that in a year's time, many will lapse because the covered technology will not justify (at the time the decision must be made) the cost of filing a further non-provisional application.

Evidence of the disproportionately higher use of provisional applications by university TTOs can be seen in the Association of University Technology Managers (AUTM) annual survey.[38] According to the survey, in fiscal year 2004, of the 8,286 new U.S. utility applications filed by U.S. universities, hospitals, and research institutes, 75% were provisional applications.[39] Conversely, the USPTO reports that provisional application filings for fiscal year 2004 accounted for only about 30% of total utility application filings across all applicants.[40]

U.S. law requires that patent applications filed in the USPTO should include an adequate written description of the invention that would enable a person of ordinary skill in the art to which the invention pertains to make and use the invention; applications also must disclose the best mode known to the inventor of practicing the invention.[41] The application must also include claims that particularly point out and distinctly claim what the inventor considers to be her invention.[42] The claims are the metes and bounds of the invention and define the inventor's ultimate right to exclude once the patent issues.

If two inventors file applications in the USPTO claiming the same invention, the Office will generally initiate an interference proceeding to determine which of the applicants is the first inventor and thus is entitled to a patent on the claimed invention. Interferences are unique to U.S. patent law, since the patent systems of other countries award patents based on which applicant was the first to file an application claiming the invention in the relevant patent office,[43] not on which applicant was the first inventor.[44] Interference proceedings are priority contests in which claimants can put forward proofs to establish either that they are the first inventor of the disputed subject matter and are entitled to the patent or that for some other reason the other party is not entitled to the patent.[45]

The term "patented invention" though commonly used, is somewhat misleading in that it suggests that each patent contains only one invention. While a patent may disclose one broad inventive concept, it will include as many inventions as it has claims, because each claim defines an invention and the written disclosure, enablement, and best mode requirements must be met for each claim.[46] In addition, the subject matter of *each* claim in a utility patent must be useful, novel (new), non-obvious to a person of ordinary skill in the art, and classifiable as a process, machine, article of manufacture, or composition of matter.[47]

Once an application is filed in the USPTO, it is examined for compliance with formal (e.g., proper fee, oath that applicant believes she is the true inventor) and substantive (e.g., novelty, non-obviousness) requirements.

Before 2000, patent applications were maintained in secrecy by the USPTO until they were either abandoned or issued as patents. However, since 2000, the USPTO has been publishing patent applications 18 months after their earliest filing date in order to facilitate early disclosure of inventive information to the public. Applicants can still avoid having their applications published if they notify the USPTO that they will not file for patent protection on the same invention in a foreign country.[48]

The patent statute provides that an applicant is entitled to a patent unless the USPTO (through its examiners) can establish that she is not.[49] Consequently, the burden is on the examiner, in the first instance, to show that a claimed invention fails to meet one or more statutory requirements. Once compliance with all requirements is established, a patent will issue from the USPTO. If compliance is not established, the applicant will have the opportunity to abandon the application or appeal the examiner's rejection(s) to the Board of Patent Appeals and Interferences and, from there, to the CAFC and, ultimately, to the U.S. Supreme Court.[50]

While this process may seem fairly straightforward, it rarely is. Patent examiners routinely reject the claims initially filed in an application based on combinations of prior art references, usually patents or other published documents that, in the examiner's view, disclose the claimed invention. The cycle of examiner rejections and applicant responses to rejections can go on for years and can easily consume tens of thousands or even hundreds of thousands of dollars before an examiner concludes a patent should be issued on a claimed invention or the applicant either appeals or gives up and abandons the application.[51]

After a patent issues, a patentee must pay escalating maintenance fees to the USPTO at 4-, 7-, and 11-year intervals to keep the patent in force.[52] An issued patent can also be the subject of a request for reexamination filed by the patentee or a third party.[53] Anyone can file a request for the USPTO to reexamine a patent based on patents or printed publications that raise a substantial new question regarding the patentability of one or more patent claims. Filing the request does not guarantee that a patent will be reexamined; only if the USPTO determines that a substantial new question of patentability in fact has been presented will such a proceeding be initiated.

Once a patent issues, its owner can use it to exclude others from making, using, selling, offering to sell, or importing the patented invention for the term of the patent. Moreover, the patent has a presumption of validity, which means that clear and convincing evidence will be required to invalidate it. This standard has been criticized because of the perception that many patents issuing from the USPTO currently are of low quality and do not deserve the presumption. Critics argue, among other things, that in recent years the standards for obtaining a patent have been lowered and the resources available to the USPTO to examine patents are insufficient.[54] Examples of patents cited as emblematic of the problem include patents for a method of swinging on a swing, a crustless peanut butter and jelly sandwich, and a well-known options pricing method.[55]

In addition, as patentees have garnered large financial awards from enforcing their patents, interest in obtaining patents has increased. This confluence of factors has created a crisis situation at the USPTO. In testimony before Congress in 2005, USPTO Director Jon Dudas noted the following:

> Patent applications in the U.S. have more than doubled since 1992. ... [T]he USPTO issued more patents last year alone (173,000) than it did during the first 40 years of its existence. While the sheer volume of applications is staggering, the technical complexity of patent applications is escalating rapidly. In 1905, more than 1/3 of U.S. patent filings were bicycle related. Today, the USPTO routinely examines patent applications in areas such as nanotechnology, bioinformatics, and combinatorial chemistry – art areas that did not even exist one hundred years ago. Some patent applications are received on CD-ROMs, containing literally the equivalent of millions of pages of data on paper.[56]

While the USPTO and concerned groups are exploring ways to ease the burden (the backlog is apparently approaching one million applications), no easy solution is in sight. In 1982, Congress created the CAFC to hear appeals in all patent cases and bring uniformity to patent law.[57] The CAFC is widely seen as having increased the lure of patents by strengthening and broadening patentee rights, upholding large damages awards, and lowering the standards for obtaining and enforcing patents. The result has been likened to "convert[ing] the weapon that a patent represents from something like a handgun or a pocket knife into a bazooka, and then... handing out the bazookas to pretty much anyone who asked for one, despite the legal tests of novelty and non-obviousness."[58] As a result, it arguably is now "easier to get patents, easier to enforce patents against others, easier to get large financial awards from such enforcement, and harder for those accused of infringing patents to challenge the patent's validity."[59]

Not surprisingly, patent infringement litigation also has increased, and the cost of defending against such a suit, even if the patent is believed to be invalid, can be prohibitive. According to a survey by the American Intellectual Property Law Association, the median cost of defending against a large ($25+million) patent infringement suit was $5 million in 2006.[60] While reexamination by the USPTO is a lower cost option available to third parties seeking to challenge a patent, the U.S. reexamination system is widely seen as deficient and inferior to, for example, an opposition system such as that used by the EPO. Several commentators have proposed the adoption of a post-grant opposition system in the U.S. to improve patent quality and lower the costs and uncertainty of the present system. Such a proceeding would allow challengers to oppose a granted patent on a more level playing field than in reexamination and at a lower cost than district court litigation.[61] A recent patent reform bill under discussion by Congress included a post-grant opposition provision, but it remains to be seen whether such a system ultimately will be introduced in this country.[62]

PATENTS AND TECHNOLOGY TRANSFER: THE BAYH-DOLE ACT

As noted earlier, universities obtain, license, and enforce patents on university-generated research and, as a result, are moving products from the lab bench to the marketplace. For example, the website of the AUTM contains a 25 + page listing of "product stories" describing successful university-generated products and programs.[63]

However, these achievements have not come without a cost to academia. Historically, universities have existed for the purpose of promoting inquiry and advancing the sum of human knowledge.[64] To further these goals, university researchers published and presented their scientific findings as soon as possible, in accordance with communal norms promoting the prompt and open sharing of data. But today, many academic researchers are being encouraged by TTO and industry sponsors to delay publishing and presenting their work until after filing a patent application and sometimes even longer than that.[65] In addition, the growth in patent-related litigation involving universities[66] and the much hyped "tragedy of the anticommons" in the patenting of basic research tools are both costs attributable, at least in part, to technology transfer initiatives.[67] While not amenable to precise quantification, both the stifling of discourse and the erosion in the norms of sharing and colloquy historically associated with the scholarly enterprise are costs that must be balanced against technology transfer gains.

Both the impressive numbers and the negative side effects are usually traced to the Bayh-Dole Act of 1980.[68] When Congress passed the Bayh-Dole Act, it gave universities presumptive title to inventions produced with federal funds, as long as the universities complied with specific requirements.[69] By allowing patent title to initially vest in universities, the Bayh-Dole Act paved the way for more interaction between universities and companies that could now obtain exclusive licenses to such patents and commercialize academic research that previously might have lain dormant and unused.[70]

In a prepared statement before a congressional subcommittee, Dr. Phyllis Gardner, Associate Professor of Medicine at Stanford University, succinctly outlined the pre-Bayh-Dole problem:

> Prior to Bayh-Dole, federal agencies would rarely relinquish ownership of federally funded inventions to academic and private institutions, even when private sector scientists and engineers actually contributed to the inventions. Valuable technology was left languishing on the shelves of research institutions. For example, in the 1960s, the U.S. government asserted that it owned rights to 5-fluorouracil (an important anti-cancer drug) even though it had provided merely a fraction of the funding that went into discovery. As a result, market entry of this critical product was unnecessarily delayed and industry distanced itself from federally funded university research.[71]

The impetus for Bayh-Dole was the belief that a wealth of basic, useful research developed in U.S. universities was languishing in those ivory towers because it took, on average, 15–20 years for basic research disclosed in publications to result in marketed products.[72] This delay was attributed to reluctance by private industry to invest in commercializing federally funded research because industry could not obtain exclusive rights to it.[73] Such reluctance created a "death valley" between publicly funded research and its commercialization by the private sector. The Bayh-Dole Act provided a type of "bridge" over this valley, by allowing universities to take title to inventions developed with federal funds and to grant exclusive licenses to entities willing to commercialize such technology.[74] While not without critics, Bayh-Dole is widely viewed as a success; in fact, many foreign countries are implementing changes to their laws to mirror its policies.[75]

But appearances can be deceiving. The Act brought to universities the lure of new money, a potential influx of new capital from licensing revenue derived from transferred technology. In order to capitalize on the opportunity, however, universities had to comply with the myriad rules mandated by Bayh-Dole, such as seeking patents on inventions and seeking licensees to commercialize the inventions.[76] With increasing frequency, universities began establishing TTOs to perform these functions. In 1980, 25 institutions of higher learning were involved in technology transfer; by 1992, that number had climbed to 200. The number of patents issued during that period also jumped – from an average of 250 a year to 1,500.[77] Research by Rogers, Ying, and Hartman suggested a likely impetus for the rapid and widespread adoption of the TTO model by many universities across the country:

> The diffusion of technology transfer offices may have been influenced by the so-called "big winner" technologies that have occurred at some universities. Examples are the $160 million that Michigan State University has earned over the life of two cancer-related patents ..., the $37 million that the University of Florida has earned from the sports drink Gatorade, the $27 million that Iowa State University has been paid for the fax algorithm, and the $143 million earned by Stanford University for the recombinant DNA gene-splicing patent. ... A "big winner" can dominate the total license income at a research university; for example, $18 million of Michigan State University's $18.3 million license income in FY 1997 came from the two cancer-related drugs.[78]

But very few universities setting up TTOs have seen these types of blockbuster successes. In 2000, about half of the total licensing income generated by all universities was earned by the top five grossing institutions.[79] Creating a patenting culture in a university requires a substantial, long-term investment of resources with no guarantee of success. On average, it takes from 5 to 10 years before a TTO breaks even, and poor management of the office can result in researchers having negative experiences with the technology transfer process that can create ill will and hinder the development of productive relationships.[80]

Bayh-Dole and other enabling legislation are evidence of a Congressional desire to facilitate technology transfer between universities and industry by using patent policy, with the ultimate goal of benefiting the public.[81] But luring academics into this brave new world of patents and royalties has created some additional unintended side effects. For example, university research often progresses in stages, and the traditional model of scholarly discourse involves the presentation and publication of research conclusions and insights at those various stages. Bayh-Dole and universities' resulting desires for patent-related revenues have altered that model.

Moreover, the Bayh-Dole Act mandates that universities share royalties from patented inventions with researchers.[82] This requirement has created a pathway for some faculty to become millionaires, thus eroding, to some extent, the pull of the publication incentive structure.[83] Also, many researchers receive study funding from industry sources, and such sponsored research agreements often specify a term of secrecy for results generated under the agreement.[84] Yet the rigid patent novelty rules directly conflict with this model by requiring an inventor to file a patent application either before or within 12 months after exposing the invention to the public (depending on the country) to avoid losing the right to obtain a patent.[85]

These rules constrain researcher behavior in ways that are not conducive to academic discourse.

The unforgiving nature of patent novelty rules also encourages a culture in which dissemination of even very early stage research, sometimes no more than a proof of concept, is delayed while a provisional patent application is prepared by the university TTO. As a result, secrecy is on the rise among academic researchers, particularly in the life sciences, with many university scientists choosing to limit and/or delay disclosures of their work in order to participate in the patent/technology transfer arena.[86]

For example, in 1966, 50% of surveyed experimental biologists felt safe in sharing information on current research with others; only 26% felt that way by 1998.[87] In a recent study of geneticists, 35% perceived academic scientists as somewhat or much less willing to share information and data than a decade ago, 58% reported adverse data withholding effects on their own research, and 56% reported adverse data withholding effects on the education of students and post-doctoral researchers.[88] Not all of these results are due to patents. Difficulties in obtaining research materials requested in material transfer agreements (MTAs) is perhaps an even larger problem for researchers and is likely influenced more by competitive pressure and the burden of complying with the request than by patent concerns.[89]

Whether benefits associated with patenting or obtaining sponsored research funds are causing many researchers to shift from a focus on basic to applied research is unclear.[90] Nevertheless, the incentives of the patent system appear to affect the publication norms and practices of some academics. Consider the following fact-based scenario:[91]

Peter, a 23-year-old PhD student in Chemistry at Big X University, discovers some interesting properties of a class of compounds with which he is experimenting and decides to publish an article disclosing some of his early findings. Based on counsel from the Big X University TTO, Peter waits until a provisional patent application covering his results is on file with the USPTO before publishing his article. Peter's research continues to proceed but not as quickly as he had hoped, and, 12 months after the filing of the provisional application, he still has several technical hurdles to clear, and commercial applications of his work are still years away.

Forced to make a prediction of the commercial potential of Peter's work, the TTO chooses not to file a non-provisional application at the end of 12 months, and the provisional application becomes abandoned. Peter makes more progress over the next several months but is then counseled by his advisor to significantly change the direction of his research. This is because the publication of the article covering his early findings is now prior art to any future patent application he might file on his new, related discoveries, which probably would not be considered to be different enough from the

earlier public disclosure to overcome an obviousness rejection. Despite Peter's great
interest in the area, he follows the instruction and changes his research focus.

Peter's predicament is troubling for a variety of reasons. First, Peter's
delay in publishing his results until after the filing of a provisional
application is part of a growing trend of secrecy among university
researchers in scientific disciplines (life sciences in particular) that runs
counter to traditional academic and scientific community norms of open
discourse and knowledge sharing. By delaying publication of his research
until after the filing of the provisional patent application, Peter potentially
has retarded the expansion of knowledge in his area by limiting the pool of
information available for others to build upon.

Second, by failing to file a non-provisional application before the
provisional application lapsed, the Big X University TTO inadvertently
may have led Peter to believe he had protection that he really did not have,
and he may be 1) more secretive in the future regarding his research results
or 2) more hesitant to participate in the patent process.[92] These are both
detrimental effects, but for different reasons. Greater secrecy on the part of
university researchers further stifles discourse and delays third parties in
building on information, an important concern in light of the cumulative
nature of most scientific advances. Hesitation by university researchers to
participate in the patent process, while not facially a negative result, is
harmful if patents are important to the commercialization of university-
generated research, which quite a bit of data suggest they are.

This problem could be mitigated through better TTO education of, and
communication with, academic inventors regarding the patent application
timeline and the percentage of provisional applications that are normally
converted to non-provisionals at that university. Such communication could
help the inventor make a more informed decision about, for example,
whether to engage in prior-art generating presentation or publication
activities on the strength of a provisional application filing. But all the
information a TTO can provide would not change the fact that 12 months
simply may be an insufficient period in which to assess the commercial
potential and technical difficulty of a discovery.

A proposal for addressing this issue made by the author elsewhere would
involve injecting more flexibility into the patent system, by creating an
opt-in extended grace period that would provide more time for academic
researchers to publish and present early stage research before having to file a
patent application. Such an extension, coupled with early application
publication (i.e., publication of designated applications immediately after

filing, instead of after an 18-month delay), would allow researchers to engage in traditional academic discourse while retaining the ability to obtain proprietary rights necessary for commercialization of their inventions. Importantly, it would also provide early disclosure of discoveries for other scientists to build upon. However, it would not address other concerns related to patenting upstream research in the university context such as those discussed below.

RESEARCH TOOL PATENTING
AND EXPERIMENTAL USE

In the same year in which Congress put technology transfer on the university map with the Bayh-Dole Act, the U.S. Supreme Court gave it a further boost with its decision in *Diamond v. Chakrabarty*.[93] This case expanded the scope of patent-eligible subject matter to include living organisms, there genetically engineered bacteria, thus jump-starting the fledgling biotechnology industry and further fueling government funding of university research in the life sciences.

The importance of the combined impacts of the *Chakrabarty* decision and the Bayh-Dole Act on the increase in technology transfer-related patenting is significant. As one commentator notes, "At roughly the same time universities were permitted to claim intellectual property rights to the fruits of federally funded research as a matter of course, the universe of potentially patentable research results expanded and the potential value of intellectual property increased."[94] For example, the relaxation of patent subject matter standards meant that universities, often engaged in upstream, early-stage research, could patent embryonic discoveries that, prior to the *Chakrabarty* decision, likely would not have been eligible for patent protection.

However, it also meant that many types of research tools – methods or products used in the process of scientific experimentation – used by scientists in their work might now be the subject of patents. As noted earlier, the substantial increase in the overall level of patenting in the U.S. is problematic for the USPTO, and the expansion in patent-eligible subject matter is a significant factor in that increase. But the increase in patenting, along with what is perceived to be a low inventiveness requirement for patentability, creates an opportunity for "patent thickets," many over-lapping patents covering an area, to form in certain technology areas.

While the actual presence of significant patent thickets in biotechnology research has not been confirmed empirically and is the subject of much debate, commentators have identified several challenges that such thickets could create for university research. For example, research may be hindered if access to needed tools is too costly because of patent license fees, is too complex to obtain because of the need to negotiate with multiple patent holders, or is simply denied altogether.[95] This is a particular concern in relation to MTAs, where onerous terms in the agreements – such as reach-through claims to products developed with the material, limitations on disclosure, and more – can end or delay negotiations and thus hinder research.

Another challenge created by the increased patenting of upstream research inputs relates to increased patent-infringement liability exposure for researchers if they use patented tools without obtaining permission. One of the complicating factors in the increase in patenting of upstream research tools is the lack of a clear experimental use exemption for patented inventions. Unlike the laws of many other countries that allow scientists to experiment on or with an invention for the purpose of research, U.S. law does not contain a broad statutory exemption for such activities. According to the CAFC:

> On its face, 35 USC 271(a) prohibits any of "making, using or selling." Any one act of the three is enough to create liability. A mere "use" which doesn't result in a sale is still actionable: Thus, the patentee does not need to have *any* evidence of damage or lost sales to bring an infringement action.[96]

In fact, in the 2001 *Duke v. Madey* case, which dealt with the unauthorized use of a patented invention by researchers at Duke University, the CAFC held that regardless of whether the allegedly infringing act is performed for commercial gain, "so long as the act is in furtherance of the alleged infringer's legitimate business and is not solely for amusement, to satisfy idle curiosity, or for strictly philosophical inquiry," the act is infringing.[97]

Various commentators have proposed the creation of a limited experimental use exemption for researchers. For example, Professor Strandburg has proposed a scheme that would provide a period of exclusivity for the patent holder after which the invention could be experimented "on" and perhaps "with" by researchers without fear of infringement liability.[98] However, under the current situation, university researchers engaged in the "business" of teaching students and conducting research are not automatically entitled to an experimental use exemption to patent infringement. While the likelihood of an academic researcher's being sued for patent infringement may be quite low, the uncertainty created by lack of a clear exemption may hinder some research activities.

Much has been written on problems associated with the Bayh-Dole Act in relation to over-zealous patenting, litigation, and licensing practices of some university TTOs and the potential for access issues for upstream research tools, increased secrecy among university scientists, and more.[99] To address these perceived problems, several commentators have called for reformation of the Act, as well as other changes to the patent system such as heightening the subject matter and utility standards and creating a statutory experimental use exemption to patent infringement.[100] These meritorious proposals could, if implemented, have the effect of improving some aspects of the current patenting regime.[101] However, it should be noted that there is not a consensus that there even is a problem; other commentators question these same contentions and argue that no, or at most minimal, changes are required.[102]

Despite these countervailing views, change seems likely to come from one or more of the three main bodies engaged in patent matters: Congress, the USPTO, and the U.S. Supreme Court. A variety of patent reform bills has been considered in Congress of late, and more are expected to be introduced.[103] The USPTO has also proposed dramatic changes to patent prosecution to deal with its backlog and quality issues. The U.S. Supreme Court in times past was seen as detached from patent matters but has, since 2005 at least, evidenced a renewed appetite for patent appeals and is now poised to make further significant changes to patent law jurisprudence with its decisions.

PATENT LICENSING AND ENFORCEMENT

Patent owners often choose licensing as a vehicle to extract value from their patents. The influential book "Rembrandts in the Attic" by Rivette and Kline encouraged companies to analyze their patent portfolios for hidden value in the form of patents that could be licensed to increase revenue or provide a competitive advantage.[104] IBM's aggressive efforts in this area are legendary: the company, which for many years has obtained more U.S. patents than any other company in the world, boosted its annual patent licensing revenue 3,300% – from $30 million in 1990 to nearly $1 billion in 2000.[105] In another approach to extracting value from patents, Dell Computers, which obtained numerous patents relating to its system for selling, distributing, and providing support for computers, used its patent portfolio as collateral in a $16 billion cross-licensing deal with IBM.[106]

Monsanto has developed a particularly creative way to extract maximum value from its patents on genetically modified seeds. The company uses two main types of license agreements to confer rights in relation to its intellectual property. First, it licenses seed producers to make and sell seed containing its proprietary traits. Seed companies pay royalties to Monsanto in accordance with these licenses. Second, it licenses growers to plant transgenic seeds covered by its patents, but only for planting a commercial crop in a single season, and prohibits growers from saving any seed from that single crop for replanting or supplying to third parties in the future.[107] These two agreements, together, allow Monsanto to capture maximum value from its intellectual property investment and maintain control of its technology. Without the agreement with the end user, the grower, Monsanto would be capturing value only from one user of the technology, the seed producer, who would then be free to capture additional value from the grower.

Thinking about patents strategically early in the development process can also provide a competitive advantage for a company. When Gillette set out to design its Sensor® shaver, it included patent attorneys on the R&D team who conducted a full patent analysis of various designs for the shaver, examining the strengths and weaknesses of the patent position of each design.[108] The company ultimately chose to go forward with the design that competitors would have the most difficulty designing around from a patent standpoint. Gillette then identified, and sought patents on, 22 different inventions related to various aspects (e.g., handle, springs, container, blade angles) of the product.

Such strategic approaches to patents can create significant problems not only for competitors but also for innovation in a technology area. For example, in the semiconductor industry, companies routinely cross-license each other's patent portfolios; otherwise, very little innovation could take place, because a single product may be covered by a plethora of patents owned by different entities.[109] However, because the terms of the cross-license agreements are a function of the size and quality of each company's patent portfolio, each company still has an incentive to accumulate as many patents as possible, even if the patents are covering only marginal advances. This not only creates waste and adds to the backlog at the USPTO, but it also creates problems for small innovators who lack a large patent portfolio for negotiations and thus may be unable to maneuver through this "patent thicket" without incurring patent infringement liability.

As noted earlier, the cost of defending against a patent infringement suit can be considerable, and until recently, patent owners could routinely obtain an injunction to shut down a business if they won a patent infringement suit. These facts, combined with the expansion of the scope of patent subject matter and the seemingly lower standards for obtaining and enforcing patents, have resulted in increased assertions of patent infringement by patent owners who do not themselves practice the invention covered by their patent and who may, in fact, have obtained the patent, by purchase or otherwise, for the sole purpose of extracting rents.

This phenomenon, denominated "patent trolling," has created considerable controversy, especially since many of the patents asserted appear to relate to business methods, which may be more likely to be of suspect quality because of the USPTO's lack of familiarity with the subject matter and prior art in that area. The U.S. Supreme Court decision in *eBay v. MercExchange*, eliminating the CAFC's rule that injunctions should routinely issue if patent infringement is found, is widely seen as a positive step in dealing with the troll problem, because the threat of an injunction is a huge stick used by patent owners to extract a settlement.[110] Now, courts can consider, among other things, whether money damages would be sufficient to compensate the patent owner for infringement, when deciding whether an injunction should issue.

It is worth noting that, while aggressive patent licensing efforts are widespread, open-source models are gaining traction as well. For example, in 2005, IBM announced the creation of a commons initiative in which it pledged not to assert 500 patents if the technologies covered by the patents are used in projects falling under an open-source initiative license.[111] Moreover, several open-source initiatives are underway in the biotechnology area, such as the Public Project in Genomics (P3G) consortium, which promotes collaboration between researchers using population genomic databases, and other initiatives have been proposed.[112] Having a variety of approaches available to researchers should be a boon to innovation in the academy and beyond.

CONCLUSIONS

Patents are important as incentives for discovery, innovation, investment, disclosure, and more. An important question under consideration in many quarters is whether the patent incentive is necessary or desirable for a variety of inventions for which protection is sought, or whether there are areas of technology and endeavor, such as upstream research tools and business methods, for which the patent system should be off limits. This chapter has also highlighted a variety of other issues associated with the procurement, use, and enforcement of patents that will continue to be analyzed and addressed in the coming years. So much is in flux in the patent system today that aspects of this chapter will surely be obsolete as soon as it is published. Yet one thing is certain: the U.S. will continue to have a patent system that can provide meaningful opportunities and obstacles for researchers for many years to come.

NOTES

1. Adam B. Jaffe and Joshua Lerner, *Innovation and its Discontents: How Our Broken Patent System is Endangering Innovation and Progress and What to Do About It*, 3 (2003).

2. Association of University Technology Managers, AUTM Licensing Survey: FY 2004 Survey Summary ii, 22, 26 (Ashley J. Stevens et al. (Eds), 2005), available at http://www.autm.net/events/File/FY04%20Licensing%20Survey/04AUTM-USLicSrvy-public.pdf

3. See Clifton Leaf, *The Law of Unintended Consequences*, Fortune, at http://www.fortune.com/fortune/print/0,15935,1101810,00.html (Sept. 7, 2005).

4. The impact on state and local economies can be quite important. The Wisconsin Alumni Foundation also boasts that "[t]o date, more than 30 companies based on WARF technology have spun out of the university, with all but one of them based in Wisconsin." *Guide Offers Aid to Campus Entrepreneurs* (Apr. 14, 2004). http://www.news.wisc.edu/9666.html

5. See Association of University Technology Managers, *Product Stories* (last visited Sept. 21, 2005). http://www.autm.net/abourtTT/aboutTT_prodStory.cfm

6. See *Patent Law Reform: Hearings Before the Subcommittee on Courts, the Internet, and Intellectual Property of the House Judiciary Committee* (June 9, 2005) (statement of Carl Gulbrandsen, Managing Director, WARF).

7. See Stephen A. Merrill et al., *A Patent System for the 21st Century*, National Academies Press (2004), available at http://www.nap.edu; *The Patent System: Today and Tomorrow: Hearings Before the Subcommittee on Intellectual Property Committee on the Judiciary*, 108 Cong. (2005) (statement of the Honorable Jon Dudas, Under Secretary of Commerce for Intellectual Property and Director of the USPTO).

8. Both agreements are available at http://www.wipo.org

9. Agreement on Trade-Related Aspects of Intellectual Property Rights, including trade in counterfeit goods, Final Act embodying the results of the Uruguay Round of trade negotiations, Apr. 15, 1994, I.L.M. 1 (1994), available at http://www.wto.org

10. Convention on the Grant of European Patents, Oct. 5, 1973, as amended by Decision of the Administration Council of the European Patent Organization of Dec. 21, 1978, 13 I.L.M. 268 (1974). The EPC went into effect in 1977.

11. Some issues include differences in views on the proper subject matter of patents, the language of the patent document and proceedings, the location and jurisdiction of such a patent office and court, compulsory licensing provisions and traditional knowledge protection, sovereignty issues, and much, much more.

12. Suzanne Scotchmer, *Innovation and Incentives*, MIT Press, 66 (2004).

13. 35 U.S.C. §§ 271(a), 154 (2000).

14. No less than a reasonable royalty, see 35 U.S.C. §§ 282, 283 (2000).

15. 35 U.S.C. §§ 284 (2000).

16. See Kathleen Gallagher, *Wisconsin May Reap Stem Cell Royalties*, Milwaukee J. Sentinel Online, http://www.jsonline.com/story/index.aspx?id = 303097 (last modified Feb. 20, 2005). However, recently initiated USPTO review of WARF's stem cell patents may reduce or eliminate the value of those patents.

17. See 35 U.S.C. §§ 101, 156, 161 (2000).

18. Antitrust Guidelines for the Licensing of Intellectual Property, DOJ/FTC, 2 (1995).

19. See, e.g., Jasmine C. Chambers, *Patent Eligibility of Biotechnological Inventions in the United States, Europe, and Japan: How Much Patent Policy is Public Policy?*, 34 Geo. Wash. Int'l L. Rev. 223, 225 (2002) ("Patents help attract the investments needed to continue research and facilitate the relationship between government, academia and the private sector ... [T]he potential to protect the fruits of expensive research speeds up the research process as well."); Clarissa Long, *Patent Signals*, 69 U. Chi. L. Rev. 625, 653 (2002) ("Among venture capitalists, both the quantity and quality of patents have long been factors that are taken into consideration when deciding whether to invest in a company, particularly in its early stages."); Mark A. Lemley, *Reconceiving Patents in the Age of Venture Capital*, 4 J. Small Emerging Bus. L. 137, 144 (2000) (suggesting that "one of the reasons people are patenting at a very early stage in the process is precisely in order to attract or appease venture capital. That is, they get patents in order to define their market model for their financiers.").

20. See, e.g., Rebecca S. Eisenberg, *Patents and the Progress of Science: Exclusive Rights and Experimental Use*, 56 U. Chi. L. Rev. 1017, 1037 (1989) (discussing theories that patents provide incentives to innovate and obtain future patents).

21. Kevin G. Rivette and David Kline, *Rembrandts in the Attic: Unlocking the Hidden Value of Patents*, 5 (2000).

22. See *Diamond v. Chakrabarty*, 447 U.S. 303, 313 (1980) ("Congress intended statutory subject matter to include 'anything under the sun that is made by man.'") citing S. Rep. No. 1979, 82nd Cong., 2nd Sess., at 5 (1952), H. R. Rep. No. 1923, 82nd Cong., 2nd Sess., 6 (1952), U.S. Code Cong. Admin. News 1952, pp. 2394, 2399.

23. Chakrabarty, 447 U.S. 303. A much earlier decision, *Parke-Davis & Co. v. H.K. Mulford & Co.*, 196 F. 496 (1926), in combination with *Chakrabarty*, set the stage for the patenting of genes, DNA, and other naturally occurring biological material isolated from, and in a purified state relative to, its natural condition. While abstract ideas, natural phenomena, and products of nature are still nominally excluded from patent eligibility, the allowance of patents covering isolated genes and purified DNA narrows the scope of "natural phenomena" that is in the public domain and not eligible for patent protection. For a more in-depth discussion of

patent eligibility standards in the U.S., see Margo A. Bagley, *Patent First, Ask Questions Later: Morality and Biotechnology in Patent Law*, 45 William & Mary L. Rev. 469 (2003).

24. The term "prior art" used generically refers to the body of information against which a claimed invention is compared in the determination of whether it is new and non-obvious.

25. *Kimberly-Clark Corp. v. Johnson & Johnson*, 745 F.2d 1437, 1453 (Fed. Cir. 1984); 35 U.S.C. § 103. Pursuant to paragraph (c) of Section 103, subject matter that qualifies as prior art only under Section 102(e), (f), or (g) cannot preclude the patentability of an invention where that subject matter and the invention, at the time the invention was made, were commonly owned or subject to an obligation of assignment to the same person. It is worth noting that an applicant need not be aware of prior art for the information to be used against her patent application. Knowledge of all of the relevant art is presumed on the part of the hypothetical person of ordinary skill. See In re Carlson, 983 F.2d 1032, 1035–1037 (Fed. Cir. 1992). "Section 102 has as one objective that only the first inventor obtain a patent ... Foreign 'patents' and foreign 'printed publications' preclude the grant of a patent whether or not the information is commonly known. Under [section] 102 a conclusive presumption of knowledge of such prior art is, in effect, a statutorily required fiction." In re Howarth, 654 F.2d 103, 106 (C.C.P.A. 1981).

26. 35 U.S.C. § 102 (2000). Subsections (a), (e), (f), and (g) are considered novelty provisions, while subsections (b), (c), and (d) are loss of right provisions by which an inventor loses the right to a patent because the invention is legally deemed to lack novelty. Subsection (b) is also a prior art provision like the novelty provisions, while subsections (c) and (d) are generally not considered to be prior art provisions. See *Oddzon Prods., Inc. v. Just Toys, Inc.*, 122 F.3d 1396 (Fed. Cir. 1997).

27. See In re Hall, 781 F.2d 897, 898 (Fed. Cir. 1986) (noting that the phrase printed publication "has been interpreted to give effect to ongoing advances in the technologies of data storage, retrieval, and dissemination.").

28. In re Klopfenstein, 380 F.3d 1345, 1352 (Fed. Cir. 2004).

29. *Ibid.* at 1352.

30. *Ibid.*

31. See, e.g., European Patent Convention, supra note 10 Article 52; Japan Patent Act Article 29 (1999).

32. 35 U.S.C. § 102(b) (2000).

33. See Margo A. Bagley, *Academic Discourse and Proprietary Rights: Putting Patents in Their Proper Place*, 47 B.C.L. Rev. 217, 266–269 (2006).

34. See Jerry G. Thursby, Richard Jensen, and Marie C. Thursby, *Objectives, Characteristics and Outcomes of University Licensing: A Survey of Major Universities*, 26 J. Tech. Transfer 59, 63 (2001) ("Products and processes based on early stage technologies are often years away from commercialization ... it is difficult to specify royalty income based on sales ... for very early stage technologies since the nature of the final product is often unknown.").

35. See 35 U.S.C. §§119(e), 111(b) (2000).

36. Paris Convention, Section 119(e).

37. *United States Patent and Trademark Office Fiscal Year 2006 Fee Schedule*, http://www.uspto.gov/web/offices/ac/qs/ope/fee2005oct01.htm. The $500.00 includes

filing, search, and examination fees, all of which are required for non-provisional applications.

38. See Association of University Technology Managers, AUTM Licensing Survey: FY 2004 Survey Summary ii, 22, 26 (Ashley J. Stevens et al. (Eds), 2005), available at http://www.autm.net/events/File/FY04%20Licensing%20Survey/04AUTM-USLicSrvy-public.pdf

39. *Ibid.* at 16.

40. U.S. Patent and Trademark Office, Performance and Accountability Report for Fiscal Year 2004, at 116 tbl.1 (2004), available at http://www.uspto.gov/web/offices/com/annual/2004/060401_table1.html

41. 35 U.S.C. § 112, 1 (2000).

42. 35 U.S.C. § 112, 2 (2000).

43. Robin Coster, *From First-to-Invent to First-to-File: The Canadian Experience*, American Intellectual Property Law Association (Apr. 2002), available at http://www.torys.com/publications/pdf/ARTech-19T.pdf (last visited Feb. 5, 2007).

44. "Making" an invention in the patent law sense involves two parts: conception and reduction to practice. Conception is the "formation in the mind of the inventor of the complete and operative invention as it is later reduced to practice." *Oka v. Youssefyeh*, 849 F.2d 581 (Fed. Cir. 1988). Reduction to practice can be either actual – making a prototype of the invention that works for its intended purpose – or constructive – filing an application with the USPTO that adequately discloses how to make and use the invention to a person having ordinary skill in the art to which the invention pertains.

45. For example, an applicant can seek to show that an opponent derived the invention from someone else and is thus not a true inventor, or that the subject matter is unpatentable and that no one is entitled to a patent on it. See 37 CFR 641.121. Interferences are not limited to two parties, or to pending applications. As long as at least one pending application is involved and the same subject matter is being claimed, there can be multiple applications or even patents involved in the interference. If only patents are involved in a priority dispute, the dispute is beyond the jurisdiction of the USPTO and must be resolved in federal district court. See 35 USC § 291 (2000).

46. 5 U.S.C. § 112 (2000).

47. 35 U.S.C. §§ 101–103 (2000).

48. 35 U.S.C. § 122 (2000).

49. 35 U.S.C. § 102 (2000).

50. 35 U.S.C. § 141 (2000). Alternatively, an applicant can appeal to the District Court for the District of Columbia before appealing to the Court of Appeals for the Federal Circuit. See 35 USC § 145.

51. Average application pendencies in the USPTO vary based on technology.

52. 35 U.S.C. § 41(b) (2000).

53. 35 U.S.C. §§ 301 et. seq. (2000).

54. See footnote 1.

55. *Ibid.* at 34 (2003).

56. *The Patent System: Today and Tomorrow: Hearings Before the Subcommittee on Intellectual Property Committee on the Judiciary*, 108 Cong. (2005) (statement of

the Honorable Jon Dudas, Under Secretary of Commerce for Intellectual Property and Director of the USPTO).

57. See, Rochelle Cooper Dreyfuss, *The Federal Circuit: A Case Study in Specialized Courts*, 64 N.Y.U. L. Rev. 1 (1989). This is a bit of an overstatement. The CAFC has jurisdiction over appeals of cases in which the plaintiff's complaint contained a claim "arising under" the Patent Act.

58. Adam B. Jaffe and Joshua Lerner, *Innovation and its Discontents: How Our Broken Patent System is Endangering Innovation and Progress and What to Do About It*, 2 (2003).

59. Adam B. Jaffe and Joshua Lerner, *Innovation and its Discontents: How Our Broken Patent System is Endangering Innovation and Progress and What to Do About It*, 35 (2003).

60. American Intellectual Property Law Association, Report of the Economic Survey (2007).

61. See Patent Reform Act of 2005, H.R. 2795, 109th Cong. (2005).

62. See Stuart J.H. Graham and Dietmar Harhoff, *Can Post-Grant Reviews Improve Patent System Design? A Twin Study of U.S. and European Patents* (2006), available at http://papers.ssrn.com/sol3/papers.cfm?abstract_id = 921826 (last visited Feb. 5, 2007); Jonathan Levin and Richard Levin, *Patent Oppositions* (2002), available at http://lsr.nellco.org/cgi/viewcontent.cgi?article = 1005&context = yale/lepp (last visited Feb. 5, 2007).

63. See footnote 5.

64. *1915 Declaration of Principles on Academic Freedom and Academic Tenure*, In: American Association of University Professors (AAUP), Policy Documents and Reports 3 (9th ed., 2001), cited in Robert C. Post, *The Structure of Academic Freedom* (draft book chapter on file with the author). The two other purposes are "to provide general instruction to the students and to develop experts for various branches of the public service." See also Charles C. Caldert, *Industry Investment in University Research*, 8 Sci. Tech. Hum. Values 24, 30 (Spring 1983) (noting a fundamental tension between the proper role of universities and the profit motive), cited in Joshua A. Newberg and Richard L. Dunn, *Keeping Secrets in the Campus Lab: Law, Values, and Rules of Engagement for Industry–University R&D Partnerships*, 39 Am. Bus. L.J. 187, 188 (2002).

65. See, e.g., Lana M. Knedlik, *Publishing: How Your Rights could Perish* (Sept. 2, 2004) http://www.stinsonmoheck.com/ns/ArticleDetail.cfm?AID = 26 ("Whether you are a sophisticated university or a lone inventor, the point is that publishing your work may not always be a good idea. ... university researchers should be careful about making any sort of public disclosure or risk losing patent rights (and ability to profit from them) forever."); Lauren MacLanahan, *Technology Transfer Buzz: Things to Know About Information Disclosures*, at 6 (Fall 2004), www.otl.gtrc. gatech.edu/OTL_Fall_2004.pdf; Laura Heisler, *Be Aware: Public Disclosure Can Affect Patentability*, Wisconsin Alumni Research Foundation, at http://www.warf. org/news/newsletters-article.jsp?articleid = 175 (Feb. 7, 2005).

66. See, e.g., *Madey v. Duke Univ.*, 307 F.3d 1351 (Fed. Cir. 2002), *cert. denied*, 123 S. Ct. 2639 (2003); *Iowa State Univ. Research Found., Inc. v. Wiley Organics, Inc.*, 2005 U.S. App. LEXIS 3694 (Fed. Cir. 2005); *Eolas Techs. v. Microsoft Corp.*, 399 F.3d 1323 (Fed. Cir. 2005); *Univ. of Rochester v. G.D. Searle & Co.*, 375 F.3d 1303

(Fed. Cir. 2004); Eli Kinitsch, *Yale Wins Suit Against Nobel Laureate*, 215 Science Now 1 (2005), at www.sciencenow.sciencemag.org/cgi/content/full/2005/214/1

67. See, e.g., Rebecca S. Eisenberg and Michael A. Heller, *Can Patents Deter Innovation? The Anticommons in Biomedical Research*, 280 Science 698–701 (1998); Arti K. Rai, *Regulating Scientific Research: Intellectual Property Rights and the Norms of Science*, 94 Nw. U. L. Rev. 77, 79 (1999) (noting that changes in intellectual property law have undermined scientific research norms), Rebecca S. Eisenberg, *Academic Freedom and Academic Values in Sponsored Research*, 66 Tex. L. Rev. 1363 (1988) (discussing sponsored research agreement restrictions on dissemination of academic results). Other costs, also difficult to quantify, include the loss to U.S. universities and the domestic economy of jobs and industry research funds as U.S. companies, frustrated by the difficulty of working with U.S. university TTOs, send jobs and dollars to overseas institutions with their growing corps of highly skilled researchers. See, e.g., Wayne C. Johnson, *Globalization of Research and Development in a Federated World*, In: Reinventing the Research University 159, 164 (2004) ("[L]arge U.S. based corporations have become so disheartened and disgusted with the situation [i.e. negotiating intellectual property rights with U.S. universities] they are now working with foreign universities, ... which are more than willing to offer extremely favorable intellectual property terms"); Robert Killoren and Susan B. Butts, *Industry–University Research in Our Times*, National Academies Government–University–Industry Research Roundtable, at http://www7.nationalacademies.org/guirr/ip_background.html (June 26, 2003).

68. Pub. L. No. 96-517, 94 Stat. 3015–3028 (codified, as amended, at 35 U.S.C. §§ 200–211, 301–307 (1980)) (commonly known as the Bayh-Dole Act).

69. See 35 U.S.C. §§ 200–211 (2000).

70. Useful summaries of the history of the Bayh-Dole Act and the varying forces leading up to its enactment can be found in: David C. Mowery, Richard R. Nelson, Bhaven N. Sampat, and Arvids A. Ziedonis, *Ivory Tower and Industrial Innovation: University–Industry Technology Before and After the Bayh-Dole Act*, 9–34 (2004); and Rebecca S. Eisenberg, *Public Research and Private Development: Patents and Technology Transfer in Government-Sponsored Research*, 82 Va. L. Rev. 1663 (1996).

71. *NIH: Moving Research from the Bench to the Bedside: Hearings Before the Subcommittee on Health of the Committee on Energy and Commerce*, 108 Cong. (2003) (statement of Dr Phyllis Gardner, representing the Biotechnology Industry Organization).

72. David C. Mowery, Richard R. Nelson, Bhaven N. Sampat, and Arvids A. Ziedonis, *Ivory Tower and Industrial Innovation: University–Industry Technology Before and After the Bayh-Dole Act*, 9–34 (2004).

73. While the funding agency could make the decision to allow licensing, such decisions were rare and were made on a case-by-case basis resulting in significant uncertainty regarding the likelihood of a favorable result. It was well understood, of course, that commercialization was well beyond the mission, resources, and expertise of university researchers and should be handled by the private sector.

74. See also Stevenson-Wydler Technology Innovation Act of 1980, Pub. L. No. 96–480, 94 Stat. 2311–2320 (codified, as amended, at 15 U.S.C. 3701–3714 (1994)) (addressing technology transfer in government laboratories).

75. See, e.g., *AUTM Licensing Survey: FY 2003 Survey Summary*, Association of University Technology Managers, at http://www.autm.net/surveys/dsp.surveyDetail. cfm?pid = 16 (visited Oct. 9, 2005) (citing announcements by the United Kingdom, Canada, Germany, and Japan of investment programs and/or statutory changes to enhance the commercialization of research from academic institutions as foreign countries "continue to strive to emulate U.S. success in harnessing the intellectual output of its academic institutions."); *Patent Law Reform: Hearings Before the Subcommittee on Courts, the Internet, and Intellectual Property of the House Judiciary Committee* (June 9, 2005) (statement of Carl Gulbrandsen, Managing Director, WARF) (noting that "at WARF, we receive numerous visitors each year from around the world. Invariably our foreign visitors ask about Bayh-Dole and express the wish that their own countries would adopt such forward-thinking legislation.").

76. See *The Bayh-Dole Act: A Guide to the Law and Implementing Regulations*, Council on Governmental Relations, at 4, at http://www.cogr.edu/docs/Bayh_Dole. pdf (last modified Oct. 1999).

77. David C. Mowery, Richard R. Nelson, Bhaven N. Sampat, and Arvids A. Ziedonis, *Ivory Tower and Industrial Innovation: University–Industry Technology Before and After the Bayh-Dole Act* (2004).

78. Everett M. Rogers, Jing Yin, and Joern Hoffmann, *Assessing the Effectiveness of Technology Transfer Offices at U.S. Research Universities*, Association of University Technology Managers, at http://www.autm.net/pubs/journal/00/assessing.pdf (visited Oct. 9, 2005).

79. AUTM Licensing Survey: FY 2000 Survey Summary, available at http://www.autm.net/events/File/Surveys/3_FY2000summary_public.pdf (last visited Oct. 9, 2005).

80. See Jason Owen-Smith and Walter W. Powell, *To Patent or Not: Faculty Decisions and Institutional Success at Technology Transfer*, 26 J. Tech. Transfer 99, 112 (2001) ("faculty decide to patent because of their beliefs about the positive personal and professional outcomes of establishing IP protection ... the decision to disclose a new finding ... depends upon conceptions of the patent benefits, framed by the costs of interacting with licensing professionals and technology transfer offices.").

81. Congress' most recent effort in this area, the Collaborative Research and Technology Enhancement Act of 2004 ("the CREATE Act"), is designed to encourage research collaborations between academic institutions and private enterprises by making it easier for the partners to obtain patents on inventions created by joint inventors from both organizations.

82. 35 U.S.C. § 202(c)(7).

83. For example, under Emory University's Intellectual Property Policy, inventors receive 100% of net royalties up to $25,000, 33% of net revenue up to $4 million, and 25% of net revenue over $4 million. Consequently, Emory's $540 million Emtriva sale made the three faculty inventors millionaires. See Emory University Intellectual Property Policy, document on file with the author.

84. See Jerry G. Thursby and Marie C. Thursby, *Who Is Selling the Ivory Tower? Sources of Growth in University Licensing*, 00 Mgmt. Sci. 1, 4 (2001) As reported by Thursby and Thursby: "Half of the firms in our industry survey noted that they

include delay of publication clauses in at least 90% of their university contracts ... The average delay is nearly four months, and some firms require as much as a year's delay."

85. 35 U.S.C. §§ 102(b).

86. See, e.g., Jeremy M. Grushcow, *Measuring Secrecy: A Cost of the Patent System Revealed*, 33 J. Legal Stud. 59, 82 (2004) (presenting data on the increased secretiveness of university researchers between 1980 and 1990); John P. Walsh and Wei Hong, *Correspondence: Secrecy is Increasing in Step with Competition*, 422 Nature 801, 802 (2003).

87. John P. Walsh and Wei Hong, *Correspondence: Secrecy is Increasing in Step with Competition*, 422 Nature 801, 802 (2003), available at http://www.nature.com

88. Eric G. Campbell et al., *Data Withholding in Academic Genetics*, 287, No. 4, J. Am. Med. Assoc. 473, 478 (Jan. 23/30, 2002). This is not to suggest that increasing secrecy is solely, or even predominantly, the result of the patent novelty rules. There are a variety of contributing factors, such as the widespread inclusion of secrecy clauses in industry sponsorship agreements, and the increasingly competitive nature of academic research in general. Nevertheless, the potential of the patent novelty rules to encourage this kind of behavior cannot be ignored.

89. John P. Walsh, Charlene Cho, and Wesley M. Cohen, *View From the Bench: Patents and Material Transfers*, 309 Science 2002 (2005).

90. See Jerry G. Thursby and Marie C. Thursby, *Who Is Selling the Ivory Tower? Sources of Growth in University Licensing*, 00 Mgmt. Sci. 1, 3 (2001) (noting that "[m]uch of the concern of those who question [Bayh Dole's] impact comes from fears that financial returns to licensing would divert faculty from basic to applied research ... we cannot reject the notion that faculty research has shifted.").

91. Based on an actual event. Names and identifying features have been changed.

92. See Jason Owen-Smith and Walter W. Powell, *To Patent or Not: Faculty Decisions and Institutional Success at Technology Transfer*, 26 J. Tech. Transfer 99, 110 (2001) ("The failure to pursue smaller scale 'bread and butter' disclosures limits future chances for commercial success by encouraging faculty to bypass the TTO or avoid commercial activities altogether.").

93. 447 U.S. 303, 313 (1980).

94. Joshua A. Newberg and Richard L. Dunn, *Keeping Secrets in the Campus Lab: Law, Values, and Rules of Engagement for Industry–University R&D Partnerships*, 39 Am. Bus. L.J. 187, 196 (2002).

95. See Stephen A. Merrill, Richard C. Levin, and Mark B. Myers, *A Patent System for the 21st Century*, p. 27, National Academies Press (2004), available at http://www.nap.edu

96. *Roche v. Bolar*, 733 F.2d 858, 861 (Fed. Cir. 1984).

97. *Madey v. Duke Univ.*, 307 F.3d 1351 (Fed. Cir. 2002), *cert. denied*, 123 S. Ct. 2639 (2003).

98. See Katherine J. Strandburg, *What Does the Public Get? Experimental Use and the Patent Bargain*, 2004 Wis. L. Rev. 81 (2004). See also Janice M. Mueller, *The Evanescent Experimental Use Exemption From United States Patent Infringement Liability: Implications for University and Nonprofit Research and Development*, 56 Baylor. L. Rev. 917 (2004); and *Merck v. Integra, Brief for Amicus Curiae Bar Association of the District of Columbia – Patent, Trademark, & Copyright Section*, 2005 WL 435891.

99. See, e.g., Rebecca S. Eisenberg, *Public Research and Private Development: Patents and Technology Transfer in Government-Sponsored Research*, 82 Va. L. Rev. 1663, 1727 (1996); Arti K. Rai and Rebecca S. Eisenberg, *Bayh-Dole Reform and the Progress of Biomedicine*, 66 L. Contemp. Probs. 289, 291 (2003) (arguing for reformation of Bayh-Dole to give funding agencies greater discretion in mandating non-exclusive licensing of federally funded inventions); David C. Mowery, Richard R. Nelson, Bhaven N. Sampat, and Arvids A. Ziedonis, *Ivory Tower and Industrial Innovation: University–Industry Technology Before and After the Bayh-Dole Act*, 9–34 (2004) (proposing changes both to Bayh-Dole and other areas of patent law such as heightened subject matter and utility requirements and a statutory experimental use exemption); Diane M. Sidebottom, *Updating the Bayh-Dole Act: Keeping the Federal Government on the Cutting Edge*, 30 Pub. Cont. L.J. 225 (2001); Scott D. Locke, *Patent Litigation Over Federally Funded Inventions and the Consequences of Failing to Comply with Bayh-Dole*, 8 Va. J.L. Tech. 3 (2003); Peter Mikhail, *Hopkins v. CellPro: An Illustration that Patenting and Exclusive Licensing of Fundamental Science is Not Always in the Public Interest*, 13 Harv. J.L. Tech. 375 (2000); Clovia Hamilton, *University Technology Transfer and Economic Development: Proposed Cooperative Economic Development Agreements Under the Bayh-Dole Act*, 36 J. Marsh. L. Rev. 397 (2003); William L. Geary, *Protecting the Patent Rights of Small Businesses: Does the Bayh-Dole Act Live Up to Its Promise?*, 22 Pub. Cont. L.J. 101 (1992); Clifton Leaf, *The Law of Unintended Consequences*, Fortune, at http://www.fortune.com/fortune/print/0,15935,1101810,00.html (Sept. 7, 2005) (arguing for amendment of Bayh-Dole to require broad licensing of federally funded inventions).

100. See *ibid.*

101. Bayh-Dole's perceived successes have made it quite popular with members of Congress, universities and other interest groups, and more than minimal changes to the current Act seem unlikely in the near term. For example, patent reform legislation currently pending before Congress does not include meaningful changes to Bayh-Dole. Moreover, the CREATE Act of 2004 provided the ideal opportunity for Congress to address issues with the Bayh-Dole Act since the legislation specifically related to enhancing the Act's technology transfer mandate, yet none of the abovementioned commentator reforms were included in that legislation. Instead, the Bayh-Dole Act was uniformly praised in congressional remarks. See, e.g., The Cooperative Research and Technology Enhancement Act of 2004, S. 2192, 108th Cong. (enacted) (statements of Senators Spector and Leahy, and Representative Berman).

102. See F. Scott Kieff and Troy Parades, *Engineering a Deal: Toward a Private Ordering Solution to the Anti-Commons Problem*, available at www.ssrn.com/abstract + 948468 (2006); Richard A. Epstein and Bruce N. Kulik, Navigating the Anticommons for Pharmaceutical Patents: Steady the Course on hatch-Waxman, available at http://www.law.uchicago.edu/lawecon/WkngPprs_201-25/209.rae-bk.anticommons.pdf (2004).

103. See, e.g., The Patents Depend on Quality Act of 2006, H.R. 5096 109th Cong. (2006); The Patent Reform Act of 2005, H.R. 2795, 109th Cong. (2005).

104. Kevin G. Rivette and David Kline, *Rembrandts in the Attic: Unlocking the Hidden Value of Patents* (2000).

105. *Ibid.* at 124.

106. *Ibid.* at 36.

107. *Monsanto v. McFarling*, 302 F.3D 1291, 1293 (Fed. Cir. 2002).

108. Kevin G. Rivette and David Kline, *Rembrandts in the Attic: Unlocking the Hidden Value of Patents*, pp. 109–113 (2000).

109. See Adam B. Jaffe and Joshua Lerner, *Innovation and its Discontents: How Our Broken Patent System is Endangering Innovation and Progress and What to Do About It*, pp. 59–64 (2003).

110. *eBay v. MercExchange*, 126 S. Ct. 1837 (2006).

111. *IBM Statement of Non-Assertion of Named Patents Against OSS*, available at http://www.ibm.com/ibm/licensing/patents/pledgedpatents.pdf (last visited Feb. 5, 2007).

112. See, e.g., Yann Joly, *Open Source Approaches in Biotechnology: Utopia Revisited* (forthcoming Maine L. Rev., copy on file with the author); Arti K. Rai, *Open and Collaborative Research: a New Model for Biomedicine*, In: Intellectual Property Rights in Frontier Industries, 131, 140–145 (Robert w. Hahn (Ed.) 2005); Sara Boettinger and Dan Burk, *Open Source Patenting*, 1 J.I.B.L. 221 (2004).

CHAPTER 5

BEYOND PATENTS: THE ROLE OF COPYRIGHTS, TRADEMARKS, AND TRADE SECRETS IN TECHNOLOGY COMMERCIALIZATION

Stuart J. H. Graham

ABSTRACT

This chapter suggests that, while researchers and teachers of university technology transfer often think exclusively in terms of patents and the Bayh-Dole Act, we ought to adopt a more nuanced view of intellectual property rights (IPRs). In the text, I discuss the primary non-patent types of intellectual property (IP) protection, copyright, trademark, and trade secret, and argue that while patents are normally the "default" position when we think about protecting technologies and profiting from them, evidence suggests that patents are among the least *important means of capturing value from innovation. Moreover, I suggest that while many consider that IP protections act as substitutes for one another, thinking about IPRs as complements is a more relevant approach to this issue. Adopting this more nuanced view better reflects reality and does a superior job of alerting our audiences to the opportunities available in the technology commercialization process.*

Technological Innovation: Generating Economic Results
Advances in the Study of Entrepreneurship, Innovation and
Economic Growth, Volume 18, 149–170
Copyright © 2008 by Elsevier Ltd.
ISSN: 1048-4736/doi:10.1016/S1048-4736(07)00005-7

1. INTRODUCTION

When considering intellectual property (IP) protections in the context of technology commercialization, university actors, and those studying the phenomenon, often think first of the Bayh-Dole Act, and of patents. University patenting of federally funded inventions is permitted under the Bayh-Dole Act of 1980, and the proliferation of university technology transfer offices, and the regime of disclosure and licensing under which many universities operate today, are largely built upon patents and the process of patenting. However, a complete understanding of the commercialization of university knowledge assets is incomplete without addressing other non-patent types of IP protection. These protections play an important role in the successful commercialization of many technologies, protecting the entrepreneur when taking the technology from idea to proof-of-concept to market. Without understanding these non-patent protections, we cannot completely appreciate the incentives that drive risk-taking and success in the commercialization game.

The purpose of this chapter is to introduce scholars and teachers to these non-patent forms of IP, and to discuss why we should care about them, particularly in the context of technology commercialization. The argument I make in this chapter is that, while patents are normally the "default" position when we think about protecting technologies and profiting from them, we should instead develop a more nuanced view of the IP environment and of opportunities facing technology entrepreneurs. Indeed, evidence I present below, principally from influential surveys (Levin, Klevorick, Nelson, & Winter, 1987; Cohen, Nelson, & Walsh, 2000), suggests that patents are among the *least* important means of capturing value from innovation, as reported by managers actually engaged in technology commercialization, albeit on a scale generally different from the entrepreneurial firm.

The other preconception held by many scholars and teachers is that IP protections act as substitutes for one another. Again, I suggest herein that a more nuanced view is appropriate. By abstracting away from our focus on single "inventions" to a broader view of innovation and commercialization as a dynamic and complex process, we can begin to think of using different types of IP together, in ways that may indeed be complementary (Graham & Somaya, 2006). I will offer evidence that entrepreneurs are examining the problem in exactly this sense, and are using patents, copyrights, trade secrets, and trademarks together, throughout the commercialization process, in ways that appear to complement one another, and that may offer a greater force of protection and more opportunities to capture value from technology products or services.

This chapter is organized as follows: Following the Introduction, Section 2 will describe the uses of IP protections by entrepreneurs, demonstrating that patents are at best secondary in many technology and industry sectors in terms of their effectiveness at earning value from innovation. Section 3 introduces the three major types of non-patent protection, namely copyright, trademark, and trade secret. In Section 4, I offer an argument against the IP-as-substitutes view, suggesting that our view of innovation ought to be expanded, particularly in the era of cumulative and complex technologies, to permit of thinking about IP-protections as complementary to one another. Section 5 offers a concrete example, analyzing how the IP-as-complements view can be extended to one important sector, namely software. Section 6 introduces the IP issues related to commercializing technologies under a "community innovation" model, while Section 7 provides a note on the role of increasingly strong IP in university research. Section 8 concludes, discussing how these issues add to our understanding and may be used to influence our teaching of technology commercialization.

2. USING IP TO APPROPRIATE VALUE FROM INNOVATIONS

Since Schumpeter (1934), we have understood that the innovation process is much more than mere "invention." Innovation encompasses all the elements necessary to bring a new technology or product to market, such as arranging capital, building the needed complementary resources, and finding success in the marketplace. When considering the profits that may be captured from an innovation, we are often interested in "supernormal" profits, those profits that can be sustained and protected from being competed away by normal market forces.

When describing the environment faced by innovators interested in securing such profits, scholars have spoken of "the appropriability regime" (Rumelt, 1984; Teece, 1986). Teece (1986) suggests that the ability of innovators to capture profits is influenced by two sources – the technological characteristics of the good and the existing legal environment (largely in terms of IP protections). In terms of the former, goods that are easily replicable provide few barriers to competitors, while characteristics that are hidden (e.g., manufacturing processes) offer hurdles difficult for competitors to overcome. When considering the legal environment, stronger rights in, and more active enforcement of, IP laws provide superior advantages to innovators attempting to keep competitors at bay and secure supernormal returns.

The relationship between patenting and technology commercialization is addressed at length in Chapter 4 by Margo Bagley. While leaving most of the details to that chapter, it is necessary to stress the prominent role that patents have played in our thinking as regards appropriating profits from innovation. Patents have long been a primary focus of researchers in management, economics, and law when analyzing the commercialization of technology – to the neglect of other forms of IP. This "patent focus" has been driven by the notoriety inside the university of the Bayh-Dole regime, and the growth of university technology transfer offices in response. Outside the university setting, research into commercialization has also tended to be overly focused on patents. This "patent focus" has been driven by the notorious growth in patenting over the last two decades, primarily in the information and biotechnology sectors, and by the reported use of patents by small firms, both as a means of protecting themselves from competitors and as a signal to venture capital. This treatment in the scholarship – made less costly by the wide availability of patent data and increased computing power – has contributed to patents' being considered in isolation and (too often) as the "gold standard" of IP protections.[1]

This chapter focuses on those things that patents are *not*. While patents are without question a strong and useful means of protecting technologies from competition, the weight of scholarly evidence over the last two decades suggests that appropriating value from innovation involves much more than mere patenting – and indeed that patents play a minor role in many circumstances.

Initial evidence of the use of patents by firms came in the so-called "Yale survey" (Levin et al., 1987). The authors employed a survey instrument to inquire into the usefulness of different legal and non-legal mechanisms for capturing value from innovation. After collecting the responses from top managers in large publicly traded firms across numerous industries, the authors demonstrated that patents are generally considered as relatively ineffective in terms of profiting from innovations when compared to secrecy, lead time, learning curve advantages, and marketing efforts.

Then the "CMU survey" (Cohen et al., 2000) followed. This more extensive survey, conducted in 1994, was aimed at the R&D managers of nearly 1,100 companies in over 30 industry sectors. Some of the survey results are excerpted in Table 1 and demonstrate that, in both product and process

Table 1. Effectiveness of Different Appropriability Mechanisms.

	N	Secrecy	Patents	Other Legal	Lead Time	Sales/ Service	Manufacturing
Process innovation							
Basic chemicals	35	58	30	12	26	27	40
Drugs	48	68	36	16	36	25	44
Computers	20	43	30	17	40	24	36
Semiconductor	18	58	23	8	48	32	43
⋮							
All 33 sectors	1087	51	23	21	45	31	38
Product innovation							
Basic chemicals	35	48	39	12	38	46	45
Drugs	49	54	50	21	50	33	49
Computers	25	44	41	27	61	40	38
Semiconductor	18	60	27	23	53	42	48
⋮							
All 33 sectors	1118	51	35	21	53	43	46

Responses scored 0–100 reflect answers to the question "During the last three years, for what percent of your [product/process] innovations [was Secrecy] effective in protecting your firm's competitive advantage from those innovations?"
Source: Adapted from Cohen et al. (2000).

innovation, secrecy was a much more important means of profiting from innovation than was patent. In fact, in the aggregate statistics, patenting was ranked significantly below lead time, complementary sales/service, and complementary manufacturing in terms of the factor's importance in securing profits from new technologies. The only category reportedly less vital than patent was "other legal," although it is not clear whether the survey's individual respondents thought "other legal" meant anti-trust, copyright, contract, litigation, or some other manifestation of law. Similarly, we do not know whether the respondents interpreted "secrecy" as trade secret protection, or as some other, more general type of non-disclosure.

The sum of this recent scholarship suggests that scholars interested in technology commercialization should take a much more nuanced view of the mechanisms available to capture value from innovations. Managers in corporate suites, and those working with scientists and engineers in the labs, report that patents are at best of secondary importance as compared with the other tools available to companies for capturing and sustaining supernormal profits. While these surveys were not detailed enough for us to know definitively whether the terms "secrecy" and "other legal" were interpreted by respondents to include copyright, trademark, and trade secret protection, other scholarly research has demonstrated that these non-patent protections continue to be useful methods for competing effectively in the knowledge economy (Graham, 2004; Graham & Mowery, 2003, 2005b; Graham & Somaya, 2006).

3. NON-PATENT FORMS OF IP PROTECTION

With an appreciation of the limits of patenting in the commercialization process, we can pursue a more detailed discussion of non-patent forms of IP. In the United States, the principal types of IP protection available in addition to patent include (a) copyright, (b) trademark, and (c) trade secret protection. While this chapter will discuss only these three types at length, other protections are available at common law (such as misappropriation[2]) and in statute (such as those available under the Semiconductor Chip Protection Act[3]), offering other valuable safeguards for innovators' commercialization activities.

3.1. Copyright

Copyright protection in the United States is granted by federal statute.[4] Copyright protects original expressions, not ideas or processes, so long as the expression is fixed in some concrete, tangible medium, such as a writing.[5] Allowable expressions under the statute may be literary, musical, dramatic, graphic, audio-visual, or architectural, among others.[6] The protection granted is against others who engage in unauthorized copying, distribution, or display of the work, and copyright has a duration equal to the life of the author plus 70 years or, in the case of works created for hire, 95 years from publication or 120 years from creation, whichever is shorter.[7]

Unlike patent protection, copyright law imposes no requirement that the expression be novel, useful, or non-obvious – only that it originates with the creator, and not copied from another. Because copyright protection begins from the moment that the expression is fixed in a tangible medium (e.g., as pen is put to paper), there is no formal registration requirement. Registration is, however, available from the Federal Government after deposit of a copy of the work with the Library of Congress. Registration is relatively inexpensive ($45)[8] and affords the copyright holder certain legal advantages, including a presumption of validity (if registered within five years after original publication),[9] the option of filing an infringement suit (which may not be brought absent registration),[10] and enhanced infringement damages.[11]

Copyright protection became more relevant in the context of technology commercialization after 1980, when software "writings" became allowable subject matter. During the 1970s, copyright protection was promoted by policymakers as the preferred protection for software inventions (Menell, 1987). In its 1979 report, the National Commission on New Technological Uses of Copyrighted Works (CONTU), charged with making recommendations to Congress regarding software protection, chose copyright as the most appropriate form of protection for computer software (CONTU, 1979). Because copyright protection adheres to an author/innovator with relative ease and has a long life – now upwards of 125 years for works created for hire – the Commission determined that copyright was the preferred type of IP protection for software (Samuelson, 1984). Congress adopted the Commission's position when it wrote "computer program" into the Copyright Act in 1980, and computer databases and programs are considered protected "literary works" under the Act.[12]

In a very real sense, one cannot understand the application of copyright to software "writings" without understanding that patent protection was extended to software "ideas" at roughly the same time (Graham & Mowery, 2003). The federal courts' initial interpretation of copyright protection as applied to software suggested strong sweeping protection for inventors.[13] While the development of court precedent over time has somewhat weakened this sweep (while patent protection for software was becoming generally accepted),[14] copyright remains an important protection for software innovators. In fact, survey evidence suggests that software engineers prefer to rely upon copyright protection as compared to patent protection, partly on philosophical grounds (Samuelson & Glushko, 1990). Given the ease, speed, and low cost of securing a copyright as compared to a patent, the latter of which can cost from $5,000 to $100,000 to prosecute (Graham, Hall, Harhoff, & Mowery, 2003), copyright offers distinct advantages to software entrepreneurs with limited time and financial resources.

In the university context, the treatment of copyrightable materials is mixed. The University of Washington, for example, specifically provides in its policy documents that certain copyrightable materials are property of the university, subject to restrictions for "scholarly works" (University of Washington, 2007). Anecdotal discussion between this author and officers at the University of California's technology transfer office suggest that certain universities, like Washington, have historically been relatively aggressive at trying to capture value on copyrightable materials from their faculty. Others, like California, have been almost completely inactive.

3.2. Trademark

Trademark protection is not an IP protection per se. Unlike patent and copyright protections, which emanate from the U.S. Constitution and are intended to reward creators and promote the useful arts, trademark is intended to protect the consumer from fraud. That said, the reality is that trademark has become a de facto form of IP, and thus it is useful to innovators in protecting marketing capabilities, brands, and goodwill. These assets may be among the most valuable assets of companies (e.g., the Microsoft brand name alone was valued in 2002 at $64.1 billion).[15]

Trademark, like copyright, is protected in the United States primarily under federal law. Nevertheless, common law elements of trademark do exist in the individual states, and in fact, the current federal regime is largely a validation of these state-granted rights. As such, common law trademark rights can be valuable protections against sales of competing products that lead to consumers' confusion or mistake as to the origin, quality, or advertising of the good.[16]

Federal law provides for the registration of marks used in commerce, and federal protection is predicated upon successful registration.[17] Registered marks may be trademarks, service marks, or other marks providing information about the origin of the commercial activity.[18] The registration process is overseen by the U.S. Patent and Trademark Office, which requires that the mark be owned, be used – or intended to be used – in commerce, and that the applicant believes that the mark is both not in use and is not confusingly similar to another mark in use.[19] Successful completion of the registration process leads to the mark's being recorded on the Principle Register, serves as notice to all other later users of confusingly similar marks in the United States, and can earn the mark the status of being incontestable.[20] Thus, registration can convert state-based common law rights into a truly strong and national IP protection.

Given that consumer protection is the underlying policy motivation for trademark protection, to be valid the mark must be distinguishable from other marks. Marks are considered distinguishable if they either (1) have the characteristic of being arbitrary or, at most, suggestive of the product, or

(2) are descriptive of the product, but have acquired "secondary meaning" after prolonged commercial association. Marks that are merely "generic" are never protectable.[21] The mark "Intel" for micro-processors may be considered suggestive of the intelligence or intellect needed to produce, or use, the product, while the mark "Blue Martini" for customer-relations management systems may be considered arbitrary as regards the commercial activity.

The protection afforded to the holder of a distinctive mark is to prevent others from employing confusingly similar marks, and to allow the holder to use the federal courts both to enforce that limitation on competitive uses and to safeguard the value of the mark itself. Courts will prevent the use of other marks that tend to associate the holder's product with other goods of lower quality.[22] Trademark law has thus developed to give the holder of the mark valuable geographic protections that prevent others from using marks that tend to confuse consumers or to dilute the value of the mark – protections that offer entrepreneurs an important shelter from competition when engaging in vital sales and marketing functions of technology commercialization.[23]

3.3. Trade Secret

Trade secret protection in the United States is derived primarily from the common law and as such is protected under the several states' laws. Trade secrets do, however, have a set of more-or-less general characteristics, regardless of the state jurisdiction in question. The subject matter of trade secrets is "valuable information," which differs from the subject matter of both patent and copyright. The information must generally be commercial information that affords some advantage or has independent economic value derived from its secrecy.[24] Moreover, the information cannot be obvious to a person trained in the relevant technical field. To keep the trade secret protection, the holder of the trade secret must also take reasonable steps to ensure that the valuable information remains a secret. Thus, many companies demand non-disclosure agreement of their employees and take care to institute policies on the treatment of secrets.

The legal remedy available to the holders of a trade secret is to prevent others from misappropriating the valuable information. "Misappropriation" derives from tort law, and as such, the concept involves some morally suspect behavior, such as stealing the information or enticing persons to disclose the information wrongfully.[25] Unlike the remedies available under patent law, trade secret law does not require courts to intervene to prevent others' use of the secret information unless the information was "misappropriated": thus, if the valuable information was independently discovered, trade secret law offers no remedy.

Trade secrets are unique among IP protections in that, in theory, they have no limit to their duration. So long as the information remains valuable and the holder takes reasonable steps to keep the information secret, there is no limit to the protection duration. Furthermore, the protection may extend not only to "positive" knowledge (e.g., customer lists) but also to "negative" knowledge (e.g., a process that was tested and found *not* to work) – both forms of information may provide advantage or value, so both are capable of trade secret protection.

4. THE RELATIONSHIP AMONG PATENT AND NON-PATENT IP PROTECTIONS

As stated above, scholars have tended to consider patenting in isolation, without considering other types of IP. Nevertheless, when the relationships among different types of IP have been considered, these protections have often been viewed as substitutes for one another. So, the question is often posed: Is patent *or* copyright appropriate for protecting software? Or, when is the appropriate point at which to *stop* trade secret protection and *start* patent protection?

The view of intellectual properties as substitutes is common in much of the management and economic literature (Graham & Somaya, 2006). Because intellectual property rights (IPRs) are creatures of the law, and because economists began analyzing IP protection quite early (Plant, 1934a, 1934b), it is not surprising that these disciplines had a strong influence on later notions of the relationships among types of IP. In the law, the substitutes view was supported by precedent. In *Kewanee Oil v. Bicron Corp.* (1974),[26] the U.S. Supreme Court declared that trade secrets protected "lesser or different inventions" than did patents. On the other hand, Friedman, Landes, and Posner (1991), in an analysis of the economics of trade secret use, provide a strong rebuttal to the Court's notion that patents are preferred for "better" inventions, arguing that the likelihood of imitation, life of the invention, and relative costs of patenting and secrecy determine the choice of IP protection. Nevertheless, the authors continued the notion advanced in *Kewanee Oil* that it is natural to think in terms of substituting patent for trade secret protection.

This IP-as-substitutes view has been strongly influenced by the importance of patent and trade secret protections in the early decades of the 20th century, driven by their significance in protecting innovation in important turn-of-the-century industries like chemicals and machinery. Because the patent laws require disclosure, it is natural that trade secret would be extinguished when a patent application was filed. Driven largely by the natural substitution that seems required by an innovator's switch from secrecy to patent, many theoretical studies of appropriability have analyzed this tradeoff (Horstman, MacDonald, & Slivinsky, 1985; Teece, 1986; Friedman et al., 1991; Arora, 1995).

But this view of patents and trade secrets as substitutes for one another considers only the individual "invention." If we are to expand our manner of thinking, considering a complex product or a complex innovation process, the IP-as-substitutes view can be relaxed (Graham & Somaya, 2006). In reality, in today's world, the innovation process has many layers, and often involves complex technologies, with potentially thousands of individual "inventions" embodied in a single product. The concepts of "cumulative innovation" and "complex technologies" have entered our lexicon, suggesting that the commercialization of technology is dynamic in terms of both time and space. If we abstract away from the single "invention," to the innovation process or the complex product, it becomes apparent that different types of IP may serve in a complementary manner. Accordingly, these different mechanisms may bring benefits to the entrepreneur simply through their coincident use.

By way of example, Pilkington, Plc employed both patent and trade secret in ways that complemented one another. Pilkington, the innovator of the "float glass" process that revolutionized the production of pane glass – and in so doing lowered production costs by orders of magnitude – used both patent and secrecy in its appropriation strategy.[27] After gaining patent protection on the "float glass" process, Pilkington engaged in worldwide licensing, giving licensees exclusive territories, but including a knowledge grant-back provision. Pilkington closely guarded its trade secrets over process innovations (tacit knowledge not included in the patent documents), and after the patents expired in the early 1980s, the company continued to collect royalties under its licenses based on its perpetual trade secrets.[28]

Results reported from an analysis of the "CMU survey" in Cohen et al. (2000) lend support to the notion that different appropriability mechanisms may be complementary in use. The authors report correlations of industry-level mean effectiveness scores of the various surveyed mechanisms (e.g., lead time, secrecy, patenting), demonstrating that in the case of process technologies, the use of patenting and secrecy are positively correlated at significant levels. Moreover, their factor analyses show that, in some circumstances, secrecy loads with patenting, leading the authors to suggest that there may be a premium to keeping to-be-patented innovations secret until the patent actually issues (Cohen et al., 2000). Another explanation may be that trade secrets are being used as a complement to patents.

In other work (Graham, 2004), I hypothesize that innovators may be using legal process inside the patent office to take advantage of longer secrecy during the patent-granting procedure. An allowance, called the "continuing application," has been used by patent applicants to extend the period of pre-grant secrecy. Logistic regressions verify that, after controlling for technology, time, and firm characteristics, patentees in industries that responded on the CMU survey that "secrecy" was more valuable were significantly more likely to use the "continuation application" procedure (Graham, 2004).

5. THE CASE OF SOFTWARE

Information Communication Technologies (ICTs) have been an important source of entrepreneurial dynamism for the last several decades. In fact, research has demonstrated that ICTs have the characteristic of a "general purpose technology," suggesting that these technologies have been broadly adopted and widely practiced throughout the economy (Hall & Trajtenberg, 2004). The introduction and wide adoption of the personal desktop computer during the 1970s and 1980s created a large installed base and offered entry opportunities for many small innovators in the software space (Graham & Mowery, 2003). Because the software market has been an important and economically relevant sector for technology commercialization, software as subject matter may offer opportunities that others do not for the complementary use of IP protections. Accordingly, this section offers a brief case study of the application of the logic of IP-as-complements view to innovation in the software sector.

The software industry, which topped $185 billion in worldwide revenues in 2001,[29] was born when International Business Machine, in the face of government anti-trust action, unbundled software from its hardware in the late 1960s. By the 1970s and 1980s, wide adoption of the desktop computer (PC) created demand for specialized software applications, a demand met principally by new market entrants like Microsoft, Symantec, and Adobe

Systems. Software differs from other industrial products in that all major types of IP (patents, copyright, trade secrets, and trademarks) are available as IP protection to software innovators.

The commercialization of these software technologies occurred in a shifting IP environment. As cataloged in Section 2, copyright protection (for source code writings) was deemed appropriate for software by Congress in 1980, although patent protection (for software ideas) has been growing in importance and use since the mid-1980s, made only more notable with the advent of the Internet and "business method patents" in the 1990s (Graham & Mowery, 2005b). During the same period, both trade secret (for valuable and secret information) and trademark (for logos and brands) have been available to software innovators.

When studying the role of IP in software commercialization, the debates that occurred in legal scholarship throughout the 1980s and 1990s concerning whether patent *or* copyright is most effective in protecting software innovation add to our perception that different forms of IP act as substitutes. Menell (1987), for instance, suggested that copyright protection might be ill-suited to software, suggesting that patent protection might create stronger incentives. Samuelson (1984) also found copyright an inappropriate protection for software, but suggested instead a sui generis form of IP. Lemley and O'Brien (1997) followed by arguing in favor of patent protection because copyrights would interfere with well-functioning markets.

Evidence suggests, however, that small firms engaged in the commercialization of software technologies are using the different types of IP in combination. For instance, HiddenMind Technology, Inc., a mobile-workforce information management software specialist, obtained a patent for its ActiveUniverse® software application (granted 2002) and registered the ActiveUniverse® trademark (in 2000), while also enjoying copyright protections in the software. Similarly, Magnitude Information Systems, Inc., an e-commerce transaction-monitoring firm, protected its E-Fuel® trademark in 1999 while seeking a U.S. patent on the underlying software algorithm (granted in 2000), while also enjoying copyright protection on its software innovation. A close reading of the patents and trademarks held by these firms reveals that the wording is quite similar, suggesting that complementarity may be running not only to use, but also to the IP protections themselves.

In Graham and Somaya (2006), we develop an empirical test of the complementarity-in-IP hypothesis, employing data collected from software-specialist firms. Using as our empirical setting the PC software application industry, we test for complementarities in the use by some 400 firms of different types of IP. Defining "use" of IP as litigation, we are able to demonstrate through a seemingly-unrelated-regression (SUR) technique that copyright and trademark, when "used" together by software specialists, exhibit the characteristics of complements. We suggest that this complementarity may be emanating from the firms' employing of certain common inputs, such as resources and expertise (Graham & Somaya, 2006).

6. OPEN OR COMMUNITY INNOVATION

IP protections are also critical, both as enablers and as obstacles, to a model of innovation called "open innovation" or "community innovation" (CI).[30] In this model, a community of individuals collaboratively creates some technological advance and cedes some portion of their ownership rights in the intellectual capital to the community. One well-known example occurs in the creation of "open-source software," although the CI development model is being used increasingly in other technology settings. A recurring theme in discussions of CI is the need to limit the availability of proprietary IPRs in order to ensure open access and design freedom to both creators and users of the innovation output (Graham & Mowery, 2005a).

Proponents of the CI development model point to developers' need to access and build upon the efforts of others, arguing that this freedom is undermined when the development community is blocked from using "fountainhead" innovations. In fact, the software innovation process may be particularly sensitive to IP roadblocks due to software's character as a "cumulative innovation" technology, meaning that innovation is closely linked to and builds upon prior generations of the technology. Moreover, the simple economics to organizations of adopting and tailoring open-source software could also be substantially altered if the open-source code, once adopted, were subject to third-party IPRs employed ex post to extract royalties after the adopting firm had made investments in deploying, learning, and modifying the software. The plain truth is that strong property rights are considered an anathema by many developers and gurus of CI.

Considering the risk that IPRs are thought to pose to the CI movement, it is useful to examine the IP-assignment licenses (such as the General Public License [GPL or "copy left"] from the Free Software Foundation) under which developers create and adopters are allowed to use the technologies. In open-source software, while licenses vary, they generally prohibit the exercise of proprietary IPRs over improvements to the software made by individual developers. In fact, at the core of the GPL open-source software model is a limit on individuals' ability to "take the code private" by exercising proprietary IP (Graham & Mowery, 2005a).

But IPRs in software may be awarded to third parties, and thus would fall outside the bilateral and multilateral scope of these open-source licenses. Therefore, rights that allow U.S. patent and copyright owners to prevent the "use" and "copying" by all others could pose substantial risks to the open-source development model. While such IPRs present a downside risk to adopters of open-source software, developers in open-source software may nevertheless benefit from the public disclosure of new art promised as the quid pro quo for the public monopoly that copyright (and for that matter, patent) affords. Furthermore, so long as information disclosure is complete and timely (by no means certain in software patenting, let alone patenting more generally), boundary searching by CI developers could be used to lessen the risk that the innovation could be the target of "hold-up." Nevertheless, it is reasonable to assume that these additional costs may lead to some reduction in the supply of CI projects.

Open-source licenses create a legal relationship between the creator of the software and its voluntary users, but the open-source license cannot preclude the existence of others' IPRs in the software. Open-source software users may relinquish certain IPRs in their derivative works under the terms of the license, but because property rights define a relationship between the property holder and the world, these "outside" rights cannot be superseded by a bilateral license.

In fact, the restrictive character of IPRs creates the foundation for the operation of the open-source license. Copyright and patent rights – to the extent that the latter have been sought – are held by the inventor of the open-source software. The inventor subsequently "passes" these rights on to other developers, allowing these later voluntary adopters to use the rights under the terms of the open-source license.

Commercial opportunities flowing from the CI model are varied. Some entrepreneurs, like Red Hat Software, rely principally upon selling services to adopters of the CI product, the latter (Linux) being available as shareware. Alternatively, the texts of different open-source licenses demonstrate that proprietary innovations arising from or built upon the core open-source software are anticipated, even though "taking open-source code private" strikes at the heart of the bargain that open-source adopters make with the CI community. For instance, LizardTech, Inc., a Seattle software company specializing in scan-to-Web publishing, contends that it has built proprietary tools, documentation, and implementations in its open-source DjVu software under the restrictive GPL, while apparently adopting the relatively unrestrictive terms of the Mozilla Public License (MPL) as regards patent rights.[31] Likewise, International Business Machines (IBM), while avoiding any code distributed under the restrictive GPL, has included a modified open-source Apache Web server in its WebSphere product under the less-restrictive terms of the Apache open-source license.[32] These examples suggest that firms may be "cherry picking" among the available open-source software licenses for favorable commercialization and appropriation conditions for proprietary innovations that complement open-source products (Graham & Mowery, 2005a).

The 2003 copyright and trade secret lawsuit filed by SCO against IBM further illustrates the hazards to which developers and adopters of open-source software may be exposed.[33] In March 2003, the SCO Group filed a $1 billion infringement action against IBM, accusing IBM of violating SCO's trade secrets in its open-source Linux code. The demand has subsequently been amended to $5 billion. SCO contends it acquired the IPRs to the UNIX operating system in 1995, and alleges in its suit that IBM has appropriated and impermissibly used the UNIX code in its LINUX products, based on the origins of LINUX as a variant of the UNIX system in the early 1990s.[34] SCO's contention that no adopters of open-source software, including IBM, had the legal standing to enforce the GPL license may invite further complication in future open-source controversies that find their way to the courts.[35] In fact, it appears that SCO was successful at demanding licensing royalties on its UNIX software from both small firms (Ev1-Rackshack) and large firms (Microsoft, Computer Associates, and SUN Microsystems) in the wake of its lawsuit.[36]

7. A NOTE ON IP POLICY AND THE UNIVERSITY

Complaints about the "kept university" (Press & Washburn, 2000) are only one element of a larger discussion concerning the proper role of the university in the national innovation system (Mowery & Sampat, 2004). The legislative history of the Bayh-Dole Act makes clear that university ownership over federally funded research was meant to create incentives to commercialize what would otherwise remain dormant discoveries.[37] However, concerns were voiced at the time of the bill's passage, questioning whether this mechanism would lead to negative consequences by shifting the focus of federally funded research away from creating new knowledge to generating profits for enterprises.[38]

The Bayh-Dole Act was one of several changes in the U.S. patent regime that altered the environment in which corporate innovation occurs in the United States. Chesbrough (2004) has referred to a rise in the in-sourcing of technology by firms, pointing to the university as a supplier of technologies. While the Bayh-Dole Act changed the rules by which universities were allowed to play in the technology game, the 1982 creation of a specialized appellate patent court is widely believed to have heralded a "strong-patent" regime in the United States (Jaffe & Lerner, 2004). Universities were thus permitted by law to secure patent rights precisely when those rights were about to become stronger.

Controversy over the proper role for IP, and the knowledge-creating function of the university, extends beyond patents. At its heart, the social contract upon which IP protections are based is built upon a quid pro quo. Society agrees to suffer a loss of consumer welfare by granting monopolies to inventors, and in return is benefited with an increased supply of invention. But society puts restrictions upon the monopoly holder, limiting the scope and duration of the exclusive rights, and also requires disclosure of the invention, thus lowering the cost and increasing the likelihood of follow-on cumulative innovation.

In copyright, the public's offer in this quid pro quo has traditionally been limited in terms of duration and scope. Scope has traditionally been narrowed by such doctrines as "Fair Use," which permits copying for purposes like parody or education, and "First Sale," which bounds the commercial reach of the copyright holder. These limitations have been eroding, however, both through legislation and court rulings, with the result that copyright, like patent, has become a stronger IPR.

The impact of this strengthening of IPRs upon university technology transfer, and the university research environment more generally, is not well understood. To the extent that strong monopoly rights create greater profit incentives for entrepreneurs, one would expect technology transfer from the university lab to the external market, with concomitant social benefits, to be encouraged. However, the profit motive may create incentives inside the university to shift focus from basic research to more applied, commercially relevant research. This result would have the effect (if research is a zero sum game) of limiting the amount of basic research completed in the university, thus reducing the output from what has been historically one of the more important engines of foundational knowledge (Mowery & Sampat, 2001).

8. CONCLUSION

This chapter has argued that scholars and teachers of university entrepreneurship must take a broader view of IP protections, beyond mere patents. When considering IP protections in the context of technology commercialization, those in the university often think first of the Bayh-Dole Act, and of patents. In this chapter, I introduced in a technology commercialization setting the relevance of non-patent forms of IP, such as copyright, trademark, and trade secret, and offered a framework for thinking about these protections, and the opportunities they offer to entrepreneurs both inside and outside the university.

While patents are normally the "default" position when we think about protecting technologies and profiting from them, I argue that, since evidence from the "Yale" and "CMU" studies suggest that patents are among the *least* important means of capturing value from innovation, we should expand the way in which we think about protecting and capturing value from innovations. I also argue against the other preconception held by many scholars and teachers that IP protections act as substitutes for one another. I suggest that we take a more nuanced view, abstracting away from our focus on single "inventions" to a broader view of innovation as a dynamic and complex process – one that permits the use of different types of IP together, in ways that may indeed be complementary (Graham & Somaya, 2006). I also offer evidence that entrepreneurs are examining the problem in exactly this sense, and are using patents, copyrights, trade secrets, and trademarks together, throughout the innovation process, in ways that appear to complement one another. In so doing, I suggest that we as scholars and teachers of commercialization ought to internalize these views, in order to bring greater value to our students who seek to understand, and to be successful in, technology innovation. As such, we do a more complete job of opening the world to our audience when we show them the complementarities among different forms of IP, and the importance of non-patent forms of IP in the technology commercialization process.

NOTES

1. Patent protection has been called a relatively strong type of protection when compared to other species of IP. For example, patent protection will block copying uses even if the technology was invented independently, unlike trade secret

protection. But cf., copyright and trade secret protections have a much longer life than does patent protection.

2. Collectors of valuable information can prevent competitors from using the information. *International News Service v. Associated Press*, 248 U.S. 215 (1911).

3. Protection is available for software embodied in semiconductor chips – so-called mask works. *E.F. Johnson v. Uniden Corp. of America*, 653 F. Supp. 1485 (D. Minn. 1985).

4. Copyright, like patent, protection emanates from the U.S. Constitution. Article I §. 8.

5. 17 U.S.C. § 102 (2006).

6. *Ibid.*

7. 17 U.S.C. § 106, § 302 (2006).

8. 37 CFR Part 201, 202, and 212 (2006).

9. 17 U.S.C. § 410 (2006).

10. 17 U.S.C. § 411 (2006).

11. The holder of a registered copyright is entitled to the recovery of attorney fees and statutorily defined damages, including those for willful infringement, only for the period after registration. Ordinarily, the owner cannot collect these damages for the period between the time of publication and registration of the copyright, but the law offers an incentive for registering *early*: damages are available from the date of publication *only* if the owner registers the copyright within three months of publication of the work. 17 U.S.C. §§ 412, 504, 505 (2006).

12. 17 U.S.C. §§ 101, 117 (as amended 1980), included commentary. For a more complete discussion, see Menell (1987).

13. See *Computer, Inc. v. Franklin Computer Corporation*, 714 F.2d 1240 (3rd Cir. 1983).

14. See, e.g., the series of Lotus-Borland cases. *Lotus Development Corp. v. Borland Int'l, Inc.*, 788 F. Supp. 78 (D. Mass. 1992) (finding *Quattro* a virtual copy of Lotus' menu structure); *Lotus Development Corp. v. Borland Int'l, Inc.*, 799 F. Supp. 203 (D. Mass. 1992); *Lotus Development Corp. v. Borland Int'l, Inc.*, 831 F. Supp. 202 (D. Mass. 1993); *Lotus Development Corp. v. Borland Int'l, Inc.*, 831 F. Supp. 223 (D. Mass. 1993); *Lotus Development Corp. v. Borland Int'l, Inc.*, 49 F.3d 807 (1st Cir. 1995), *aff'd* 116 S. Ct. 804 (1996).

15. Interbrand-Business Week Survey, *Business Week*, August 5, 2002, pp. 95–99.

16. *Reddy Communications v. Environmental Action Foundation*, 477 F. Supp. 936 (D.D.C. 1979).

17. 15 U.S.C. § 1051 *et seq.* (2006).

18. 15 U.S.C. §§ 1053, 1054, 1127 (2006).

19. 15 U.S.C. § 1051 (2006).

20. 15 U.S.C. §§ 1072 (2006).

21. *Zatarian's, Inc. v. Oak Grove Smokehouse, Inc.*, 698 F.2d 786 (5th Cir. 1983).

22. *Scarves by Vera v. Todo Importa Ltd., Inc.*, 544 F.2d 1167 (2nd Cir. 1976).

23. Trademark protection may be lost, however. If the holder fails to "use" the mark in commerce, or fails to "police" the mark by attempting to prevent others from using the mark in diluting ways, the mark may be lost. It may even be converted to the public domain. Famous examples of the latter include aspirin and cellophane.

24. *Metallurgical Industries, Inc. v. Fourtek, Inc.*, 790 F.2d 1195 (5th Cir. 1986); Uniform Trade Secrets Act (1985).

25. *E.I. DuPont de Nemours & Co. v. Christopher*, 431 F.2d 1012 (5th Cir. 1970).

26. 416 U.S. 470.

27. *United States v. Pilkington, Plc*, 1994-2 Trade Cas. (CCH); 70,842, 1994 WL 750645 (D. Ariz. 1994).

28. The Department of Justice considered this use of trade secret as the maintenance of unwarranted monopoly power. See *ibid.*

29. International Data Corp. (online: http://www.siia.net/divisions/research/growth.asp). This estimate is for packaged software only, and thus underestimates all global revenues, missing important elements such as embedded software. The packaged personal computer-based software market in the United States alone is estimated at nearly $30 billion.

30. The phrase "open innovation" is used differently here than as used in Chesbrough (2004). Chesbrough uses the phrase to describe the increasing phenomenon of firms reaching outside their boundaries to in-source technology.

31. According to the company: "LizardTech has chosen to use the GNU GPL [but] we believe the GNU GPL is a flawed license because it does not satisfactorily address all issues necessary for release of the code. ... On the issue of patents, LizardTech believes the approach taken in the Mozilla Public License [] is preferable to that in the GNU GPL, because the MPL explicitly provides for contributors to grant patent rights to users of the open source software." *Ibid.*

32. Galli, P. (2004). "CA moves with new open-source licensing for content, database projects," *eWeek*, May 24.

33. IBM has filed a countersuit against SCO claiming patent infringement. Lyman, J. (2003). "Big Blue hits SCO with patent counterclaim," *TechNewsWorld*, August 7.

34. Both Redhat and Novell have since joined the suit, with Novel claiming that the UNIX property transferred to SCO in 1995 did not include the copyrights that SCO is now asserting against IBM. Vaughan-Nichols, S. (2004). "Novell pushes for end to SCO's suit," *eWeek*, November 11.

35. "The Free Software Foundation is the only entity that can enforce the GPL so, in effect, IBM is barred from trying to enforce the GPL with SCO," according to Blake Stowell, a SCO spokesperson. Quoted in McMillan, R. (2003). "SCO: IBM cannot enforce GPL," *InfoWorld*, October 27.

36. O'Gara, M. (2004). "Texas Hoster pays SCO Linux tax," *Linux Business Week*, March 5; McMillan, R. (2004). "CA named as SCO licensee," *InfoWorld*, March 4; McMillan, R. (2003). "Sun revealed as SCO mystery licensee," *ComputerWorld*, July 11.

37. From the Bayh-Dole Act. "An Act to Amend the Patent and Trademark Laws." PL 96-517 (HR 6933). "It is the policy and objective of the Congress to use the patent system to promote the utilization of inventions arising from federally supported research or development; to encourage maximum participation of small business firms in federally supported research and development efforts; [and] to promote collaboration between commercial concerns and nonprofit organizations, including enterprise ... ."

38. *Ibid.* Comments of Representative Jack Brooks: "The policies and objectives of government funding of research and development should be determined on the basis of what is in the best interest of the public. [Introducing commercial motives] would change the direction of federal research and development from a process of intellectual and technological innovation for the general welfare of the people to one which emphasizes the profit incentive underlying commercialization in the market-place."

ACKNOWLEDGMENTS

I would like to thank Marie Thursby for her comments on a previous draft, as well as participants at the Kauffman Workshop on teaching university entrepreneurship held at the College of Management at Georgia Institute of Technology, February 8–10, 2007. Funding for this chapter was provided by the Ewing Marion Kauffman Foundation.

REFERENCES

Arora, A. (1995). Licensing tacit knowledge: Intellectual property rights and the market for know-how. *Economics of Innovation and New Technology, 4,* 41–59.

Chesbrough, H. W. (2004). *Open innovation: The new imperative for creating and profiting from technology.* Cambridge, MA: Harvard Business School Press.

Cohen, W. M., Nelson, R. R., & Walsh, J. (2000). *Protecting their intellectual assets: Appropriability conditions and why U.S. manufacturing firms patent (or not).* Unpublished manuscript, NBER Working Paper 7552. Cambridge, MA.

CONTU (National Commission on New Technological Uses of Copyrighted Works). (1979). *Final report.* Washington: USGPO.

Friedman, D. D., Landes, W. M., & Posner, R. A. (1991). Some economics of trade secret law. *Journal of Economic Perspectives, 5*(1), 61–72.

Graham, S. J. H. (2004). *Continuation, complementarity, and capturing value: Three studies exploring firms' complementary uses of appropriability mechanisms in technological innovation.* Unpublished doctoral dissertation. University of California, Berkeley.

Graham, S. J. H., Hall, B. H., Harhoff, D., & Mowery, D. C. (2003). Exploring the effects of patent oppositions: a comparative study of US and European patents. In: W. M. Cohen & S. Merrill (Eds), *Patents in the knowledge-based economy.* Washington, DC: National Academies Press.

Graham, S. J. H., & Mowery, D. C. (2003). Intellectual property protection in the U.S. software industry. In: W. M. Cohen & S. Merrill (Eds), *Patents in the knowledge-based economy.* Washington, DC: National Academies Press.

Graham, S. J. H., & Mowery, D. C. (2005a). The use of USPTO 'continuation' applications in the patenting of software: Implications for free and open source. *Law & Policy, 27*(1), 128–151.

Graham, S. J. H., & Mowery, D. C. (2005b). Software patents: Good news or bad news? In: R. Hahn (Ed.), *Intellectual property rights in frontier industries: Software and biotechnology*. Washington, DC: AEI-Brookings Joint Center.

Graham, S. J. H., & Somaya, D. (2006). *Vermeers and rembrandts in the same attic: Complementarity between copyright and trademark in software firms' IP leveraging strategies*. Unpublished manuscript, GER Working Paper. Georgia Institute of Technology TI.

Hall, B. H., & Trajtenberg, M. (2004). *Uncovering GPTS with patent data*. Unpublished manuscript, NBER Working Paper no. 10901. Cambridge, MA.

Horstman, I., MacDonald, G., & Slivinsky, A. (1985). Patents as information transfer mechanism. *Journal of Political Economy, 93*, 837–858.

Jaffe, A. B., & Lerner, J. (2004). *Innovation and its discontents: How our broken patent system is endangering innovation and progress, and what to do about it*. Princeton, NJ: Princeton University Press.

Lemley, M. A., & O'Brien, D. W. (1997). Encouraging software reuse. *Stanford Law Review, 49*(2), 255–305.

Levin, R. C., Klevorick, A. K., Nelson, R. R., & Winter, S. G. (1987). Appropriating the returns from industrial research and development. *Brookings Papers on Economic Activity, 3*, 783–820.

Menell, P. (1987). Tailoring legal protection for computer software. *Stanford Law Review, 39*, 1329–1372.

Mowery, D. C., & Sampat, B. N. (2001). University patents and patent policy debates in the USA, 1925–1980. *Industrial and Corporate Change, 10*(3), 781–814.

Mowery, D. C., & Sampat, B. N. (2004). *Universities in national innovation systems*. Mimeo, Working paper presented at Global ICS, Lisbon, May–June.

Plant, A. (1934a). The economic theory concerning patents for inventions. *Economica, 1*(1), 30–51.

Plant, A. (1934b). The economic aspects of copyright in books. *Economica, 1*(2), 167–195.

Press, E., & Washburn, J. (2000). The kept university. *Atlantic Monthly, 285*(3), 39–54.

Rumelt, R. P. (1984). Towards a strategic theory of the firm. In: R. B. Lamb (Ed.), *Competitive strategic management*. Englewood Cliffs, NJ: Prentice-Hall.

Samuelson, P. (1984). CONTU revisited: The case against copyright protection for computer programs in machine-readable form. *Duke Law Journal*, 663–752.

Samuelson, P., & Glushko, R. J. (1990). Survey on the look and feel lawsuits. *Communications of the ACM, 33*(5), 483–495.

Schumpeter, J. A. (1934). *The theory of economic development; an inquiry into profits, capital, credit, interest, and the business cycle*. Cambridge, MA: Harvard University Press.

Teece, D. J. (1986). Profiting from technological innovation: Implications for integration, collaboration, licensing and public policy. *Research Policy, 15*(6), 285–305.

University of Washington. (2007). Patent, invention, and copyright policy (Chapter 7). In: *University of Washington handbook*. Seattle: University of Washington.

PART III:
STRATEGY FOR INNOVATION

CHAPTER 6

MARKETING STRATEGY CONSIDERATIONS IN THE COMMERCIALIZATION OF NEW TECHNOLOGIES: AN OVERVIEW AND FRAMEWORK FOR STRATEGY DEVELOPMENT

Leslie H. Vincent

ABSTRACT

This chapter provides an overview of the marketing strategy development process in the commercialization of breakthrough technologies. Important concepts and elements that are considered critical when developing market applications are presented with emphasis on three key decisions: target market selection, segmentation, and positioning. These strategic decisions will guide the more tactical considerations relating to the specific elements, or marketing mix, of the product's marketing strategy. Marketing strategy development is a dynamic process impacted by many factors. This chapter highlights the dynamic nature of this process as well

Technological Innovation: Generating Economic Results
Advances in the Study of Entrepreneurship, Innovation and
Economic Growth, Volume 18, 173–200
ISSN: 1048-4736/doi:10.1016/S1048-4736(07)00006-9

as provides insight into the fundamental considerations in strategy formulation.

INTRODUCTION

Successful technology commercialization is dependent upon there being a market for that technology. While on the surface this seems rather intuitive, one of the most cited reasons behind start-up and product failures stems directly from market considerations (Cooper, 2001). To further illustrate, at any given time approximately 5.6 million potential new ventures are struggling for survival, yet the percentage of those actually succeeding in their commercialization efforts is relatively small (only 30 percent survive their first five years in business) (Reynolds, Carter, Gartner, & Greene, 2004). Perhaps one of the most cited reasons behind this high failure rate is a lack of planning or direction for the venture (i.e., no clear strategy). Moreover, high-technology start-ups are particularly prone to this failure because they focus on the technology and tend to ignore the market (www.glocalvantage.com). Venture capitalists estimate that as many as 60 percent of new venture failures could have been prevented through better pre-launch marketing analysis (Lodish, Morgan, & Kallianpur, 2001).

The focus of this chapter is on the marketing strategy considerations that must be addressed in the commercialization of a new product, with particular emphasis on products that are high-tech in nature. By addressing the important concepts and elements to consider when developing market applications for breakthrough technologies, effective upfront market planning can alleviate or avoid altogether these potential marketing-related pitfalls. This chapter begins by providing an overview of marketing strategy in general, as well as the performance implications associated with effective strategy development and implementation. A general framework for strategy development is presented that will guide the remainder of the chapter. From this, the discussion focuses on three critical decisions that must be made early on in the strategy development process that will provide the foundation for all of the other decisions regarding the go-to-market strategy – segmentation, target market selection, and positioning. These strategic decisions will guide the more tactical considerations relating to the specific elements, or marketing mix, of the product's marketing strategy. This chapter provides an overview of these different considerations in developing a marketing strategy or roadmap in the commercialization of the technology.

MARKETING STRATEGY

What is Marketing Strategy?

In general, strategy can be defined as a firm's positioning to gain a competitive advantage in the marketplace (Teece, Pisano, & Shuen, 1997; Juga, 1999). The primary objective of a strategy is to secure organizational effectiveness by performing the right activities at the right time. The central focus of a strategy is that the organization, or in this case the commercialization team, achieves the right fit between the technology and the external environment. Building upon this high-level definition, more specifically a marketing strategy allows firms to develop a plan that enables them to offer the right product to the right market with the intent of gaining a competitive advantage. In other words, a marketing strategy provides an overall vision of how to correctly position products in the marketplace to the right set of customers, while accounting for both internal and external constraints.

More formally, marketing strategy can be defined as the selection and analysis of *target markets* and the creation and maintenance of an appropriate *marketing mix* to satisfy the needs of the target market (Ferrell, Hartline, & Lucas, 2002). Here, the target market represents the group of customers that the product will reach, while the marketing mix includes product attributes, distribution channels, promotion, and pricing considerations. The specifics associated with these different elements are discussed in greater detail later in this chapter. Essentially, a marketing strategy is developed by selecting the "right" strategy from all possible alternatives. Marketing strategy research has focused primarily on one of two arenas: marketing strategy formulation or marketing strategy implementation. The next section discusses these two different areas of marketing strategy.

Marketing Strategy Formulation

Marketing strategy *formulation* research examines the impact of certain variables on the development of marketing strategies themselves. In addition, this stream of research tends to focus on what should be done or the role of marketing strategy in practice (Mintzberg, 1994). Study of marketing strategy variables within this domain can focus on the marketing strategy itself, and includes variables such as strategy comprehensiveness, resource commitment, and emphasis on capabilities (Menon, Bharadwaj,

Adidam, & Edison, 1999). Furthermore, some studies have investigated antecedents to marketing strategy formulation, with an innovative culture emerging as the key antecedent to effective marketing strategy development (Menon et al., 1999). Finally, marketing strategy formulation has been linked to several key organizational outcomes, including strategy creativity, implementation performance, financial performance, and organizational learning (Menon et al., 1999; Slotegraaf & Dickson, 2004; Atuahene-Gima & Murray, 2004). There has been a large debate within the literature as to whether formal strategic planning has value. Strategic planning is most useful in situations characterized by large changes, high uncertainty, inefficient markets, and highly complex tasks (Armstrong, 1982). Several review papers have shown that under such conditions, strategic planning results in superior performance (Armstrong, 1982; Sinha, 1990; Powell, 1990).

Armstrong (1982) posits two guidelines for the development of strategies. First, strategies should be comprehensive in nature and thus consider all important factors. Second, strategies should recognize uncertainty and have flexibility within the plan. For high-technology start-ups, the technologies themselves are at such an early stage that simply being able to formulate a marketing strategy is a significant performance milestone that must be met. In addition to developing a complete and comprehensive strategy, the literature suggests that strategy development should also foster learning that can be incorporated into the strategy development process (Menon et al., 1999; Atuahene-Gima & Murray, 2004). In other words, the strategy should be a living concept: as new information is uncovered, the strategy should be refined and updated so as to ensure the right fit between the strategy and the environment. This learning and evolution of the strategy is of particular importance in unstable environments, such as those that characterize technology commercialization.

The role of information in innovation and strategy development is critical. Past research has suggested that information plays a critical role in the planning or development of strategy (Mintzberg, 1981, 1994; Steiner, 1979). Along with information regarding the different alternatives available to the firm, strategies should contain information regarding strengths, weaknesses, and opportunities (Grant, 1995; Menon et al., 1999). Furthermore, within the new product development domain, research has suggested that knowledge, including information regarding both the customer and the market, is critical during the pre-launch phase of development (Joshi & Sharma, 2004; Griffin & Hauser, 1993). This knowledge development occurs as an evolutionary process that is on-going throughout development.

Therefore, the role of knowledge creation and dissemination is not a one-time effort, but rather a dynamic process that must be managed during technology commercialization.

Marketing Strategy Implementation

The second major stream of marketing strategy research examines organizations' implementation of marketing strategies. Marketing strategy *implementation* research treats the strategy as given and examines the outcomes associated with the successful implementation of the strategy. Variables associated with marketing strategy implementation primarily focus on the financial performance of the chosen strategy and how well the implementation efforts occurred (Bonoma, 1984; Noble & Mokwa, 1999).

The focus of this chapter is on the development of the marketing strategy, rather than the effective implementation of the strategy. Recall that the number one factor in explaining the failure of commercialization efforts is poor market strategic planning, and in particular marketing planning; therefore, this chapter focuses on the elements necessary in the development of the strategy itself (Cooper, 2001). The remaining part of the chapter presents an overall framework for developing marketing strategies (see Fig. 1 for an overview). The next section of this chapter will prove essential to the effective development of marketing strategies, because the discussion turns to three critical decisions that must be made early in the development process. These three decisions will provide the foundation from which all other marketing decisions are made – segmentation, targeting, and positioning considerations.

SEGMENTATION, TARGET MARKET SELECTION, AND POSITIONING

Segmentation, targeting, and positioning are often referred to as the building blocks of marketing, in that they provide the overall definition of the market space in which organizations or new ventures will compete (Bearden et al., 2004). Each of these strategic decisions provides guidance in terms of the remaining tactical decisions that must be made regarding the market introduction of a product. Furthermore, these decisions go hand-in-hand and cannot be made in isolation from one another. Together, these decisions determine *what* product will be sold and to *whom* (Lodish et al., 2001).

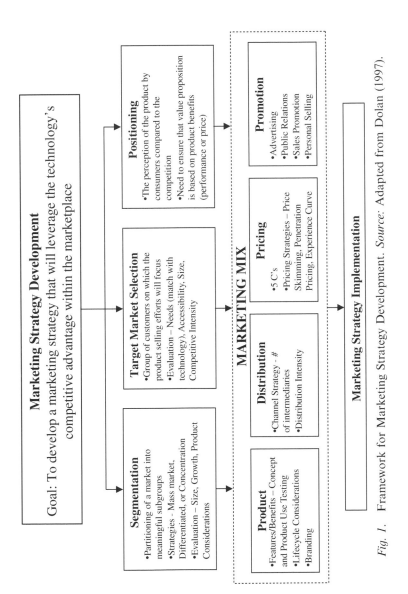

Fig. 1.   Framework for Marketing Strategy Development. *Source:* Adapted from Dolan (1997).

We will take a more in-depth look at each one of these important considerations in the strategy formulation process.

Segmentation

Segmentation is the process by which a market is partitioned into meaningful subgroups such that specific marketing efforts can be tailored to these specific groups of customers (Lodish et al., 2001). Thus, segmentation includes dividing the market into homogeneous subgroups such that the marketing mix can be tailored to each group's specific needs as they relate to the product or technology. Market segmentation not only can be useful for established organizations, but also can provide performance benefits for new ventures as well (Bearden et al., 2004). While there are several different approaches to segmentation, in this chapter we focus on the three traditional approaches used to segment the market: mass marketing, differentiated marketing, and niche marketing.

Mass Marketing
Mass marketing is a segmentation strategy in which the market is not segmented into subgroups. The entire market is treated as one segment. This approach assumes that the market itself is homogeneous with respect to the technology or product and that consumers belonging to this market have similar needs that can be satisfied with one marketing mix (i.e., the same product, price, promotion, and distribution channel is used to reach the entire market). Mass marketing is most appropriate for commodity products; however, very few firms use a mass-marketing approach (Ferrell et al., 2002). Because mass marketing relies on one product, or in this case, one technology application, firms relying on mass marketing are vulnerable to competing products that are more differentiated in nature and therefore have the potential to provide better solutions to the market's needs.

Differentiated Marketing
Differentiated marketing involves dividing the marketplace into homogeneous subgroups based on needs and then tailoring the marketing program to those different subgroups. For a differentiated marketing strategy to work in practice, the characteristics and needs of consumers within each subgroup must be similar while at the same time having different needs and characteristics across the different groups. Firms using this segmentation strategy must develop a unique marketing mix for each of

the segments identified within the market. Medium to large organizations use this approach, because they have the resource base in place to manage both offering multiple products and developing many different marketing mixes to best suit the needs of the many segments (Ferrell et al., 2002).

Market Concentration Strategy or Niche Marketing
The final segmentation strategy focuses on only one segment and develops a marketing plan suited for that particular subsegment. This market concentration strategy is more likely to be used by start-ups that simply do not have the resources available to develop multiple products, each with a tailored marketing mix, for multiple segments. In this approach to segmentation, marketing efforts are focused on one small, well-defined market segment or niche with a unique, specific set of needs. This approach requires a complete understanding of the segment's needs so that the potential for high market share within this market space can overcome the small size of the market and make this approach profitable to pursue. Firms competing with a market concentration strategy are more focused on providing novel and innovative solutions to consumers and are less likely to compete based on price (Bearden et al., 2004). While a market concentration approach to segmentation is not as resource-intensive as the multisegment approach, the risk associated with specialization can be substantial. A firm that focuses on a single segment must select that segment and develop the marketing mix to provide a best fit for the needs of that group. Failing that, the firm will have no other segment to fall back on if conditions in the environment change or if the initial definition of the market space was not done well.

Criteria for Segmentation
Effective segmentation requires several criteria to be met (Bearden et al., 2004). The first of these is *measurability*, or the degree to which the size and purchasing power of the segment can be assessed. If the size of the segment itself cannot be estimated, then the firm will not be sure of the true market potential associated with this particular customer segment and therefore will be unable to assess the potential opportunity of targeting this select group within the marketplace. This leads to the second criterion that must be considered – whether the segment is *substantial*. This criterion is imperative because a firm wants a segment large enough to have sufficient sales and profit potential to offset the cost of developing a unique product and marketing campaign geared to that segment. Furthermore, the segment itself must be *accessible*. Accessibility refers to the degree to which a firm can reach the segment efficiently. In addition to reaching the segment, the firm must

consider the *stability* of the segment itself. This criterion focuses on the durability of the needs within the segment over time. Ideally, the needs within each segment will remain homogeneous over time, while at the same time the needs between segments will be heterogeneous. If this is not the case, then segmentation will not be as effective. Finally, it is important that each segment *responds differently* to different marketing mixes and product or technology bundles. Otherwise, segmentation will not produce the desired results, and marketing to the entire market as a whole may be a more suitable approach.

Segmenting the Market

Given these different considerations, the next issue is how to go about segmenting the market meaningfully. In determining which segmentation strategy will be most effective for a new technology, a firm should consider many factors. The first is the appropriate segmentation base. Many different options are available to segment the market into homogeneous subgroups (see Table 1 for an overview). Depending on the nature of the product, the appropriate base for segmentation can differ. For example, if a technology or product is targeted to individuals within the market (i.e., selling the product in a B-to-C context), then it may be more appropriate to segment

Table 1. Segmentation Bases.

Business-to-consumer	
Demographics	Age, gender, race, income, education, occupation, household size
Psychographics	Conservative, values, lifestyles
Culture	Religion, nationality
Geographic	Country, state, urban versus rural
Benefits desired	Desired product attributes
Usage rate	Users versus nonusers, heavy versus light
Buying situation	Store type, occasion
Brand loyalty	Loyal versus nonloyal
Business-to-business	
Business size	Employees, annual sales, customer base
Usage rate	Users versus nonusers, heavy versus light
Product application	Resale versus production component
Industry type	Industry organization belongs to
Organizational type	Manufacturing, service, government
Geography	Country, region, state
Purchase type	New versus repeat customers

Source: Bearden, Ingram, and LaForge (2004), Boone and Kurtz (2006), and Wind and Cardozo (1974).

the market based on consumer needs, demographics, or geographic location. However, if a technology is more likely to come into play in the business-to-business setting, then these same segmentation approaches may not be appropriate. In the latter case, it is better to consider factors such as customer size, type of organization, and industry characteristics.

The second, critically important consideration includes estimating the market potential of different segments before selecting the target market to pursue. Two factors come into play in this decision: the size and the growth of the segment. Segmentation is not appropriate when the overall market is so small that targeting different customer groups will not provide substantial performance benefits. Therefore, the size and growth of potential market segments must be assessed. To determine the size of the potential segment, a firm can estimate the potential sales volume that can be achieved within each segment. To do this, a firm must collect secondary data or information regarding the market size and also develop estimates of the new product's market penetration. In doing this, the first step is to estimate the market potential of the segment, or the maximum sales possible for a product within this industry or segment in a given time period. From this, the sales potential can be calculated, which estimates the total sales the firm can obtain within that market. Note that the sales potential can never be larger than the market potential for a segment. In addition to assessing the overall size of the different segments, a firm should consider the growth associated with each, as well. Segments that are growing are attractive, because the new venture can grow as the market grows and can capture new customers as they come into the market, rather than having the entire product demand come from the current market in which competitors already offer products that meet customer needs (Gatignon & Xuereb, 1997).

Finally, characteristics of the product or technology itself can impact the segmentation strategy selected. The first such characteristic is the product's current life cycle stage. Research suggests that, for very new products or technologies, a market concentration approach to segmentation may work best. Under this scenario, only one product offering is initially developed and offered to one segment, providing an opportunity for the firm to learn from this initial market offering before expanding into other markets (Moore, 1995). In addition to product life cycle considerations, it is also important to consider the potential for modifications to the core technology or product. Early on, the firm's focus may be on one product application; but as demand for the product grows, and the firm has increasing resources available to put back into the development of product extensions, the segmentation strategy may shift from a concentration approach to a multisegment segmentation strategy.

Target Market Selection

After a firm identifies and evaluates its product's different segments, this information will form the basis from which the target market for the new technology is selected. The target market is the group of customers, either individuals or organizations, on which the firm will focus its selling efforts. In addition, selection of the target market will impact the marketing mix that the firm must manage in order to reach this market efficiently and effectively. Thus, selection of a target market is a critical decision for firms. In selecting the target market, the firm's most important consideration is whether the target segment wants the value derived from the firm's product offering more than other potential segments (Lodish et al., 2001). Other factors that can impact the ultimate decision of the target market include accessibility, size, and current and future competition.[1] The target market's fit with the value proposition of the technology must be assessed, because this fit will provide the real value to potential customers. Furthermore, the importance of whether the technology provides something this market segment truly needs cannot be overestimated. There is no one right answer when selecting a target market and often managers must make tough decisions regarding the best approach to marketing their product.

Positioning

Positioning represents how the firm wants its product or service to be perceived by the target market relative to the competition's product or service. Positioning is categorization of a new product or technology in consumers' minds. To create a product positioning statement, a firm must be able to implicitly state why buyers in the target market should buy its product rather than others being offered. Positioning new products is somewhat unique, in that the end user has no preconception of what the technology or product is; this provides a real opportunity to create a particular positioning of the technology without fear of how it will compare to previous positioning attempts of competitive product offerings. This is the best chance to create an effective positioning of the new technology, and therefore great care should be taken when considering how to position the product in consumers' minds.

As with segmentation and target market selection, a multitude of factors can impact the positioning decision. In general, several different positioning strategies can be used to distinguish one's product from others in the market (Boone & Kurtz, 2006). These include product attributes, price/quality, competitors, application, product user, and product class. To determine market positioning for new technologies, a firm must consider the competitive advantage of its product or technology and then attempt to leverage this advantage with consumers. Thus, competitive advantage facilitates how consumers will derive value from a firm's technology – whether that is through increased performance and greater benefits, or lower price, or both. The key to winning customers is to understand their needs better than competitors and to incorporate those needs into the firm's market offering. Furthermore, for competitive advantage to persist over time, a firm's technology should be protectable and difficult for others to emulate (Barney, 1991). When a firm commercializes high-technology products, the technology and benefits derived from the technology are the likely source of the competitive advantage; thus, the positioning of the product likely will focus on the technology. Therefore, it is critical that the technology fits with customer needs in the target market in order to effectively position the product in the consumer's mind.

The biggest mistake firms make when positioning products is to focus on product attributes/features and not product benefits. Recall that positioning refers to consumer perceptions and that consumers make purchase and adoption decisions based on product benefits, not features. Therefore, when thinking of the value derived from a technology, it is imperative that a firm considers the benefits its target market will derive from using the product (i.e., shorter cycle time, reduced waste, and increased performance), rather than focusing on the technical attributes or features associated with the product. Furthermore, the product's positioning must be complete, such that customers have enough information to categorize the technology in their mind. At the same time, the firm must balance complete positioning with over-positioning the technology, whereby consumers have too narrow a picture of the technology or product. The rule of thumb is that consumers can at most perceive two or three differentiating attributes or benefits at a time. Any more than that can lead to confusion in consumers' minds, which ultimately impacts their decision whether to adopt or purchase the technology.

Only after the positioning decision of the product/technology is complete can a firm tackle all of the other marketing-related decisions. The product, brand, price, promotion, and distribution (i.e., the marketing mix) must all be consistent with the product positioning statement.

Summary

While most of this section has focused on general marketing frameworks designed to aid in developing a marketing strategy for a new product or technology, some research suggests that certain approaches to these strategic considerations are better suited for new ventures. Recall that the link between strategy and new venture performance has been well documented within literature (Sandberg & Hofer, 1987). Furthermore, certain types of strategies seem to foster higher levels of performance. A market concentration strategy, in which the firm focuses on one particular market segment with one product offering, seems to provide the best performance returns for new ventures (Dess, Lumpkin, & Covin, 1997; Stuart & Abetti, 1987). The rationale behind this is simple – firms that focus on one market segment have fewer market elements to manage and therefore can focus all of their energy and limited resources on that one market segment (Simon, Houghton, & Lumpkin, 2001). Furthermore, new ventures that utilize a market concentration strategy are better positioned to collect and adapt to new information or changes within their environment due to the limited arena in which they are competing. This facilitates the feedback process, making these firms better able to adapt and implement changes that can ultimately lead to increased success in the marketplace. On the other hand, new ventures that seek out a multisegment strategy are less nimble, having all of their resources focused on managing multiple segments without the flexibility necessary to respond to environmental changes.

Segmentation, target market selection, and positioning are critical strategic decisions that must be considered before other marketing strategy elements can be addressed. Segmentation and positioning is a dynamic process. There should be constant feedback and adjustment to the positioning and segmentation decisions as other elements of the marketing mix unfold and as environmental conditions change.

THE MARKETING MIX

For breakthrough technologies, the focus of the marketing mix is to develop an entry strategy that will stimulate primary demand, which will in turn foster the diffusion of the technology to the marketplace (Crawford & DiBenedetto, 2005). Given that the technology itself will drive the product to be offered to the market, this chapter will briefly discuss different considerations regarding the product application that will be offered to the target market. The primary focus of this section is on the other elements of the marketing mix – distribution, pricing, and promotion.

Product

Once the target market is selected and a positioning statement created, a firm can then return to the product and look for ways to enhance its value for the target market. Two marketing tasks are considered critical to ensuring that the product put in front of consumers is actually the product they need: concept testing and product use testing. The number one cause of new product failures in the marketplace is missing the market (Cooper, 2001; Crawford & DiBenedetto, 2005). To minimize this risk, it is advisable for new ventures to conduct both a concept test and a product use test during the product's development. A concept test involves contacting potential customers within the target market, describing the product application of the technology, and determining whether the market really has a need for this product. Concept testing should occur before the actual prototype is developed so that customer feedback can be incorporated into the product design. Concept testing helps to identify the key features and benefits that the target market considers most important as they relate to the product. After the prototype has been constructed, it is time again to gather market feedback with a product use test. In this customer test, the firm presents the actual product, or prototype, to the consumer and asks whether the product meets the needs described in the concept test. This market feedback is invaluable and can mean the difference between a successful new product that meets the needs of the market versus a product that, while it incorporates a novel technology, does not provide any real value to the consumer.

When developing the marketing strategy, the firm must also consider stage of the product life cycle. In most cases, the technologies being developed are in the early stages of the product life cycle, before market adoption has occurred. This can present both unique challenges and opportunities in developing an effective go-to-market strategy. At this stage in the product life cycle, efforts primarily focus on understanding the needs of the target market as well as the actual development of the product itself.

Again, at this stage, new ventures have an opportunity to conduct research within the market that can help shape future marketing activities. In other words, products that match market needs are much easier to market when the new product is introduced into the marketplace (Ferrell et al., 2002).

When considering the specific features and benefits of a product, it is important to also consider the brand the firm wants associated with its venture and product. A brand is simply the set of attributes that consumers associate with a company and is a foundation to building a relationship with consumers in the target market. The brand created by a firm can be one of its most valuable assets in that consumers are willing to pay a higher price for a set of product attributes for a given brand (Srivastava, Shervani, & Fahey, 1998). A company's brand and its positioning strategy differ, in that the brand is about attributes that individuals associate with the company, while positioning focuses on the benefits derived from the product. An effective brand can lead to increased name recognition, higher perceptions of product performance and quality, and loyalty among the target market (Keller, 1993). Start-ups must build a brand from scratch, and it is imperative that the brand appeals to the target market and provides value to those consumers . In building a strong brand, new ventures should have a polished image from the beginning and start by building credibility with both customers and potential investors. Furthermore, the product itself does not comprise the brand, and therefore when considering how to go about developing the brand, a firm should not focus solely on product features and benefits but rather should provide an overall message about the company. A firm's name, logo, website, and even letterhead become part of the brand. Brands are best built through strong product performance and effective promotion techniques, which we will discuss later in the chapter.

Distribution

Product distribution comprises getting the physical product or technology to the consumer. The distribution decision includes deciding upon the actual players involved in moving the product from the place of production to the place of purchase or consumption by the end user. When deciding upon the right distribution strategy, a firm must keep in mind both the efficiency and effectiveness (i.e., does the channel provide the product to the target market in a timely fashion) of potential distribution alternatives (Ferrell et al., 2002). When evaluating the alternatives available to get a product into the marketplace, a firm must constantly consider how the distribution channel can provide value to the consumer. The distribution channel decision stems directly from the decisions regarding the target market segment and how the product is to be positioned in the consumer's mind. The key is for the channel of distribution to enhance the perceived value associated with the product.

Distribution channels can be either direct or indirect in nature. With a direct channel, the product offering moves from the producer to the consumer without any intermediaries. Indirect channels, on the other hand, involve intermediaries in the distribution of the product to the end user. Intermediaries often perform several key functions that are important to consider when selecting the right distribution strategy for a technology. Intermediaries provide both inventory management and physical distribution capabilities to the producer, in that they are responsible both for ordering and storing the merchandise and for delivering the products to, and return of products from, the final consumer. Channel members can also play a critical role in communication of information to potential customers about a product that will impact their likelihood to purchase. Oftentimes, the channel members themselves are advertising or promoting a product through either their sales force or their point-of-purchase displays. Furthermore, intermediaries are a great source of market feedback: they can pass along information about consumer satisfaction with the product, and competitive activity, and also provide insight into unmet market needs.

Identifying the type of distribution channel that will work best for the placement of a technology is not easy. Direct channels are primarily best suited for certain industries including services, medical and professional services, banking and finance, business-to-business markets, as well as Internet-based business models. Direct distribution is advisable when the target market comprises mainly business users or when the market itself is geographically concentrated. Direct distribution is also better suited to complex products where extensive technical knowledge is required in the selling of the product. Furthermore, where a new venture has a very limited product line, it is more beneficial to use direct distribution (Ferrell et al., 2002).

In contrast, indirect distribution is primarily used when selling consumer products and especially when the target market is geographically diverse. In this case, the new venture is unlikely to have adequate resources to perform all of the channel functions necessary to reach a broad consumer target market, so the venture relies upon intermediaries to complete this task. Indirect channels are better suited for products that are relatively simple, inexpensive, durable, and standardized in nature. Whereas with direct channels, a new venture has control over all elements of the marketing effort that will reach the ultimate consumer, when using intermediaries the venture trades off control for a wider distribution effort. Furthermore, for a small player like a new venture, the power is primarily held by the other intermediaries, in that they already have established relationships within the channel. Moreover, breaking into the channel can be a difficult process and difficult to implement in practice.

A firm that decides to use intermediaries to distribute its product to the market must also consider distribution intensity – the number of intermediaries through which its product will be distributed. Distribution intensity offers three options: intensive, selective, and exclusive. Intensive distribution attempts to saturate the market with the product by allowing many outlets within a specified area to carry the product. This approach provides extensive market coverage and potential exposure for the product and is best suited for convenience type goods. Intensive distribution is appropriate for firms that utilize a mass-market segmentation strategy (Ferrell et al., 2002). An alternative to giving every potential outlet in a geographic area the right to sell the product is selective distribution – selecting several outlets in the area and giving them the right to sell the product within a defined area. This distribution approach is appropriate for consumer products, where consumers benefit from comparison shopping and after-sales service is important. The final alternative available for consideration is exclusive distribution, which gives only one outlet the right to sell a product within a defined geographic area. Prestige products with exclusive images are primarily distributed through exclusive retailers. This approach to distribution works well for firms targeting one market segment with clearly defined needs (Ferrell et al., 2002).

Pricing

A firm's determination of its product's price will directly impact the profit potential of a new venture. Pricing of the product is the one aspect of the marketing mix that is most easily changed and with which results are seen immediately. The fastest and most effective way a company can realize its maximum profit is to get its pricing right so that customer demand is sufficient. Five objectives should guide pricing decisions: (1) ensuring market survival, (2) enhancing sales growth, (3) maximizing profits, (4) deterring competition, and (5) establishing a product quality image (Bearden et al., 2004).

While on the surface determining the optimal price of a new product seems rather straightforward, in reality the decision is much more complex. Furthermore, for radically new products this decision is even more challenging, in that there are no current substitutes in the market from which to benchmark. Therefore, a firm with such a radical product must try to develop both financial estimates of the value derived to consumers from the use of the product (i.e., in terms of either cost savings or increased productivity), and the costs incurred in producing the product. Both of these estimates provide a starting point from which the pricing decision can occur.

When deciding how to price the new product, the firm must evaluate several factors. These factors are referred to as the five Cs of pricing: costs, customers, channels of distribution, competition, and compatibility (Bearden et al., 2004). To establish the minimum price that a venture can charge for the new product, the firm must consider the costs associated with developing and marketing the product. In this estimation, it is necessary to include costs associated with production, distribution, and promotion. The selected price must cover the investment and support behind the product at a minimum in order for the product offering to make sense; in other words, the price set must cover both direct and indirect costs. Otherwise, there is no possibility of the survival of the firm if revenue coming in from sales of the product cannot cover the incurred cost of development, marketing, and everyday operations.

After costs, a firm should assess customers' price expectations and willingness to pay for the product. Because much of this consideration centers around the value derived from the product's use, it is imperative that the target market's needs be well understood, so that an attempt to quantify the value consumers receive through the use of the technology can be included in this consideration. For new ventures using an indirect channel of distribution, the same consideration must be made for channel intermediaries. The product's price must be set so that other members within the channel are able to earn adequate returns from the sale of the product. If this return is not sufficient, one of two things will likely happen. Either the channel member will not elect to be part of the distribution channel or the product will be neglected and not marketed to its full potential.

Pricing considerations are also impacted by the competition present within the market. When setting prices for a product, a firm must do a competitive analysis of competitors' charges for similar products. When a technology or product is a radical departure from the status quo, the firm still has to assess what consumers are paying for the current value they receive from alternative products. Furthermore, competitors will react to the introduction of a new product that they see as a threat. Finally, the price set for a product provides a signal to consumers in the marketplace about the quality associated with the product. A firm must ensure that its price conveys the right information about product quality, technology, and brand. The price that is determined should fit in with the long-term strategic goals of the venture.

Many different strategies can be used in pricing the product. For the purpose of this chapter, we focus only on those strategies that are used for new product introductions and those that primarily occur within a business-to-business context. The rationale behind this is that the majority of the breakthrough technologies developed will initially target markets that consist primarily of organizations as customers. Three different pricing strategies are useful when determining the price of a new product: price skimming, penetration pricing, and experience curve pricing (Bearden et al., 2004; Noble & Gruca, 1999). Price skimming occurs when the initial price of the product is set high and then decreases systematically over time. Price skimming works well for products that have a significant performance advantage (i.e., provide greater value to the market) over current technologies and also have low switching costs (therefore, lower hurdles to overcome for customer adoption to occur) (Crawford & DiBenedetto, 2005). Price skimming assumes relatively inelastic demand with an attempt to recover, early on, the fixed costs of developing the product (Cannon & Morgan, 1991). Penetration pricing, on the other hand, is the exact opposite: the initial price is set low so as to stimulate demand for the new product and preempt competition from entering the market. Firms use penetration pricing primarily to drive sales growth, based on the notion that consumers will try new products with low prices. In this case, the emphasis is on future growth at the expense of short-term profits (Cannon & Morgan, 1991). Experience curve pricing is similar to penetration pricing in that the initial price is low so as to facilitate adoption and build sales volume; as time passes, the organization is able to reduce costs through experience, thus resulting in no change in the price.

A firm's selection of a pricing strategy for a new technology can be informed by past research, which has highlighted when certain approaches to pricing may be more appropriate. Price skimming is recommended for new products when there is a high degree of differentiation in the marketplace (Jain, 1993). The rationale behind this choice is fourfold. First, the likelihood of another product's providing the same value as the new product is low. Second, customers will be willing to pay a higher price for the new product. Third, technologies that provide a major improvement over the current products can support charging a higher price in the marketplace (Mercer, 1992). Fourth, price skimming can be used effectively by new ventures facing a cost disadvantage due to their limited size and resources (Noble & Gruca, 1999). In contrast, penetration pricing is best suited for products where speed of adoption is important. Both penetration pricing and experience curve pricing are better suited for markets with low levels of differentiation in which building sales volume is a critical objective, and for products that offer only minor improvements in value for customers (Mercer, 1992; Schoell & Guiltinan, 1995; Tellis, 1986).

Promotion

The final element of the marketing mix to consider when developing a go-to-marketing strategy is promotion. In general, promotion is the mechanism by which information regarding a new product is conveyed to its target market. Promotion creates awareness of the product with the consumer and is also important in converting that awareness into product trial. Several different approaches can be used when promoting a new product: advertising, public relations (PR), sales promotions, and personal selling (Ferrell et al., 2002). The product itself will determine which of these different types of promotion may be more beneficial. For example, when promoting a product that is complex in nature, personal selling tends to be more effective than advertising (Lilien, 1979). This is further complicated by the fact that, at different times in the product purchase process, different promotion tools may be necessary. Again, for breakthrough technologies that provide significant value to organizations, PR may be a useful tool in generating awareness within the target market. The following sections briefly describe the four techniques that comprise a promotion strategy. When developing a marketing strategy, be aware of the different tools that will help convey the product's value to the intended target market.

Advertising
Advertising is defined as any new product promotion that is nonpersonal in nature and is paid for by an identified organization. Advertising is primarily used for consumer products and helps create awareness for the product along with building brand and product recognition within the marketplace. A good advertisement is based on a strong product positioning statement

and effectively conveys the product's benefits relative to other comparative offerings within the market. In determining where to place the advertisement, a firm must consider the nature of the target market as well as the message content. For new ventures or start-ups with a limited budget, advertising is most effectively utilized when part of coordinated marketing campaign. While advertising does create awareness in a large target audience, it is not without weaknesses. In general, advertisements have low credibility with consumers because ads are paid for by the organization trying to sell the product. Furthermore, the fact that an advertisement reaches the target audience does not mean the audience will be interested in the product or even pay attention to the ad. Advertising can be very expensive compared to other promotion techniques, and the reward may not be worth the expense. Therefore, a firm must perform a cost–benefit analysis in which the ultimate test is whether the ad will increase sales, before determining whether advertising is the most appropriate tool for conveying information regarding a product to its target market.

Public Relations

Public relations (PR) includes the promotion of an organization and its people, products, or ideas to potential customers. PR is effective in creating and enhancing the image associated with a new venture and can effectively convey an image associated with innovativeness as well as high quality. PR allows a firm to tell its story through a third party, making consumers more likely to try the firm's products. Whereas advertisements are paid for directly by the firm, PR is not paid for directly by the organization, thus increasing the credibility of this promotion technique with consumers. PR does impose an indirect cost, including the time and effort of the organization to interest influential others in saying or writing good things about the company or the product.

PR offers many different ways to convey information about the organization or its products. The first is to issue press releases or have a news conference when something positive happens, such as the introduction of a new product with a novel value proposition. Media coverage can also be used effectively by start-up firms with breakthrough products. Alternatively, articles in industry press that focus on the positive aspects of a new firm's product can also have a significant impact on generating awareness of and interest in the product. Finally, getting involved in the community can help get the company's name and product out there while at the same time cultivating a positive image.

Many new ventures should strive to utilize PR over advertising when developing their marketing strategy. PR is much cheaper than advertising, a benefit for a new firm with limited resources. Furthermore, PR can help build credibility not only for the product itself but also for the firm. PR can serve two purposes for new ventures: (1) it can help the product to be perceived as a winner and (2) it can help the new venture find funding from external parties.

Two approaches can be effectively used to get an organization or venture noticed by the press. First, create a press kit that contains background information about the company as well as the specific details of the product or technology. This information can be given directly to journalists or made available online. The second approach is to present the technology or product at industry trade shows.

Sales Promotions

Sales promotions are activities that provide incentive for consumers to try a product; they include free samples, free trials, or giveaways of the new product in the hopes that ultimately the consumer will purchase that product in the future. Sales promotions can be effective when used in conjunction with the other promotional techniques and can represent a rather large portion of the marketing budget (Blattberg, Briesch, & Fox, 1995). Sales promotion works well for both consumer and business products in large and small organizations: it pulls a product through the distribution channel by stimulating demand for the product (Bearden et al., 2004). While sales promotion can be beneficial in stimulating product trial and purchase, it is not without limitations. Sales promotions cannot overcome an inferior product or problems with the product's positioning in the marketplace. Again, there must be congruence and fit between the promotion utilized and the positioning of the product for the target market.

Personal Selling

Personal selling comprises personal communication about the product or technology that attempts to inform customers within the target market while also persuading them to purchase the product (Ferrell et al., 2002). Personal selling provides the most detailed product information to the consumer, as compared with other promotion techniques. Personal selling is very useful for highly complex products that require a great deal of technical knowledge in order to convey the products' benefits. The advantages of personal selling are substantial, but the major downside is cost. A great deal of resources must be expended to recruit, select, and train an effective sales force.

However, in the initial stages of a new venture, oftentimes the inventor or founding management team performs this role in order to foster initial sales of the technology.

Summary

Now that all of the building blocks of developing a marketing strategy have been presented, the purpose of this section is to examine how high-tech ventures can put these different elements together to formulate an effective marketing strategy. One of the primary difficulties facing new ventures is deciding which product (or form of the technology) to launch when and to whom. Most high-tech innovations have the potential to become platform technologies, meaning that there are many different options available in terms of the product-form, which can complicate marketing strategy development considerably. There may be many different target market options with different marketing mix configurations. The work by Moore (1995, 1999) provides some unique insights regarding the introduction of disruptive technologies into the marketplace.

Initially, high-tech ventures should go after those technology enthusiasts who will help foster diffusion of the technology within the marketplace (Moore, 1995). During this time, segmentation may not necessary; instead, the marketing strategy should focus on generating sales from early visionaries of the new technology, or those consumers who will gain a significant competitive advantage through the technology and are willing to pay for it. Early on, the goal of the marketing strategy is to create product awareness and trial, and technology enthusiasts are of critical importance in achieving this goal. During this introductory phase, new firms will want to introduce the basic product through selective distribution in order to induce trial among those enthusiasts and early adopters of the technology. Sales during this introductory phase are often deal driven (i.e., the product itself is tailored to meet the individual consumer's need), and the performance of the technology itself is critical to these initial customers. In other words, marketing strategies are built around the core benefit derived from the use of the technology.

As technology adoption occurs within this first segment, initial customers can provide valuable feedback and insight into the performance and benefits associated with the technology. This feedback can provide the impetus for product extensions of the basic product, thus tailoring the product to different market needs (i.e., segmentation). Thus, the nature of the marketing strategy will change to that of a concentrated marketing strategy. During this time, the focus shifts from product awareness and trial to actually growing the market. Initially this growth will occur through niche-based marketing efforts by which the firm will target specific segments of the market with a tailored product offering. Firms can take advantage of specialized distribution and concentrate their limited resources on offering a complete solution to different subsegments of the market. Niche marketing can provide valuable returns to the venture before it attempts to introduce the product to the mass market. Recall that niches are small homogeneous segments of the market where network effects are strong in that consumers within these small segments tend to know each other. Therefore, word-of-mouth among potential consumers within the segment is very powerful marketing tool that new firms can capitalize upon and should consider when developing a marketing strategy at this stage.

As both the firm and product sales grow, the firm may have to shift from a niche-based marketing strategy to one that is aimed towards the overall market. This will require the firm to once again revisit the elements of the marketing mix. In other words, the firm may want to adopt a mass-market approach regarding the product offerings of the technology, which will provide substantial market share and financial returns to the firm. At this point, the firm is likely to be growing in both size and resources and will have the capabilities required by a mass-market strategy. It is during this time that marketing strategies should facilitate the technology's becoming the industry standard, thus creating high switching costs for customers. Marketing strategies are concerned with maximizing the distribution of the product and getting it to as many consumers as possible. In addition, competition increases considerably as growth occurs and as the technology is adopted in the mainstream market; competition thus becomes a greater consideration when adapting the marketing strategy. Once this marketplace acceptance of the technology has occurred, the firm can once again adjust the marketing strategy to consider product derivations among the core technology (Moore, 1999).

In developing the marketing strategy for a new technology, it is important to consider where in the process that technology falls. Most new ventures focused on commercializing a new technology will target enthusiasts first and then follow a market concentration strategy by which the technology is customized into different product offerings that best meet the needs of specific market segments. A mass-market approach to commercialization is unlikely as an initial approach for new technologies; rather, a marketing strategy evolves over time as the technology itself is adopted within the marketplace.

CONCLUSION

It should be clear by now that marketing strategy development is a complex, dynamic process dependent upon a multitude of factors. With so many different marketing strategy options available to a new venture, the process of deciding upon the correct target market, positioning, and marketing mix can be challenging. Thus, it is no wonder that the number one cause of new venture failure results directly from ineffective marketing planning. The objective of this chapter was to provide a general overview of the different considerations that come into play when developing a marketing strategy, with the goal of alleviating some of the uncertainty associated with strategy development. The first section of the chapter provided some conceptual definitions of what constitutes a marketing strategy in general and primarily focused on the front end of the strategic process – strategy formulation and development. Given the context of technology commercialization, a framework was given to guide marketing strategy formulation efforts. While most of the tools presented apply regardless of the context, strategy development for radically new products that are commercialized through new ventures warrant special consideration.

Four primary objectives should guide marketing strategy development for new ventures: (1) it should pinpoint the specific target markets the small company will serve, (2) it should determine customer needs and wants through market research, (3) it should analyze the firm's competitive advantage and build guerrilla marketing strategies around them, and (4) it should help in creating a marketing mix that meets customer needs and wants (Lodish et al., 2001).

When developing the go-to-market strategy for any new product, the decisions made regarding segmentation, target market, and positioning will dictate all of the specific decisions relating to the marketing mix. This chapter has highlighted that, for most new ventures, a market concentration segmentation strategy that positions the new product based on the value derived from the technology itself is likely to outperform the other options. Once these key decisions have been addressed, then considerations shift more towards the specifics of the product itself, distribution, pricing, and promotion. Marketing strategy development is only half the battle of commercializing a new product; but after the game plan is set, implementation efforts will occur much more smoothly. The strategy developed will dictate the organization, staffing, and execution of the marketing efforts and provide a foundation from which a successful launch can occur.

NOTE

1. Competition can affect the decisions made during the marketing strategy formulation process. Competition will impact not only the target market selected, but also how the product is positioned within the market (i.e., the product form, pricing, distribution, and promotion considerations). A more detailed consideration of these issues is provided in Chapter 8 of this volume.

REFERENCES

Armstrong, J. S. (1982). The value of formal planning for strategic decisions: Review of empirical research. *Strategic Management Journal*, *3*, 197–211.

Atuahene-Gima, K., & Murray, J. Y. (2004). Antecedents and outcomes of marketing strategy comprehensiveness. *Journal of Marketing*, *68*(4), 33–46.

Barney, J. (1991). Firm resources and competitive advantage. *Journal of Management*, *17*(1), 99–120.

Bearden, W. O., Ingram, T. N., & LaForge, R. W. (2004). *Marketing: Principles and perspectives* (4th ed.). Boston: McGraw-Hill Irwin.

Blattberg, R. C., Briesch, R., & Fox, E. J. (1995). How promotions work. *Marketing Science*, *14*(3), G122–G132.

Bonoma, T. V. (1984). Making your marketing strategy work. *Harvard Business Review*, *62*(2), 69–72.

Boone, L. E., & Kurtz, D. L. (2006). *Contemporary marketing* (12th ed.). Mason, OH: Thomson South-Western.

Cannon, H. M., & Morgan, F. W. (1991). A strategic pricing framework. *Journal of Business and Industrial Marketing*, *6*, 59–70.

Cooper, R. G. (2001). *Winning at new products: Accelerating the process from idea to launch* (3rd ed.). New York: Perseus Publishing.

Crawford, M., & DiBenedetto, A. (2005). *New products management* (8th ed.). Boston: McGraw-Hill Irwin.

Dess, G. G., Lumpkin, G. T., & Covin, J. G. (1997). Entrepreneurial strategy making and firm performance: Tests of contingency and configurational models. *Strategic Management Journal*, *18*(9), 677–695.

Dolan, R. J. (1997). *Note on marketing strategy*. Harvard Business School Case 9-598-061.

Ferrell, O. C., Hartline, M. D., & Lucas, G. H. (2002). *Marketing strategy* (2nd ed.). Fort Worth: Harcourt College Publishers.

Gatignon, H., & Xuereb, J. M. (1997). Strategic orientation of the firm and new product performance. *Journal of Marketing Research*, *34*(1), 77–90.

Grant, R. (1995). *Contemporary strategy analysis*. Cambridge: Blackwell Publishers.

Griffin, A., & Hauser, J. R. (1993). Voice of customer. *Marketing Science*, *12*(1), 1–27.

Jain, S. C. (1993). *Marketing planning and strategy*. Cincinnati: South-Western.

Joshi, A. W., & Sharma, S. K. (2004). Customer knowledge development: Antecedent and impact on new product performance. *Journal of Marketing, 68*(4), 47–59.

Juga, J. (1999). Generic capabilities: Combining positional and resource-based views for strategic advantage. *Journal of Strategic Marketing, 7*(1), 3–18.

Keller, K. L. (1993). Conceptualizing, measuring, and managing customer-based brand equity. *Journal of Marketing, 57*(1), 1–22.

Lilien, G. L. (1979). Advisor 2: Modeling the marketing mix decision for industrial products. *Management Science, 25*(2), 191–204.

Lodish, L., Morgan, H. L., & Kallianpur, A. (2001). *Entrepreneurial marketing.* New York: Wiley.

Menon, A., Bharadwaj, S. G., Adidam, P. T., & Edison, S. W. (1999). Antecedents and consequences of marketing strategy making: A model and a test. *Journal of Marketing, 63*(2), 18–40.

Mercer, D. (1992). *Marketing.* Cambridge: Blackwell Publishers.

Mintzberg, H. (1981). What is planning anyway? *Strategic Management Journal, 2*, 319–324.

Mintzberg, H. (1994). *Rise and fall of strategic planning.* New York: The Free Press.

Moore, G. A. (1995). *Inside the Tornado: Marketing strategies from Silicon Valley's cutting edge.* New York: Harper Collins Publishers.

Moore, G. A. (1999). *Crossing the chasm: Marketing and selling disruptive products to mainstream customers.* New York: Harper Collins Publishers.

Noble, C. H., & Mokwa, M. P. (1999). Implementing marketing strategies: Developing and testing a managerial theory. *Journal of Marketing, 63*, 57–73.

Noble, P. M., & Gruca, T. S. (1999). Industrial pricing: Theory and managerial practice. *Marketing Science, 18*(3), 435–454.

Powell, W. W. (1990). Neither market nor hierarchy: Network forms of organization. In: B. M. Staw & L. L. Cummings (Eds), *Research in organizational behavior,* (Vol. 12, pp. 295–336). Greenwich, CT: JAI Press.

Reynolds, P. D., Carter, N. M., Gartner, W. B., & Greene, P. G. (2004). The prevalence of nascent entrepreneurs in the United States: Evidence from the panel study of entrepreneurial dynamics. *Small Business Economics, 23*, 263–284.

Sandberg, W. R., & Hofer, C. W. (1987). Improving new venture performance: The role of strategy, industry structure, and the entrepreneur. *Journal of Business Venturing, 2*, 5–28.

Schoell, W. F., & Guiltinan, J. P. (1995). *Marketing: Contemporary concepts and practices* (6th ed.). Boston: Allyn and Bacon.

Simon, M., Houghton, S., & Lumpkin, G. T. (2001). Making lemonade out of lemons: The role of strategy in managing misperceived start-ups. *Best paper proceedings, academy of management, annual metting.* Washington, DC, C.D. Format.

Sinha, D. K. (1990). The contribution of formal planning to decisions. *Strategic Management Journal, 11*(6), 479–492.

Slotegraaf, R. J., & Dickson, P. R. (2004). The paradox of a marketing planning capability. *Journal of the Academy of Marketing Science, 32*(4), 371–385.

Srivastava, R. K., Shervani, T. A., & Fahey, L. (1998). Market-based assets and shareholder value: A framework for analysis. *Journal of Marketing, 62*(1), 2–18.

Steiner, G. A. (1979). *Strategic planning: What every manager must know.* New York, NY: Free Press.

Stuart, R. W., & Abetti, P. A. (1987). Start-up ventures: Towards the prediction of initial success. *Journal of Business Venturing, 2*, 215–230.

Teece, D. J., Pisano, G., & Shuen, A. (1997). Dynamic capabilities and strategic management. *Strategic Management Journal, 18*(7), 509–533.

Tellis, G. J. (1986). Beyond the many faces of price: An integration of pricing strategies. *Journal of Marketing, 50*(4), 146–160.

Wind, Y., & Cardozo, R. (1974). Industrial market segmentation. *Industrial Marketing Management, 3*, 153–166.

CHAPTER 7

COMPETITIVE ADVANTAGE IN TECHNOLOGY INTENSIVE INDUSTRIES

Frank T. Rothaermel

ABSTRACT

This chapter introduces the reader to the meaning of competitive advantage and posits that a firm's strategy is defined as the managers' theory about how to gain and sustain competitive advantage. The author demonstrates how a firm creates its competitive advantage by creating more economic value than its rivals, and explains that profitability depends upon value, price, and costs. The relationship among these factors is explored in the context of high-technology consumer goods-laptop computers and cars. Next, the chapter explains the SWOT [s(trengths) w(eaknesses) o(pportunities) t(hreats)] analysis. Examining the interplay of firm resources, capabilities, and competencies, the chapter emphasizes that both must be present to possess core competencies essential to gaining and sustaining competitive advantage through strategy. Next, the chapter describes the value chain by which a firm transforms inputs into outputs, adding value at each stage through the primary activities of research, development, production, marketing and sales, and customer service, which in turn rely upon essential support activities that add value indirectly. After describing the PEST

Technological Innovation: Generating Economic Results
Advances in the Study of Entrepreneurship, Innovation and
Economic Growth, Volume 18, 201–225
ISSN: 1048-4736/doi:10.1016/S1048-4736(07)00007-0

[p(olitical) e(conomic) s(ocial) t(echnological)] Model for assessing a firm's general external environment, the chapter explains Porter's Five Forces Model. The chapter then describes the strategic group model and illustrates that model by reference to the pharmaceutical industry. The author notes that opportunities and threats to a company differ based upon the strategic group to which that firm belongs within an industry. Finally, the chapter explores the importance of strategy in technology intensive industries and emphasizes that sustained competitive advantage can be accomplished only through continued innovation.

1. WHAT IS COMPETITIVE ADVANTAGE?

Gaining and sustaining competitive advantage is the defining question of strategy. Accordingly, strategy research is motivated by attempting to answer fundamental questions like, "why do some technology start-ups succeed, while others fail?," or "what determines overall firm performance?," and "what can you as an entrepreneur or manager do about it?" The unifying element of strategy research is a focus on explaining and predicting *interfirm-performance differentials.* Thus, strategy researchers seek answers to practically relevant questions like "why is Sony, as a new entrant into the market for home video games dominating the incumbent firm Sega, who helped create the industry?," or "why is Dell continuously outperforming Gateway?"

Strategy researchers believe that the answer to these fundamental questions lies in the differences in firm strategy. A dictum of strategy, therefore, is that overall firm performance is explained by a firm's strategy. *A firm's strategy is defined as the managers' plan about how to gain and sustain competitive advantage* (Drucker, 1994). This strategic plan reflects the managers' assumptions about the company's strengths and weaknesses as well as the competitive dynamics in the external industry environment. A strategic plan is, therefore, expressed in a logical coherent framework based on an internal analysis of the company's strength and weaknesses [S(trength) W(eaknesses)] as well as of the external (environmental) opportunities and threats [O(pportunities) T(hreats)] it faces, making up the so-called *SWOT Analysis.* A firm's strategy details a set of goal-directed actions that managers intend to take to improve or maintain overall firm performance. If the managers' assumptions align closely with the competitive realities, successful strategies can be crafted and implemented, resulting in superior firm performance.

This definition of strategy highlights the pivotal role managers play in setting and implementing a firm's strategy, and thus in determining firm performance. Achieving sustained superior performance over a company's direct rivals, therefore, is the ultimate challenge in strategy.

Simply put, a firm that outperforms its competitors has a competitive advantage. If this firm is able to dominate its competitors for prolonged periods of time, the company is said to have a sustained competitive advantage. For example, through the innovative use of IT and other strategic innovations, the world's largest retailer Wal-Mart was able to outperform its competitors, Target and Costco, throughout the 1990s and early 2000 in terms of financial performance. Thus, we can say that Wal-Mart had a sustained competitive advantage during this time period. A firm that enjoys a competitive advantage not only is more profitable than its competitors, but also grows faster because it is able to capture more market share, either directly from competitors or from overall industry growth, due to the firm's stronger competitiveness.

In the simplest terms, profit (Π) is defined as total revenues (TR) minus costs (C), or $\Pi = TR - C$, where $TR = P*Q$, or price times quantity sold. Revenues, therefore, are a function of the value created for customers and the volume of goods sold. Both volume and profit margin drive overall profit, one measure of competitive advantage as depicted in Fig. 1.

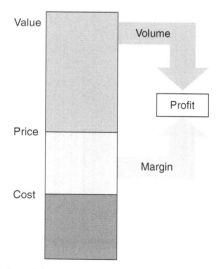

Fig. 1. Volume and Margin as Drivers of Profit.

In more abstract terms, one can say that *a firm has a competitive advantage when it is able to create more economic value than its rivals.* Economic value, in turn, is simply the difference between the perceived value of a good to a customer and the total costs per unit, including costs of capital, to produce the good. Thus, the magnitude of a firm's competitive advantage is the difference between the perceived value created and the costs to produce the good or service compared to its direct competitors. If the economic value created is greater than that of its competitors, the firm has a competitive advantage; if it is equal to the competitors, the firms are said to have competitive parity; and if it lower than its rival firms, the firm has a competitive disadvantage.

If we take a closer look at the equation $\Pi = TR - C$, where $TR = P * Q$, we realize that firm profitability depends, simply put, on three factors: (1) perceived *value* created for customers; (2) the *price* of the product or service; and (3) the total *costs* of producing the product or service. The perceived value of a good, for example, is assigned by customers based on the product's features, performance, design, quality, and so on. For example, customers value a BMW M3 sports car more than a Dodge Intrepid, and accordingly are willing to pay more for the BMW M3 (and have lots more fun driving it!). The price of a product (or service) is simply the dollar amount the customer pays to purchase the good. Indeed, trade happens because both sides, sellers and buyers, benefit. That is because buyers generally value the goods they buy at a higher dollar amount than they actually pay for it. Sellers, on the other hand, generally sell their products or services above cost.

Think about the laptop you bought for college. How much did you pay for it? Let's assume you paid $1,200 for it. But, how much do you value it? That is, how much is it worth to you? This can be determined by thinking about how productive and enjoyable college would be for you without a laptop (and assuming you do not have convenient access to a close substitute like a desktop). You quickly realize you would have been willing to pay much more for a laptop than you actually paid for it. Indeed, if you were pushed, you probably would have paid several thousand dollars for it, given the way it enhances your productivity. If you would have been willing to pay, let's say, $8,000 for your laptop, but paid only $1,200 for it, you actually captured value in the amount of $6,800. This amount is the difference between the value you place on the laptop and what you paid for it. In economics, this is called consumer surplus, because it is the value you, as the consumer, capture in the transaction of buying the laptop. Finally, the total costs C is simply the average unit costs that the manufacturing of a product incurred, including costs of capital. Let's say it costs that company $500 to make your laptop; it will capture a profit of $700 when it sells the laptop to you (this is called producer surplus in economics). Thus, trade is beneficial to both buyers and sellers, because transacting parties capture some of the overall value created.

Fig. 2 graphically illustrates how these concepts fit together. V is the value of the product to the consumer, P the price, and C the average unit cost. Thus, V-P is the value the consumer captures (or consumer surplus), P-C is the profit margin, while V-C is the value created by this transaction.

Based on these concepts, one realizes that a firm has two levers to create competitive advantage: (1) the value created to customers V; and/or (2) the costs of production C. Often higher value goes along with greater cost. Given the earlier example, while the BMW M3 creates more value than the Dodge Intrepid, the BMW M3 also costs more to create than the Dodge Intrepid. Yet, some firms were able to overcome the trade-off between value created and costs incurred to produce that value. For example, Toyota, through its lean manufacturing system, was able to produce cars that were perceived to be of higher value by customers due to superior quality and features, while at the same time the unit cost was lower, when compared to cars manufactured by U.S. or European car makers in the same class. This situation is depicted in Fig. 3, where Firm B is able to capture competitive

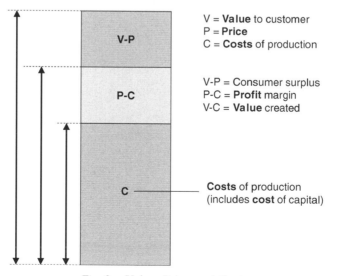

Fig. 2. Value, Price, and Costs.

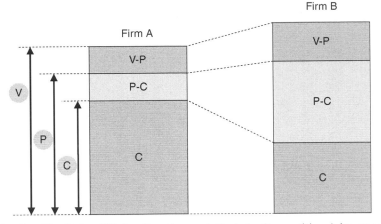

Fig. 3.   The Role of Value Creation and Costs in Competitive Advantage.

advantage on both levels, with higher perceived value created than Firm A, with, at the same time, lower costs to produce the good or service. Thus, Firm B can charge a higher price than Firm A because Firm B creates more value than Firm A. In addition, Firm B is more profitable than Firm A, because Firm B has lower cost than Firm A. While competitive advantage only requires a firm either to achieve higher value created (assuming costs are equal) or lower costs (assuming value created is equal) than its competitors, some firms are able to gain and sustain a competitive advantage through a twofold superior performance based on higher value created *and* lower costs.

2. INTERNAL AND EXTERNAL ANALYSIS (SWOT)

To create and sustain competitive advantage, the firm's managers must understand the firm's internal strengths and weaknesses as well as its opportunities and threats that present themselves in the firm's external environment. This is done through a SWOT. Internal strengths and weaknesses concern issues such as quantity and quality of the firm's resources, capabilities, and competencies. The goal here is that a firm's strategy should leverage a firm's strengths while mitigating its weaknesses, or acquire new resources and build new capabilities and competencies to turn weaknesses into strengths. To understand the external environment,

**Competitive Advantage Requires Strategic Fit between a Firm's
Internal Strengths & Weaknesses and External Opportunities and Threats**

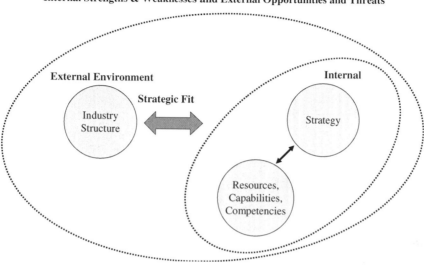

Fig. 4. Strategic Fit.

the managers must analyze the structure of the industry in which they compete, because overall firm profitability is determined not only by firm effects but also by industry effects (McGahan & Porter, 1997). The latter point implies that not all industries are equally profitable, and thus some industries are more attractive than others. For example, the average industry rate of return on invested capital is many times higher in the pharmaceutical industry than in the grocery industry, and this has been so for decades. The ultimate goal of the SWOT analysis is therefore to aid managers in formulating a strategy that allows a coherent fit between the company's resources, capabilities, and competencies, on the one hand, and its industry structure, on the other hand (as depicted in Fig. 4).

2.1. Internal Analysis: Resources, Capabilities, and Core Competencies

Superior firm profitability is the result of a firm's gaining and sustaining competitive advantage through strategy. To be able to leverage a strategy into competitive advantage, however, a firm must possess *core competencies*, that allow the managers to manipulate the underlying drives of profitability, i.e., perceived value and cost. To obtain a competitive advantage, a firm must have competencies that allow it to create higher perceived value than its competitors or to produce the same or similar products at a lower cost, or to do both simultaneously. For example, the core competence of Honda Motor Company is to produce small, highly reliable, and high-powered engines. This allows the company to create superior value in the mind of the consumer. Yet, it is important to realize that the final product (e.g., an Acura MDX, a crossover SUV in Honda's luxury line of vehicles) is only the visible side of competition. What is even more important to think about is the science, engineering, and managerial competencies needed to create the Acura MDX and its high-performing engine. While products and services are the visible side of competition, underneath are a diverse and deep set of competencies that make this success happen. This implies that companies compete as much in the product and service markets as they do on developing competencies. Superior or core competencies allow managers to create higher perceived value and/or achieve a lower cost structure (Prahalad & Hamel, 1990).

Core competencies are built through the complex interplay between resources and capabilities. *Resources* are assets on which a company can draw when executing strategy. Resources fall into two categories: *tangible* (such as land, buildings, plant, and equipment) and *intangible* (such as brand name, reputation, patents, and technical and market know-how). Finally, a firm's *capabilities* are the managerial skills necessary to coordinate and orchestrate a diverse set of resources and to deploy them strategically. A firm's capabilities are by their nature intangible, and are captured in a firm's routines, procedures, and processes (Teece, Pisano, & Shuen, 1997). As depicted in Fig. 5, the interplay between resources and capabilities allows managers to create core competencies, which are then leveraged to formulate and implement strategy with the goal of attaining a competitive advantage and thus superior profitability.

It is important to realize that competitive advantage can stem from both the resource and the capability side. To be the basis of a competitive advantage, a firm resource must be: (1) valuable (V), thus allowing the managers to exploit opportunities or mitigate threats in the firm's external environment; (2) rare in terms of scarcity (R); (3) imitation protected, so only imperfect imitation is possible (I) ; and (4) substitution protected (N), in the sense that equivalent substitutes are not readily available (Barney, 1991). In short hand, this resource-based framework is termed *VRIN*.

Yet, managers need to be aware of a critical distinction. While resources can have some or even all of the *VRIN* attributes, unless a firm has the

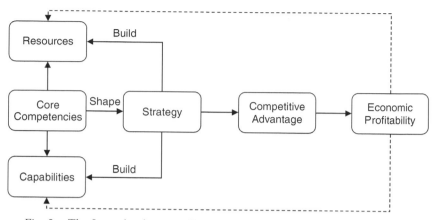

Fig. 5.   The Interplay between Resources, Capabilities, and Competencies.

(science, engineering, and managerial) capabilities to orchestrate and deploy these resources in an effective and efficient manner, the managers will not able to create a core competence and thus will fail to achieve a firm-level competitive advantage. On the other hand, the managers may be able to draw only on average resources that do not fulfill any of the *VRIN* requirements, but the firm possesses superior capabilities of coordinating, orchestrating, and deploying the average resources that results in superior performance. For example, it can be argued that McDonald's or the U.S. Army draw on average human resources, but both possess superior capabilities, systems, and structures that allow these organizations to deploy these resources globally in a superior fashion that has not been matched by their rivals. Taken together, competitive advantage requires that a firm possesses either (1) resources that can be classified by any or all of the *VRIN* attributes (e.g., an important and enforceable patent or thicket of patents) and the capability to deploy these resources or (2) average resources but superior capabilities at deploying, orchestrating, and managing the bundle of average resources. It comes as no surprise that a company that can combine *VRIN* resources with superior capabilities is in the strongest position to achieve and sustain competitive advantage.

2.2. The Value Chain and Activity Systems

The concept of the value chain captures the notion that a firm engages in a number of activities to transform inputs into outputs, and through this process adds value at each stage (Porter, 1985). This transformation process is composed of a set of distinct activities, such as research, development, production, marketing and sales, and customer service. While these so-called primary activities directly add value by transforming inputs into outputs as the firm moves a product or service horizontally along the value chain, each of the distinct primary activities along the way is supported by other activities, such as information systems, operations management, human resources, finance, accounting, and general management. Together, the latter activities are called support activities, as they add value indirectly, while primary activities add value directly. Fig. 6 depicts a generic value chain containing both primary and support activities.

Competitive advantage requires different positioning strategies through strategically choosing a different mix of value chain activities in order to deliver a unique value at a competitive price (Porter, 1996). Activities are therefore the basic units of competitive advantage. It is important to note, however, that competitive advantage or competitive disadvantage at the firm level is the outcome of the interplay among all of the firm's activities, not only a selected few.

It is critical to understand that operational effectiveness, accomplished through such programs like Six Sigma, is a *necessary but not sufficient condition for competitive advantage.* This is true because these type of

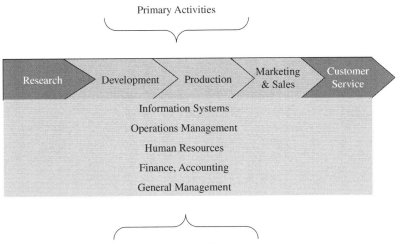

Fig. 6.   The Value Chain.

programs are available to all companies and are taught to MBAs, and thus diffuse widely and rapidly within industries. While they accomplish an absolute increase in competitiveness of each firm implementing these programs, they do not change firms' relative advantage vis-à-vis one another. To truly create competitive advantage, a firm must not only be operationally effective, but also choose a different strategic posture based on its unique system of activities. A sustainable strategic position, therefore, requires important trade-offs. For example, it is often not possible to provide innovation at low cost, because innovation requires (very) high and ongoing R&D investments over time. One could argue that Carly Fiorina's tenure at HP was brought to an end by her intended strategy of creating "high-tech at low cost." This ambitious strategy required overcoming what appears to be insurmountable obstacles due to significant strategic trade-offs between the goals of innovation and low cost.

Strategic positions are sustainable if they require trade-offs with other positions. Therefore, the essence about strategy is to choose what activities to engage in, and more importantly, what not to do. Companies with a clear strategic profile and posture outperform companies that attempt to be too many things to too many customers. Strategy therefore is about combining activities into a complex system that not only creates competitive advantage, but also protects from imitation. For example, when attempting to answer the question "what is Southwest Airlines' core competence that creates its superior performance?," one would need to identify a set of activities and how they are coordinated and orchestrated to form a coherent strategy. Ideally, the activities persued are consistent to one another, while at the same time they also reinforce one another. This implies that the interconnected system of activities is more than the sum of its parts. Understanding competitive advantage as embedded in a system of activities also explains why imitating an entire system of complex activities is so difficult. While one can easily observe several elements of an activity system, what cannot be observed are the capabilities necessary to orchestrate and manage the network of activities.

Strategic Activity Systems, such as the one for Southwest Airlines depicted in Porter (1996), show how a firm's strategic position is built on a network of diverse activities. When activity systems are developed to a mature stage, a number of core strategic themes and a number of supporting strategic activities can be identified and implemented through a network of tightly linked activities (Siggelkow, 2001, 2002).

The following is an excerpt from an interview with Kevin Rollins, Vice Chairman at Dell Computer, that highlights the complex interdependencies between strategic positioning based on a diverse set of consistent and reinforcing value chain activities (Fishburne, 1999).

Question (Q): What is it about the direct sales model and mass customization that has been difficult for competitors to replicate?

Answer (A): It's not as simple as just having a direct sales force. It's not as simple as just having a mass customization in-plant or manufacturing methodology. It's a whole series of things in the value chain: from the way we procure, the way we develop product, the way we order and have inventory levels, and manufacturer and service support. The entire value chain has to work together to make it efficient and effective.

Q: What is the competition looking at?

A: So many of our competitors are really looking at our business and saying "Oh, its the asset management model – seven days of inventory. That's what we're going to do," rather than looking at every one of 10 things and replicate those.[1]

3. EXTERNAL ANALYSIS: OPPORTUNITIES AND THREATS

Besides internal analysis, the second major input for strategy formulation is a deep understanding of the firm's external environment. This is done to identify opportunities and threats, with the goal of leveraging opportunities and mitigating threats. Events in the external environment, such as changing demographics, sociocultural norms, deregulation, globalization, technological change, macroeconomic changes, as well as political and legal changes, can all create opportunities and threats for companies. One way to understand a firm's external environment is to apply the *PEST Model*. This entails assessing the firm's general environment along the following dimensions: Political/legal, Economic, Social, and Technological (PEST).

While an accurate understanding of a firm's general external environment is necessary, many of these work through affecting the underlying structure of the firm's industry. An important first step, therefore, is to analyze the *structure of the industry* in which you are competing, or planning to compete. An industry is defined as set of companies that offer comparable products and services (i.e., substitutes); an industry is thus the supply side of the market. It is important to keep in mind, however, as industries converge (e.g., computing, biotechnology, and nanotechnology), it becomes harder and harder to produce accurate definitions of an industry. Thus, industry boundaries will be increasingly difficult to define.

As mentioned earlier, industries show different average profitabilities over time. This is due to different industry structures, some of which are clearly more favorable than others. For example, the average rate of return on invested capital for the time period between 2000 and 2003 was 22.6% for the pharmaceutical industry, 15.9% for the software industry, 11.9% for the publishing industry, 11.2% for the retail industry, 6.6% for the steel industry, and only 1.8% for the air transportation industry (Hill & Jones, 2007).

These differences in underlying industry profitability are explained by each industry's structure, which is assessed along such industry dimensions as the number and size of competitors, the similarity and differences in the product and service offerings, the height of entry and exit barriers, scale economies, and thus the cost to overcome these barriers. One simple dimension to understand industry structure is the size and number of competitors. If there are many small firms in an industry, the industry is fragmented, and generally exhibits low average profitability (what economists call "perfect competition"). If there are only a few large firms in an industry, this industry structure is more favorable and can exhibit higher industry returns ("oligopoly"). The most favorable industry structure is the monopoly, where only one firm supplies the entire market. To more deeply understand industry structure, and how it affects firm performance, we now turn to the well-known Five Forces Model developed by Michael Porter.

3.1. Porter's Five Forces Model

Porter's Five Forces Model helps managers to understand the underlying industry structure, and thus aids in identifying threats and opportunities. This model is depicted in Fig. 7, and highlights five forces that shape competition within an industry, and thus determine the overall industry profitability and its attractiveness. The viewpoint is that of an incumbent firm already active in an industry. These forces are: (1) the risk of entry by potential competitors; (2) the bargaining power of buyers; (3) the bargaining power of suppliers; (4) the threat of substitutes; and (5) the resulting intensity of rivalry among existing competitors (Porter, 1980).

The *risk of entry* concerns potential competitors that are not yet competing in your industry, but have the capability to do so if they choose.

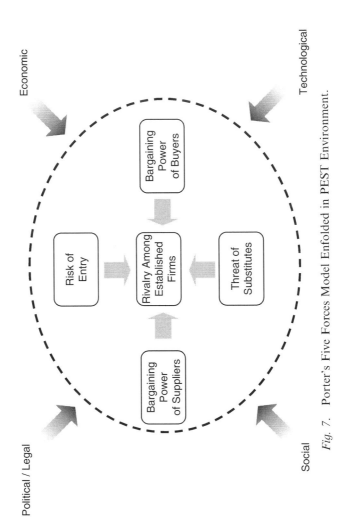

Fig. 7. Porter's Five Forces Model Enfolded in PEST Environment.

For example, in the Southeastern U.S. the TV cable company, Comcast, has entered the business for residential and commercial telephone services and Internet connectivity (as Internet Service Provider), thus emerging as a competitor for AT&T and Bell South, who recently merged. The risk of entry by potential competitors is determined by the barriers to entry, i.e., how costly an investment is it to enter the industry? Indeed, the height of barriers to entry has been found consistently to be the most significant predictor of industry profitability. For example, the pharmaceutical industry in the U.S. experienced between the end of World War II and 1975 only one entry, which was Syntex, based on the breakthrough innovation of the contraceptive pill. Thus, the industry was characterized by extremely high barriers to entry, which in turn was reflected by fairly average industry profitability (over 20% return on invested capital year after year). With the emergence of biotechnology, which represents a radical process innovation through which new drugs are discovered and commercialized, new entrants in the form of biotechnology start-ups were able to circumvent the entry barriers. As a consequence, over 2,000 new biotechnology firms entered the industry and clearly changed the underlying industry structure (Rothaermel, 2000, 2001a; Rothaermel & Hill, 2005). In general, the heights of entry barriers are determined by factors like government regulation, economies of scale, product differentiation, and customer switching costs.

The *bargaining power of buyers* concerns the pressure buyers can put on the seller's company's margin through demanding a lower price and higher product quality. Strong buyers can act to reduce the company's revenues. Buyers have strong bargaining power when they purchase in large quantities and control many access points to the final customer. For example, Wal-Mart and Home Depot can exert tremendous pressure on their suppliers to lower prices and to increase quality, because these two companies will choose not to place the suppliers' products on their shelves. Buyers also are extremely powerful when they are the only customer buying a certain product. Many modern defense technologies rely on the latest innovations, and thus are clearly technology and engineering driven, but frequently these products are bought by only one buyer, the U.S. Department of Defense, which has considerable bargaining power to demand lower prices and higher quality. Buyers are also powerful when they can credibly threaten to backward integrate. This is commonly observed in the auto component supply industry, where car manufacturers like GM, Ford, or DaimlerChrysler have the capability to backwardly integrate to produce their components in-house, should their demands for lower prices and higher product quality not be met by their suppliers. Also, if the buyers' switching costs are low, this adds to the strength of this force, because buyers can play off the suppliers against each other. This threat is particularly pronounced if the products sold to buyers are non-differentiated commodities, like agricultural products. Thus, buyers can possibly extract the profitability earned in the industry (see Chapter 1).

The *bargaining power of suppliers* attempts to capture pressures that suppliers to the industry can exert on industry profitability. Inputs into the production process concern raw materials, labor (may be individuals or labor unions, where the company faces collective bargaining), and services. While strong buyers have the power to reduce a company's revenues, a powerful supplier can raise the company's cost through demanding higher prices for its input or delivering lower quality inputs. Thus, any profits earned in the industry may actually be appropriated by the suppliers (see Chapter 1).

Suppliers are powerful, relative to the firms in the industry, if only a few substitutes are available for the products and services supplied. For example, crude oil is still a critical input in many industries, and oil suppliers are fairly powerful in raising prices and squeezing industry profitability where products and services rely heavily on oil as a critical input. Suppliers are also in a more powerful position when the extent of competition among suppliers is low, which often goes along with a small number of large suppliers. Supplier power is further enhanced when the supplied product is unique and differentiated or when the companies in the industry face significant switching costs. Supplier power is also strengthened when suppliers provide a credible threat of forwardly integrating in the companies' industry, or when the companies in the industry buy only small quantities from the suppliers. Microsoft's power as supplier of operating systems in the market for personal computing stems from the fact that Windows is the de facto standard in the industry, consumer switching costs are high, and the product is fairly unique and differentiated.

The *threat of substitutes* concern the questions whether any available products or services come close to meeting the needs of your customers. Close substitutes place limits on the ability of companies in the industry to raise prices; if they do, customers will switch. For example, if coffee prices would increase significantly, customers might switch to tea or other non-alcoholic beverages to meet their needs. One reason Microsoft has such a powerful position is that there are only few viable substitutes for the Windows operating system (e.g., Linux). Thus, the threat of this force is determined by the existence of substitutes with attractive price and performance characteristics that result in low switching costs.

These four forces conspire to determine the *rivalry among existing competitors* in the industry, and they thus determine overall industry profitability. The threat of rivalry refers to the competitive intensity within an industry, which can range from cut-throat to genteel. Competitive intensity is determined by how hard existing firms fight among themselves to gain market share from each other, or to capture a significant amount of industry growth. Competitive weapons include price discounting, product and service differentiation, and advertising spending. The stronger the rivalry in the industry, the lower the industry profitability, because intense competition leads to lower prices (and thus lower revenues) and greater costs, squeezing out profitability in the industry (which can be captured by consumers, as in the airline industry in the years following the September 11 terrorist attacks). On the other hand, firms may prefer non-price competition and compete on advertising and innovation, thus avoiding head-on competition. This scenario has been observed for extended periods in the soft drink industry (Coke vs. Pepsi) and in the automobile industry. The threat of rivalry among existing competitors is strongest (weakest) in an industry that has many (few) firms, has excess (no excess) capacity, low (high) industry growth, low (high) differentiation, low (high) switching costs, no (a) history of cooperative pricing with an emphasis on non-price competition, and high (low) exit barriers.

At this point, however, it is important to note that Andy Grove, former CEO of Intel, has suggested that Porter's Five Forces Model is incomplete in the sense that it does not consider the strength, power, and competence of *complementors* (Grove, 1996). These are companies that provide products and services (or competencies) that add value through complementing the original product offering, because when these two products (or competencies) are used in tandem they provide more value to the customer. Clearly, Grove was thinking of the complementary relationship between Microsoft's operating system, Windows, and Intel's microprocessors' chip architecture, which together built the Wintel standard in personal computing today. But Grove's idea that complementors are critical to creating firm value can be easily extended to other industries. For biotechnology start-ups that have developed new drugs due to their strength in drug discovery and early stage development, existing pharmaceutical are often complementors, because they have an existing strengths in large-scale manufacturing, in managing FDA clinical trials and regulatory approval, and in distributing drugs via armies of detail people (sales forces) to doctors, hospitals, and Health Maintenance Organizations (HMOs). This has led to a cooperative equilibrium in this industry through a division of labor in scientific discovery and commercialization, in which each partner focuses on its comparative strengths (for more detail, see Chapters 1 and 8) (Gans & Stern, 2000; Rothaermel, 2000, 2001a, 2001b; Hill & Rothaermel, 2003; Rothaermel & Hill, 2005).

In sum, the stronger a competitive force, the greater the threat it represents. On the flip side, the weaker the competitive force, the greater the opportunity it presents. The strengths (or the weakness) of the forces together determine overall industry attractiveness.

While a useful model to understand industry profitability, an important caveat is that the Five Forces Model is static, and thus it provides only a snapshot of moving target. One cannot use it to determine the speed of change in an industry or the rate of innovation. Moreover, the strength of each competitive force changes throughout the industry life cycle. Thus, managers need to repeat the Five Forces analysis over time to create a more accurate picture of their industry. In addition, both external and internal industry factors can alter industry structures. These factors include change in external environment discussed above, but also innovation or firm strategy can change the structure of an industry, and thus the Five Forces. Finally, identifying attractive industries does not imply that one can easily enter them.

Perhaps even more important is the fact that the Five Forces Model cannot say much about inter-firm differentials, because it is a model of industry profitability, not a model of predicting why one firm outperforms another *in the same industry*. Thus, the Five Forces Model cannot explain why Southwest Airlines is outperforming the legacy carriers like Delta, American, or Continental, because they all compete in the same industry. To overcome this shortcoming to some extent, scholars offer the Strategic Group Model, to which we turn next.

3.2. Strategic Group Model

When comparing Southwest Airlines to the legacy carriers, it becomes clear that firms in the *same* industry *differ along important dimensions*. While they are competing in the same industry, Southwest Airlines offers low cost, point-to-point connections, while the legacy carriers offer basically all destinations in the world via a hub and spoke system, combined with a differentiated product offering. More generally speaking, companies often use a different positioning in their strategy in terms of technological leadership, product quality, pricing policies, market segments served, distribution channels, and customer service. As a consequence of differences along such important strategic dimensions, it is often possible to identify groups of competitors in an industry, where group members pursue a similar strategy that results in a similar positioning, while at the same time that group is different from other groups of firms. In many industries such *strategic groups* can be identified along a fairly small number of dimensions. While belonging to the same industry, different rates of performance are generally observed in different strategic groups (Nair & Kotha, 2001; McNamara, Deephouse, & Luce, 2003). This implies that firm performance is partly determined by strategic group membership.

For example, in the global pharmaceutical industry, two main strategic groups have been identified (see Fig. 8) (Cool & Dierickx, 1993). One strategic group has chosen a positioning strategy based on discovering and developing new (blockbuster) drugs. This group includes companies like Aventis, Eli Lilly, Merck, and Pfizer. Developing new drugs requires consistently high R&D expenditures (generally spending upwards of 10% of sales on R&D), because it takes easily 10–15 years for a newly discovered

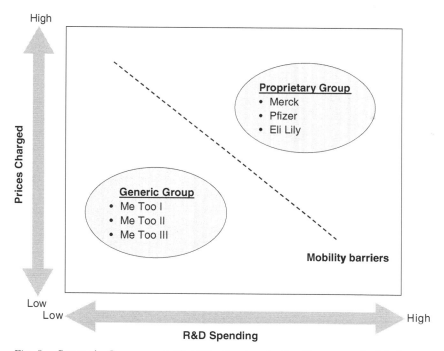

Fig. 8. Strategic Groups and Mobility Barriers in the Pharmaceutical Industry.

molecule to reach the market for drugs. Moreover, drug discovery and development costs have risen drastically, and can reach $1 billion. The strategy of focusing on the discovery and development of proprietary drugs also has an extreme risk element to it, because only one out of 10,000 discovered molecules will make it to the market for pharmaceuticals[2] (Rothaermel & Deeds, 2004, 2006). This implies that the firms in the strategic group focusing on proprietary drugs are pursuing a high risk, high return strategy. The strategy is clearly high risk, given the very low odds of discovering and developing new drugs that are also commercially viable, i.e., serve a large enough market to recoup the firm's investment (and to pay for all the other failures along the way). On the other hand, with a high risk comes a potential for high returns. Should a new drug be discovered, firms will patent protect it, and thus be able to extract monopoly rents for a considerable time (as long as exclusivity of the patent lasts, see Chapters 3–5).

While this first group is described as the *proprietary group*, a second strategic group in the pharmaceutical industry can be identified. This group is the so-called *generic group*, because their positioning strategy is to focus on the low-cost manufacturing and distribution of drugs that have come off patents (me-too products). The strategy of companies in the generic group is characterized by little R&D spending, production efficiencies (especially in large-scale manufacturing), and alternative distribution channels (e.g., over the counter). These elements combine to create a low-cost, low-risk strategy. The strategy is low cost, because the R&D investments required to understand the manufacturing behind patent-expired drugs are minimal. But this strategy is also low return; because of the lack of differentiation, these firms are unable to charge high prices; indeed, their products are commodities.

The concept of strategic groups has several implications for competitive advantage. One immediate insight is that the opportunities and threats companies face in an industry will differ based on the strategic group to which the firms belong. The threats of new entry, bargaining power of buyers and suppliers, substitutes, and rivalry among established firms are mediated by membership in a specific strategic group. For example, while the risk of entry into the generic drug group is low, it is much higher in the proprietary group. Historically, the bargaining power of buyers has been low in the proprietary drug group, because their drugs enjoy IP protection (although this appears to be changing with the rise of HMOs) and there are generally no close substitutes. In contrast, the bargaining power of buyers has been high in the generic drug group, because they are often bought in large quantities by a few buyers (large hospitals and HMOs), and substitutes are readily available. This in turn implies that a company's direct competitors are the ones within its own strategic group, because of their similar strategic positioning. Given the existence of different strategic groups, one also realizes that the strength of the different competitive forces discussed above changes based on the strategic group to which a firm belongs. This implies that each strategic group, even though they belong to the *same industry, differ along the opportunities and threats* they are facing.

Another implication of the existence of strategic groups is that some groups are more attractive than others, given the impact of the competitive forces discussed. Thus, there exists performance heterogeneity across strategic groups in the same industry. For example, companies in the proprietary drug group tend to outperform companies in the generic drug group. So, why are firms not moving from a lower performing group to higher performing groups? The answer is that strategic groups are generally separated by *mobility barriers* (Caves & Porter, 1977). These are industry-specific factors that inhibit movement from one group to another. For example, the pharmaceutical companies in the proprietary drug group have built their strong R&D competence over long periods of time through large R&D investments, but also through R&D alliances and R&D acquisitions (Rothaermel & Hess, 2007). This implies that a company in the generic group cannot easily build an R&D competence necessary to compete in the proprietary group, because not only are very high investments necessary, but also these competencies tend to be built cumulatively over long periods of time. Mobility barriers, therefore, separate strategic groups from one another.

4. DRIVERS OF ECONOMIC PROFITABILITY

We are now in a position to put together the pieces that drive economic profitability (or overall firm performance). We realize that firm performance is a function of industry *and* firm effects. Industry effects, and thus the attractiveness of different markets, can be understood with the Five Forces Model and the Strategic Group Model. Firm-level competitive advantage, on the other hand, depends on the firm's value and cost positions (which are an outflow of its competencies) relative to its competitors. A firm's strategy allows managers to choose attractive industries and build the competencies necessary to gain and sustain competitive advantage. Fig. 9 depicts the

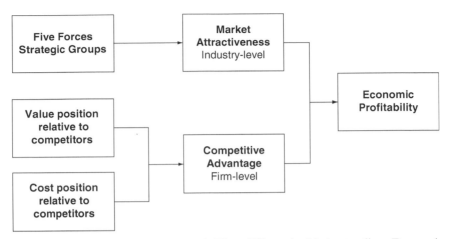

Fig. 9. The Role of Industry and Firm Effects in Understanding Economic Profitability.

individual factors that drive economic profitability, and highlights the analytical tools available to understand each factor.

5. STRATEGY IN TECHNOLOGY INTENSIVE INDUSTRIES

Today, technological innovation is in many industries the most important driver of competitive advantage. Reasons for the increasing importance of innovation in many industries include deregulation, globalization, rapid technological progress (e.g., advances in IT, biotechnology, and nanotechnology), and accelerating diffusion rates for technology-based products. These factors combine to increase the competitive intensity of almost all industries. Even in industries that are thought of as mundane, like the steel industry, technology has become one of the key differentiating factors in determining firm performance. In general, traditional industries, once considered low tech, are increasingly becoming technology intensive industries.

One could argue that technology intensive industries like the software industry change so rapidly and in such unpredictable fashion, that strategic planning is not necessary and thus a futile exercise. Nothing could be further from the truth. The opposite holds: Strategy becomes even more important in technology intensive industries. For example, Microsoft employs a formalized strategy process that is at the same time decentralized and flexible (Hill & Jones, 2007). It is formalized in the sense that it uses standard financial information to determine resource allocation for the next budget year and holds managers accountable for their actual performance compared to their intended performance. It is decentralized in the sense that many of the ideas incorporated in the strategic plan derive from a dialogue between unit heads and top management. Moreover, Microsoft is known to be a company where many strategic initiatives, like the Internet Explorer or the Xbox, have come from mid-level managers deep within the organization. The final strategic plan is decided upon, however, only after detailed scrutiny by top management, including Bill Gates and Steve Ballmer. Finally, Microsoft's strategic planning is flexible, because all managers involved realize that the assumptions underlying the strategic plan may need to be adjusted due to unforeseen circumstances that can arise in the future. This type of strategic flexibility becomes even more important since, in our fast-paced world, the only constant is change.

This type of formal, decentralized, and flexible strategic planning brings to mind the quote by General (and later President) Eisenhower, who stated: "In preparing for battle I have always found that plans are useless, but planning is indispensable." Thus, strategy making in technology intensive industries is akin to the way a fire department plans. It does not know where and when the next emergency will arise, nor does it know the magnitude thereof. Nonetheless, the managers in the fire department (e.g., fire chiefs) put contingency plans in place to address a wide range of emergencies along different dimensions. It is in the same spirit that one ought to view strategic planning in technology intensive industries. This implies that scenario planning, asking the "what if" questions, becomes imperative.

Since the only constant in technology intensive industries is change, *sustained competitive advantage can only be accomplished through continued innovation.* This in turn requires the continuous introduction of new products or services (Shay & Rothaermel, 1999). For example, the percentage of sales obtained from new products developed within the past 5 years has exceeded 40% for 3M, while Proctor & Gamble even strives for 50%. Introducing new products helps firms create more value for customers. At the same time, innovations in manufacturing (like lean manufacturing) and in business processes (e.g., re-engineering) allow firms to lower their cost structure. Thus, innovation works simultaneously to raise the overall value created and to lower the cost required to create the product or service; thus, profits margins widen and firm profitability increases.

Continued innovation creates a string of the so-called Schumpeterian rents based on temporary monopolies. The extent of how long these competitive advantages can be enjoyed depends on the speed of imitability by competitors, which is often determined by the technological and engineering difficulty of the underlying innovation (small vs. large science), the IP protection of the innovation (see Chapters 3–5), and the strategic decisions about how to appropriate returns from invention (see Chapter 1).

NOTES

1. Author's interview with a Distinguished Technologist at HP.
2. The drug discovery and development process can be broken down into distinct sequential stages. The discovery stage can take anywhere between 2 and 10 years. In the next stage, which can take up to 4 years, a lead drug candidate is developed and pre-clinical testing is undertaken. A lead candidate then enters phase I of clinical testing, which can take up to 2 years. In this phase, the lead candidate is administered to 20–30 healthy volunteers and its safety and dosage are evaluated. In phase II, which can take up to 2 years, the drug is given to 100–300 patient volunteers to check for efficacy and side effects. In phase III, which can take up to 3 years, the drug is administered to 1000–5000 patient volunteers to monitor reactions to long-term drug usage. The next stage, FDA review and approval, can take up to 2 years. This is followed by a 2-year post-marketing testing period.

ACKNOWLEDGMENTS

The author thanks Carolyn Davis and Marie Thursby for helpful comments and suggestions. This material is based upon work supported by the National Science Foundation under Grant No. 0545544. Any opinions, findings, conclusions, or recommendations expressed in this material are those of the author and do not necessarily reflect the views of the National Science Foundation.

REFERENCES

Barney, J. (1991). Firm resources and sustained competitive advantage. *Journal of Management,* *17*(1), 99–120.
Caves, R. E., & Porter, M. E. (1977). From entry barriers to mobility barriers. *Quarterly Journal of Economics, 91*(2), 241–262.
Cool, K., & Dierickx, I. (1993). Rivalry, strategic groups, and firm performance. *Strategic Management Journal, 14*(1), 47–59.

Drucker, P. (1994). The theory of business. *Harvard Business Review, 75*(September–October), 95–105.

Fishburne, R. (1999). Kevin Rollins, vice chairman, Dell Computer. *Forbes, 163*(7), 163.

Gans, J. S., & Stern, S. (2000). Incumbency and R&D incentives: Licensing the gale of creative destruction. *Journal of Economics and Management Strategy, 9*(4), 485–511.

Grove, A. S. (1996). *Only the paranoid survive: How to exploit the crisis points that challenge every company and career.* New York: Currency Doubleday.

Hill, C. W. L., & Jones, G. R. (2007). *Strategic management theory. An integrated approach* (7th ed.). Boston: Houghton Mifflin.

Hill, C. W. L., & Rothaermel, F. T. (2003). The performance of incumbent firms in the face of radical technological innovation. *Academy of Management Review, 28*(2), 257–274.

McGahan, A. M., & Porter, M. E. (1997). How much does industry matter, really? *Strategic Management Journal, 18*(1), 15–30.

McNamara, G., Deephouse, D. L., & Luce, R. A. (2003). Competitive positioning within and across a strategic group structure. *Strategic Management Journal, 24*(2), 161–180.

Nair, A., & Kotha, S. (2001). Does group membership matter? Evidence from the Japanese steel industry. *Strategic Management Journal, 22*(3), 221–235.

Porter, M. E. (1980). *Competitive strategy. Techniques for analyzing industries and competitors.* New York: Free Press.

Porter, M. E. (1985). *Competitive advantage: Creating and sustaining superior performance.* New York: Free Press.

Porter, M. E. (1996). What is strategy? *Harvard Business Review, 77*(November–December), 61–78.

Prahalad, C. K., & Hamel, G. (1990). The core competence of the corporation. *Harvard Business Review, 71*(May–June), 79–91.

Rothaermel, F. T. (2000). Technological discontinuities and the nature of competition. *Technology Analysis and Strategic Management, 12*(2), 149–160.

Rothaermel, F. T. (2001a). Incumbent's advantage through exploiting complementary assets via interfirm cooperation. *Strategic Management Journal, 22*(6–7), 687–699.

Rothaermel, F. T. (2001b). Complementary assets, strategic alliances, and the incumbent's advantage: An empirical study of industry and firm effects in the biopharmaceutical industry. *Research Policy, 30*(8), 1235–1251.

Rothaermel, F. T., & Deeds, D. L. (2004). Exploration and exploitation alliances in biotechnology: A system of new product development. *Strategic Management Journal, 25*(3), 201–221.

Rothaermel, F. T., & Deeds, D. L. (2006). Alliance type, alliance experience, and alliance management capability in high technology ventures. *Journal of Business Venturing, 21,* 429–460.

Rothaermel, F. T., & Hess, A. M. (2007). Building dynamic capabilities: Innovation driven by individual, firm, and network-level effects. *Organization Science, 18,* 898–921.

Rothaermel, F. T., & Hill, C. W. L. (2005). Technological discontinuities and complementary assets: A longitudinal study of industry and firm performance. *Organization Science, 16*(1), 52–70.

Shay, J. P., & Rothaermel, F. T. (1999). Dynamic competitive strategy: Towards a multi-perspective conceptual framework. *Long Range Planning, 32*(6), 559–572.

Siggelkow, N. (2001). Change in the presence of fit: The rise, the fall, and the renaissance of liz claiborne. *Academy of Management Journal, 44*(4), 838–857.

Siggelkow, N. (2002). Evolution toward fit. *Administrative Science Quarterly, 47*(1), 125–159.

Teece, D., Pisano, G., & Shuen, A. (1997). Dynamic capabilities and strategic management. *Strategic Management Journal, 18*(7), 509–533.

CHAPTER 8

TECHNOLOGY COMMERCIALIZATION: COOPERATIVE VERSUS COMPETITIVE STRATEGIES

Anne W. Fuller and Marie C. Thursby

ABSTRACT

This chapter presents a framework for evaluating commercialization strategies available to start-up innovators operating in high-technology industries. The chapter uses a stream of research relating to three major considerations for commercialization strategies: intellectual property rights' strength; requisite complementary assets; and licensing/alliance transaction costs. The authors describe the options available to the innovator and explain how the attractiveness of alliances increases with the strength of the innovator's IPR position and the cost of acquiring complementary assets. The four distinct commercialization environments defined by these factors then are related to the likelihood an innovator will commercialize an invention through cooperation or competition. The chapter then applies the framework to five case

Technological Innovation: Generating Economic Results
Advances in the Study of Entrepreneurship, Innovation and
Economic Growth, Volume 18, 227–250
ISSN: 1048-4736/doi:10.1016/S1048-4736(07)00008-2

studies of start-up innovators in a major research university's business incubator.

1. INTRODUCTION

In this chapter we present a framework for evaluating commercialization strategies for start-up innovators in high-technology industries. Whether firms commercialize their inventions by entering the product market, competing head to head with incumbent firms, or form some type of alliance varies significantly across industries and inventions (Gans, Hsu, & Stern, 2002). Product market competition is common in the electronics industry where start-up innovators often overtake incumbent producers, while in biotechnology, alliances between new and incumbent firms are more common (Christensen, 1997; Lerner & Merges, 1998). Patterns in electronics are consistent with the Schumpeterian hypothesis that technological change sets in motion a process of creative destruction by which new firms, whose technological identities are often aligned with radical scientific discoveries, can replace incumbent firms' market position (Schumpeter, 1942). By contrast, in the so-called biotechnology revolution, incumbent pharmaceutical firms have avoided the Schumpeterian "gale of creative destruction" by forming alliances with small biotechnology firms (Higgins, 2006; Rothaermel & Thursby, 2006).

The framework we advocate is based on a stream of research that relates three major considerations for commercialization strategies. First, the strength of intellectual property rights (IPR). Second, the ability to acquire complementary assets (CA) needed to compete in the product market. Finally, the transaction costs in negotiating alliances or licenses (Gans, Hsu, & Stern, 2000; Gans et al., 2002; Gans & Stern, 2003a; Hsu, 2006). While this framework can be used to examine strategy for incumbent as well as start-up innovators (entrants), we will focus primarily on the latter.

The chapter is organized as follows. We first present the options available to an entrant and draw on this body of work to explain why the attractiveness of alliances, as compared to product market competition, increases with both the strength of the entrant's IPR position, as well as the cost of acquiring CA. These factors define four distinct commercialization environments that can be related to the likelihood that start-up innovators commercialize their inventions through cooperation or competition. We then use this framework to discuss five case studies of start-up innovators currently residing in the business incubator of a major U.S. university.

2. STRATEGIES FOR TECHNOLOGY ENTREPRENEURS

Fig. 1 illustrates the problem of a start-up firm that has an invention with commercial potential. The firm can choose to develop, manufacture, and market, a product based on the invention, or it can choose to form some type of alliance with an incumbent firm. An alliance could be as simple as a license to the incumbent to manufacture and sell the product, or it could involve a joint venture in which the entrant continues research and development of the invention and the incumbent takes over manufacturing or marketing. Choosing an alliance is what we call "cooperation," and entering the product market is "competition." For simplicity, think in terms of a single incumbent so that if an alliance is formed, the alliance will earn monopoly profits from the invention. How the entrant and incumbent split these profits will depend on the bargaining power of the two firms. In Fig. 1, π^{coop} represents the portion of alliance profits that accrue to the entrant. If the innovator decides to enter the product market itself, it will earn monopoly profits if the incumbent does not imitate her invention, or duopoly profits if the incumbent successfully imitates. The entrant's profits from choosing to enter the product market are denoted by π^{comp}.

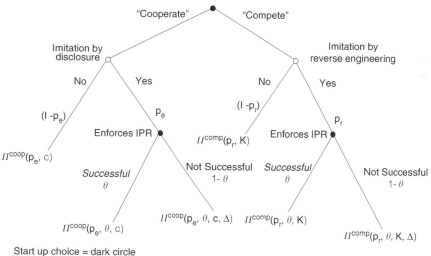

Start up choice = dark circle
Incumbent choice = hollow circle

Fig. 1. Start-up Choices and Payoffs. *Source:* Adapted from Gans et al. (2002).

Note that the entrant risks imitation by the incumbent with either route to commercialization. With probability p_r, the incumbent imitates the entrant's product by reverse engineering when the entrant chooses to compete, and with probability p_e the incumbent expropriates the technology once the entrant discloses the invention in the process of negotiating the alliance if the entrant chooses cooperation. If the entrant has patent protection on her invention, then with some positive probability (θ) she can enforce her patents through the courts. As shown in the figure, a high probability of successfully enforcing IPR increases the entrant's expected profits regardless of whether she competes or cooperates. The important point to realize, however, is that depending on the form of IPR, stronger rights will have other effects than simply raising the likelihood of successful enforcement in the courts. Clear legal rights to the invention are likely to reduce the transactions costs in negotiating an alliance. In addition, strong IPR reduces the threat of expropriation during the negotiation process since the entrant's expected profit from competing is higher. This will increase the share of monopoly profits the incumbent is willing to give the entrant in an alliance. Thus, stronger IPR raises the relative returns to cooperation.

If the entrant chooses cooperation, it bears transactions costs, which we denote by c regardless of the outcome of the negotiation. As noted above, these costs may be correlated with the clarity of property rights, but they also reflect uncertainty as to the value of the invention. For inventions that need further development before commercialization, the value of the invention will be known only with some uncertainty. In the case of university inventions, for example, almost 50% of the inventions licensed are no more than a proof of concept at the time of license; many of them are so embryonic that ultimate applications of the invention are unknown (Jensen & Thursby, 2001; Shane, 2000). In such situations, the availability of venture capital (VC) funding may serve to reduce transaction costs. Notice that these costs affect only the ultimate payoff from cooperation and not the costs associated with competition. Thus a decrease in transactions costs of negotiation increases the attraction of cooperation, *ceteris paribus*.

If the entrant chooses cooperation, it avoids the costs associated with the CA needed to directly enter the product market (see Chapter 2). If it chooses to compete, it bears these costs, denoted by K, regardless of the outcome of competition. Thus, an increase in either the importance of CA or the cost of acquiring these assets will increase the benefits from cooperation.

3. COMMERCIALIZATION ENVIRONMENTS

Whether competing or cooperating represents the more effective strategy, depends on the commercialization environment created by the interplay of all these factors. To see this, consider Gans and Stern's (2003a) rubric, which defines four distinct environments represented in Fig. 2.

Starting with the "Attacker's Advantage," IPR and CA are both considered weak. This occurs when legal means for protecting the entrant's IPR are either unavailable or considered ineffective, and the lack of CA is not an impediment to entry. In industries, such as the disk drive industry studied by Christensen (1997), incumbents may indeed be subject to the "gale of creative destruction" as innovators enter the product market with technologies that destroy the incumbent's lead. Industries in this quadrant are ones in which technological competition determines competitive advantage and that advantage is often short lived as new entrants continually threaten leadership positions. It is also important to recognize that in this environment, opportunities for contracting are limited. The relative benefits to new entrants from contracting with market leaders are few, and the entrant can gain an advantage by entering niche markets that are currently underserved by the leaders. In this environment there is an advantage to the entrant from maintaining its innovation as a secret, following a "stealth" entry strategy.

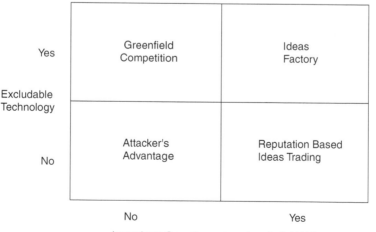

Fig. 2.   Commercialization Environments. *Source:* Gans and Stern (2003a).

This environment is quite different from the "Ideas Factory," which is defined by both strong IPR and CA that are costly to acquire and essential to product market entry. In this environment, contracting with established firms that control these assets has a substantial benefit. Moreover, formal mechanisms for protecting IPR are effective so that the risk of expropriation discussed earlier is relatively low. In this environment cooperation is the most effective strategy, and the returns to the entrant are determined in large part by the bargaining position. A strong patent portfolio allows the entrant both to disclose the new technology and to signal its value as a potential threat. Thus, when (as in contrast to Section II, where we assumed a single incumbent) there are multiple incumbents, the entrant may be able to strike an alliance with the one providing the best terms.

The pharmaceutical industry is a prime example of the Ideas Factory. In more than three decades since Cohen and Boyer's discovery of recombinant DNA in 1973 and Milstein and Kohler's discovery of cell fusion techniques for producing monoclonal antibodies in 1975, it has been common for new biotechnology firms to form alliances of various types with pharmaceutical companies. For the biotechnology firms, the alliances with pharmaceutical companies provide CA for commercialization of products; and for the pharmaceutical companies, the biotechnology firms provide critical expertise in new techniques for discovery as well as manufacturing and process development, bolstering their product pipelines (Galambos & Sturchio, 1998; Henderson, Orsenigo, & Pisano, 1999; Higgins & Rodriquez, 2006; Hoang & Rothaermel, 2005). By drawing on the expertise of biotech enterprises, incumbent firms have been able to adapt to the revolutionary innovations in molecular biology rather than becoming victims of a Schumpeterian gale of creative destruction (Gans et al., 2000; Hill & Rothaermel, 2003; Rothaermel & Hill, 2005).

In these two environments, the message for strategy is clear because the strength of IPR and complementary asset position both indicate the same strategy. As we shall see, the message is less clear in the two remaining environments, in which the strength of IPR and CA by themselves point to different strategies.

"Reputation-Based Ideas Trading" is defined by weak IPR and an environment in which CA determine the ability to succeed in the product market. In this environment, the entrant receives clear benefits from an alliance because CA are important and costly to acquire. Thus, it is difficult for start-ups to overturn incumbent firms' market position, which of course weakens the incentives for incumbents to form alliances. In this environment, whether alliances are common depends on the incumbent's attitude. At one extreme are cases like Bob Kearns, who invented the intermittent windshield wiper in the 1960s and approached Ford regarding a license. Ford rejected the license and expropriated the technology, and not until the 1990s did Kearns manage to enforce his patent (Gans & Stern, 2003a). This is in marked contrast to incumbent companies such as Cisco Systems and Intel, who in the 1990s provided internal incentives for their management that promoted alliance formation, both of whom consciously developed reputations for forming alliances.

Finally, "Greenfield Competition" is defined by strong IPR and an environment in which CA do not preclude market entry. Cooperative and competitive strategies both make sense in this environment. The entrant faces a relatively low risk of expropriation in approaching incumbent firms, but it is also feasible for the entrant to acquire the CA needed to enter the product market. Entrants in this environment continually threaten incumbents because turning technological innovations into effective products, rather than competencies per se, largely determine firm performance.

Notice that in all four environments, particularly those where alliances are beneficial but hard to arrange or negotiate, intermediaries can be important in determining the best strategy (Arora & Ceccagnoli, 2006; Hsu, 2006). For example, venture capitalists have well-established networks that improve start-up abilities, not only to find appropriate alliances, but also to reduce the threat of expropriation. Organizations such as the Association of University Technology Managers (AUTM) and the American Society of Composers, Authors and Publishers (ASCAP) provide a variety of services to promote licensing or other agreements.

4. WHEN DO WE SEE COMPETITION AND COOPERATION?

From the preceding discussion, it is clear that we would expect to see product market competition most often with the Attacker's Advantage and least often with the Ideas Factory. The likelihood of cooperation in the other two environments is less clear. While our discussion of pharmaceutical alliances, as well as Christensen's (1997) study of disk drives, are both consistent with the Gans and Stern framework, neither relates the probability of cooperative strategy specifically to strength of IPR and the importance or cost of CA.

For this we refer to Gans and Stern's (2003b) study of the commercialization strategies of 118 start-up companies that commercialized inventions. Sixty-three of the firms were backed by funding from the Small Business Innovation Research program (SBIR), and 55 were VC-funded. The study is based on a survey in which these firms provided information on their strategy for commercializing a single project as well as information on the IPR, CA, and funding associated with the project. In their statistical analysis of the results, Gans et al. (2000, 2002) labeled strategies as cooperative if the firm received revenue from either a license for its invention(s) or as part of an acquisition. Sixty-eight percent of the firms in the sample received their revenues solely from commercialization themselves, and 21% received their revenues solely from licenses or acquisition. The remainder received revenue by both means. As expected, the biotechnology firms in the sample were more likely to cooperate than others.

The study measured the IPR and complementary asset positions in several ways. The simplest measure of IPR was whether the project had at least one patent associated with it. Regarding CA, the survey asked respondents to indicate on a scale of 1–5 the importance of control over four types of assets. The four assets were manufacturing capability, distribution channels, brand name, and sales and service forces. The scores were then used to construct a measure of whether CA were of low or high importance (CA LOW or CA HIGH). Based on these measures, a firm without any patents associated with the project and CA LOW has the Attacker's Advantage. The probability a firm in this environment received any revenue from cooperation was .143. A firm with at least one associated patent and CA HIGH would be in the Ideas Factory with a .56 probability of receiving revenue from cooperation. The probability of cooperative revenue for firms in the Reputation-Based Ideas Trading quadrant was .308. With Greenfield Competition, the probability of cooperation was .346.

When practically applying the Gans and Stern rubric, it is important to realize that the number of patents may not accurately reflect the strength of the firm's IPR. Patents are only one of the legal mechanisms used to protect intellectual property and one that is often considered relatively ineffective in obtaining and sustaining a competitive advantage. For example, an early survey by Edwin Mansfield (1995) showed that, except in pharmaceuticals, manufacturing firms did not perceive the presence or absence of patent protection essential to successful innovation. Moreover, as discussed in

Chapter 1, several subsequent surveys showed that secrecy and other legal mechanisms (such as trademarks) are viewed as more effective than patents in many industries (Cohen, Nelson, & Walsh, 2000; Levin, Klevorick, Nelson, & Winter, 1987).

For this reason, Gans et al. (2002) asked respondents to indicate, on a scale of 1–5, the effectiveness of patents, litigation, and secrecy in deterring imitation of the technology. As discussed in Section II, effective patents and litigation should, all else equal, increase the relative benefits of cooperation, while secrecy favors either competition or keeping critical elements of the technology secret in the alliance. Indeed, the core result – that cooperation is more likely the stronger is IPR – holds up in the Gans et al. (2002) statistical analysis when measures based on patent and litigation effectiveness are taken into account.

Finally, in a separate study, Hsu (2006) examined the alliance behavior of 696 start-ups as a function of VC funding. As expected, he found that VC-backed firms in the sample were much more likely to engage in R&D alliances than those backed by SBIR funding. This result is robust to controlling for prior VC funding and the patent portfolio of the firms.

5. CASE STUDIES

In this section, we discuss five start-up firms with reference to the Gans and Stern rubric.[1] These case studies allow us to highlight some of the nuances that determine whether firms in the four commercialization environments decide to compete or cooperate. In particular, they allow us to highlight two important points. First, these environments are dynamic rather than static, with appropriate firm strategy changing quite rapidly in some cases. Second, both the strength of a company's IPR and its complementary asset position are endogenous, explaining some of the dynamics observed in practice.

The first two cases we describe are companies in the medical device industry, while the others operate either in software or electronics. For each case, we present a description of the company, the technology, relevant IPR, and CA needed for commercial application. We then discuss the company strategy for commercial exploitation of the technology in terms of the Gans and Stern rubric.

In all of the cases we consider, the companies have either applied for or been granted patents on the technology in question. So in evaluating their

IPR, it is important to think of these patents in the context of patent effectiveness in the industry in which the firm operates. For this we rely on results from Cohen et al.'s (2000) survey of industry views on the effectiveness of various mechanisms for protecting competitive advantage from innovations. The survey provides information on R&D managers' responses regarding the percentage of product and process innovations for which various mechanisms were effective. The mechanisms considered were patents, secrecy, other legal mechanisms (such as trademarks), as well as non-legal mechanisms such as lead time and complementary sales channels or services. Figs. 3 and 4 present the mean responses for firms in four industries: software, computers, biotech, and drugs.[2]

Several patterns should be noticed. First, patents are not considered the most effective mechanism in any of the industries. Second, except for secrecy in the biotech sector, none of the mechanisms is considered as effective for process innovations as for product innovations. Finally, the effectiveness of various mechanisms varies across industry sectors. In terms of the factors that define the Gans and Stern rubric, complementary sales channels or services are less important in the biotech sector than the others. With the exception of secrecy, which is considered relatively important in all four sectors, formal legal mechanisms are considered most important in the biotech and drug sectors.

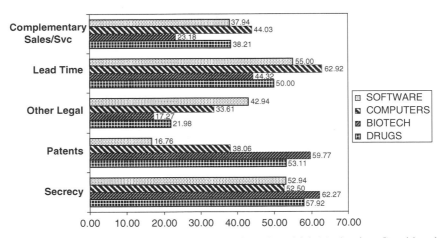

Fig. 3.   Mean Percentage of Product Innovations for which Mechanism Considered Effective (Q32). *Source:* Data provided by Wes Cohen from 1994 Carnegie Mellon Survey.

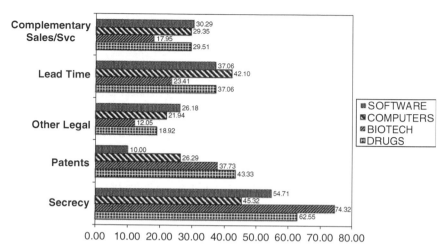

Fig. 4. Mean Percentage of Process Innovations for which Mechanism Considered Effective (Q33). *Source:* Data provided by Wes Cohen from 1994 Carnegie Mellon Survey.

5.1. BioWound

5.1.1. Company Background

Ralph Ruben was a biomedical engineering graduate student at the University of Alabama at Birmingham in the mid-1980s. He was doing research on tissue engineering and the re-growth of skin using very low-level electrical stimulation. After earning his Masters' he went to work in the health care industry but kept these ideas in the back of his mind. In October 2000 he founded this firm to commercialize a product using these ideas in the wound care industry. The firm was virtual with no full-time employees until summer 2005, when he and a colleague quit their day jobs and came on board full-time in the firm. Before having a single employee they had raised almost $6 million in seed funding. In October 2006 they raised an additional $5 million in series A venture funds. At the end of 2006 they had 10 employees, with 7 of those residing in the United Kingdom. The first product launched in the UK in November 2006 and is in post market surveillance study.

5.1.2. Technology

The core product uses very low-level electrical stimulation in both a diagnostic and a therapeutic modality for chronic wound care patients such as bed-ridden diabetes individuals. The configuration has changed markedly from beta trials with users and focus groups. The closest competing solution is a large vacuum pump arrangement solely for in-hospital use. The BioWound solution is a self-contained large bandage.

5.1.3. IPR
Three patents have been drafted by a well-known IP firm (Fish & Neave) and have been thoroughly vetted by BioWound's investors. All three are currently under examination at the U.S. Patent and Trademark Office (USPTO). As Ralph states, "Our main assets are our patents. The firm owns virtually nothing else." Also recall from the Cohen et al. (2000) study that patents are considered relatively effective in protecting competitive advantage in biotech areas. There is no university tie for the technology or patent work.

5.1.4. Competition and CA
Chronic wound healing is a $12B market worldwide and expected to continue growing. The gold standard product on the market today is a vacuum assisted closure (VAC) product sold by Kinetic Concepts Inc. (KCI). KCI started in 1976 with advanced therapeutic beds for hospitals. In 1995 they launched the VAC system based on technology they licensed from a university. The VAC product line by itself is generating nearly $1 billion in revenues yearly for KCI. Although regulatory approvals of this product are easier than in the pharmaceutical industry, significant approvals still are needed to market these wound healing devices to the public. In the U.S. a 510 (K) approval is required by the Food and Drug Administration (FDA). This technique is new to the application, so a full evaluation is expected unless the product is approved in another market first. Testing required for approval under European directives (CE mark) for medical devices can sometimes be helpful in shortening the U.S. FDA approvals. CE approval itself, however, can take three to five years with testing in Europe. A further market barrier is the medical reimbursement system, particularly in the U.S. market.

5.1.5. Strategy
Licensing was not considered because large firms only license proven technologies in this area. The original business plan was to sell through a distributor, but by 2006 the firm decided that direct sales were necessary to properly focus and optimize sales efforts with initial customers. The United Kingdom was chosen as the first market for several reasons, the primary one being a focused market served by less than 600 tissue-viability nurses. The UK market has been used by established firms such as Johnson & Johnson

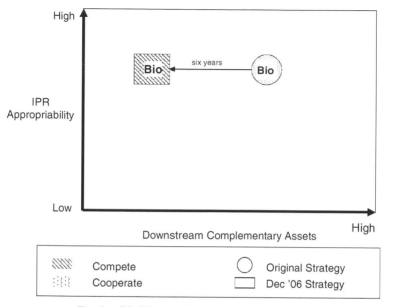

Fig. 5.   BioWound Changes from Founding.

for rollout of other new product families. Additionally, IPR control is easier in Europe than in more developing markets such as China and India. The firm considered a launch in Asia because of the projected high growth rates of the wound care market as well as the relative ease of regulatory approvals. However, the Asian nations' geographic size and marginal protection of intellectual property removed them from contention for the launch.

As shown in Fig. 5, BioWound started with a cooperative strategy and fit in the Ideas Factory quadrant of the Gans and Stern rubric. Over time, however, Ruben and his colleagues realized that by entering a market outside the U.S., they could lower the cost of acquiring CA. Thus, we have observed a change in BioWound's strategy to one of competition in the Greenfield Competition quadrant.

5.2. Medjoint

5.2.1. Company Background
The firm was started in April 2005 with a founding team of seven comprising two mechanical engineering faculty members, two graduate students, two medical doctors, and one senior executive retired from a Fortune 500 firm.

A CEO with both a scientific and a business background was brought on board towards the middle of 2006. The firm is using shape memory polymers in reconstructive surgery applications. In summer 2006 the firm received $1 million in grants and private placement funds. The firm had seven employees at the end of 2006 and expects to have medical devices for orthopedics cleared through the FDA in the next two to three years.

5.2.2. Technology
The core technology stems from research conducted with National Institutes of Health (NIH) and National Science Foundation (NSF) funding to the mechanical engineering department over the past 10 years. The principal investigator is closely involved with the firm, primarily in further development of the technology for commercial applications. The firm is developing a polymer product for knee surgery that would eliminate the need for threaded screws utilized in joint reconstruction. In addition, the company is developing an alloy-based product for ankle fusion as an alternative to limb amputation. This product has a pseudo-elastic property, which helps maintain compression during the ankle-healing process. Lack of such compression in titanium and stainless steel is a major cause for failures of ankle surgery.

5.2.3. IPR
The base IPR combines claims both on unique materials and on their application to orthopedic surgery. The firm has an exclusive license from the University of Colorado for certain IPR related to polymers and orthopedic applications. In addition, the firm has applied for patents on the use for knees and other joints and is developing patents on proprietary instrumentation and packaging. For the alloy materials, the firm has patented the application in the ankle. As in the case of BioWound, Medjoint is developing products in an industry where patents are relatively effective in protecting competitive advantage.

5.2.4. Competition and Complementary Assets
The medical device industry has several multi-billion dollar incumbent firms (i.e., J&J, Zimmer). The industry is expected to grow more than 10% each year because of aging and obesity demographics, particularly in the U.S. Currently the orthopedic fixation market space has one major device provider, and that firm is aggressive at protecting channel exclusivity. At the end of 2006, this new entrant was in discussions with several market players for strategic partnership possibilities.

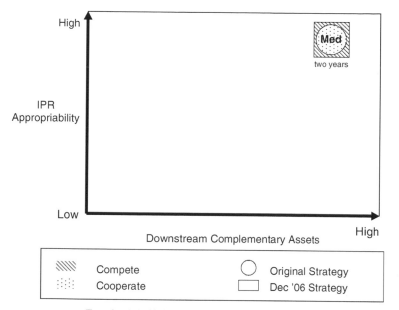

Fig. 6. Medjoint Changes from Founding.

5.2.5. Strategy

The start-up was at a decision point at the end of 2006, with two major options: (1) obtain VC funding to support FDA clearance and the development of sales and distribution channels; or (2) find a strategic partner(s) for collaboration in support of FDA clearance and to provide a channel to the market. Thus, Medjoint is in the Ideas Factory quadrant with strong IPR but also a high FDA hurdle and a need for CA. Medjoint is the only case in which the 'go to market' strategy has not markedly changed. Fig. 6 shows their location on the Gans and Stern grid. It is possible, however, that when the firm further develops its strategic direction in terms of competing or cooperating, it may find a need to move in terms of intellectual property or CA.

5.3. SensorTech

5.3.1. Company Background

Two students met during their MBA program. Each wanted to start a firm when they entered the program. They had no idea what type of firm they wanted to start and together began searching for opportunities during their MBA studies. This firm was founded in August 2004 with three founding partners: the two MBA students (COO and CEO) and one PhD student in mechanical engineering who became the CTO. At the end of 2006 they had three employees.

5.3.2. Technology

The key technology is a method of providing sensing for precision linear displacement positioning. It was developed in the machine dynamics lab of a mechanical engineering professor. A doctoral student developed this technology as an applied solution for his research. The invention was not core to the lab's research but rather was a byproduct of it. His advisor was a co-inventor on the patent and has been very helpful as an advisor to the firm. The firm was formed based on a prototype from the PhD student's research, so further development was needed by the firm in order to develop a 'market ready' product.

5.3.3. IPR

The first patent, still under review at the USPTO, is exclusively licensed from the university. The firm has applied for several additional patents on subsequent research conducted in the firm. Additionally, the electronics developed by the firm will work only with this integrated positioning system, so the founders believe the IPR position will ultimately be fairly strong even though they are still early in the process with the USPTO. Notice, however, if we assume the electronics industry is similar to the computer industry, the Cohen et al. (2000) study suggests that patents are less effective than lead time or other business strategies in protecting firm advantage. This idea is reinforced by the firm's getting a product into the marketplace while the underlying patents have not yet issued.

5.3.4. Competition and Complementary Assets

The product is in the precision sensor market space as part of the industrial automation and controls sector. Incumbent firms such as MTS Sensors, Renishaw and Kavlico are well established in the fluid power industry where precision sensing is very important. These firms have a broad range of product solutions to offer their customers. There are four different incumbent technologies, and this new technology for position sensing can work with all of them.

5.3.5. Strategy

The initial business plan for the firm was to compete in the sensor market with its own line of products. The firm strategy changed to producing solutions for original equipment manufacturers (OEMs) when the founders realized distribution of the product would be a significant challenge. The current business model is to perform customized engineering of solutions for these OEMs. They receive funds to do the up-front engineering and then sell the solution to the OEM who in turn sells it to an end user. This model provides a higher level of revenue and flexibility than a typical licensing arrangement. They intend to manufacture the core electronics in China and use the OEM path as the distribution. The firm expects to have its first products in the market in the first-half of 2007. Licensing could be a solution in different market segments where the OEM solution is not as viable.

Thus, in a relatively short period of time, SensorTech has moved from a competitive strategy to a cooperative one. As in the case with Medjoint, SensorTech needed costly downstream CA to make a profit, but SensorTech's IPR is weak relative to that of Medjoint. Thus, it is natural to think of SensorTech as positioned in the Reputation-Based Ideas Trading quadrant (Fig. 7).

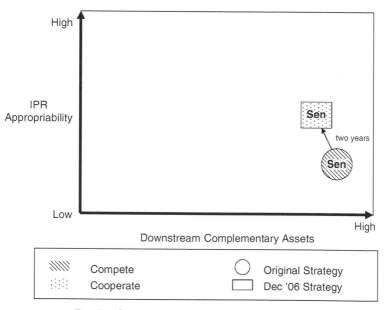

Fig. 7. SensorTech Changes from Founding.

5.4. Sync-Up

5.4.1. Company Background

A university professor and one of his graduate students started the company in April 2004 to exploit a novel approach to network multi-pathing that can be used to optimize wide area networks (WAN). In fall 2004, a skilled business partner was brought in as a consultant and he became the CEO in January 2005. At the end of 2006, the firm had four employees and three contractors. Funding of $2.5 million was received in November 2005, and plans were for a new round in early 2007. A nine-month beta test of the system was successfully completed, and a full market launch is expected for the first-half of 2007.

5.4.2. Technology

The technology was developed by an electrical engineering professor with seed funds from the NSF. The original research, completed in 2001, was to improve Internet connectivity performance in wireless applications. By 2003 the professor began to think he might have something of commercial value and went about forming a company to further develop the software algorithms needed to make his ideas work.

5.4.3. IPR

The underlying technology is owned by the university, which has applied for two patents currently under review at the USPTO. The firm has exclusive license rights for both patents. One of the patent applications included 51 claims and, if the claims remain on the issued patent, it should provide substantial IPR coverage. In addition, the firm has 10 more patents in various stages of application or review by the USPTO.

5.4.4. Competition and Complementary Assets

Security and regulatory pressures are pushing for a physical consolidation of corporate data centers using WAN connections. The incumbents in this nascent market (WAN optimization is about four years old and $500 million in size) are primarily small firms with patches and specific features to enhance particular performance problems. This firm's product can significantly improve communication performance from such data centers with its intelligent multi-pathing system, which eliminates the underlying cause of latency and delay in the network. However, the incumbents have already garnered the attention of information technology (IT) professionals and have influenced the specifications in requests for proposals (RFPs) for network improvements, making it more difficult to sell Sync-Up's radically different solution.

5.4.5. Strategy

The initial marketing efforts were to enterprise-wide IT departments. In its initial two years, Sync-Up learned that even though it is operating in a relatively young industry segment, where the standards used to generate RFPs are informal, these standards present a significant barrier to entry. This, of course, is an example of why lead time is considered the most important mechanism for attaining competitive advantage in the software products industry (recall Fig. 3). Given the significant entry barriers in the initial market segment, the firm is now evaluating alternatives. The recent growth of online gaming, voice over Internet protocol (VoIP) and video streaming sites, such as YouTube, has opened up different market opportunities for this technology to sell to Internet service providers. In this new market space, the same base technology can be packaged into a high-tier Internet application for the providers with end user software loaded to improve connectivity performance at the desktop PC level. Sync-Up's management and board of advisors are meeting in early 2007 to decide what market approach to pursue. The firm is evaluating both a distribution sales channel and selling product to an OEM under the Sync-Up brand name. Such an OEM agreement provides a revenue guarantee and fixed margin agreements which are important to a start-up firm. Fig. 8 shows the representation of this movement as the firm

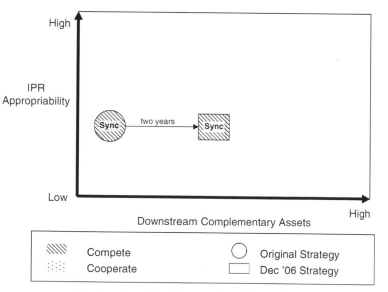

Fig. 8. Sync-Up Changes from Founding.

remains in a competitive strategy in the Attacker's Advantage quadrant but moves towards the Reputation-Based Ideas Trading with higher value on CA and cooperative strategy.

5.5. Overview

5.5.1. Company Background
The firm was started in September 2003 with five founders, after spending about four months to refine the concept and business plan for a software product to provide continual monitoring of financial transactions and alert a company if signs of exceptions or possible illicit activity are discovered. The initial funding came from angel investors followed by a VC round of funding in July 2004 after their first product sale. The firm had 25 employees and eight offshore contractors serving 30 customers at the end of 2006.

5.5.2. Technology
The core technology is in the software algorithms that provide continuous quality management of transaction data by looking for anomalies. The firm is enhancing its closed loop system with increasing functionality (coverage of areas such as travel expenses and general ledger items, in addition to the initial accounts payable module) and a more efficient core platform. The system runs as an application service provider (ASP). The software runs in the customer's data center and can be remotely accessed by Overview. This provides an enhanced level of independence needed for such audit functions rather than using customer employees to run the software directly.

5.5.3. IPR
Within the firm, all software is routinely copyrighted. Additionally, eight patents are in various stages of application and review, but the CEO noted that in software, a competitor can often write around a patent.

5.5.4. Competition and Complementary Assets
The incumbent solution is manual searches of financial records or a desktop auditor's toolkit that was originally produced about 20 years ago. Both options result in a periodic audit of a sample of the financial transactions and thus leave an opening for a continuous full audit product such as this.

5.5.5. Strategy
Overview originally planned to work in tandem with an established partner (or partners) to implement its continual monitoring system. There were

three obstacles to this approach. First, potential partners wanted Overview to show customer experience in which customers found value from using the product. Second, the large auditing firms who were most likely to partner with Overview had to be convinced that the product would not negatively impact their current business revenues. Finally, the potential partners wanted to evaluate how this monitoring system compared with something from large financial system providers such as Oracle or SAP. These concerns drove Overview to develop an internal direct sales force in competition with other firms in the market space.

Going forward, the firm can continue a direct sales channel to large organizations (their smallest current customer is $400 million in yearly sales) or move to referral from the major accounting firms (i.e., KPMG, PWC). Large software houses such as SAP and Oracle are a threat to both this technology and, more broadly, the third party accounting firms. Therefore, the importance of the independence of the audit is stressed over a possible future SAP application that could make something similar available directly to the large customers. Overview, like Sync-Up, is in a relatively weak intellectual property environment in the Attacker's Advantage quadrant. Fig. 9 shows Overview has moved from a cooperative strategy to

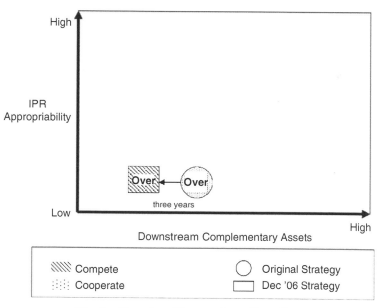

Fig. 9. Overview Changes from Founding.

a competitive one. Overview is now is a position to decide whether to stay in a competitive position and increase its installed base or to partner with a larger established firm.

6. CASE SUMMARY

Fig. 10 is a compilation of the beginning and ending positions for each of the case firms. The beginning strategy represents each firm in the business plan or incorporation stage. Three of the firms began with a plan to compete rather than cooperate, including two firms (Medjoint and SensorTech) with quite high value for CA.

Four of the five firms migrated during these early years into a different strategic position or market segment. Notice that three of the five firms initially were 'mismatched' with the prescriptions of the Gans and Stern rubric. Overview was located in Attacker's Advantage quadrant with a cooperative strategy while Medjoint and SensorTech were in the "Ideas" quadrants with strategies to compete. BioWound, Overview, and Sync-Up are now in the Greenfield Competition or Attacker's Advantage, all

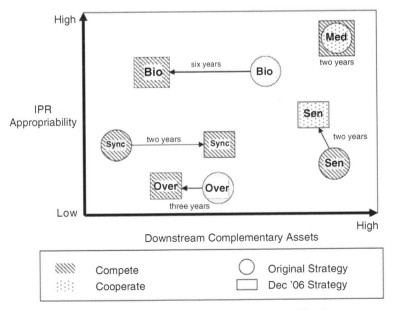

Fig. 10.   Start-up Examples (Changes Over Time).

competing with incumbents. This result is indeed what the Gans and Stern framework would have advised. SensorTech has switched to a cooperative strategy in the Reputation-Based Ideas Trading quadrant, which is also in line with the rubric. The remaining firm, Medjoint, is now in a decision process, but conversations with the CEO clearly indicate that he prefers an alliance and hopes a deal will be consummated, rather than pursuing VC funding and competing in Medjoint's chosen market space. This last result would put all five of the firms in alignment with Gans and Stern's rubric.

NOTES

1. All focal firms and individual names used here are synonyms.
2. We are grateful to Wesley Cohen for providing these data from the 1994 Carnegie Mellon Survey of manufacturers on the appropriability of R&D. Note the sample size for software is particularly small though the results shown here are consistent with our case research.

REFERENCES

Arora, A., & Ceccagnoli, M. (2006). Patent protection, complementary assets and firms: Incentives for technology licensing. *Management Science, 52*(2), 293–308.

Christensen, C. M. (1997). *The innovator's dilemma: When new technologies cause great firms to fail.* Boston, MA: Harvard Business School Press.

Cohen, W. M., Nelson, R. R., & Walsh, J. P. (2000). *Protecting their intellectual assets: Appropriability conditions and why U.S. manufacturing firms patent (or not).* Unpublished manuscript.

Galambos, L., & Sturchio, J. (1998). Pharmaceutical firms and the transition to biotechnology: A study in strategic innovation. *Business History Review, 72*(Summer), 250–278.

Gans, J.S., Hsu, D.H., & Stern, S. (2000). *When does start-up innovation spur the gale of creative destruction?* Unpublished manuscript.

Gans, J. S., Hsu, D. H., & Stern, S. (2002). When does start-up innovation spur the gale of creative destruction? *RAND Journal of Economics, 33*(4), 571–586.

Gans, J. S., & Stern, S. (2003a). The product market and the market for "Ideas": Commercialization strategies for technology entrepreneurs. *Research Policy, 32,* 333–350.

Gans, J. S., & Stern, S. (2003b). When does funding research by smaller firms bear fruit?: Evidence from the SBIR program. *Economics of Innovation and New Technology, 12*(4), 361–384.

Henderson, R. M., Orsenigo, L., & Pisano, G. P. (1999). The pharmaceutical industry and the revolution in molecular biology: Interactions among scientific, institutional, and organizational change. In: D. C. Mowery & R. R. Nelson (Eds), *The sources of industrial leadership.* Cambridge: Cambridge University Press.

Higgins, M. J. (2006). The allocation of control rights in pharmaceutical alliances. *Journal of Corporate Finance, 13*, 58–75.

Higgins, M. J., & Rodriquez, D. (2006). The outsourcing of R&D through acquisitions in the pharmaceutical industry. *Journal of Financial Economics, 80*, 351–383.

Hill, C. W. L., & Rothaermel, F. T. (2003). The performance of incumbent firms in the face of radical technological innovation. *Academy of Management Review, 28*(2), 257.

Hoang, H., & Rothaermel, F. T. (2005). The effect of general and partner-specific alliance experience on joint R&D project performance. *Academy of Management Journal, 48*(2), 332–345.

Hsu, D. H. (2006). Venture capitalists and cooperative start-up commercialization strategy. *Management Science, 52*(2), 204–219.

Jensen, R., & Thursby, M. C. (2001). Proofs and prototypes for sale: The licensing of university inventions. *The American Economic Review, 91*(1), 240–259.

Lerner, J., & Merges, R. (1998). The control of strategic alliances: An empirical analysis of the biotechnology industry. *Journal of Industrial Economics, 46*, 125–156.

Levin, R., Klevorick, A., Nelson, R. R., & Winter, S. (1987). Appropriating the returns from industrial research and development. Paper presented at the Brookings Papers on Economic Activity: Microeconomics.

Mansfield, E. (1995). Academic research underlying industrial innovations: Sources, characteristics, and financing. *The Review of Economics and Statistics, 77*, 55–65.

Rothaermel, F. T., & Hill, C. W. L. (2005). Technological discontinuities and complementary assets: A longitudinal study of industry and firm performance. *Organization Science, 16*(1), 52–70.

Rothaermel, F. T., & Thursby, M. C. (2006). The nanotech vs. the biotech revolution: Sources of productivity in incumbent firm research. *Research Policy, 36*, 832–849.

Schumpeter, J. A. (1942). *Capitalism, socialism and democracy.* New York: Harper & Brothers.

Shane, S. (2000). Prior knowledge and the discovery of entrepreneurial opportunities. *Organization Science, 11*(4), 448–469.

PART IV:
FINANCING INNOVATION

CHAPTER 9

INTRODUCTION TO FINANCE AND VALUING EARLY STAGE TECHNOLOGY

Matthew J. Higgins

ABSTRACT

The purpose of this chapter is to serve as a basic guide to introduce the reader to different types of valuation techniques utilized when valuing new technologies. The goal is to familiarize the reader with the differing techniques along with some of the issues in utilizing them. The chapter begins with the foundation of corporate finance – the time value of money – and moves through brief discussions on discounted cash flow, decision tree analysis, Monte-Carlo analysis, and real option analysis. The chapter ends with a discussion emphasizing the need to place valuation into a larger context of firm control rights and ownership.

1. INTRODUCTION

The purpose of this chapter is to serve as a basic guide to introduce the reader to different types of valuation techniques utilized when evaluating and valuing new technologies. It is meant to serve not as a comprehensive guide but rather as one that will familiarize the reader with different techniques and

Technological Innovation: Generating Economic Results
Advances in the Study of Entrepreneurship, Innovation and
Economic Growth, Volume 18, 253–285
Copyright © 2008 by Elsevier Ltd.
ISSN: 1048-4736/doi:10.1016/S1048-4736(07)00009-4

some of the issues with using them. Part of this exercise is *science* – there are clear mathematical formulas that can be used to process information. However, much of this exercise will be *art*, in that a significant amount of time will be spent trying to categorize and evaluate a new technology. The mathematical models and formulae are only as effective as the quality of the information that is supplied to them. The familiar adage "GIGO" ("garbage in, garbage out") is extremely relevant to this discussion.

Uncertainty is an on-going issue that will be continually addressed throughout this chapter. Many types of uncertainty exist: uncertainty with respect to a project's probability of success; uncertainty with respect to the actual market that will be served; uncertainty that the market will be there when a product arrives; and uncertainty with respect to project costs and revenues. These are but a few of the uncertainties faced when attempting to place a valuation on a new technology or venture.

While all of these challenges exist in the valuation of new technologies, they do not suggest that one should just simply throw their hands up in the air and not attempt a rigorous valuation exercise. Completing a valuation is something that cannot be done within a black box. It is an exercise that must be put into a larger context. Valuations become important when entrepreneurs attempt to solicit funding. Having a firm understanding of one's own value will enable valuations others place on your firm to be placed into context. In addition, valuation is often just one component of a term sheet or an alliance agreement. As a result, value should be viewed as something that can be negotiated up or down with respect to other control rights.

The rest of this chapter is organized as follows: Section 2 discusses how research and development (R&D) is funded; basic valuation concepts are discussed in Section 3; early stage valuation techniques are presented in Section 4; the influence valuation plays in the greater context of control rights is discussed in Section 5; and Section 6 concludes.

2. HOW IS R&D FINANCED?

There are several potential outlets for R&D funding for small entrepreneurial firms. Not all of these outlets will be available for entrepreneurs at any given time. However, they will often become available as firms or technologies mature. In general, nine venues are available for financing: (1) friends/family/ bootstrap investors, (2) "angel" investors, (3) government, (4) internal corporate funds, (5) banks, (6) public debt markets, (7) public equity markets, (8) strategic alliance partners, and (9) venture capitalists (Metrick, 2006).

For early-stage technologies and firms, many of these options are not available. For example, banks will often not provide financing unless owners are willing to commit personal assets as collateral. The public debt markets are mostly closed for early-stage research, which is viewed as too risky. Internal funds are often lacking, which necessitates looking for financing in the first place. Public equity markets become a possible option, but only at a more mature point in a firm's product life cycle. This leaves individuals, angel investors, government, venture capitalists, and strategic alliance partners.

Individuals and angel investors are probably the earliest places where financing becomes available. As the technology or firm progresses, there is the potential to enter the venture capital (VC) market. VC money can be expensive in terms of control rights and ownership of a firm. Notwithstanding this cost, VCs can often help provide complementary activities to aid in the general management of a small firm. In addition, if the firm or technology matures far enough, VCs can position the firm for an initial public offering. Unfortunately, even VCs may not be interested in investing in some projects due to risk of failure. For example, in the case of many biotechnology firms, projects in the earliest stages of pre-clinical testing often have trouble finding VC funding.

In this type of situation, strategic partnerships with large firms in an industry have helped fill this research funding gap (Higgins, 2007). For example, pharmaceutical firms provided over $1 billion in alliance financing to biotechnology firms in 2000.[1] Most often these alliance agreements involve combinations of upfront payments, milestone payments, and royalties that further add to this figure (Higgins, 2007).

These different sources of funding will not necessarily alter the valuation made on a project or a firm. However, as will be discussed in Section 5, valuation should not be done in a vacuum. Very often valuation is tied to other types of control rights whereby firms give up ownership in specific aspects of a product or firm. This makes the initial valuation, which can be used as a starting point, all the more important.

3. BASIC VALUATION CONCEPTS

3.1. Time Value of Money

The first building block to understanding valuation is the concept of time value of money or TVM. TVM will help provide an understanding of why a dollar received at some point in the future is worth less than a dollar received today, or, why one can invest less than a dollar today and receive one dollar in the future. Many of us were unknowingly introduced to the general concept of TVM as a child if you were a fan of Popeye. The phrase, "I will gladly pay you Tuesday for a hamburger today" was oft spoken by hamburger lover J. Wellington Wimpy. Clearly, however, he was wiser than he was given credit for, because he went around consuming hamburgers today while paying for them "on Tuesday" at today's prices. While the time difference ("future") is minimal, the example still illustrates the general underlying notion.

Assume for a moment that you own a piece of beach property and you want to sell it. Yesterday your realtor called and presented you with an offer of $100,000. You were ready to accept the offer when you received a second offer of $114,240. This second offer, however, is payable in one year from the time of sale. Which offer should you choose? Your decision will be based on whether the additional $14,240 in the second offer sufficiently compensates you for the use of $100,000 for one year. If the answer is no, then you should take the first offer. However, if the answer is yes, then you should accept the second offer. Let us evaluate the options.

If you accept the first offer you will be paid $100,000 today. Assume that you can invest that money at an insured rate of return of 8 percent for the next year. At the end of the year you would have

$$\$100,000 + (0.08 \cdot \$100,000) = \$100,000 + \$8,000 = \$108,000$$

$$\text{Principal} + \text{Interest} = \text{Payoff}$$

This first offer has a next year pay off of only $108,000 versus the second offer of $114,240. As a result, you would be better off in taking the second offer. One issue overlooked in this analysis is the probability of default in the second option. Clearly, if the buyer defaults then you would receive no money in the following year. Such complications are easily dealt with through the use of insurance. The cost of the insurance would simply be deducted from the overall payment and the new value would then be compared with $108,000.

This example serves as a demonstration of the *future value* (FV) of money for one time period. The FV of money can be generalized to n periods by the equation:

$$FV = PV \cdot (1 + r)^n \tag{1}$$

where PV (*present value*) is the value of a dollar at time, $t = 0$; FV the value of a dollar at time, $t = n$ in the future; r the interest rate that would be compounded for each period of time; and n the period of time you want to equate.

The previous example could also have been considered in terms of PV instead of FV. In that case the analysis would have been performed slightly differently. The concern would be what the second offer was worth today versus what the first offer was worth at the end of the year. This is derived by simply re-arranging Eq. (1) and solving for PV:

$$PV = FV/(1 + r)^n \qquad (2)$$

In the previous example this would equate to

$$PV = \$114,240/(1 + 0.08)^1$$
$$PV = \$105,777.78$$

The second offer has a larger PV than the first offer. Regardless of the way in which the two offers are analyzed, either in terms of PV or FV, the end result is the same: offer two remains the better choice.

This analysis answers an important question: what rate of return would have to be offered in order to make one offer better than the other? Again, the answer can be found by re-arranging Eq. (1):

$$(1 + r)^n = FV/PV$$
$$(1 + r) = (FV/PV)^{(1/n)}$$
$$r = (FV/PV)^{(1/n)} - 1 \qquad (3)$$

This would suggest an insured return of

$$r = (\$114,240/\$100,000)^{(1/1)} - 1$$
$$r = 14.24\%$$

in order to equate the two offers. The specific determination of r will be discussed later. Clearly, when thinking about the valuations of new technologies, the risks associated with these types of projects will have an impact on the magnitude of r.

One caveat needs to be remembered when using these derivations. In the example above the time period was arbitrarily set to one year. N does not necessarily need to be in years; however, the value for r needs to be expressed in the same time units as n. Assume for a moment that in the above example n is two years instead of one. This would imply a PV of

$$PV = \$114,240/(1 + 0.08)^2$$
$$PV = \$97,942.38$$

N can also be expressed in months, so instead of n equaling 2, n would now equal 24. If the units of n are changed then r needs to be converted from an annualized value to a monthly value as well. In this case r would be divided by 12 to generate a monthly interest rate of 0.67 percent. The new PV becomes

$$PV = \$114,240/(1 + 0.0067)^{24}$$
$$PV = \$97,400.61$$

N can also be expressed as a daily rate in which case n would grow to 730 (daily for two years) and r would fall to 0.000219 generating a PV:

$$PV = \$114,240/(1 + 0.000219)^{730}$$
$$PV = \$97,363.91$$

If the rate of return is continuous then the PV becomes

$$PV = FV \cdot e^{-(r \cdot n)}$$
$$PV = \$114,240 \cdot e^{-(0.08 \cdot 2)}$$
$$PV = \$97,348.90$$

This caveat demonstrates two important ideas. First is the need to ensure that the time period is consistent between n and r. Second, the PV of the investment continues to fall as the compounding period decreases from discrete (e.g., annual or monthly) to continuous time.

3.2. Discounted Cash Flow

In corporate finance, discounted cash flow (DCF) is nothing more than the application of the TVM to valuing a project or a stream of income. DCF analysis is the gold standard of valuation techniques and is used extensively throughout corporate America. DCF analysis simply determines the PV of future cash flows by discounting them using an appropriate discount rate or cost-of-capital. However, like all models, the valuations will only be as good as the assumptions made with respect to projected cash flows and the discount rate. Incorrect valuations do not imply the model is "wrong," but rather imply that the assumptions made are inaccurate. Forecasting the future, never an easy prospect, is made all the more difficult when dealing with valuations for high-risk projects. Expect to utilize relatively high discount rates for high-risk ventures.

The first step in conducting a DCF analysis is to project actual cash flows. This is an accounting exercise and is beyond the scope of this chapter. Suffice it to say, with almost all new ventures there will be a period, often significant in the case of the biopharmaceutical industry, of negative cash flows before the project or venture becomes cash flow positive.

The next step is to determine an appropriate value for r or, as Razgaitis (2003) refers to it, the "risk-adjusted hurdle rate" or (RAHR). On one extreme, r can take the value of a *risk-free* rate of return – often associated with the 10-year Treasury. While this is deemed risk-free in that it is backed by the U.S. government, its rate has changed dramatically over time. For example, in the 1980s, the 10-year rate peaked at over 15 percent. Over the last five years, however, the rate has been below 5.5 percent. This shows that the notion of risk-free rate of return can change over time. If r is allowed to simply equal the rate of inflation, for example 2.5 percent, then the value of $1,000 received three years from now is

$$DCF = \$1,000/(1 + 0.025)^3$$
$$DCF = \$928.60$$

In other words, assuming inflation stayed constant over this time period, one should be indifferent between receiving $928.60 now or $1,000 three years from now.

If the example is slightly modified such that $1,000 is received in each year for the next three years, given the same rate of inflation, DCF becomes

$$DCF = \$1,000/(1 + 0.025)^1 + \$1,000/(1 + 0.025)^2 + \$1,000/(1 + 0.025)^3$$
$$DCF = \$2,856.12$$

In this case, the *net present value* (NPV) of receiving $1,000 payments in each of the next three years using only the rate of inflation is $2,856.12. The term "NPV" is now used since multiple cash flows (which can be positive or negative) are summed over time.

Returning to the previous example, if r increases to reflect the T-Bill rate of 5.5 percent, the PV becomes

$$DCF = \$1,000/(1 + 0.055)^3$$
$$DCF = \$851.61$$

As the value of r or the RAHR begins to increase, the initial investment required to generate that return gets smaller. In terms of valuation of a new venture or technology, the higher value placed on r – primarily due to risk – the *lower* will be that project's current valuation. Clearly, along with the projections made for a project's future cash flows, another area which is debatable is the correct value for r. Investors have the incentive to push r up as high as possible, while entrepreneurs have the incentive to push r as low as possible.

As one moves up the spectrum in terms of costs of capital, investment grade corporate bonds are a logical next step beyond the 10-year T-bill. Over the past 30 years, the average Moody's Aaa rated bond had a rate of 8.77 percent.[2] Move down the investment ladder to Moody's Bbb rated bonds and the rate increases slightly to an average of 9.84 percent over the same time period. These rates are consistent with the cost of borrowing for higher quality firms. Rates of borrowing or the required rate of return for an individual project, even within these firms, *should* exceed the firm's cost of borrowing.[3] As such, an entrepreneur can expect values for r for new technologies or ventures to greatly exceed these lower bound references.

One often-used rate in a broader corporate finance context is the weighted-average cost of capital or WACC (Brealey, Meyers, & Allen, 2005). WACC is a firm's cost of capital based on a combination of equity and debt and is defined as follows:

$$
\begin{aligned}
\text{WACC} = &[(\% \text{ debt}) \bullet (\text{after} - \text{tax cost of debt})] \\
&+ [(\% \text{ equity}) \bullet (\text{cost of equity})]
\end{aligned}
\tag{4}
$$

The value generated can serve as a floor with respect to expected rates of return for projects. Unfortunately, WACC is of little use to a start-up or entrepreneurial firm. These firms are not involved, for the most part, in the public equity or debt markets. The underlying variables needed to generate a WACC are just not realistic for these types of firms. That said, the discussion involving WACC will be returned to when discussing the use of industry comparables below.

Several authors have suggested broad values of r based on varying degrees of risk. Brealey et al. (2005) offer four recommendations:

30%	for speculative ventures
20%	for new products
15%	for expansion of existing business
10%	for cost improvement of known technology

Razgaitis (2003), however, provides a much more complex range of values. His values range from 10 to 18 percent (approximating the cost of corporate borrowing) for risk-free types of projects, for example, plant expansion for an existing product to 20 to 25 percent for a new product utilizing a well-understood technology. He offers ranges of 30–40 percent and 35–45 percent for projects for new technologies servicing existing and new market segments. Most, if not all, early stage technologies will fall into these latter two categories.

Fig. 1 demonstrates the impact these ranges of *r* can have on an NPV calculation. The example is similar in length to the product development time faced in the pharmaceutical industry where the average development time runs approximately 12–15 years (DiMasi, 2001). Negative cash flows during periods 1–10 correspond to expenditures on R&D. Positive cash flows occur over time periods 11–16. If *r* equals zero percent, the NPV of the project is $2.9 billion; however, this is obviously not realistic. By looking at the impact of values for *r* that range between 12 and 35 percent, the project's NPV swings from positive to negative. Fundamentally, following the NPV method, the choice to invest or not invest in a project would depend on the choice of *r*. The importance in its determination cannot be overstated.

Assume for a moment that a correct *r* can be determined (and agreed upon by all concerned). The next logical question is: should this *r* be used in valuing the entire project? Does a project's risk profile remain constant throughout its entire development process? Clearly, in the case of drug development, the probability that a drug candidate makes it to market significantly increases as it advances through the various stages of clinical testing. If risk changes through time, it seems logical that the value of *r* should change to reflect these changes in risk. One solution to this problem is to use a weighted-NPV or decision tree-type analysis that will reflect changing risk parameters. This issue will be explored in more detail later.

4. VALUATION TECHNIQUES FOR EARLY STAGE TECHNOLOGY

4.1. Comparables

Projecting financials for an established firm is still not an exact science. Attempting to do so for an early stage technology is much less a science than

	r	1	2	3	4	5	6	7	8	9	10	11	12	13	14	15	16	NPV
Cash Flow	0%	-25	-25	-30	-30	-45	-45	-50	-50	-75	-150	250	500	750	850	800	300	2925
DCF	12%	-22.32143	-19.92985	-21.35341	-19.06554	-25.53421	-22.7984	-22.61746	-20.19416	-27.04575	-48.29599	71.86903	128.3375	171.8806	173.9268	146.157	48.9365	491.9514
DCF	25%	-20	-16	-15.36	-12.288	-14.7456	-11.79648	-10.48576	-8.388608	-10.06633	-16.10613	21.47484	34.35974	41.23169	37.3834	28.1475	8.444249	35.8045
DCF	35%	-18.51852	-13.71742	-12.19326	-9.032047	-10.03561	-7.433783	-6.11834	-4.532104	-5.035671	-7.460253	9.210189	13.64472	15.16081	12.72759	8.873265	2.464796	-31.99564

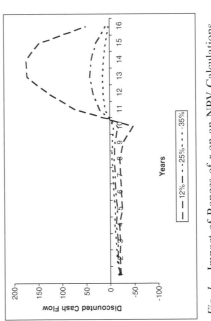

Fig. 1. Impact of Ranges of *r* on an NPV Calculations.

an art. Clearly, some "practical" rules based upon experience can be applied, but these are general and their applicability to varying technologies is questionable, at best. One of the easiest ways – but not without serious concerns – around this problem is simply to try to find a firm or project that is very similar and use that firm's financials or valuations as an initial starting point (Boer, 1999).

Recall that WACC is defined as

$$\text{WACC} = [(\% \text{ debt}) \bullet (\text{after-tax cost of debt})] + [(\% \text{ equity}) \bullet (\text{cost of equity})]$$

The cost of equity (cost of equity = risk-free rate + risk premium) contains a calculation for risk premium. This risk premium is determined as the product of a firm's beta, β, and market premium:

$$\text{Risk premium} = \beta \bullet \text{market premium} \qquad (5)$$

The market premium is easily obtained from the capital asset pricing model (CAPM). However, while the determination of market premium is relatively straightforward, where does one get a beta for a firm that is private? Options are limited and include finding a comparable firm that is publicly traded and using that firm's beta value.

There are several problems with this approach. First, by using the comparables method, there is a strong assumption of similarity between the two firms. However, given possible life-cycle differences between very early stage technology ventures and public firms, these "similarities" should be viewed suspiciously. Second, if the goal is to value a technology versus an entire firm, then using a firm-level beta value may be problematic. Beta measures the correlation between stock movements with respect to a benchmark index. Using a firm-level beta to indirectly generate a WACC for a project that in all likelihood has a much higher risk profile may not be appropriate.

This is not to suggest that the comparable method is without some merit. It has its uses, for example in trying to generate projected financials, ratios, and/or sales and marketing data. This use becomes more relevant if the technology competes with or replaces an existing product. Looking at comparable firms, especially over time, may give the entrepreneur some indication of the type of sales projections they might reasonably expect.

Comparables are used extensively in two situations. First, venture capitalists will often generate a valuation for a firm or technology based on similar past experiences. This is advantageous if the venture capitalist believes that the risk/reward profile matches that of the previous venture which was funded. At a minimum, use of comparables provides the venture capitalist a starting point at which to begin a valuation analysis. Second, firms that utilize real options analysis, discussed later, are able to build up a portfolio of risk profiles on which they can draw upon to generate volatility measures, which will be a necessary condition for this type of analysis. Pharmaceutical firms are a good example of firms that conduct large amounts of R&D and as a result are able to build a relatively large risk profile for research.

The use of comparables has a place in analyzing or determining where a firm or technology *may* end up. However, one should be cautious in looking to public or more established firms and trying to use their financials and risk profiles for purposes of valuation.

4.2. Discounted Cash Flow/Decision Tree Analysis

RAHR or r played an important role in the resulting NPV of the previous hypothetical drug development project. As r increases in value, which reflects a more adequate level of risk for projects utilizing new technologies, the NPV of the project turns negative. Traditionally, if a potential project has a positive NPV value, then it should be considered by the firm for investment (Brealey et al., 2005). However, if the project has a negative NPV value, then the investment should be rejected. As a result, under a traditional analysis, the hypothetical drug development project would be rejected for r values at or above 30 percent.

An important assumption implicit in this type of analysis is not appropriate for most, if not all, early stage technology valuation. The assumption is that each of the projected cash flows, either positive or negative, will be realized with certainty (Metrick, 2006). Clearly, this is an overly strong assumption, especially when dealing with nascent technologies. In general, the failure rates of these projects tend to be very high. As a result, it is not appropriate to assume that cash flows will be realized with certainty. In addition to failure, this basic analysis overlooks the firm's ability to terminate a project at each stage of development. This flexibility has value.

One possible solution to this problem is to build a decision tree and generate probabilities for each stage. Doing so, however, adds another layer of complexity into the analysis. Assumptions have to be made regarding development time and costs, projected cash flows, and values for r.

Probabilities that a technology will actually advance from one stage to the next have to be derived. This task is more difficult in some industries than in others. Largely, it is a function of the volume of R&D taking place and the kind of information being disseminated. For example, in the pharmaceutical industry, probabilities (or at least ranges of probabilities) are available for some drug candidates within specific therapeutic categories based upon prior experience. Unfortunately, even in the pharmaceutical industry, probabilities become suspect when considering newer biotechnology-based therapies. The failure rate in this area is relatively high. As a result, the ability to generate reliable probabilities is generally low.

With this caveat in mind, let's begin to build a decision tree. First, consider the following example:

Example: Rubicon Inc. is a small biotech firm serving a niche market, developing a product to treat a rare disease. The development process is long – estimated to be 10 years before potential launch. Unfortunately, Rubicon Inc. is cash-constrained. Thus, management has decided to approach a large pharmaceutical company for alliance financing; however, first they want to value the potential product so they are better able to evaluate an offer.

Because the example deals with the hypothetical development of a drug, the individual stages of development are consolidated into pre-clinical, phase I, phase II, phase III, and FDA approval. The three stages of phase testing correspond to the three stages of human clinical trials, and FDA approval corresponds to the submission process to the FDA.[4] We will also assume that the firm will incur some start-up manufacturing and marketing expense in year 10.

Table 1 consolidates the DCFs from Fig. 1 and combines them into these five more-defined stages of development. For demonstrative purposes, the pre-clinical stage will take three years and cost $51.4 million; phase I will last two years and cost $27.0 million; phase II will last two years and cost $22.3 million; phase III will last two years and cost $18.5 million; and finally, FDA application and launch will last one year and cost $16.1 million. Recall that these costs are all summed across the respective years and then *discounted back to the present*. The NPV of the project from pre-clinical to launch is an estimated *negative* $135 million.

Assume that the product has only five viable years of regulatory protection before a generic is able to come on the market and compete.[5] We will also

Table 1. Cumulative Report of DCFs from Fig. 1 and Combines them
into Five More-Defined Stages of Development.

	Year	Cash Flow (Million, $)	Discount Factor	DCF (Million, $)	Sum of DCF by Stage (Million, $)
Pre-clinical	1	−25	0.8	−20.0	−51.4
	2	−25	0.64	16.0	
	3	−30	0.512	−15.4	
Phase I	4	−30	0.4096	−12.3	−27.0
	5	−45	0.32768	−14.7	
Phase II	6	−45	0.262144	−11.8	−22.3
	7	−50	0.209715	−10.5	
Phase III	8	−50	0.167772	−8.4	−18.5
	9	−75	0.134218	10.1	
FDA application	10	−150	0.107374	−16.1	−16.1
Base sales	11	250	0.085899	21.5	
	12	500	0.068719	34.4	
	13	750	0.054976	41.2	
	14	850	0.04398	37.4	
	15	800	0.035184	28.1	
	16	300	0.028147	8.4	171.0
					35.8

assume that there are some sales still in the sixth year but those then fall off to zero after that year.[6] The discounted value of these cash flows is a *positive* $171 million. Combining the outflows with the inflows results in a *positive* NPV; hence it is in the company's interest to pursue the project.

For comparative purposes (and to demonstrate the influence of the choice of *r*), Table 2 replaces *r* with 12 percent, instead of 25 percent. With the same exact assumptions on cash inflows and outflows the NPV rises to almost $500 million. A little over 50 percent reduction in the value of *r* results in a dramatic increase in NPV from $35 million to almost $500 million. This should solidify the importance that *r* holds in the overall valuation of a project and/or technology.

Instead of one base projection for sales, now let us assume some variance in projected sales. R&D costs may be relatively predictable; however, sales that are realized many years in the future are less so. As a result, three assumptions are made with respect to sales. In Table 3, when *r* is equal to 25 percent, the three assumptions will be an average case, a low case, and a high case with respect to sales. The average case will assume discounted total revenues of $171 million. The low case will

Table 2. For Comparative Purposes *r* is Replaced with 12 Percent Instead of 25 Percent.

	Year	Cash Flow (Million, $)	Discount Factor	DCF (Million, $)	Sum of DCF by Stage (Million, $)
Pre-clinical	1	−25	0.892857	−22.3	−63.6
	2	−25	0.797194	−19.9	
	3	−30	0.71178	−21.4	
Phase I	4	−30	0.635518	−19.1	−44.6
	5	−45	0.567427	−25.5	
Phase II	6	−45	0.506631	−22.8	−45.4
	7	−50	0.452349	−22.6	
Phase III	8	−50	0.403883	−20.2	−47.2
	9	−75	0.36061	−27.0	
FDA application	10	−150	0.321973	−48.3	−48.3
Base sales	11	250	0.287476	71.9	
	12	500	0.256675	128.3	
	13	750	0.229174	171.9	
	14	850	0.20462	173.9	
	15	800	0.182696	146.2	
	16	300	0.163122	48.9	741.1
					492.0

assume revenues of $112 million, and the high case, revenues of $233 million. Table 4 presents these same three categories but for an *r* of 12 percent.

Introducing a variance to sales is reasonable – one truly never knows how the market will respond to a product. In addition, as will be shown below, introducing a variance in sales will actually generate additional value, even if the probabilities associated with the variance are small. This is primarily due to the amount of value that is captured in the right tail in the high case (Metrick, 2006).

The hypothetical project's various stages are now aggregated. The next order of business is to determine the probability of moving from one stage to the next. For some products in some industries these probabilities will be more easily obtained. In other industries, for example biotechnology, the probabilities might be much more difficult. For an oncology drug, the probability that a drug candidate moves from one stage to the next will be much smaller than that probability for a cholesterol or allergy drug. This information, however, will become critical in order to complete a weighted NPV/decision tree analysis.

Table 3.   Three Assumptions Namely Average Sales, Low Sales and
High Sales when *r* is 25 Percent.

	Year	Cash Flow (Million, $)	Discount Factor	DCF (Million, $)	Sum of DCF by Stage (Million, $)
Base sales	11	250	0.085899	21.5	
	12	500	0.068719	34.4	
	13	750	0.054976	41.2	
	14	850	0.04398	37.4	
	15	800	0.035184	28.1	
	16	300	0.028147	8.4	171.0
Low sales	11	185	0.085899	15.9	
	12	350	0.068719	24.1	
	13	500	0.054976	27.5	
	14	500	0.04398	22.0	
	15	500	0.035184	17.6	
	16	200	0.028147	5.6	112.6
High sales	11	400	0.085899	34.4	
	12	750	0.068719	51.5	
	13	900	0.054976	49.5	
	14	1,100	0.04398	48.4	
	15	1,000	0.035184	35.2	
	16	500	0.028147	14.1	233.0

A decision tree based upon the various research stages is presented in Fig. 2. Assume for the hypothetical product in development the following probabilities of proceeding to the next stage are reasonable:

Pre-clinical to phase I	33%
Phase I to phase II	50%
Phase II to phase III	75%
Phase III to FDA approval	85%

From this chart, there is a 67 percent chance that the product is terminated after the pre-clinical stage. Likewise, there is a 16.5 percent chance that the candidate clears pre-clinical testing and then is terminated after phase I testing ($0.33 \times 0.50 = 0.165$). Continuing with the same methodology, we can generate the remaining probabilities that a drug

Table 4. Three Assumptions Namely Average Sales, Low Sales and High Sales when *r* is 12 Percent.

	Year	Cash Flow (Million, $)	Discount Factor	DCF (Million, $)	Sum of DCF by Stage (Million, $)
Base sales	11	250	0.287476	71.9	
	12	500	0.256675	128.3	
	13	750	0.229174	171.9	
	14	850	0.20462	173.9	
	15	800	0.182696	146.2	
	16	300	0.163122	48.9	741.1
Low sales	11	185	0.287476	53.2	
	12	350	0.256675	89.8	
	13	500	0.229174	114.6	
	14	500	0.20462	102.3	
	15	500	0.182696	91.3	
	16	200	0.163122	32.6	483.9
High sales	11	400	0.287476	115.0	
	12	750	0.256675	192.5	
	13	900	0.229174	206.3	
	14	1,100	0.20462	225.1	
	15	1,000	0.182696	182.7	
	16	500	0.163122	81.6	1,003.1

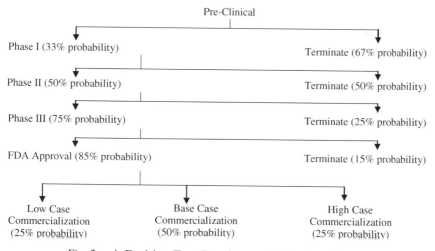

Fig. 2. A Decision Tree Based upon the Various Stages.

candidate reaches a particular stage and then terminates:

Pre-clinical/stop	67.00%
Phase I/stop	16.50%
Phase II/stop	4.12%
Phase III/stop	1.85%

With respect to projected revenues, assume that if the drug candidate receives FDA approval, there will be a 50 percent probability that the revenues will be the "average" case. The remaining 50 percent is equally distributed across the low and high cases. This analysis suggests that a drug candidate has a 5.25 percent chance of making it all the way from pre-clinical development to the market and generating "average" sales. Likewise, there is a 2.62 percent chance of making it all the way from pre-clinical development and then being either a flop in terms of sales or a surprise.

Once again, it should be noted that these probabilities are for demonstrative purposes only. Clearly, the point is made that in order to conduct this type of analysis, similar probabilities must be generated with some confidence. The decision tree itself can get far more complicated with many more branches.

Finally, the aggregated DCFs for each of the stages of development must be combined with the newly created cumulative probabilities. In Table 5, the two are combined and then summed to arrive at an overall weighted NPV of *negative* $23.8 million. Using this weighted approach, we would *not* choose to pursue the project given that its NPV is negative. What went wrong or what changed? The culprit could be our assumption on revenues, time period involved, the probabilities utilized, or the cost of capital (r).

Depending on the technology or product being valued, revenue assumptions may or may not be difficult to ascertain. This is similarly true with the assumptions on costs. However, given the influence of the other factors, fairly large changes to either the cost structure (decline) or revenue stream (increase) would have to occur in order to shift the NPV toward positive territory. Time also has an impact on the valuation: it influences the discount factor. The longer the time frame, the lower the discount factor will be, which pushes down the corresponding DCF. Being able to decrease the development time to market would increase the resulting DCF; however, to do so would require a change in original assumptions on development or a possible change in technology.

Recall that in the original standard DCF analysis the stream of cash flows, both positive and negative, are assumed to occur with certainty. By moving to

Table 5. The Aggregated DCFs for Each of the Stages of Development when Combined with the Newly Created Cumulative Probabilities.

	Year	Cash Flow (Million, $)	Discount Factor	DCF (Million, $)	Sum of DCF by Stage (Million, $)	Probability	Weighted Sum of DCF by Stage (Million, $)
Pre-clinical	1	−25	0.8	−20.0	−51.4	0.670	−34.4
	2	−25	0.64	−16.0			
	3	−30	0.512	−15.4			
Phase I	4	−30	0.4096	−12.3	−27.0	0.165	−4.5
	5	−45	0.32768	−14.7			
Phase II	6	−45	0.262144	−11.8	−22.3	0.041	−0.9
	7	−50	0.209715	−10.5			
Phase III	8	−50	0.167772	−8.4	−18.5	0.019	−0.3
	9	−75	0.134218	−10.1			
FDA application	10	−150	0.107374	−16.1	−16.1		
Base sales	11	250	0.085899	21.5			
	12	500	0.068719	34.4			
	13	750	0.054976	41.2			
	14	850	0.04398	37.4			
	15	800	0.035184	28.1			
	16	300	0.028147	8.4	154.9	0.053	8.1
Low sales	11	185	0.085899	15.9			
	12	350	0.068719	24.1			
	13	500	0.054976	27.5			
	14	500	0.04398	22.0			
	15	500	0.035184	17.6			
	16	200	0.028147	5.6	96.5	0.026	2.5
High sales	11	400	0.085899	34.4			
	12	750	0.068719	51.5			
	13	900	0.054976	49.5			
	14	1,100	0.04398	48.4			
	15	1,000	0.035184	35.2			
	16	500	0.028147	14.1	216.9	0.026	5.7
							−23.8

this regime we are now assuming that movement from one stage to the next occurs with some probability less than one. In fact, there is only a slightly better than 10 percent chance that a drug candidate survives all the way from pre-clinical to market. The initial potential revenues are large; however, there exists a fairly low probability that these cash flows come to fruition.

The final factor has a fairly large impact on the resulting decision. In this example, *r* was determined to be 25 percent. Arbitrarily decreasing the value of r to 12 percent produces two impacts, which can clearly been seen in Table 6. First, the cumulative R&D costs almost double (since they are not being discounted so heavily). However, and more striking, there is a dramatic increase in projected revenues. Baseline sales jump from around $155 million to almost $700 million. As a result, the overall weighted NPV for the project has turned positive. Clearly, facing these projections, the project would now be accepted.

Table 6. Two Impacts are Formed when Arbitrarily Decreasing the Value of r to 12 Percent.

	Year	Cash Flow (Million, $)	Discount Factor	DCF (Million, $)	Sum of DCF by Stage (Million, $)	Probability	Weighted Sum of DCF by Stage (Million, $)
Pre-clinical	1	−25	0.892857	−22.3	−63.6	0.670	−42.6
	2	−25	0.797194	−19.9			
	3	−30	0.71178	−21.4			
Phase I	4	−30	0.635518	−19.1	−44.6	0.165	−7.4
	5	−45	0.567427	−25.5			
Phase II	6	−45	0.506631	−22.8	−45.4	0.041	−1.9
	7	−50	0.452349	−22.6			
Phase III	8	−50	0.403883	−20.2	−47.2	0.019	−0.9
	9	−75	0.36061	−27.0			
FDA application		−150	0.321973	−48.3	−48.3		
Base sales	11	250	0.287476	71.9			
	12	500	0.256675	128.3			
	13	750	0.229174	171.9			
	14	850	0.20462	173.9			
	15	800	0.182696	146.2			
	16	300	0.163122	48.9	692.8	0.053	36.4
Low sales	11	185	0.287476	53.2			
	12	350	0.256675	89.8			
	13	500	0.229174	114.6			
	14	500	0.20462	102.3			
	15	500	0.182696	91.3			
	16	200	0.163122	32.6	435.6	0.026	11.4
High sales	11	400	0.287476	115.0			
	12	750	0.256675	192.5			
	13	900	0.229174	206.3			
	14	1,100	0.20462	225.1			
	15	1,000	0.182696	182.7			
	16	500	0.163122	81.6	954.8	0.026	25.0
							20.1

This simple exercise of decreasing the discount rate fundamentally changes the perception of the project or technology in question. And with this we also return full circle to the original discussion relating to the appropriate choice for r. Obviously, entrepreneurs would like to see a lower r, which raises the overall valuation. Firms, VCs, or others making investments will argue for a larger r, which effectively decreases overall valuation. One partial solution to this dilemma is to use the technique, discussed in the following section, in the order to generate a range of assumptions instead of a solitary value. With this approach, many of the assumptions and choices that have been made up to this point can be relaxed and considered over a broader spectrum. This allows, for example, for a discussion with respect to the *range* of r instead of one finite value. More importantly, the values or ranges on the assumptions made that will cause NPV or weighted-NPV valuations to flip from positive to negative can now be determined.

4.3. Monte-Carlo Analysis

Up to this point all the decisions that have been made have been singular and non-random in nature. The "best" value to use in the respective models was based on some underlying assumption. We now consider a powerful analytical method called Monte-Carlo analysis or Monte-Carlo simulation. Instead of being constrained to a singular decision, a range of outcomes or variables with associated probabilities can now be determined. In the examples above, this would include the assumptions on costs, revenues, probabilities, and r. Once a range of values are determined for the variables in question, computer packages, such as Crystal Ball® by Decisioneering Inc., will randomly select values from these ranges and generate a forecast of outcomes. Usually, these iterations are done several thousand times. The NPV calculation then becomes the average of these many thousand simulated outcomes.

Consider a very basic example to demonstrate the methodology before reconsidering the previous example. Assume a simple profit calculation of total revenues minus total cost. Total revenues are projected to be $100 million with corresponding total cost of $75 million, resulting in a net profit of $25 million. Now, assume that revenues follow a triangular distribution. With this distribution we need fairly good knowledge with respect to minimum and maximum sales. Assume that minimum sales could

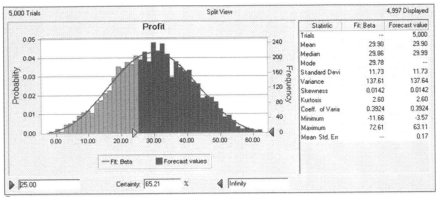

Fig. 3. Forecast Values when Plugging the Assumptions into Crystal Ball® and
Setting the Iterations to 5,000 Random Trails.

be $75 million and the maximum sales could be $125 million, with the most
likely sales being $100 million. For costs, assume a uniform distribution
with the minimum cost level being $60 million and maximum cost level
being $80 million. Plugging these assumptions into Crystal Ball® and setting
the iterations to 5,000 random trials produces the forecast values shown in
Fig. 3.

The program generates a mean profit forecast of $29.90 million with a
median value of $29.99 million. The standard deviation is $11.73 million.
From the output there is a 65.21 percent chance that the forecasted profit
will exceed $25 million or the value from the discrete analysis. Consider
what happens if the distribution for revenues is swapped from a triangular
distribution to a normal distribution. Fig. 4 shows the forecast values over
5,000 iterations.

Mean forecast revenues increase slightly to $30.17 million and median
forecast revenues rise to $30.05 million. The standard deviation falls to
$11.56 million and the probability that revenues will exceed $25 million
increases to 66.24 percent. Overall the underlying distribution had a minor
impact on forecast profit and underlying certainty. The choice of which
exact underlying distribution can come from an understanding of what the
distribution *means* in terms of projections. For example, the use of the
triangular distribution implies we have a relatively high level of certainty
with respect to the most likely sales figure. Looking at previous revenues or

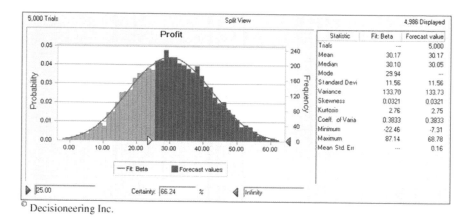

© Decisioneering Inc.

Fig. 4. The Forecast Values over 5,000 Iterations.

revenues from competing products may give some insight into which underlying distribution to choose. With these types of programs and tools, it is cost-less to change the underlying assumption and test the impact on forecast revenues and certainty.

This example was relatively basic in that only current revenue, cost, and forecast-projected profit were considered. Turning attention back to the Rubicon example, we can see whether the opinion or investment/valuation decision changes when utilizing this valuation tool. The first case considered will keep the discount rate at 12 percent (consistent with Tables 2, 4, and 6. Each of the first 10 years of costs (negative cash flows) will be assigned a uniform distribution. Lognormal distributions are placed on each of the cumulative probabilities such that the distribution is skewed to the left (or toward a lower probability of success). Sales from years 11 to 16 are assigned a normal distribution. As a robustness check, sales are also assigned a triangular distribution with the previous sales ranges being used as extreme values. The forecast NPV, over 5,000 iterations, has an 88 percent chance of being greater than zero (Fig. 5).

The analysis can be complicated once again. A distributional assumption can be placed on the discount rate. Placing a uniform distribution on the discount rate produces little divergence in our forecast NPV (Fig. 6).

Overall, the forecast NPV falls slightly from a mean value of $25.11 million to $18.81 million and the probability that forecast NPV is positive falls from 88 percent to 81 percent. Under either of these forecasts, with the

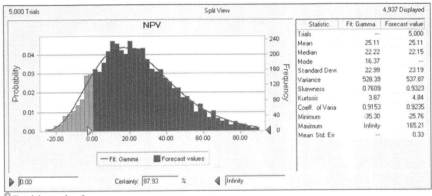

© Decisioneering Inc.

Fig. 5. The Forecast of NPV over 5,000 Iterations.

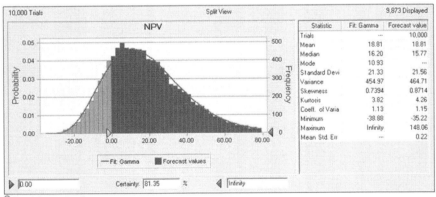

© Decisioneering Inc.

Fig. 6. Divergence in Forecast NPV is Produced when a Uniform Distribution on the Discount Rate is Placed.

associated assumptions on distributional forms, the project has over an 80 percent chance of producing a positive NPV.

4.4. Real Options Analysis

Before jumping into a discussion on real options, let's start by briefly discussing what a financial option is and how it differs from a real option.

Financial options come in two forms – calls and puts. Options, unlike equities, are two-sided, legally binding contracts. Each option contract has a seller and a buyer. Each contract also represents 100 shares of an underlying equity. For example, if you were to purchase 10 call option contracts, you would have the legal right to buy 1,000 shares of an underlying equity. If one person's option increases in value, the other person's option declines in value by the same amount. Call options give the buyer the legal *right* – not obligation – to buy an underlying equity for a specific price at or by a specific time in the future. Options contracts have specific expiration days or "ex-days". After the expiration day, an option becomes worthless.

There are two types of call and put contracts – American and European options. These types of options differ in the ability to exercise the option before the expiration day. A European call contract can be exercised only on the expiration day. This means that an investor has the right to buy an underlying equity for a specific price on a specific expiration day. If the investor chooses not to exercise the option or buy the underlying equity, then the contract just expires, worthless. In contrast, an American call contract allows an investor the right to exercise the option any day up to and including expiration day. This flexibility has value and, as a result, American call contracts are usually more expensive than European call contracts.

Moving from financial options to *real* options, many things become much fuzzier. For example, there is no underlying legal contract in real options. As a result, there are no exact expiration days or finite strike prices at which an asset can be bought or sold. In fact, unlike financial options whose underlying assets are equity, the underlying asset is real – an R&D project, for example. Notwithstanding the fundamental differences in structure and underlying assets, we will borrow from the financial option toolbox in order to value real options.

Up until this point, a major assumption has been ignored. Until now we have assumed that once management sets a research trajectory and starts down a particular path, they continue along this path until the product either fails or reaches the end of the path. Traditional valuation techniques (such as the NPV rule) do not properly capture management's flexibility to adapt and revise later decisions in response to unexpected market developments. Traditional approaches assume an expected scenario of cash flows and presume management's passive commitment to a certain static operating strategy. Moreover, these valuation strategies do not allow for the possibility that management changes course or responds to unexpected

Table 7. Examples of Different Types of Real Options a Firm Faces.

Option	Description	Examples
Defer	To wait before taking an action until more is known or timing is expected to be more favorable	When to enter a new market, acquire a partner, build a plant, develop land, and hire permanent employees
Expand or contract	To increase or decrease the scale of an operation in response to demand	Adding or subtracting to a service offering, or adding memory to a computer, mining, and oil development
Abandon	To discontinue an operation and liquidate the assets	Discontinuation of a research project, or product/service line
Stage investments	To commit investment in stages giving rise to a series of valuations and abandonment options	Staging or R&D projects, or venture investments in a new venture
Switch	To alter the mix of inputs or outputs of a production process in response to market prices	Process flexibility, global location flexibility, input mix flexibility, output mix, and volume flexibility
Grow	To expand the scope of activities to capitalize on new perceived opportunities	Extension of brand names to new products or marketing through existing distribution channels and platform investments

market events. The real world is characterized by change, uncertainty, and competitive interaction. As new information arrives and uncertainty is resolved, management may have valuable flexibility to alter its initial operating strategy in order to capitalize on favorable future opportunities or to react so as to mitigate losses. This managerial operating flexibility is like financial option and is valuable to a firm.

If today's decisions affect what you can do tomorrow, then tomorrow's decisions have to be analyzed before you can act rationally today. Table 7 lists six examples of different types of real options a firm faces (it is by no means complete).

4.4.1. Binomial Pricing Model and Black–Scholes
One of the most basic, discrete, valuation methods for financial options is the Binomial Pricing Model (BPM). The BPM is based on the premise that a

value of a call option can be obtained by building a replicating portfolio composed of some proportion of a share of equity and debt (borrowing or lending) (Bodie, Kane, & Marcus, 2004). The BPM can simply be expressed as

$$C = N \cdot S - B \tag{6}$$

where C is the value of a European call option; N a proportion of a share of equity, between zero and one; S the price of the underlying equity; and B is either borrowing or lending.

The BPM valuation equation is designed to determine the value of a call option. European Put–Call Parity can be used to equate the relationship between a European put and a European call (Bodie et al., 2004). It can be shown that American calls have the same exact value as a European call. The missing element is the European put value. While these derivations and relationships are beyond the scope of this chapter, the general strategy of deriving American and European option values using the BPM is as follows: (1) use the BPM to find the value of a European put option (this is accomplished by working through the discrete branches backwards through time); (2) re-evaluate the previous derivation at stage for early exercise; doing so will allow you to generate the value of an American put option; (3) use the value derived in (1) along with the European Put–Call Parity formula to derive a European call value; and (4) it can be shown that the American call option is equal to the European call option.[7]

Black and Scholes (1973) took the next step and generated a continuous time options pricing model. The option pricing model is defined as

$$C = \{P \cdot N(d_1) - [e^{-rt} \cdot X \cdot N(d_2)]\} \tag{7}$$

where d_1 and d_2 equal

$$d_1 = [\ln(P/X) + T(r + 0.5\sigma^2)]/(\sigma^2 \cdot t)^{1/2}$$
$$d_2 = d_1 - (\sigma^2 \cdot t)^{1/2}$$

The value of a European call option, C, is equal to current stock price, P, times the normal distribution evaluated at d_1 minus the product of three components. These components consist of the exercise price, X, a discount factor e^{-rt} (where r is the risk-free rate of return and t is defined as the time, in years, to expiration date), and the normal distribution evaluated at d_2. Intuitively this equation can be related to the BPM in the following manner. The product $N(d_1)$, which will be a number between zero and one, times P is similar to $N \cdot S$ and the second product, $e^{-rt} \cdot X \cdot N(d_2)$, is a PV, acting similar to B.

The model makes the following assumptions: (1) the stock pays no dividends over the course of the options life; (2) European exercise terms are used; (3) markets are efficient; (4) no commissions are charged; (5) interest rates remain constant and known; and (6) returns are lognormal distributed. While these assumptions are strict, they do not preclude the use of the Black–Scholes model in option valuations.

Several factors can increase (decrease) the underlying value of a call option: (1) increase (decrease) in the variance of the underlying asset; (2) increase (decrease) in the value of the underlying asset; (3) increase (decrease) in the time to expiration; (4) increase (decrease) in the risk-free rate; and (5) decrease (increase) in the exercise price (Bodie et al., 2004). In dealing with real options, the first and third factors are the most important. The issues surrounding variance will become apparent in the example.

4.4.2. Real Options Example

This valuation technique is now applied to an example typical in the high-tech sector. Pharmaceutical, software, or types of high-tech companies often engage in strategic alliances with multiple smaller firms. The hope is that, as time goes by, some of these smaller firms will produce a technology or product that becomes valuable to the firm. In a sense, these firms outsource a potion of their R&D. By doing so, they are able to access new technologies, approaches, and platforms. Over time, as the underlying technologies and research progress, it may become beneficial for the larger firm to acquire the smaller technology firm. This scenario is seen widely in the pharmaceutical industry (Higgins & Rodriguez, 2006). With this outsourcing R&D approach in mind, consider the following example:

Example: Elfloo is a large high-tech company that sells networking equipment. To fuel its growth, it is in constant need of new people and new products. Elfloo's strategy is to obtain these by investing in smaller companies with good products and then, if things go well, to acquire a controlling interest. You are in charge of identifying potential investment targets for the firm. In your research you come across a small, publicly traded firm, Evolutia, which appears to have some promising new technologies. How much should you recommend Elfloo invest in Evolutia today in exchange for the option to acquire 51 percent of Evolutia in two years for $33.2 million?

Evolutia currently has a market capitalization of $60 million, currently pays no dividends, and has stock price volatility over the past year of 45 percent.

Solution: When utilizing the Black–Scholes option pricing formula, as discussed above, we only need to determine the equivalents to five key pieces of information:

1. P = current stock price
2. X = exercise price
3. r = annualized risk-free rate of return
4. σ^2 = variance (per year) of stock return
5. t = time (in years) until expiration

In our example, we get the following:

1. P = 51 percent of Evolutia's current market value or $30.6 million
2. X = the cost to acquire 51 percent of Evolutia in two years, $33.2 million
3. r = risk-free rate of return, 5 percent
4. σ^2 = annual stock price volatility, 45 percent
5. t = two years until "expiration"

Plugging these values into the Black–Scholes equation:

$$C = \{P \cdot N(d_1) - [e^{-rt} \cdot X \cdot N(d_2)]\}$$

where d_1 and d_2 equal

$$d_1 = [\ln(P/X) + T(r + .5\sigma^2)]/(\sigma^2 \cdot t)^{1/2}$$
$$d_2 = d_1 - (\sigma^2 \cdot t)^{1/2}$$

We get a value for "C" or our call option to acquire Evolutia of $8.4 million. Therefore, you should recommend an investment of $8.4 million today in exchange for the right to acquire 51 percent of Evolutia in two years for a cost of $33.2 million.

In this example, the valuation was for an entire firm, which was publicly traded. However, if one is interested in valuing a potential licensing opportunity for a drug, then we are not dealing with a full-firm valuation. In this case public equity values are not available to be relied upon. More importantly, the measure of volatility, σ^2, is lost. In the previous example, variance was simply derived from annual stock price volatility.

The values of P and X can be determined with a bit of work. For example, P becomes the value of the project. This is the value of the projected revenues times the probability these revenues are realized. There is a caveat in the calculation of P. If a firm injects an additional investment at the time of commercialization, say for example marketing, then this value is also added to the value of the project. This sum is then multiplied by the probability of realization. This accounts for monies that the firm has or will commit to the project at this later date. It is similar to selling a \$10,000 car with a \$50,000 bag of money in the front seat. The value of the combined package would be \$60,000. X is a summation of all working and fixed capital along with R&D expenses. It is the easier of the two values to determine.

The more complex issue is what value to use for volatility, σ^2. In the previous example, when the valuation of a publicly traded firm was considered, this was relatively easy because volatility was simply variance of the underlying equity. However, in order to derive the volatility measure of a research project, a firm is going to have extensive experience in R&D. For example, many pharmaceutical firms have extensive portfolios of both successful and failed R&D projects. As a result, they are able to generate volatility measures for different types of research. This raises a major limitation in the use of real options analysis. For firms that do not have this type of experience, the decision on what to use for volatility becomes much more uncertain. We know from option theory that an increase (decrease) in variance increases (decreases) the overall value of the option. As such, an inaccurate variance measure will result in an inaccurate options value. Overall, however, if a firm has relevant experience, then real option becomes one more tool in the valuation toolbox.

5. PUTTING VALUATIONS IN PERSPECTIVE

As was suggested earlier, the difficult process of valuation cannot be conducted in a vacuum. Depending on the source of funds (e.g., venture capitalists or strategic partners), a valuation of a technology or venture is conducted as one portion of a much larger agreement. These agreements often include provisions of other control rights including rights pertaining to intellectual property, testing, marketing, manufacturing, and distribution. A valuation often becomes just one bargaining tool in a much more complicated negotiation process. For example, research has shown that biotechnology firms are often willing to take substantial discounts in terms of valuation in order to get their first alliance with a large pharmaceutical firm (Nicholson, Danzon, & McCullogh, 2005). This first alliance serves as a signal of quality, and these authors find that the biotechnology firms that engaged in this practice received higher subsequent valuations in future rounds of financing. Clearly, this is a case where the signal of quality was worth a diminished initial valuation. However, this also demonstrates the importance of determining an accurate and reflective *initial* valuation from which one can negotiate.

Research has shown that biotechnology firms engaging in their first alliance are also more likely to give up more control rights (Higgins, 2007). Biotechnology firms also tend to give up more rights in periods of limited availability of public financing (Aghion & Bolton, 1992; Holmstrom & Tirole, 1997; Lerner, Shane, & Tsai, 2003; Higgins, 2007). Overall, *relative bargaining* position matters in how strategic alliance agreements are negotiated. This is similarly true when negotiating with a VC firm. If a firm or entrepreneur is in a weakened bargaining position, then they can expect to relinquish additional rights and/or value to the other firm. This, once again, not only makes valuations important, but also stresses the importance of firm or entrepreneur preferences for specific control rights. Clearly, an entrepreneur may be willing to give up certain rights, but others, for example those involving intellectual property, may need to be protected.

6. CONCLUSION

Valuation of private firms or new technologies entails a mixture of both art and science. While there is no one-way to approach valuation of these types of assets, a combination of several of the techniques is often needed – and suggested. Given the large amount of uncertainty involved in new technologies and small firms, it is certainly the case that reasonable people can disagree on valuation. Clearly, the parties involved will have their own best interests in mind. Moreover, valuation should not be considered in a vacuum. Valuation should be seen as one component of a larger negotiation involving ownership issues and other relevant control rights. Having a better understanding of a project's or venture's value will allow for a better negotiating position.

As was initially cautioned, this chapter is meant not as an inclusive guide to valuation techniques, but rather as a primer to introduce the lay person to the broad issues and methods involved and available. An extended list of additional resource materials is included in the reference section for the interested reader.

NOTES

1. Author's calculations based on data from Recombinant Capital.
2. Author's calculation based on the Federal Reserve's Statistical Release H.15 "Selected Interest Rates".
3. A firm can be viewed as a bundle of individual projects, with risk spread out across this portfolio. As such, the rate at which a firm can borrow will reflect this lower risk profile.
4. Phase I involves safety testing, phase II is concerned with small-scale human efficacy trials, and phase III focuses on large-scale human efficacy trials.
5. Again, this is for demonstrative purposes only.
6. Note, this is an oversimplified assumption just for demonstrative purposes. We could compute perpetuity in year 6 that account for some small amount of on-going sales in the future. This assumption is valid in the drug industry since even when a drug loses patent protection and a generic comes on the market, there will still be some minimal sales due to such factors as the inability to take the generic drug by some patients.
7. Interested readers can see Bodie et al. (2004) for a more complete discussion on financial option pricing.

REFERENCES

Aghion, P., & Bolton, P. (1992). An incomplete contract approach to financial contracting. *Review of Economic Studies, 59*, 473–494.
Black, F., & Scholes, M. (1973). The pricing of options and corporate liabilities. *Journal of Political Economy, 81*(3), 637–654.
Bodie, Z., Kane, A., & Marcus, A. (2004). *Investments*. New York: McGraw-Hill.
Boer, F. P. (1999). *The valuation of technology: Business and financial issues in R&D*. New York: Wiley.
Brealey, R., Meyers, S., & Allen, F. (2005). *Principles of corporate finance*. New York: McGraw-Hill.
DiMasi, J. A. (2001). New drug development in U.S. 1963–1999. *Clinical Pharmacology and Therapeutics, 69*, 286–296.
Higgins, M. J. (2007). The allocation of control rights in pharmaceutical alliances. *Journal of Corporate Finance, 13*, 58–75.
Higgins, M. J., & Rodriguez, D. (2006). The outsourcing of R&D through acquisition in the pharmaceutical industry. *Journal of Financial Economics, 80*, 351–383.
Holmstrom, B., & Tirole, J. (1997). Financial intermediation, loanable funds, and the real sector. *Quarterly Journal of Economics, 112*, 663–691.

Lerner, J., Shane, H., & Tsai, A. (2003). Do equity financing cycles matter? Evidence from biotechnology alliances. *Journal of Financial Economics, 67,* 411–446.

Metrick, A. (2006). *Venture capital and the finance of innovation.* New York: Wiley.

Nicholson, S., Danzon, P., & McCullogh, J. (2005). Biotech-pharma alliances as a signal of asset and firm quality. *Journal of Business, 78*(4), 1433–1464.

Razgaitis, R. (2003). *Valuation and pricing of technology based intellectual property.* New York: Wiley.

CHAPTER 10

VENTURE CAPITAL FINANCING AND DOCUMENTATION

William J. Carney

ABSTRACT

The purpose of this chapter is to outline the steps involved in obtaining venture capital funding for a start-up business. The chapter first discusses access to Venture Capitalists (VCs) and provides the reasons behind VCs' preference for investing in a traditional C corporation rather than a limited liability company or other pass-through entity. The chapter then describes both the due diligence performed by VC's counsel and the documentation a start-up must provide to satisfy that diligence need. Next, the chapter addresses typical terms of financing deals with VCs, including the types of securities issued and the rights, preferences, and pricing of those securities. Finally, the chapter concludes with a chart identifying the VC financing terms available before and after a significant market downturn and a sample term sheet summarizing the terms of preferred stock to be issued to a hypothetical VC or VC group investing in a start-up business.

Technological Innovation: Generating Economic Results
Advances in the Study of Entrepreneurship, Innovation and
Economic Growth, Volume 18, 287–311
ISSN: 1048-4736/doi:10.1016/S1048-4736(07)00010-0

1. AFTER THE ANGEL ROUND: FINDING THE VENTURE CAPITALISTS

We assume here that a business corporation has been properly organized by competent counsel, and that initial financing has been obtained. Some of this may have come from friends and family, or in some cases from angel investors knowledgeable in the business being financed.

Once the business has progressed to the point where it will need more money to progress, the search should start immediately. It may take many months to arrange another round of financing, and the early funds may be exhausted before you get the new money. Does that mean laying off any employees? Or giving up leased space? Or stopping development of your product until new funds are received? None of these options is desirable.

Web searches will reveal the identity of venture capital (VC) firms interested in investing in your area. Your attorney, if experienced in start-up businesses, and your accountant may also have contacts with VCs that should be explored. But identification is only part of the job: getting the attention of VCs may be just as hard. In some areas, organizations bring entrepreneurs together to learn about the process, to hear presentations from advisers, angels, and VCs, and to provide networking opportunities. Finally, some investment banks are willing to search for early round financing.

Several factors affect the decision whether to use an investment bank for this process. There are thousands of investment banks, some of them quite small boutiques that specialize in early stage financings. Some are run by escapees from larger firms and have considerable experience at seeking early stage capital, as well as many contacts with VCs, wealthy individuals, and potential strategic-partner investors. Finding an investment bank with expertise in your business area is obviously important. Beware of boutiques run by relative neophytes, who may lack the contacts they claim, lack the experience to present your opportunity effectively, and tie you up for months without actually raising any capital. While larger investment banks may have more contacts, your risk getting lost in the shuffle when bigger deals appear. Whatever size of bank you work with, choose a quality investor capable of serving as a lead investor for a round of financing in which other VCs will participate. Typically, VCs share in each round, thus reducing the risk for each VC. A quality lead investor will establish a relationship, probably including board membership, that can provide you with experienced counsel and advice throughout the business's development stage. If the business succeeds through a first round of financing, having a quality lead investor in the first round sends a positive signal to other VCs for subsequent rounds. Because later investors will expect earlier round investors to continue to invest in the later rounds, the first round lead investor as well as the other first round investors should have the capacity to continue through several rounds.

Fee arrangements should be thoroughly discussed and reduced to writing. Expect to pay an up-front retainer ranging from $25,000 to $125,000 and to pay a commission ranging between 3% and 7% of the proceeds. Some investment banks will also want an interest in your firm, perhaps involving a warrant to purchase an amount of stock up to 10% of the offering, as part of their fee. While this is costly, investment bankers can assist you in placing a value on your business, and they will know and understand the terms of the financing that will be demanded by VCs. Further, as they generate interest from multiple investors, competition will enable them to chip away at harsh term sheets.

2. STRUCTURING THE CORPORATION FOR FINANCING

This chapter does not address the business side of the transaction – having a coherent business plan and a clear idea about use of proceeds. Instead, it addresses more legal aspects of the structure of the entity that will be used to exploit your idea and raise capital.

Many start-up enterprises that expect to lose money during the development stage are formed as "pass-through" entities, typically limited liability companies. Pass-throughs are not tax-paying entities, but simply report their income or losses to the Internal Revenue Service (IRS), and report the shares of that income allocated to each investor. Investors can then use their respective shares of reported losses as an offset to their own taxable income. Where individual investors are involved, the use of these losses in this way is an attractive feature of the investment. At the initial stage, angel investors may find this an attractive benefit. But when VC firms become involved, this tax scenario typically is not the case, and any pass-through entity (or corporation electing Subchapter S pass-through treatment) will have to convert to the corporate form (or terminate its Subchapter S election). VCs' investors are frequently entities that pay no taxes, such as university endowment funds and retirement plans. Accordingly, the traditional business corporation is the form of choice for these investments. In most cases, the state of incorporation will not matter, because corporate laws have a great deal of uniformity across the nation. When a company contemplates going public through an initial public offering, some advisers will suggest reincorporation, often into Delaware, but in some cases into Nevada. This author does not generally regard that as good advice, but concedes that this is a minority position.

Incorporation can be handled by any skilled business attorney and is a relatively simple process at the beginning. Angel investors will typically take common stock for their investments, so a capital structure with all common stock makes sense at the beginning. The charter should contain indemnification provisions that empower the corporation to indemnify officers and directors to the full extent of the law, and exculpatory provisions that relieve directors from liability for breaches of the duty of care – features that will be essential should the company ultimately go public, but valuable protection at any stage.

Even at an early stage, the company should seek knowledgeable outsiders for its board, in addition to the principals in the firm. Outsiders can bring objectivity that may moderate the founders' excess enthusiasm for the project, and also can bring complementary knowledge to the deliberations. The company should anticipate reserving a board seat for venture capitalists – probably one additional place for each round of financing, as new VCs enter the arena. To keep the board from reaching a cumbersome size, some of the early stage directors may anticipate stepping aside as new outsiders are added. The structuring of the management team is beyond the scope of this chapter, but note that many inventors lack the management experience and training to carry through the development of their business; thus, they should seek out others with complementary skills. VCs will pay close attention to the quality of the entire management team in their evaluations, because it is not enough to have a great business plan; you have to be able to execute it.

Corporate record-keeping is critical from the outset. Venture capitalists will do thorough due diligence and will carefully examine financial records, corporate records (e.g., minutes and bylaws), evidence of your property rights in your IP, as well as agreements with suppliers, customers, major shareholders, officers, and other employees. (We omit the investigation of the product or invention here as, again, it is beyond the scope of this chapter.) The corporation should work with an accountant at an early stage to secure accounting software to provide good financial records. While some of this VC due diligence will necessarily take place before a VC commits to a term sheet, in many cases the bulk of the due diligence will be reserved for after agreement on a term sheet. The term sheet may commit the company to deal exclusively with the VC during the due diligence period, to assure that the VC's efforts will not be wasted. This period often lasts 30–45 days, which can be problematic for the company: if the VC decides not to go ahead after completing due diligence, or suggests renegotiating the terms to much less favorable ones, the company's bargaining position has weakened, as it is that much closer to running out of cash, with less remaining time to find investors. Here the company must rely on the good faith and good reputation of the VC.

If the company has valuable trade secrets and proprietary information, it should obtain confidentiality agreements from any prospective investor at the outset, before due diligence reaches the stage of investigating such information. In some cases, the company may want to exclude some details from the disclosures, probably after consulting with counsel.

3. WHAT VENTURE CAPITALISTS WANT

3.1. Due Diligence

The VC's counsel will send a request for documentation to the company at an early stage. The company, in consultation with counsel, will want to anticipate much of this by assembling the anticipated documents in a single room where VC's counsel and other representatives can examine them efficiently and without disturbing company personnel in their regular duties. Here we deal primarily with the legally oriented issues. Obviously, the business plan and financial records will be an important part of this review. What follows is a list of the documents the company can anticipate will be required, together with some indication of the information that will be sought in these documents.

3.1.1. Review of Seller's Corporate Documents
3.1.1.1. Articles of Incorporation. Have preemptive rights ever existed, either by default under the corporation act or by charter, and not been honored? Are there records of waivers?

What shareholder approvals are required for this round of VC financing?

If this is not the "A Round," and a class or series of preferred stock is already outstanding, what rights will the earlier class have as a result of this financing? If it is a "down round," will it have an effect on conversion ratios of earlier classes, and thus on the number of shares of common stock outstanding after conversion on a liquidity event?

Are there any restrictions on the transfer or voting of stock?

Have full rights of exculpation and indemnification of directors been provided?

3.1.1.2. Bylaws. Are there any restrictions on the transfer or voting of stock?

Are there any unusual provisions governing powers of officers, votes required for merger or sale, notice of shareholders' meetings, and similar corporate governance matters?

Do bylaws require amendment to accommodate new directors?

Can both director and shareholder action be taken by written consent?

3.1.1.3. Minute Books. Are there any restrictions on the transfer or voting of stock?

Are any powers of attorney outstanding with respect to voting securities?

Provide a summary description of the rights of each class of outstanding security approved by the board under any "blank preferred" authority, or of debt issues.

Are there outstanding warrants, options, or conversion rights that must be honored, or can they be canceled or redeemed?

If preemptive rights ever existed, have they been honored? Are there records of waivers?

Was stock validly issued, fully paid, and non-assessable?

3.1.1.4. Major Contracts. Do any employment agreements impose long-term obligations on seller, or provide for severance payments on a change in control?

Do any officer or employee benefit plans impose long-term obligations on the seller? Are there bonus plans, profit-sharing agreements, retirement plans, and other fringe benefit agreements, such as life insurance, hospitalization, and major medical? Does the company have any contracts providing special retirement payments to former officers or employees, or any contracts providing consulting payments?

Are there voting agreements among shareholders, or agreements that restrict transfer or voting of stock?

Verify the number of stock options and their exercise prices and expiration dates.

3.1.1.5. Stock Books. Verify the number of outstanding shares.

Verify the number of shareholders and their names and addresses, and the amount each holds.

Is there any record of pledges of outstanding shares?

Is there evidence of compliance with exemptions from securities registration (within applicable statutes of limitation), including investment letters and restrictive legends on certificates?

3.1.2. Representations and Warranties

The Stock Purchase Agreement will be required to contain representations and warranties covering, at a minimum.

- The company is duly organized and in good standing in its state of incorporation, and qualified to do business in other states where it does business.
- The company has legal power to enter into all agreements connected with the financing, and will not violate any other agreements by doing so.
- The capitalization of the company is as represented, and the number of outstanding shares is as represented, and all shares are duly authorized and validly issued. Representations about the number of stock options outstanding will also be required.
- The company's financial statements are true and correct in all material respects, and there have been no material adverse changes since the date of the last financial statements.
- There are no liabilities, contingent or otherwise, not disclosed on the financial statements, except those in a schedule, and liabilities for taxes not yet due and payable.
- All taxes owing have been fully paid.
- There are no contractual obligations exceeding some specified dollar threshold, or agreements obligating the company for longer than a specified period, often 1 year, except as disclosed in a schedule.
- All employees have entered into appropriate confidentiality agreements with respect to the company's intellectual property.
- The acts required to enter into the financing agreements and to close the transaction have been authorized, and the officers are authorized to execute agreements.
- When the new preferred shares are issued, and upon conversion of the preferred into common stock, the shares of common stock, will be duly and validly issued, and fully paid and non-assessable, and, along with the common stock to be issued, will be free and clear of any liens or restrictions on transfer, other than transfer restrictions under state and federal securities laws.

- The offer and sale of the securities does not violate state or federal securities laws.
- The company has good title to its properties, which are subject to no undisclosed liens or mortgages, except those disclosed in an attached schedule.
- The company has sufficient legal rights to all intellectual property (disclosed on a schedule) to conduct its business.

3.1.3. Certifications
The company's attorneys will be required to give opinion letters to the VCs to the effect that

- the company is duly organized and in good standing in its state of incorporation and in other states where it does business;
- the company holds good title to its patents, patent applications, and provisional applications; and
- the company use and exploitation of its patents will not be subject to restriction because of patent rights of others (except as disclosed).

3.2. Terms of Deals

Preferred stock is a stock that has some contract rights superior to those of the common stock. That superiority may be in rights to dividends, voting rights, or liquidation rights, or some combination of them. The contract rights of the preferred are set forth in the articles of incorporation or (in Delaware) the certificate of incorporation. Typically amendments to these documents require approval of both the board of directors and the shareholders. All states have provided a simpler procedure, should companies elect to follow it. The articles or certificate of incorporation may provide authority for the company to issue a class of preferred stock, without initially specifying its terms. The articles or certificate may also specify that the class can be divided into one or more series. In these cases, the articles or certificate will delegate to the board of directors the power to determine the rights and preferences of the preferred, and the number of shares in each series. When the board does so, its action constitutes an amendment of the articles or certificate of incorporation when the proper document is filed with the Secretary of State.

What follows is an outline of some of the basic terms of VC investments, with some explanation, and use of the jargon of the industry.

- *Type of security.* Venture capitalists almost always want convertible preferred stock. Preferred stock provides the investors with a priority over the founders upon liquidation of the company, if things go badly, and, in some cases on a sale, with a guaranteed return, based on accumulated arrearages on the specified dividend rate on the preferred stock.
- *Dividend preference.* While preferred stock may have a specified dividend rate, the board of directors has the option to choose whether to declare and pay these dividends when the terms specify they are declarable. If they are not declared (and they almost never are in this type of financing), they are cumulative. This means: (1) these dividends accumulate until paid, (2) no dividends or distributions may be paid on the common stock unless and until all past dividends are paid on the preferred, and (3) on redemption of the preferred or liquidation of the company, these accrued dividends must be paid (along with the original price of the preferred) before any payments are made on the common stock. These preferences justify the higher price the VCs will pay for their shares over the price paid by the founders.
- *Price.* Venture capitalists will determine the company's "pre-money" value, and thus the price they are willing to pay for their shares, based on some form of discounted cash flow based on expected future revenue streams anticipated by the company (see Chapter 9). Part of the pricing calculation may be based on the amount of money anticipated for the company to reach certain milestones.
- *Liquidation preference.* If the company is liquidated, the preferred will receive both a specified amount, represented by the original purchase price, plus accrued dividends, and, in some cases, an additional amount. If the preferred stock is "participating preferred," it may receive an additional amount determined in some manner with reference to what the common shareholders receive.
- *Redemption.* Preferred stock may be redeemable. In some cases it will be redeemable at the option of the holders, who can "put" the stock to the company for a specified redemption price, which will include a premium over the initial purchase price (e.g., the accrued and unpaid dividends). This provides an exit for the VCs when they perceive that things are not going well, and this right may force the founders to agree to a sale of the company. The forced redemption may well lead to a liquidation. In some cases the company may have an option to redeem. Where this option exists, the VCs will have the option to remain in the company by converting their preferred stock into common stock.

- *Conversion rights.* The holders will have the option of converting their preferred stock into common stock of the company at any time. Typically the original conversion ratio is one share of common for each share of preferred, subject to adjustments set out below. The circumstances in which this conversion right will be exercised are relatively rare, since by converting the preferred holders relinquish their liquidation preferences. Ordinarily, they will retain their preferred until an exit event, which will require mandatory conversion.
- *Exit events-mandatory conversion.* Preferred stock will automatically convert into common stock at such time as the VCs have the opportunity to exit at a profit. Mandatory conversion is required when the company makes a public offering at or above a specified price (a "Qualified Initial Public Offering," or "IPO"). Similarly, if the company is sold at or above that price, the preferred will automatically convert into common.
- *Anti-dilution protection.* When new shares are sold at prices below the conversion price of a series of convertible preferred stock, anti-dilution language generally kicks in. After the NASDAQ market index dropped from over 5,000 in early 2,000 to a low of below 1,500 in 2002, valuations for many small companies that had been anticipating public offerings plummeted, and public offerings were no longer feasible. These companies were forced to engage in new rounds of private financing through venture capitalists at lower valuations than before. These transactions, called "down rounds," triggered anti-dilution clauses by which conversion rights on earlier rounds of convertible preferred stock were reset at lower prices. Venture capitalists often have considerable bargaining power in negotiating the terms of these clauses, especially in down rounds.

The toughest of these clauses is called the "full ratchet" clause. Here the conversion price is reduced to give the holders the same lower price paid by the most recent investor (there is no upward ratchet if stock is sold for a higher price). The tough part of this clause is that the conversion price ratchets down to this price regardless of how many shares are sold in the down round. To illustrate how this clause can be extremely favorable to investors, consider the following example. A company has one million shares of common stock owned by founders, who paid one penny per share. The company also has outstanding 250,000 shares of convertible preferred stock outstanding, which convert into common stock at $1.00 per share. Thus, if all the preferred shares were converted, the VC investors would own 20% of the company (250,000 of 1,250,000 outstanding shares of common stock).

Now assume that the company's board of directors invites a new person to join the board and issues him one share of common stock for one cent. At this point, the anti-dilution rights adjust so the venture capitalists are entitled to buy new shares at $0.01 per share; their 250,000 shares of $1.00 preferred now convert into 25,000,000 shares of common stock. The venture capitalists own 25,000,000 out of 26,000,001 shares, or over 96% of the common stock! This is obviously an extreme example, and the effect is more modest when, for example, the A series round of preferred stock is at $5.00 per share and the following B round is at $4.00.

The clause that is more desirable for the company and existing shareholders is the "weighted average" clause, which takes into account the number of shares issued. This clause works as follows:

$$\frac{[(\text{Number of shares previously outstanding})(\text{Conversion price}) + (\text{Consideration for additional shares})]}{\text{Number of shares outstanding after additional issue}}$$

Under this formula, which is much more widely used, the results in the first example would be as follows:

$$\frac{(1,000,000)(\$1.00) + \$0.01}{1,000,000.01} = \$0.999999$$

These provisions may contain an exception for a specified number of shares sold under employee stock option plans.

- *Pay to play provisions.* When issuers have some bargaining power, they may insist that holders of convertible preferred must "pay to play" in any subsequent down round of financing. Under this scheme, convertible holders *must* purchase a pro rata share of any down round before the anti-dilution protection becomes applicable.
- *Right of first refusal.* Conversely, when the company engages in subsequent rounds of financing, the earlier investors will generally have a right of first refusal to buy additional shares at the offering price. In both this case and under the pay to play provisions, the right to purchase (or the obligation to purchase) is usually specified as the percentage of the total equity of the company held by the investor.
- *Voting rights.* The preferred stock will vote share for share with the common stock on most matters. But by contract (and often by state law), the preferred will have the right to vote separately as a class or series to approve the issuance of any new class or series of preferred, particularly

where the rights or preferences of the new class or series will be equal to or superior to those of the existing class, and thus dilutive of its rights. Separate class voting rights will also be provided (by contract or by law) for votes on mergers and charter amendments. The preferred will also obtain the right to elect one or more directors to the board.

- *Co-sale ("Tag-Along") right.* This provides that if the founders commit to sell their common stock, the preferred holders have the right to sell their stock on the same terms. Tag-along rights are one form of protection from having the founders bail out, leaving the company without critical leadership.
- *Restrictions on sales of founders' stock.* Another way of protecting the preferred holders from a bailout is to provide that founders' stock vests over a period of time, leaving the balance of it subject to repurchase by the company at cost if a founder terminates his or her employment.
- *"Drag-Along" right.* This provides that, if the preferred shareholders find a willing buyer, the founders will agree to sell their shares on the same terms.
- *Registration Rights.* This assures that the company will register the VCs' shares with the Securities Exchange Commission ("SEC") for sale to the public. A "demand registration" provision obligates the company to register shares at the demand of holders of a specified minimum percentage of the VCs' shares. A "piggy-back" registration requires the company to include VCs' shares in any registered offering initiated by the company.

3.3. Pitfalls for Founders

Conflicts do arise between venture capitalists on the one hand and founders and angel investors on the other.

If VCs control the board, they may be able to fire the founder, which triggers the right of the corporation to cancel unvested stock, and may require the founder to resell even vested stock to the company at cost. In addition, some VCs in control of a board can dilute founders' interests by causing the corporation to sell cheap stock to the VCs, to the exclusion of the founders and angel investors. This may be in the form of a second round of financing at a bargain price, in which VCs exercise their right to purchase the entire offering, to the exclusion of the founders and angels. VCs can put the company in a position where it has no other choice by delaying a new financing round until the company is desperate for cash and lacks the time to engage in a broad search for outside sources of funding.

VCs also can negotiate the sale of control of the company by selling their own shares at a premium, without including founders and angel investors in the deal.

Some VCs may be in a position to appropriate value from founders and angels through self-dealing, in which other companies they control transact with the company at prices that shift wealth from the company to the VCs' controlled entities. VCs having such control could cannibalize the company's intellectual property by licensing it or transferring it to controlled entities at bargain prices. Also, a VC controlling another enterprise could cause a merger of the two firms and freeze the founders of the company out, by cashing out all company common stockholders at low values.

While founders may have legal remedies for some of these abuses, those remedies are costly to enforce. Litigation may be required to occur in some distant jurisdiction under the terms of the stock purchase agreement. Such litigation involves factual issues with which many judges are unfamiliar. Pre-trial discovery will be extensive, and motions filed by defendants will add to the delays and costs for plaintiffs. As you read the term sheet in Part V, make a list of issues about which you would warn founders that you see if you are representing them in the negotiations, and suggest your preferred resolution. The chances of getting a favorable resolution of many of them will depend on market conditions and whether your company has the prospect of negotiating better terms with other VCs.

4. OVERVIEW: THE TERM SHEET AND THE DOCUMENTATION

The following chart demonstrates the need for expert advice in negotiating financing. Terms change depending on market conditions. The following "then and now" chart describes conditions in a "down market" following the market crash of 2000–2001 (Bartlett, 2002, pp. 281, 293–295). Obviously, knowledge of current conditions and term sheet terms is critical to getting the best result (Table 1).

The term sheet will be submitted to the company by the lead investor in a VC round. Once it is agreed to, the other documents will follow. They will include: (1) a Stock Purchase Agreement, (2) a Shareholders' Agreement, (3) amendments to the charter (articles of incorporation) to reflect the rights of the preferred series, and (4) a Registration Rights Agreement.

Table 1. Variance in Term Sheets.

Term	Then	... and, in many cases, now
Valuations	$15–$100 million pre-money	$3–$10 million pre-money
Investment amount	$5–$30 million	$2–$15 million
Number of investors	Single VC investor	At least 2 VC investors, with a "known" lead investor
Closing cycle	1–2 months	3–4 months
Dividends	Non-mandatory, non-cumulative 8% per year	Mandatory, cumulative payable in kind up to 15% per year
Liquidation preference	1× purchase price, plus participation rights up to a 3× cap	3×purchase price (and sometimes significantly higher), plus participation rights with no cap
Redemption	None	At option of holders, after 5 years at purchase price plus accrued dividends
Automatic conversion	Upon qualified IPO of $50 million, no price limit	Upon qualified IPO of $75 million, with at least 5×purchase price
Anti-dilution protection	Standard broad-based weighted average adjustment	Full ratchet adjustment for a period; then weighted average
Board composition	2VC; 2 common; 1 outsider	Same
Protective provisions	Investor approval of: senior and pari passu securities; sale of company; payment of dividends; liquidation; and change of rights	Investor approval of: senior and pari passu securities; sale of company; payment of dividends; liquidation, change of rights; change of business; incurrence of debt over specified limit; annual budgets and variances; acquisitions of other businesses; grant of exclusive rights in technology; and appointment or termination of CEO
Preemptive rights	Right to maintain pro-rata ownership in later financings	Right to invest up to 2×pro-rata ownership in later financings
Pay to play provisions	Not often used; preferred loses anti-dilution protection if do not participate in later financing at lower price	More common now; preferred automatically converts to common if do not participate in later financing at lower price
First refusal rights	Right to purchase any shares proposed to be sold by employees	Right to purchase any shares proposed to be sold by any shareholder
Co-sale rights	Right to sell alongside any founder that sells shares	Right to sell alongside any shareholder that sells shares
Drag-along rights	None	Right to force all shareholders to sell company upon board and majority shareholder approval
Founder vesting	Standard 4-year vesting with some up-front vesting	Moving to 4-year vesting
Representations and warranties	From company only	Some reps and warranties from founders individually as to IP

5. A SET OF DOCUMENTS

5.1. A Sample Term Sheet

[Company Name]
PROPOSED SERIES A PREFERRED STOCK ("SERIES A PREFERRED") TERM SHEET

REVISED

SUMMARY OF TERMS

Issuer:	[Company Name] (the "Company")
Purchasers:	Massive Ventures. LP ("MVI") and other investors (collectively the "Investors") mutually acceptable to MVI and the Company. Subject to the conditions contained herein, MVI will commit to invest $1 million of the total financing, and will endeavor to find additional Investors to complete the total financing.
Amount of Total Financing:	$1,000,000 (which may increase up to $3,000,000)
Price:	The Series A Preferred shall represent a pre-money valuation of $5,000,000 million and a post-money valuation of $8,000,000 million, assuming an aggregate investment of $3,000,000.
	If the audited net revenues in 2007 are less than 80% of the net revenues as Projected in the Business Plan dated July 2006 (80% of the Plan net revenues being defined as $4,000,000), then the Investors shall receive additional Series A shares to adjust the effective pre-money valuation on this round to $3.5 million.
Securities Issued:	That number of shares of Series A Preferred that, upon conversion, equal 37.5% post-financing fully diluted ownership of the Company.

Continued

Option Pool:	Immediately prior to the Series A financing, there are to be shares of Common Stock equal to at least 11.5% of the fully diluted shares of the Company available for issuance to officers, directors, and employees ("Option Pool"). All options issued under the Option Pool will be issued at an exercise price not less than fair market value and vest in equal annual installments over not less than 4 years. Any changes to the terms of the Option Pool or any increase in the amount of shares in the Option Pool must be approved by the Compensation Committee.
Closing Date:	Anticipated not later than 45 days following the acceptance of this term sheet.
Use of Proceeds:	To fund (a) expanded sales, marketing and administrative infrastructure; and (b) operating losses.
Dividends:	The Series A Preferred dividends will be 8% per annum, will accrue on a daily basis (whether or not declared), and will be cumulative. The dividends will be payable when and if declared by the board. The Series A Preferred dividends will be paid in preference to any dividends on Common Stock.
Liquidation Preference:	In the event of any liquidation, sale, or winding up of the Company or any merger or consolidation of the Company with another entity resulting in the shareholders of the Company owning less that 50% of the capital stock of the resulting company (a "Liquidation Event"), the holders of the Series A Preferred shall be entitled to receive, in preference to the holders of the Common Stock, a per share amount equal to the original purchase price plus accrued but unpaid dividends (the "Liquidation Preference").

Continued

	Following such distributions to the Series A Preferred, the remaining assets shall be distributed ratably to holders of the Common Stock and Series A Preferred on an as-if-converted basis (provided that the maximum distribution to the holders of the Series A Preferred shall be an aggregate of four (4) times the total amount invested by the holders of the Series A Preferred).
A merger, acquisition or sale of substantially all of the assets of the Company in which the shareholders of the Company do not own a majority of the outstanding shares of the surviving corporation shall be deemed a Liquidation Event.
Conversion:	The holders of the Series A Preferred shall have the right to convert their Series A Preferred, at any time, into shares of Common Stock. The initial Conversion Rate shall be 1:1, subject to anti-dilution adjustments as provided below.
Automatic Conversion:	The Series A Preferred shall be automatically converted into Common Stock, at the then applicable conversion price, by (i) written consent or agreement of the holders of greater than 75% of the outstanding shares of Series A Preferred voting together as a class; or (ii) upon the closing of a firmly underwritten public offering of Common Stock of the Company in which (A) the aggregate cash proceeds to the Company equal or exceed $35 million, net of underwriters commission and expenses, (B) the market capitalization of the Company upon a public offering is in excess of $150 million; and, (C) the share price of the offering is at least three times the share price of the Series A Preferred (together a "Qualified Public Offering").

Continued

Anti-Dilution Provisions:	Proportional anti-dilution protection for stock splits, stock dividends, combinations, recapitalization, etc. The conversion price of the Series A Preferred shall be subject to adjustment to prevent dilution, on a full ratchet basis, in the event that the Company issues additional shares of Common Stock or Common Stock equivalents at a purchase price less than the applicable conversion price, other than common stock issued

    (i)   upon conversion of any Preferred Stock;
    (ii)   to the Company's employees, officers, directors or consultants pursuant to stock options approved by the Compensation Committee;
    (iii) as a dividend distribution on any Preferred Stock;

Redemption:	The Series A Preferred shares shall be redeemed, at the option of the Investors, at any time after 5 years from the closing of the Series A Preferred financing at a redemption price that is the greater of fair market value (with no discount for minority interest) or the Liquidation Preference, as defined above.
Voting Rights:	The Series A Preferred will vote on an as-if-converted basis and not as a separate class, except as specifically provided herein or as otherwise required by law. Each share of the Series A Preferred shall have a number of votes equal to the number of shares of Common Stock then issuable upon conversion of such shares of the Series A Preferred.
Board of Directors:	The Board of Directors of the Company (the "Board") will consist of five directors, to be comprised of the following: the Company's CEO and COO; one member to be designated

Continued

	by the CEO with the Board of Directors' approval; one member from MVI; and, one member from other Investors in the Series A Preferred.
	In addition, each Investor not electing a director shall have observation rights.
	The Compensation Committee of the Board will consist of three directors, one of which will be a Series A representative; one of which will be MVI; and, one of which will be the CEO.
	The Company will pay reasonable expenses incurred by directors in attending the meetings.
Observation Rights:	Customary Observation Rights will be granted to any investor not on the Board of Directors who holds at least 15% of the Series A Preferred, if so desired.
Protective Provisions:	For so long as any shares of Series A Preferred remain outstanding, consent of greater than 75% of the Series A Preferred voting together as a single class shall be required for any action that

(i)   Alters or changes the rights, preferences, or privileges of the Series A Preferred;

(ii)   Amends or waives any provisions of the Company's Certificate of Incorporation or Bylaws that adversely affects the rights of the Series A Preferred.

For so long as any shares of Series A Preferred remain outstanding, consent of greater than two-thirds of the Series A Preferred voting together as a single class shall be required for any action that

(i)   Results in the repurchase of shares of Common Stock or Series A Preferred;

(ii)   Results in the payment or declaration of any dividend on any shares of Common Stock or Series A Preferred;

Continued

(iii)   Increases the authorized or issued number of shares of any class of Preferred Stock or Common Stock or other security or right convertible into equity of the Company;

(iv)   Creates (by reclassification or otherwise) any new class or series of shares having rights, preferences, or privileges senior to on or a parity with the Series A Preferred; or,

(v)   Results in any merger, other corporate reorganization, change of control of the Company, or any other transaction in which all or substantially all of the assets of the Company are sold, transferred, or otherwise disposed of, or a substantial portion of the assets are licensed.

In addition, for so long as any shares of Series A Preferred remain outstanding, consent of greater than two-thirds of the Series A Preferred voting together as a single class shall be required for any action that

(i)   Permits any subsidiary or affiliate of the Company to sell or issue any stock to any party other than the Company;

(ii)   Changes the Board size;

(iii)   Increases the authorized or issued number of shares of any class of Preferred Stock or Common Stock or other security or right convertible into equity of the Company;

(iv)   Creates or commits the Company to enter into a joint venture, licensing agreement or exclusive marketing or other distribution agreement with respect to the Company's products, or a material asset sale, other than in the ordinary course of business;

	Continued
	(v) Results in the Company acquiring equity or results in a material change in the Company's line(s) of business;
	(vi) Enters the Company into material business activities not contemplated in the original business plan presented to the Investors;
	(vii) Commences or settles any material litigation.
Events of Non-Compliance and Remedies:	An event of non-compliance shall occur if (i) the Company breaches in any material respect any of the covenants or any of its obligations to the holders of the Series A Preferred shares and fails to cure such breach after notice and a reasonable opportunity to cure; or (ii) the Company incurs a bankruptcy, receivership, assignment for the benefit of creditors or any unsatisfied judgment in a material amount. If any event of non-compliance occurs and continues for 90 days, and until such event of non-compliance is cured, the holders of a majority of the Series A, B, and C Preferred shares shall have the right to elect a majority of the Company's board of directors.
Capital Expenditures, Assumption of Debt and Guarantees:	A capital budget will be approved by the Board. Approval of the Board is required for any capital expenditure beyond $50,000 greater than the total approved in the annual capital budget (i.e., if the budget is $1,000,000 in total, then board approval is needed for $1,050,001 and greater). Approval of the holders of the Series A Preferred is required for any assumption of debt in excess of a total of $1 million outstanding at any one time and any guarantees of debt or other obligations of another entity, or a grant of a lien or other encumbrance on the assets of the Company.

Continued

Information Rights:	So long as an investor continues to own 5% or more of the Series A Preferred or Common Stock issued upon conversion thereof, the Company shall provide Investors;

1) Audited annual financial statements;
2) Quarterly financial and operating statements;
3) Annual operating plan;
4) Standard inspection and visitation rights;
5) Monthly reports of operations.

Representations and Warranties:	Standard representations and warranties of the Company for transactions of this type.
Registration Rights:	Standard Registration Rights for transactions of this type, to include two demand rights for the Series A Preferred and unlimited piggyback and short-form registration rights.
Rights of First Refusal:	The Company will have the right of first refusal to purchase any shares offered for sale by shareholders. Should the Company not exercise the right in full, said shares must be offered to the holders of the Series A Preferred on a pro-rata basis.
Tag Along Rights:	The holders of the Series A Preferred will have standard TagAlong Rights on any proposed sale of shares by any other holder of outstanding common stock or common stock equivalents, with customary exceptions.
Founders Shares:	The Founders (John Smith and Melissa James) are prohibited from selling any of their shares of the Company prior to a Qualified Public Offering.
Preemptive Rights:	The holders of the Series A Preferred shall have the right in the event the Company proposes to offer equity securities to any person (subject to customary exclusions) to purchase up to its pro-rata portion of such shares (based on the shareholder's percentage of the fully diluted

Continued

	outstanding shares of the Company). Such right of first refusal will not apply to a Qualified Public Offering, and will terminate upon a Qualified Public Offering. In addition, the Company will grant the holders of the Series A Preferred any rights of first refusal or registration rights granted to subsequent purchasers of the Company's equity securities to the extent that such subsequent rights are superior, in good faith judgment of the Company's Board, to those granted in connection with this transaction.
Conditions Precedent:	The following conditions to the Series A Closing must be satisfied prior to the Closing Date:

(i)   Completion of all due diligence to the satisfaction of the Investor;

(ii)   Completion of mutually satisfactory legal documentation;

(iii)   No material adverse change in the Company's business prospects shall have occurred prior to the Closing Date;

(iv)   Satisfaction of other customary closing conditions as set forth in the Stock Purchase Agreement;

(v)   Necessary committee/Board approvals for each Investor.

Non-Competition Agreements:	John Smith and Melissa James will enter into an Employment and Non-competition Agreement with the Company in form and substance reasonably satisfactory to the Investors.
Confidential Information and Invention Assignment Agreement:	Each employee of the Company will enter into a Confidential Information and Invention Agreement with the Company in a form and substance reasonably satisfactory to the Investors.

Continued

Legal and Due Diligence Expenses:	The Company agrees to pay reasonable fees and expenses of the legal counsel for the Investors, together with the Investors' other reasonable due diligence out of pocket expenses.
Exclusivity:	For a period of 45 days from the date of acceptance of this letter, the Company and its shareholders (i) shall deal exclusively with MVI in connection with the issue or sale of any equity or debt securities or assets of the Company or any merger or consolidation involving the Company, (ii) shall not solicit, or engage others to solicit (unless as part of this financing to parties acceptable to MVI and under terms acceptable to MVI) offers for the purchase or acquisition of any equity or debt securities or assets of the Company or for any merger or consolidation involving the Company, (iii) shall not negotiate with or enter into any agreements or understandings with respect to any such transaction without the approval of MVI, (iv) shall inform MVI of any such solicitation or offer; and (v) shall use its best efforts to close the Series A financing as soon as possible.
Other Terms:	Other terms and conditions as the parties shall mutually agree.
Expiration:	This term sheet shall expire unless executed by the Company prior to 9:00 am EST on January 31, 2007.

[Company Name]   Massive Ventures

By: _____   By: _____
Its: _____   Its: _____
Date: _____   Date:_____

B. A Stock Purchase Agreement[1]
C. Shareholders' Agreement[1]
D. Amended Articles of Incorporation[1]
E. Registration Rights Agreement[1]

---

[1] Available from the author.

REFERENCE

Bartlett, J. W. (2002). Trends in venture capital financing terms. In: S. Viello (Ed.), *Venture capital 2002: Getting financing in a changing environment.* New York: Practising Law Institute.

CHAPTER 11

THE ANATOMY OF CONTRACTS IN LICENSING: THE CONTEXT OF BAYH–DOLE

Anne M. Rector and Marie C. Thursby

ABSTRACT

This chapter explains the structure of two contracts commonly involved in university licensing: the license granting a company (or companies) outside the university rights to make, sell, or lease products or processes based on a university invention, and the nondisclosure agreement (NDA) that plays a role in the license negotiation process. In the context of the Bayh–Dole Act, the chapter explains that license contracts often contain a complex combination of payment terms intended to provide sufficient incentives for licensees to undertake the (often risky) development of embryonic research. The authors relate the intent of the Bayh–Dole Act to the concerns of university licensing professionals who often negotiate licensing agreements. The chapter then examines the same incentive issues (and the universal contract issues of money, risk, control, standards, and endgame) in the context of NDAs, used by potential licensing partners to protect their respective interests while sharing information about a licensable technology. The chapter concludes with an assignment that

Technological Innovation: Generating Economic Results
Advances in the Study of Entrepreneurship, Innovation and
Economic Growth, Volume 18, 313–347
Copyright © 2008 by Elsevier Ltd.
All rights of reproduction in any form reserved
ISSN: 1048-4736/doi:10.1016/S1048-4736(07)00011-2

provides students with an opportunity to evaluate a license, not from the
university's perspective but from that of a client interested in licensing an
invention owned by the university.

1. INTRODUCTION

This chapter explains the structure of common contracts involved in
university licensing. We focus on two types of contracts: the license contract,
which grants a company (or companies) outside the university rights to make,
sell, or lease products or processes based on a university invention, and a
nondisclosure agreement (NDA), which plays a role in the license negotiation
process. The nature of both types of agreements is dictated largely by the fact
that the inventions in question are typically quite embryonic, needing substantial development on the part of the licensee before products or processes
can be commercially viable. Typical license contracts tend to involve a
complex combination of payment terms intended to provide sufficient
incentives for licensees to undertake this development, which is often quite
risky. Before reaching the point of negotiating payment terms, however, the
potential licensing partners must share information about the technology at
issue. Their attorneys will attempt to protect the university licensor's interest
in keeping the technology confidential, while also allowing the prospective
licensee access to enough information to evaluate the technology. A confidentiality agreement or NDA is the simplest way to achieve both licensor's and
licensee's goals in the initial discussions.

Section 2 discusses university licensing in the context of the Bayh–Dole
Act, the law underlying much of the licensing that occurs – that is, the
licensing of federally funded inventions. This law was, in large part,
motivated by concerns that, because of the substantial investment needed on
the part of potential licensees, many university inventions would remain
undeveloped. As discussed in Sections 3–5, the intent of the Act was to
provide incentives for licensing and development and, consequently, it
provides a useful framework for understanding the concerns of university
licensing professionals when they structure draft agreements. Section 6
discusses many of the same incentive issues in the context of NDAs. Finally,
Section 7 outlines an assignment in which TI:GER® students evaluate a
license agreement, not from the university's perspective, but from that of a
client interested in licensing an invention.

2. THE BAYH–DOLE ACT

Commercial use of university inventions that are not in the public domain, including use by the inventor(s), typically requires obtaining a license from the university. This is the result of employment policies in US universities which, with rare exception, specify that inventions based on faculty, student, or staff research using university resources belong to the university. When research is partially or wholly funded by the federal government, the licensing of resulting inventions is governed by the Bayh–Dole Act of 1980,[1] which gives universities the right to take title to and exclusively license results from federal funding. Congress intended the Act to provide incentives for universities to market their inventions and for firms to license those inventions, while at the same time protecting the need for wide dissemination of research results. Thus, universities can collect license revenue, which they are required to share with the inventor(s), but in return they must file for patents on inventions that are patentable. As discussed in Chapter 4, exclusive licenses were thought to be necessary for firms to be willing to license and develop inventions from federally funded research because of the inventions' embryonic nature. To prevent the monopoly power created by such exclusivity from standing in the way of an invention's public availability, under Bayh–Dole, the federal government retained the right to "march-in" if a licensee did not take "effective steps to achieve practical application of the subject invention."[2]

Since the passage of Bayh–Dole, patenting and licensing by US universities has increased dramatically. By 1992 over 150 universities reported more than 1,500 patents granted.[3] Since the early nineties, over 200 US universities report having dedicated technology transfer offices (TTOs) devoted to soliciting disclosures by employees and licensing their inventions. The most recent Association of University Technology Managers (AUTM) Annual Survey (2004) reported 3,090 patents issued, 9,247 patent applications, and 3,867 licenses executed by the 158 responding universities. For the 109 institutions responding in both 1996 and 2004, the number of inventions disclosed increased 72.5%, from an average of 66.9 per institution to 115.4. The average number of new patent applications filed increased 231%, from an average of 22.8 per institution to an average of 73.4. The number of license and option agreements executed by universities rose 71.6%, from an average of 18.7 to an average of 32.1. Roughly 70% of these licenses were to small firms or start-up firms. Of the licenses to small firms, 42% were exclusive, and 90% of the licenses to start-ups were exclusive.

Although data on the portion of license agreements that result from federal funding are not available from AUTM, an earlier survey of 62 university TTOs showed that over 60% of the licenses executed were the result of federal funding.[4] Thus, it is not surprising that Bayh-Dole has heavily influenced TTO missions and operations. All TTOs responding to the survey reported having multiple objectives, including earning revenue and sponsored research, as well as simply executing licenses and encouraging commercialization. Although the TTOs' most important objective was earning revenue, with 98% of the respondents noting that revenue was either moderately or extremely important to them, next in importance was the number of inventions commercialized, with 92% noting commercialization was either moderately or extremely important to them. In response to open-ended questions, the TTO professionals noted that their two greatest challenges were obtaining cooperation from faculty inventors and due diligence to ensure licensees pursue commercialization. This attitude of TTO professionals factors prominently in the types of contracts offered to potential licensees.

3. LICENSE CHARACTERISTICS

Appendix B provides a base template used for exclusive licenses offered by the TTO of a major US university. The sections most relevant to this chapter are those on company diligence obligations and payment terms. Section 3 includes six separate diligence requirements. The first stipulates a time period within which the licensee company must furnish the licensor university with a written plan for research and development aimed at bringing a product or process based on the licensed invention to market, and the second requires a yearly update on progress toward that plan. The last four specify dates by which the company must meet development or commercial milestones, such as working prototype, first commercial sale, net sales, and a number of products sold.

As shown in Section 4 of the template, the university also seeks multiple payment terms, including a nonrefundable license issue fee and patent reimbursement by a particular date, as well as annual license fees to be paid each year the license is maintained. The latter fees are also nonrefundable, but may be credited against running royalties paid in the same year. Running royalties are payments as a percent of the value of the company's net sales.

This template is an example from a single university and is in draft form, so particular items may or may not appear in final negotiated agreements. Nonetheless, the complexity of payment terms is consistent with results from several university license surveys.[5] For example, Jensen and Thursby (2001)[6] estimate that license issue fees and running royalties appear in 84 % of the contracts executed; annual maintenance fees and patent reimbursement appear in 78% of the contracts; and fees paid when milestones are reached are included in 58% of the contracts. Notice that the last of these includes, not only the due diligence requirements mentioned in Section 3 of the form license agreement in Appendix B, but also a payment when the milestone is reached.

4. STAGE OF DEVELOPMENT

The rationale for such complicated payment terms lies in the early stage of development of the majority of university inventions. In this section we consider the stage of invention development, and in Section 5 we relate development stage to payment terms.

The first column of Table 1 gives estimates, provided by TTO personnel responding to the Thursby et al. (2001) survey, of the percentage of university inventions at various stages of development at the time they were licensed. On an average, these professionals estimate, slightly less than half of these inventions were no more than a proof of concept at the time of license, and another 37% were no more than a lab scale prototype. For the subset of inventions requiring animal or clinical trials before public use, less than one-fourth had data available at the time of license. Manufacturing feasibility was known for only 15% of the inventions. Only 12% were considered ready for commercial use. Thus, 88% of the inventions licensed required further development by the licensee, making shelving a potential issue for most inventions licensed out by universities. Shelving in this context refers to a licensee's failure to pursue development and/or applications of a licensed technology, as discussed in Section 5.

Table 1. Licensing Survey Results (Thursby et al., 2001).

Stage of Development	TTO (%)	Business (%)
Proof of concept (no prototype)	45	38
Prototype (only lab scale)	37	36
Preclinical stage	26	15
Clinical stage	10	5
Manufacturing feasibility known	15	9
Ready for commercial use	12	7

The second column of Table 1 gives similar estimates from a survey of 112 companies that license in university inventions. While the percentages given by companies differ somewhat, they paint the same picture. The majority of inventions licensed required substantial development before products or processes based on them were commercialized.

This need for further development, after execution of the license contract, means that the TTO's ability to meet its Bayh–Dole obligation to ensure reasonable efforts to commercialize an invention depends on the licensee's effort. This dependence explains the list of due diligence provisions in the typical license. Notice in the appended template that failure to fulfill any of the diligence requirements constitutes material breach and, according to Section 12.3, also constitutes grounds for the university to terminate the agreement. An important point to realize, however, is that in practice it is costly and probably impossible for the university to perfectly monitor development effort by the licensee. Although, for example, Subsections 3.1(a) and (b) ask for statements of the number of employees working on development and intended levels of sales, such reports can be inflated and may well not reflect true company commitment to commercializing the licensed invention.

Another key to explaining payment terms is that, in addition to company's effort, successful commercialization often requires inventor collaboration with the licensee. According to the TTO professionals, roughly 70% of the inventions licensed required inventor cooperation with the licensee for successful development. On the licensee side, the business executives estimated that inventor cooperation was critical for development of the inventions they licensed 40% of the time. The inventor's role in development is notably highest for those inventions in the proof of concept phase and lowest for those inventions ready for commercial use. For example, business executives said that inventor collaboration was needed for only 20% of the inventions that were ready for commercial use. Sixty-seven percent of the business executives responding said that faculty collaboration was critical because they have specialized knowledge of the technology.

Finally, developing university inventions is quite risky, because respondents to the business survey report the failure rate of licensed university inventions as 46%. Of those, nearly half (47%) failed for purely technical reasons.

5. PAYMENT TERMS

The need for inventor and licensee effort in further development, effort which is hard if not impossible to observe and therefore monitor, presents a problem of contractibility. So, while in the appended license, Section 3, Diligence Obligations, specifies deliverables during the development process, those obligations are imperfect monitoring mechanisms. Universities therefore need to structure payments in a way that provides appropriate incentives for all of the parties involved in development.

For example, consider the need for inventor collaboration. If inventors prefer conducting original research, they are unlikely to spend time working with the licensee unless their own financial incentives are tied to commercial success. This is because, under the provisions of Bayh–Dole, an inventor receives a portion of the university's license revenue regardless of that inventor's efforts toward commercialization. If the total license payment were to be made upfront (i.e., if the total payment made by the licensee were a license issue fee), then the inventor could collect her/his share immediately and regardless of her/his effort in development. This conflict arises with license maintenance fees as well. However, license payments in the form of milestone payments or running royalties will accrue to the inventor only if technical milestones are met and/or the invention is commercially successful. This, then, is known as the moral hazard problem: the outcome of a contracting problem depends on an agent's effort, which is unobservable. As a result, the principal who offers the contract must design it so as to provide sufficient incentives for the agent to contribute the desired effort.

The need for licensee effort implies that, in addition to inventor moral hazard, there is a second problem, known as adverse selection, in which firms may "shelve" inventions. Shelving occurs where the licensee's intent in licensing was simply to block other firms from developing them or, more innocently, because by the time the invention's development is completed, expected profits are less than originally anticipated.

Suppose a firm expresses interest in an invention because it simply wants to bar a rival's access to the invention. Such a firm obviously has no intention of assigning employees to development, or if it were to conduct experiments to determine technical success, it would not commercialize the invention. The ideal contract for such a firm would impose only one form of payment – a running royalty – because the firm has no intention of selling a product based on the invention. Thus, one justification for the license issue fee is that, if high enough, the fee discourages shelving firms from trying to obtain a license.

A second problem with regard to licensee incentives arises because development takes time and strategic directions of companies change. By the time the company determines the invention to be technically successful, the direction of the company may have changed. This was true in the march-in case of Cell Pro and Johns Hopkins. In 1997, Bayh and Cutler petitioned the National Institutes of Health to take back the Johns Hopkins license for the My-10 antibody originally licensed to Becton Dickinson. While the latter company had invested in development, over time it decided to withdraw from the therapeutic business, so developing the licensed antibody had no economic value to the company. Cases such as these motivate universities to demand the annual maintenance fees included in the attached template. These fees provide an incentive for the licensee to return the license to the university if the firm no longer intends to commercialize it.

6. UNDERSTANDING NONDISCLOSURE AGREEMENTS AND LICENSES

While the TTO or the licensee of a university invention may expect their attorneys to simply "paper the deal" – that is, transfer the terms of a negotiated business deal into written form – transactional attorneys must be more than scriveners to accomplish their clients' needs. In fact, they have to understand the client's business needs and then *translate* those needs into contract concepts.[7]

Understanding the licensor motivations described above in Sections 2–4 can move the transactional attorney down the road toward successfully representing a university TTO or a technology licensee. In fact, some of the same core issues will arise in every business transaction, whether a license out from a university to an established company, or an NDA between two parties considering a joint venture or partnership, or a lease of business premises, or a contract of employment. As implied in part by earlier sections of this chapter and as noted by one legal author, each of these agreements addresses the core issues of *money, risk, control, standards*, and *endgame.*[8]

The remainder of this chapter discusses how these five core issues might play out in the context of an NDA or a license agreement. Assume that a TI:GER® student team is about to negotiate terms with a company interested in licensing the PhD student's technology. First, though, the potential licensee firm (TechLicensee, Inc. or TLI) wants to learn all about the technology. The licensor (Montana Institute of Technology or MIT) has two interests: licensing the technology and preventing TLI from expropriating that technology (see Chapter 8). Thus, the TI:GER® student team has sent TLI the draft NDA in Appendix A. We will examine how the five core issues play out in that document.

As discussed in Sections 2–5, *money* is central to most business deals, and it is the driver behind many contract provisions. When parties enter into an NDA, however, they are exchanging not funds, but information. Thus, the sample NDA makes no provision for payments between the parties.

Beyond the clearly stated financial provisions of most contracts are the parts that more subtly allocate *risk*. Risk allocation is accomplished most often by financial provisions such as the license issue fee, royalty, and milestone payments discussed in Section 5. But risk also is assigned in contracts through use of conditions precedent, covenants, and representations and warranties.[9]

A representation is simply a fact statement made at a particular moment in time; its maker intends the statement to cause the recipient to rely upon it and, based on that reliance, to act or to refrain from acting.[10] A warranty, on the other hand, is a promise by the person making the statement that it is true. Because most contracts list "representations and warranties" in the same section, one could infer the two terms are interchangeable.[11] They are not: a representation gives rise to different remedies than does a warranty. In the sample NDA, for example, we find one representation and warranty from the prospective licensor, MIT and MTRC, to the prospective licensee, TLI: "MTRC and MIT represent and warrant that neither of them has disclosed the Proprietary Information to any person or entity for the purpose of investigating a licensing arrangement."[12] This representation, if false but made honestly or negligently by MTRC and MIT, gives TechLicensee (who relied upon it) a right to rescind the NDA and to receive restitution. In contrast, if that false representation is made fraudulently, then TechLicensee can sue MTRC and MIT to receive money damages. In addition, because MTRC and MIT also gave a warranty as to that same false statement, TLI can receive money damages *regardless of whether TLI knew the statement was false, and regardless of whether TLI actually relied on the statement.*[13] Thus, representations and warranties lower the riskiness of a transaction to the party receiving them.

In contrast to reps and warranties, a covenant allocates risk by addressing actions of the parties or changes in circumstances that either may or must occur between the contract's signing and the deal's closing. Covenants create common law contract remedies of damages and specific performance (i.e., a court can require the other party both to pay money and to perform the actions it promised to do).[14] In the sample NDA, for example, the prospective licensee TLI could ask for a covenant from MRTC and MIT that "prior to the date Proprietary Information is disclosed to TLI pursuant to this Agreement, the Proprietary Information will not be disclosed to any other person or entity."

A condition precedent, our final contract provision for allocating *risk*, is a specific set of facts that must exist before one party is obligated to close the deal[15] or, where a closing is not necessary, to perform its part of the contract.[16] If that factual requirement never occurs (the condition is unsatisfied), then the party requiring it can refuse to perform and thus has what is called a "walk-away right." In addition, the party that fails to fulfill the condition precedent cannot bring a breach of contract lawsuit if first party does choose to walk away. A condition precedent to performance by MTRC and MIT under our NDA could involve securing the Proprietary Information: "TLI agrees that, as a condition precedent to the obligation of MTRC and MIT to disclose the Proprietary Information, TLI will create a secure room at its principal place of business (the "Site"), at which Site the Proprietary Information will be delivered by MTRC and held and evaluated by TLI."

Risk can, of course, reach beyond the purely financial and affect reputation or creditworthiness. Most risk-allocation provisions, however, are simply a way to shift present or potential future financial hazards from one side of a transaction to the other. For example, as noted in Section 5, a licensing contract creates a risk to the licensing university that the licensee will shelve the licensed technology. The government retains "march-in" rights under Bayh–Dole but prefers to avoid exercising them. Thus, a financial provision such as a license issue fee to discourage shelving often is at heart a risk-allocation device and is needed to provide incentives when actions by either the licensor or licensee are, in effect, noncontractible. Risk allocation also occurs by means of liability and indemnification provisions. Thus, for example, a licensor and licensee must agree upon the degree of tort liability exposure each is willing to assume once the licensed technology reaches its market.[17] Parties also can agree not to impose liability upon each other: for example, in Section 3 of the NDA, TLI, MTRC, and MIT agree they are not liable to each other if one of them is forced to disclose Proprietary Information by a court.

Control is another key component of virtually all contracts. In the NDA, control of the Proprietary Information is the central issue between the parties. MTRC and MIT might ask for the following additional language that makes more explicit TLI's obligation to control access to the Proprietary Information it receives: "TLI further covenants and agrees that Proprietary Information will not be removed from the Site by TLI except pursuant to §7 of this Agreement." This is a logical follow-on to the condition precedent and is a risk-allocation device intended, among other things, to reduce MTRC and MIT's risk that the Proprietary Information will not be kept confidential by TLI. A further example of a control provision appears in

Section 5: "The Proprietary Information shall not be used by TLI for any purpose other than evaluation and negotiation of a possible license with MIT." This is an attempt by MTRC and MIT to avoid the risk that the prospective licensee, TLI, will simply expropriate the Proprietary Information, or its most valuable component, for TLI's own use. In a licensing agreement, control is expressed in the essential terms of the contract: is it an exclusive or non-exclusive license? Beyond that core question, parties to a license may want either more, or less, control depending upon whether having control redounds to their potential benefit or to their potential harm. For example, a license out may include a provision requiring the licensor to submit reports *and* to permit the licensor to visit the licensee's facilities in order to confirm the licensee's performance under the license and the accuracy of the licensee's reports to the licensor.[18]

Arguably, the same Section 5 of the NDA that is a control device also sets a *standard* for TLI's performance under the NDA. Standards are created by most words that appear in a contract.[19] In the NDA, for example, the definitions in §1 state the parties' agreed-upon standard for information to which the NDA applies. Similarly, §6 creates the standard of "immediate" return of Proprietary Information upon MTRC's request. That standard could have been made even more vague by substituting "promptly" for "immediately," or more precise by substituting return "within 48 hours." A license agreement also will establish standards, whether for timeliness of submitted reports or the exercise of one party's discretion (e.g., "in its reasonable judgment"[20]). Attorneys must learn to recognize standards language, to decide whether their client can or will perform up to the standard created by that language, and, if necessary, to negotiate a different standard that better meets the client's business needs.[21] Failure to create appropriate standards can result in contract breaches that could have been avoided.

Endgame refers to how the parties will end their contractual relationship, whether mutually or unilaterally.[22] Often this issue is addressed in "event of default" provisions, by which the parties define in advance certain situations that will be a basis for terminating their contract. Endgame also encompasses the contract language describing the steps, if any, each party may or must take before declaring the contract terminated. While the NDA does not explicitly address endgame, it does provide in §7 that TLI will return all Proprietary Information to MTRC immediately upon request. In addition, §9 of the NDA creates a two-year term for the entire agreement, but goes on to impose confidentiality obligations on TLI, for five years with respect to Confidential Information and perpetually with respect to Trade Secrets. Thus, while the term of an agreement (i.e., the time period it remains in force) may seem an aspect of *endgame*, this NDA provision also imposes *control* obligations on TLI, thereby lowering *risk* for MTRC and MIT.

The license template in Appendix B handles *endgame* both explicitly and implicitly: explicitly in Sections 10 ("Assignment"), 12 ("Termination"), and 13 ("Dispute Resolution"); and implicitly in Section 4 ("Royalties and Payment Terms"). Section 4 reflects many of the license characteristics described above in Section 2 of this chapter. For example, Section 4.1 imposes both a license issue fee and reimbursement of the licensor's patent costs upon the licensee. Adverse selection also may be avoided by imposition of the license issue fee, as discussed earlier in Section 5 of this chapter. Also as noted in Section 5, the problem of adverse selection motivates licensors to include other payment provisions, such as those in Section 4.1 requiring the licensee to pay both annual maintenance fees and running royalties.

Returning to our initial consideration from Section 2, university-to-industry licensing reflects limitations and requirements imposed by government regulation of technology transfer. The Bayh–Dole Act[23] has, as one stated objective, "protect[ing] the public against nonuse or unreasonable use of inventions."[24] As noted in Section 2, this objective then motivates licensors to include payment terms that encourage licensees not to shelve a licensed technology. The Act also imposes reporting obligations and sets limits on universities' rights to retain title to inventions stemming from federally funded research.[25] In addition, Bayh–Dole requires universities and their licensees to agree that the invention will be manufactured substantially in the US.[26] Finally, as mentioned in Section 2, the Act gives the government the right to "march- in" and reallocate rights to an invention to "a responsible applicant" if the university or its assignee fails "to achieve practical application" of the invention.[27] Language throughout the Exclusive Patent License Agreement in Appendix B reflects these requirements of federal law.[28] The assignment that follows in Section 7 asks students to identify that language in the Exclusive Patent License Agreement from the viewpoint of our potential licensee, TLI.

7. EVALUATING AN EXCLUSIVE PATENT LICENSE AGREEMENT DRAFT FROM THE LICENSEE'S PERSPECTIVE

Assume that your TI:GER® team is, or that as attorneys you represent, TechLicensee, Inc. – the public company that signed the NDA, evaluated the technology, and now wants to license that technology. This is a shift from your team's usual viewpoint as a potential licensor.

Read and think through the practical impact of each provision of the Exclusive Patent License Agreement Draft in Appendix B. Identify terms that reflect issues of *money, risk, control, standards,* and *endgame* discussed in Section 6. As noted in this chapter, contractual provisions often are driven by government regulation of technology transfer. Thus, please identify language in the Exclusive Patent License Agreement Draft that may be included as a response to the Bayh–Dole Act.

As a team, write a short memorandum to opposing counsel (who represents the licensor – MIT, its TTO, and the inventor). Identify the provisions of this agreement to which you object. Draft the language you want opposing counsel to use in place of the original. Do not completely rewrite the draft license agreement: instead, select the portions for negotiation and revision that your team identifies as of most importance to TLI, the licensee. Be prepared to discuss your team's drafting experience during the next class meeting, including explaining each language change you request.

NOTES

1. 35 U.S.C. §200 et seq. (2001).
2. Id. at §203.
3. R. Henderson, A. Jaffe, M. Trajtenberg, *Universities as a Source of Commercial Technology: A Detailed Analysis of University Patenting, 1965–1988,* 80:1 Rev. Econ. Statistics 119 (1998).
4. R. Jensen, M. C. Thursby, *Proofs and Prototypes for Sale: The Licensing of University Inventions,* 91:1 Am. Econ. Rev. 240 (2001); J. G. Thursby, R. Jensen, M. C. Thursby, *Objectives, Characteristics and Outcomes of University Licensing: A Survey of Major U.S. Universities,.* 26:1–2 J. Tech. Transfer 59 (2001).
5. R. Jensen, M. C. Thursby, *Proofs and Prototypes for Sale: The Licensing of University Inventions,* 91:1 Am. Econ. Rev. 240 (2001); J. G. Thursby, R. Jensen, M. C. Thursby, *Objectives, Characteristics and Outcomes of University Licensing: A Survey of Major U.S. Universities,.* 26:1–2 J. Tech. Transfer 59 (2001); E. Dechenaux, M. C. Thursby, J. G. Thursby, *Shirking, Sharing Risk, and Shelving: The Role of University License Contracts* (2007).
6. R. Jensen, M. C. Thursby, *Proofs and Prototypes for Sale: The Licensing of University Inventions,* 91:1 Am. Econ. Rev. 240 (2001).
7. T. L. Stark, *Thinking Like a Deal Lawyer,* 54 J. Leg. Educ. 223, 223 (2004). See also C. M. Fox, Working with Contracts: What Law School Doesn't Teach You 33–63 (2002). New York: Practicing Law Institute.
8. Id. at 228. See also discussion of confidentiality and license agreements in H. B. Wellons, E. S. Ewing, R. Copple, W. Wofford, and E. Leitzan, Biotechnology and the Law 122–124, 156–158 (2007). Chicago: ABA Publishing.
9. Id. at 229.
10. T. L. Stark, Drafting Contracts: How and Why Lawyers Do What They Do, Chap. 3 (2007). New York: Aspen Publishers.

11. Indeed, attorneys still fall prey to the old custom of using paired, duplicative words in contracts: for example, a debt is "due and owing." See Appendix B, Montana Institute of Technology Exclusive Patent License Agreement Draft, §13.2, which refers to "sole and exclusive procedures."

12. See Appendix A, Nondisclosure Agreement between TechLicensee, Inc. and the Montana Institute of Technology and Montana Tech Research Corporation, §4. This unequivocal statement is called a "flat representation." Risk could be shifted from the licensor to the licensee by adding words that hedge, creating a "qualified representation" – "MTRC and MIT represent and warrant that, except for the disclosure listed on Exhibit A to this Agreement, neither of them has disclosed the Proprietary Information to an person or entity except pursuant to agreements substantially similar to this Agreement."

13. For a detailed discussion of the damages available, see T. L. Stark, Drafting Documents: How and Why Lawyers Do What They Do, Chap. 3 (2007). New York: Aspen Publishers. See also Appendix B, Montana Institute of Technology Exclusive Patent License Agreement Draft, §9, "No Representations or Warranties."

14. T. L. Stark, Drafting Contracts: How and Why Lawyers Do What They Do, Chap. 3 (2007). New York: Aspen Publishers.

15. K. A. Adams, Legal Usage in Drafting Corporate Agreements, 44–45 (2001). Westport, CT: Quorum Books.

16. T. L. Stark, Drafting Contracts: How and Why Lawyers Do What They Do, Chap. 4, (2007), Aspen Publishers.

17. See Appendix B, Montana Institute of Technology Exclusive Patent License Agreement Draft, §8, "Indemnification and Insurance."

18. See Appendix B, Montana Institute of Technology Exclusive Patent License Agreement Draft, §5, "Reports and Records " and §3.1, "Diligence Requirements."

19. Stark, supra note 7, at 231.

20. See Appendix B, Montana Institute of Technology Exclusive Patent License Agreement Draft, §13.2, "Dispute Resolution."

21. Stark, supra note 7, at 231.

22. Id.

23. 35 U.S.C. §200 et seq. (2001).

24. Id. at §200.

25. Id. at §202 (requiring the university, among other things, to report inventions to the government within a reasonable time; to elect within two years after disclosure to retain title to the invention; to file a patent application and to disclose in the patent application that the invention was made with federal government support and that the government has rights in it; to make periodic reports on use or efforts at using the invention; to share royalties with the inventor; to license, where feasible, to small business firms; and to reinvest royalties or income from an invention in scientific research, development, and education.).

26. Id. at §204.

27. Id. at §203.

28. For example, read the "Recitals" portion of Appendix B, Montana Institute of Technology Exclusive Patent License Agreement Draft.

APPENDIX A

NONDISCLOSURE AGREEMENT
BETWEEN
TECHLICENSEE, INC.
AND
THE MONTANA INSTITUTE OF TECHNOLOGY
AND THE MONTANA TECH RESEARCH CORPORATION

This Agreement is effective as of the _____ day of _____, 200_ ("Effective Date"), by and between TechLicensee, Inc., a Montana corporation, and Montana Institute of Technology ("MIT"), and Montana Tech Research Corporation, a Montana Corporation ("MTRC").

Whereas TechLicensee, Inc., together with its employees and agents (collectively, "TLI") may receive information about certain MTRC technology (the "Technology"), and whereas MTRC or MIT may disclose to TLI Proprietary Information (as hereinafter defined) to facilitate such observation; now, therefore, in consideration of the foregoing and the mutual promises contained herein, TLI, MIT and MTRC hereby agree as follows:

1. Definitions
(a) Trade Secrets - As used in this Agreement the term "Trade Secrets" shall mean any scientific or technical information, design, process, procedure, formula, or improvement that is commercially valuable and secret in that it is not generally known in the industry in the areas in which it is utilized.
(b) Confidential Information - As used in this Agreement the term "Confidential Information" shall mean any data or information having commercial value that may include but not be limited to data, data bases, product plans, strategies, forecasts, research procedures and development, marketing techniques, procedures and materials, customer names and other information related to customers, price-lists, pricing policies, and financial information that the parties consider sensitive and is not generally known to the public.
(c) Proprietary Information - As used in this Agreement, the term "Proprietary Information" shall mean Trade Secrets and Confidential Information, as defined above.

2. TLI agrees to hold Proprietary Information received hereunder in confidence and to utilize its best efforts to avoid disclosure of such Proprietary Information to any person, firm, corporation or individual. TLI shall have no obligation of confidentiality with respect to information received hereunder that:
(a) is already known to TLI at the time of disclosure, as evidenced by written records of the TLI produced for MTRC's inspection within 14 days after disclosure of the information; or
(b) is or becomes publicly known without the wrongful act or breach of this Agreement; or
(c) is rightfully received by TLI on a non-confidential basis from a third party with a lawful right to disclose; or
(d) is approved for release to a third party by the written authorization of MTRC.

3. Neither party shall be liable to the other for the disclosure of Proprietary Information that the party is obligated to disclose by order of a court of competent jurisdiction.

4. MTRC and MIT represent and warrant that neither of them has disclosed the Proprietary Information to any person or entity for the purpose of investigating a licensing arrangement.

5. Any information pertaining to the Technology that is disclosed by MTRC or MIT to TLI shall be treated as Proprietary Information. The Proprietary Information shall not be used by TLI for any purpose other than evaluation and negotiation of a possible license with MIT. All other information disclosed by MTRC or MIT to TLI shall not be considered Proprietary Information unless MTRC indicates to TLI at the time of such disclosure that the information is Proprietary and within thirty (30) days after such disclosure provides TLI with an appropriately-marked writing setting forth such Proprietary Information.

6. Nothing in this Agreement shall be construed to grant TLI any right, title or license in or to any Proprietary Information received hereunder, other than the right to receive such Proprietary Information for the purpose of evaluating such Proprietary Information in anticipation of a licensing transaction with MTRC.

7. TLI agrees to return all Proprietary Information received under this Agreement to MTRC immediately upon request.

8. This Agreement shall be governed by and construed in accordance with the laws of the State of Montana, without giving effect to principles of conflicts of laws.

9. The term of this Agreement shall be two (2) years from the Effective Date of this Agreement, provided that the term of confidentiality with respect to Confidential Information received by TLI hereunder shall be five (5) years after the date of disclosure of Confidential Information, and the term of confidentiality with respect to Trade Secrets received by TLI hereunder shall be perpetual.

THE MONTANA INSTITUTE OF TECHNOLOGY
MONTANA TECH RESEARCH CORPORATION   **TECHLICENSEE, INC.**
BY_____   BY_____
Makawi Magone, III, PhD   ITS_____
Director, OTT
DATE_____   DATE_____

APPENDIX B

*Last Modified:*_____

OTT: _____

MONTANA INSTITUTE OF TECHNOLOGY

EXCLUSIVE PATENT LICENSE AGREEMENT*

DRAFT

Offer to continue negotiations based upon this
draft agreement open until_____

*Used with permission.

MONTANA INSTITUTE OF TECHNOLOGY
EXCLUSIVE PATENT LICENSE AGREEMENT

DRAFT

This Agreement, effective as of the date set forth above the signatures of the parties below (the "EFFECTIVE DATE"), is between the Montana Institute of Technology ("M.I.T."), a Montana corporation, with its principal office at 101 East Main Street, Missoula, MT 59802-4458 and TechLicensee, Inc. ("COMPANY"), a Montana corporation, with a principal place of business at _____.

RECITALS

WHEREAS, M.I.T. is the owner of certain PATENT RIGHTS (as later defined herein) relating to M.I.T. Case No. _____, "_____" by _____ and has the right to grant licenses under said PATENT RIGHTS;

WHEREAS, M.I.T. desires to have the PATENT RIGHTS developed and commercialized to benefit the public and is willing to grant a license thereunder;

WHEREAS, COMPANY has represented to M.I.T., to induce M.I.T. to enter into this Agreement, that COMPANY shall commit itself to a thorough, vigorous and diligent program of exploiting the PATENT RIGHTS so that public utilization shall result therefrom; and

WHEREAS, COMPANY desires to obtain a license under the PATENT RIGHTS upon the terms and conditions hereinafter set forth.

NOW, THEREFORE, M.I.T. and COMPANY hereby agree as follows:

1. DEFINITIONS.

1.1 "AFFILIATE" shall mean any legal entity (such as a corporation, partnership, or limited liability company) that is controlled by COMPANY. For the purposes of this definition, the term "control" means (i) beneficial ownership of at least fifty percent (50%) of the voting securities of a corporation or other business organization with voting securities or (ii) a fifty percent (50%) or greater interest in the net assets or profits of a partnership or other business organization without voting securities.

1.2 "EXCLUSIVE PERIOD" shall mean the period of time set forth in Section 2.2.

1.3 "FIELD" shall mean [definition of field].

1.4 "LICENSED PRODUCT" shall mean any product that, in whole or in part:
    (i)   absent the license granted hereunder, would infringe one or more claims of the PATENT RIGHTS; or
    (ii)   is manufactured by using a LICENSED PROCESS or that, when used, practices a LICENSED PROCESS.

1.5 "<u>LICENSED PROCESS</u>" shall mean any process that, absent the license granted hereunder, would infringe one or more claims of the PATENT RIGHTS or which uses a LICENSED PRODUCT.

1.6 "<u>NET SALES</u>" shall mean the gross amount billed by COMPANY and its AFFILIATES and SUBLICENSEES for LICENSED PRODUCTS and LICENSED PROCESSES, less the following:

(i) customary trade, quantity, or cash discounts to the extent actually allowed and taken;

(ii) amounts repaid or credited by reason of rejection or return;

(iii) to the extent separately stated on purchase orders, invoices, or other documents of sale, any taxes or other governmental charges levied on the production, sale, transportation, delivery, or use of a LICENSED PRODUCT or LICENSED PROCESS which is paid by or on behalf of COMPANY; and

(iv) outbound transportation costs prepaid or allowed and costs of insurance in transit.

No deductions shall be made for commissions paid to individuals whether they be with independent sales agencies or regularly employed by COMPANY and on its payroll, or for cost of collections. NET SALES shall occur on the date of billing for a LICENSED PRODUCT or LICENSED PROCESS. If a LICENSED PRODUCT or a LICENSED PROCESS is distributed at a discounted price that is substantially lower than the customary price charged by COMPANY, or distributed for non-cash consideration (whether or not at a discount), NET SALES shall be calculated based on the non-discounted amount of the LICENSED PRODUCT or LICENSED PROCESS charged to an independent third party during the same REPORTING PERIOD or, in the absence of such sales, on the fair market value of the LICENSED PRODUCT or LICENSED PROCESS

Non-monetary consideration shall not be accepted by COMPANY, any AFFILIATE, or any SUBLICENSEE for any LICENSED PRODUCTS or LICENSED PROCESSES without the prior written consent of M.I.T.

1.7 "<u>PATENT RIGHTS</u>" shall mean:

(a) the United States and international patents listed on Appendix A;

(b) the United States and international patent applications and/or provisional applications listed on Appendix A and the resulting patents;

(c) any patent applications resulting from the provisional applications listed on Appendix A, and any divisionals, continuations, continuation-in-part applications, and continued prosecution applications (and their relevant international equivalents) of the patent applications listed on Appendix A and of such patent applications that result from the provisional applications listed on Appendix A, to the extent the claims are directed to subject matter specifically described in the patent applications listed on Appendix A, and the resulting patents;

(d)   any patents resulting from reissues, reexaminations, or extensions (and their relevant international equivalents) of the patents described in (a), (b), and (c) above; and

(e)   international (non-United States) patent applications and provisional applications filed after the EFFECTIVE DATE and the relevant international equivalents to divisionals, continuations, continuation-in-part applications and continued prosecution applications of the patent applications to the extent the claims are directed to subject matter specifically described in the patents or patent applications referred to in (a), (b), (c), and (d) above, and the resulting patents.

1.8 "REPORTING PERIOD" shall begin on the first day of each calendar quarter and end on the last day of such calendar quarter.

1.9 "SUBLICENSE INCOME" shall mean any payments that COMPANY receives from a SUBLICENSEE in consideration of the sublicense of the rights granted COMPANY under Section 2.1, including without limitation license fees, milestone payments, license maintenance fees, and other payments, but specifically excluding royalties on NET SALES.

1.10 "SUBLICENSEE" shall mean any non-AFFILIATE sublicensee of the rights granted COMPANY under Section 2.1.

1.11 "TERM" shall mean the term of this Agreement, which shall commence on the EFFECTIVE DATE and shall remain in effect until the expiration or abandonment of all issued patents and filed patent applications within the PATENT RIGHTS, unless earlier terminated in accordance with the provisions of this Agreement.

1.12 "TERRITORY" shall mean [fill-in territory or world-wide.]

2. GRANT OF RIGHTS.

2.1 License Grants. Subject to the terms of this Agreement, M.I.T. hereby grants to COMPANY and its AFFILIATES for the TERM a royalty-bearing license under the PATENT RIGHTS to develop, make, have made, use, sell, offer to sell, lease, and import LICENSED PRODUCTS in the FIELD in the TERRITORY and to develop and perform LICENSED PROCESSES in the FIELD in the TERRITORY.

2.2 Exclusivity. In order to establish an exclusive period for COMPANY, M.I.T. agrees that it shall not grant any other license under the PATENT RIGHTS to make, have made, use, sell, lease and import LICENSED PRODUCTS in the FIELD in the TERRITORY or to perform LICENSED PROCESSES in the FIELD in the TERRITORY during the period of time commencing on the EFFECTIVE DATE and terminating with the first to occur of:

(i)   the expiration of _____(__) years after the first accrual of NET SALES or SUBLICENSE INCOME for a LICENSED PRODUCT or LICENSED PROCESS; or

(ii)   the expiration of _____(__) years after the EFFECTIVE DATE ("EXCLUSIVE PERIOD").

Upon expiration of the EXCLUSIVE PERIOD, the license granted hereunder shall become nonexclusive and shall extend to the end of the TERM, unless sooner terminated as provided in this Agreement.

2.3 Sublicenses. COMPANY shall have the right to grant sublicenses of its rights under Section 2.1 only during the EXCLUSIVE PERIOD. Such sublicenses may extend past the expiration date of the EXCLUSIVE PERIOD, but any exclusivity of such sublicense shall expire upon the expiration of the EXCLUSIVE PERIOD. COMPANY shall incorporate terms and conditions into its sublicense agreements sufficient to enable COMPANY to comply with this Agreement. COMPANY shall promptly furnish M.I.T. with a fully signed photocopy of any sublicense agreement. Upon termination of this Agreement for any reason, any SUBLICENSEE not then in default shall have the right to seek a license from M.I.T. M.I.T. agrees to negotiate such licenses in good faith under reasonable terms and conditions.

2.4 U.S. Manufacturing. COMPANY agrees that any LICENSED PRODUCTS used or sold in the United States will be manufactured substantially in the United States .

2.5 Retained Rights.

(a)   M.I.T. M.I.T. retains the right to practice under the PATENT RIGHTS for research, teaching, and educational purposes.

(b)   Federal Government. COMPANY acknowledges that the U.S. federal government retains a royalty-free, non-exclusive, non-transferable license to practice any government-funded invention claimed in any PATENT RIGHTS as set forth in 35 U.S.C. §§ 201-211, and the regulations promulgated thereunder, as amended, or any successor statutes or regulations.

2.6 No Additional Rights. Nothing in this Agreement shall be construed to confer any rights upon COMPANY by implication, estoppel, or otherwise as to any technology or patent rights of M.I.T. or any other entity other than the PATENT RIGHTS, regardless of whether such technology or patent rights shall be dominant or subordinate to any PATENT RIGHTS.

3. COMPANY DILIGENCE OBLIGATIONS.

3.1 Diligence Requirements. COMPANY shall use diligent efforts, or shall cause its AFFILIATES and SUBLICENSEES to use diligent efforts, to develop LICENSED PRODUCTS or LICENSED PROCESSES and to introduce LICENSED PRODUCTS or LICENSED PROCESSES into the commercial market; thereafter,

COMPANY or its AFFILIATES or SUBLICENSEES shall make LICENSED PRODUCTS or LICENSED PROCESSES reasonably available to the public. Specifically, COMPANY or AFFILIATE or SUBLICENSEE shall fulfill the following obligations:

(a)   Within _____ months after the EFFECTIVE DATE, COMPANY shall furnish M.I.T. with a written research and development plan describing the major tasks to be achieved in order to bring to market a LICENSED PRODUCT or a LICENSED PROCESS, specifying the number of staff and other resources to be devoted to such commercialization effort.

(b)   Within sixty (60) days after the end of each calendar year, COMPANY shall furnish M.I.T. with a written report (consistent with Section 5.1(a)) on the progress of its efforts during the immediately preceding calendar year to develop and commercialize LICENSED PRODUCTS or LICENSED PROCESSES. The report shall also contain a discussion of intended efforts and sales projections for the year in which the report is submitted.

(c)   COMPANY shall develop a working model on or before _____, 200___, and permit an in-plant inspection by M.I.T. on or before _____, 200___, and thereafter permit in-plant inspections by M.I.T. at regular intervals with at least _____ ( ) months between each such inspection.

(d)   COMPANY shall make a first commercial sale of a LICENSED PRODUCT and/or a first commercial performance of a LICENSED PROCESS on or before _____, 200___.

(e)   COMPANY shall make NET SALES according to the following schedule:

_____	$_____;
_____	$_____;
_____ and each year thereafter	$_____.

(f)   COMPANY shall sell the following numbers of LICENSED PRODUCTS according to the following schedule:

200___	_____ units;
200___	_____ units;
200___ and each year thereafter	_____ units.

In the event that M.I.T. determines that COMPANY (or an AFFILIATE or SUBLICENSEE) has failed to fulfill any of its obligations under this Section 3.1, then M.I.T. may treat such failure as a material breach in accordance with Section 12.3(b).

4. ROYALTIES AND PAYMENT TERMS.

4.1 Consideration for Grant of Rights.

(a) License Issue Fee and Patent Cost Reimbursement. COMPANY shall pay to M.I.T. on the EFFECTIVE DATE a license issue fee of [number] dollars ($#), and, in accordance with Section 6.3, shall reimburse M.I.T. for its actual expenses incurred as of the EFFECTIVE DATE in connection with obtaining the PATENT RIGHTS. These payments are nonrefundable.

(b) License Maintenance Fees. COMPANY shall pay to M.I.T. the following license maintenance fees on the dates set forth below:

[January 1, year]	**[dollar amount]**
[January 1, year]	**[dollar amount]**
[and each January 1 of	
every year thereafter]	**[dollar amount]**

This annual license maintenance fee is nonrefundable; however, the license maintenance fee may be credited to running royalties subsequently due on NET SALES earned during the same calendar year, if any. License maintenance fees paid in excess of running royalties due in such calendar year shall not be creditable to amounts due for future years.

(c) Running Royalties. COMPANY shall pay to M.I.T. a running royalty of [number] percent (#%) of NET SALES by COMPANY, AFFILIATES and SUBLICENSEES. Running royalties shall be payable for each REPORTING PERIOD and shall be due to M.I.T. within sixty (60) days of the end of each REPORTING PERIOD.

(d) Sharing of SUBLICENSE INCOME. COMPANY shall pay M.I.T. a total of fifty percent (50%) of all SUBLICENSE INCOME received by COMPANY or AFFILIATES, excluding running royalties on NET SALES of SUBLICENSEES. Such amount shall be payable for each REPORTING PERIOD and shall be due to M.I.T. within sixty (60) days of the end of each REPORTING PERIOD.

(e) No Multiple Royalties. If the manufacture, use, lease, or sale of any LICENSED PRODUCT or the performance of any LICENSED PROCESS is covered by more than one of the PATENT RIGHTS, multiple royalties shall not be due.

4.2 Payments.

(a) Method of Payment. All payments under this Agreement should be made payable to "Montana Institute of Technology" and sent to the address identified in Section 14.1. Each payment should reference this Agreement and identify the obligation under this Agreement that the payment satisfies.

(b)   Payments in U.S. Dollars. All payments due under this Agreement shall be drawn on a United States bank and shall be payable in United States dollars. Conversion of foreign currency to U.S. dollars shall be made at the conversion rate existing in the United States (as reported in the Wall Street Journal) on the last working day of the calendar quarter of the applicable REPORTING PERIOD. Such payments shall be without deduction of exchange, collection, or other charges, and, specifically, without deduction of withholding or similar taxes or other government imposed fees or taxes, except as permitted in the definition of NET SALES.

(c)   Late Payments. Any payments by COMPANY that are not paid on or before the date such payments are due under this Agreement shall bear interest, to the extent permitted by law, at two percentage points above the Prime Rate of interest as reported in the Wall Street Journal on the date payment is due.

5. REPORTS AND RECORDS.

5.1 Frequency of Reports.

(a)   Before First Commercial Sale. Prior to the first commercial sale of any LICENSED PRODUCT or first commercial performance of any LICENSED PROCESS, COMPANY shall deliver reports to M.I.T. annually, within sixty (60) days of the end of each calendar year, containing information concerning the immediately preceding calendar year, as further described in Section 5.2.

(b)   Upon First Commercial Sale of a LICENSED PRODUCT or Commercial Performance of a LICENSED PROCESS. COMPANY shall report to M.I.T. the date of first commercial sale of a LICENSED PRODUCT and the date of first commercial performance of a LICENSED PROCESS within sixty (60) days of occurrence in each country.

(c)   After First Commercial Sale. After the first commercial sale of a LICENSED PRODUCT or first commercial performance of a LICENSED PROCESS, COMPANY shall deliver reports to M.I.T. within sixty (60) days of the end of each REPORTING PERIOD, containing information concerning the immediately preceding REPORTING PERIOD, as further described in Section 5.2.

5.2 Content of Reports and Payments. Each report delivered by COMPANY to M.I.T. shall contain at least the following information for the immediately preceding REPORTING PERIOD:

(i) the number of LICENSED PRODUCTS sold, leased or distributed by COMPANY, its AFFILIATES and SUBLICENSEES to independent third parties in each country, and, if applicable, the number of LICENSED PRODUCTS used by COMPANY, its AFFILIATES and SUBLICENSEES in the provision of services in each country;

(ii) a description of LICENSED PROCESSES performed by COMPANY, its AFFILIATES and SUBLICENSEES in each country as may be pertinent to a royalty accounting hereunder;

(iii) the gross price charged by COMPANY, its AFFILIATES and SUBLICENSEES for each LICENSED PRODUCT and, if applicable, the gross price charged for each LICENSED PRODUCT used to provide services in each country; and the gross price charged for each LICENSED PROCESS performed by COMPANY, its AFFILIATES and SUBLICENSEES in each country;

(iv) calculation of NET SALES for the applicable REPORTING PERIOD in each country, including a listing of applicable deductions;

(v) total royalty payable on NET SALES in U.S. dollars, together with the exchange rates used for conversion;

(vi) the amount of SUBLICENSE INCOME received by COMPANY from each SUBLICENSEE and the amount due to M.I.T. from such SUBLICENSE INCOME, including an itemized breakdown of the sources of income comprising the SUBLICENSE INCOME; and

(vii) the number of sublicenses entered into for the PATENT RIGHTS, LICENSED PRODUCTS and/or LICENSED PROCESSES.

If no amounts are due to M.I.T. for any REPORTING PERIOD, the report shall so state.

5.3 <u>Financial Statements</u>. On or before the ninetieth (90th) day following the close of COMPANY's fiscal year, COMPANY shall provide M.I.T. with COMPANY's financial statements for the preceding fiscal year including, at a minimum, a balance sheet and an income statement, certified by COMPANY's treasurer or chief financial officer or by an independent auditor.

5.4 <u>Records</u>. COMPANY shall maintain, and shall cause its AFFILIATES and SUBLICENSEES to maintain, complete and accurate records relating to the rights and obligations under this Agreement and any amounts payable to M.I.T. in relation to this Agreement, which records shall contain sufficient information to permit M.I.T. to confirm the accuracy of any reports delivered to M.I.T. and compliance in other respects with this Agreement. The relevant party shall retain such records for at least five (5) years following the end of the calendar year to which they pertain, during which time M.I.T., or M.I.T.'s appointed agents, shall have the right, at M.I.T.'s expense, to inspect such records during normal business hours to verify any reports and payments made or compliance in other respects under this Agreement. In the event that any audit performed under this Section reveals an underpayment in excess of five percent (5%), COMPANY shall bear the full cost of such audit and shall remit any amounts due to M.I.T. within thirty (30) days of receiving notice thereof from M.I.T.

6. PATENT PROSECUTION.

6.1 <u>Responsibility for PATENT RIGHTS</u>. M.I.T. shall prepare, file, prosecute, and maintain all of the PATENT RIGHTS. COMPANY shall have reasonable opportunities to advise M.I.T. and shall cooperate with M.I.T. in such filing, prosecution and maintenance.

6.2 <u>International (non-United States) Filings</u>. <u>Appendix B</u> is a list of countries in which patent applications corresponding to the United States patent applications listed in <u>Appendix A</u> shall be filed, prosecuted, and maintained. <u>Appendix B</u> may be amended by mutual agreement of COMPANY and M.I.T.

6.3 <u>Payment of Expenses</u>. Payment of all fees and costs, including attorneys fees, relating to the filing, prosecution and maintenance of the PATENT RIGHTS shall be the responsibility of COMPANY, whether such amounts were incurred before or after the EFFECTIVE DATE. As of _____, M.I.T. has incurred approximately $_____ for such patent-related fees and costs. COMPANY shall reimburse all amounts due pursuant to this Section within thirty (30) days of invoicing; late payments shall accrue interest pursuant to Section 4.2(c). In all instances, M.I.T. shall pay the fees prescribed for large entities to the United States Patent and Trademark Office.

7. INFRINGEMENT.

7.1 <u>Notification of Infringement</u>. Each party agrees to provide written notice to the other party promptly after becoming aware of any infringement of the PATENT RIGHTS.

7.2 <u>Right to Prosecute Infringements</u>.

(a)   COMPANY Right to Prosecute. So long as COMPANY remains the exclusive licensee of the PATENT RIGHTS in the FIELD in the TERRITORY, COMPANY, to the extent permitted by law, shall have the right, under its own control and at its own expense, to prosecute any third party infringement of the PATENT RIGHTS in the FIELD in the TERRITORY, subject to Sections 7.4 and 7.5. If required by law, M.I.T. shall permit any action under this Section to be brought in its name, including being joined as a party-plaintiff, provided that COMPANY shall hold M.I.T. harmless from, and indemnify M.I.T. against, any costs, expenses, or liability that M.I.T. incurs in connection with such action.

Prior to commencing any such action, COMPANY shall consult with M.I.T. and shall consider the views of M.I.T. regarding the advisability of the proposed action and its effect on the public interest. COMPANY shall not enter into any settlement, consent judgment, or other voluntary final disposition of any infringement action under this Section without the prior written consent of M.I.T.

(b)   M.I.T. Right to Prosecute. In the event that COMPANY is unsuccessful in persuading the alleged infringer to desist or fails to have initiated an infringement action within a reasonable time after COMPANY first becomes aware of the basis for such action, M.I.T. shall have the right, at its sole discretion, to prosecute such infringement under its sole control and at its sole expense, and any recovery obtained shall belong to M.I.T.

7.3 <u>Declaratory Judgment Actions</u>. In the event that a declaratory judgment action is brought against M.I.T. or COMPANY by a third party alleging invalidity, unenforceability, or non-infringement of the PATENT RIGHTS, M.I.T., at its option, shall have the right within twenty (20) days after commencement of such action to take over the sole defense of the action at its own expense. If M.I.T. does not exercise this right, COMPANY may take over the sole defense of the action at COMPANY's sole expense, subject to Sections 7.4 and 7.5.

7.4 <u>Offsets</u>. COMPANY may offset a total of fifty percent (50%) of any expenses incurred under Sections 7.2 and 7.3 against any payments due to M.I.T. under Article 4, provided that in no event shall such payments under Article 4, when aggregated with any other offsets and credits allowed under this Agreement, be reduced by more than fifty percent (50%) in any REPORTING PERIOD.

7.5 <u>Recovery</u>. Any recovery obtained in an action brought by COMPANY under Sections 7.2 or 7.3 shall be distributed as follows: (i) each party shall be reimbursed for any expenses incurred in the action (including the amount of any royalty or other payments withheld from M.I.T. as described in Section 7.4), (ii) as to ordinary damages, COMPANY shall receive an amount equal to its lost profits or a reasonable royalty on the infringing sales, or whichever measure of damages the court shall have applied, and COMPANY shall pay to M.I.T. based upon such amount a reasonable approximation of the royalties and other amounts that COMPANY would have paid to M.I.T. if COMPANY had sold the infringing products, processes and services rather than the infringer, and (iii) as to special or punitive damages, the parties shall share equally in any award.

7.6 <u>Cooperation</u>. Each party agrees to cooperate in any action under this Article which is controlled by the other party, provided that the controlling party reimburses the cooperating party promptly for any costs and expenses incurred by the cooperating party in connection with providing such assistance.

7.7 <u>Right to Sublicense</u>. So long as COMPANY remains the exclusive licensee of the PATENT RIGHTS in the FIELD in the TERRITORY, COMPANY shall have the sole right to sublicense any alleged infringer in the FIELD in the TERRITORY for future use of the PATENT RIGHTS in accordance with the terms and conditions of this Agreement relating to sublicenses. Any upfront fees as part of such sublicense shall be shared equally between COMPANY and M.I.T.; other revenues to COMPANY pursuant to such sublicense shall be treated as set forth in Article 4.

8. INDEMNIFICATION AND INSURANCE.

8.1 Indemnification.

(a)   Indemnity. COMPANY shall indemnify, defend, and hold harmless M.I.T. and its trustees, officers, faculty, students, employees, and agents and their respective successors, heirs and assigns (the "Indemnitees"), against any liability, damage, loss, or expense (including reasonable attorneys fees and expenses) incurred by or imposed upon any of the Indemnitees in connection with any claims, suits, actions, demands or judgments arising out of any theory of liability (including without limitation actions in the form of tort, warranty, or strict liability and regardless of whether such action has any factual basis) concerning any product, process, or service that is made, used, sold, imported, or performed pursuant to any right or license granted under this Agreement.

(b)   Procedures. The Indemnitees agree to provide COMPANY with prompt written notice of any claim, suit, action, demand, or judgment for which indemnification is sought under this Agreement. COMPANY agrees, at its own expense, to provide attorneys reasonably acceptable to M.I.T. to defend against any such claim. The Indemnitees shall cooperate fully with COMPANY in such defense and will permit COMPANY to conduct and control such defense and the disposition of such claim, suit, or action (including all decisions relative to litigation, appeal, and settlement); provided, however, that any Indemnitee shall have the right to retain its own counsel, at the expense of COMPANY, if representation of such Indemnitee by the counsel retained by COMPANY would be inappropriate because of actual or potential differences in the interests of such Indemnitee and any other party represented by such counsel. COMPANY agrees to keep M.I.T. informed of the progress in the defense and disposition of such claim and to consult with M.I.T. with regard to any proposed settlement.

8.2 Insurance. COMPANY shall obtain and carry in full force and effect commercial general liability insurance, including product liability and errors and omissions insurance which shall protect COMPANY and Indemnitees with respect to events covered by Section 8.1(a) above. Such insurance (i) shall be issued by an insurer licensed to practice in the State of Montana or an insurer pre-approved by M.I.T., such approval not to be unreasonably withheld, (ii) shall list M.I.T. as an additional insured thereunder, (iii) shall be endorsed to include product liability coverage, and (iv) shall require thirty (30) days written notice to be given to M.I.T. prior to any cancellation or material change thereof. The limits of such insurance shall not be less than One Million Dollars ($1,000,000) per occurrence with an aggregate of Three Million Dollars ($3,000,000) for bodily injury including death; One Million Dollars ($1,000,000) per occurrence with an aggregate of Three Million Dollars ($3,000,000) for property damage; and One Million Dollars ($1,000,000) per occurrence with an aggregate of Three Million Dollars ($3,000,000) for errors and omissions. In the alternative, COMPANY may self-insure subject to prior approval of M.I.T. COMPANY shall provide M.I.T. with Certificates of Insurance evidencing compliance with this Section. COMPANY shall continue to maintain such insurance or self-insurance after the expiration or termination of this Agreement during any period in which COMPANY or any AFFILIATE or SUBLICENSEE continues (i) to make, use, or sell a product that was a LICENSED

PRODUCT under this Agreement or (ii) to perform a service that was a LICENSED PROCESS under this Agreement, and thereafter for a period of five (5) years.

9. NO REPRESENTATIONS OR WARRANTIES.

EXCEPT AS MAY OTHERWISE BE EXPRESSLY SET FORTH IN THIS AGREEMENT, M.I.T. MAKES NO REPRESENTATIONS OR WARRANTIES OF ANY KIND CONCERNING THE PATENT RIGHTS, EXPRESS OR IMPLIED, INCLUDING WITHOUT LIMITATION WARRANTIES OF MERCHANTABILITY, FITNESS FOR A PARTICULAR PURPOSE, NONINFRINGEMENT, VALIDITY OF PATENT RIGHTS CLAIMS, WHETHER ISSUED OR PENDING, AND THE ABSENCE OF LATENT OR OTHER DEFECTS, WHETHER OR NOT DISCOVERABLE. Specifically, and not to limit the foregoing, M.I.T. makes no warranty or representation (i) regarding the validity or scope of the PATENT RIGHTS, and (ii) that the exploitation of the PATENT RIGHTS or any LICENSED PRODUCT or LICENSED PROCESS will not infringe any patents or other intellectual property rights of M.I.T. or of a third party.

IN NO EVENT SHALL M.I.T., ITS TRUSTEES, DIRECTORS, OFFICERS, EMPLOYEES AND AFFILIATES BE LIABLE FOR INCIDENTAL OR CONSEQUENTIAL DAMAGES OF ANY KIND, INCLUDING ECONOMIC DAMAGES OR INJURY TO PROPERTY AND LOST PROFITS, REGARDLESS OF WHETHER M.I.T. SHALL BE ADVISED, SHALL HAVE OTHER REASON TO KNOW, OR IN FACT SHALL KNOW OF THE POSSIBILITY OF THE FOREGOING.

10. ASSIGNMENT.

This Agreement is personal to COMPANY and no rights or obligations may be assigned by COMPANY without the prior written consent of M.I.T. M.I.T. shall have the right to terminate this Agreement immediately upon written notice to COMPANY upon a purchase of a majority of COMPANY's outstanding voting securities in a single transaction by a third party without M.I.T.'s prior written consent.

11. GENERAL COMPLIANCE WITH LAWS

11.1 Compliance with Laws. COMPANY shall use reasonable commercial efforts to comply with all commercially material local, state, federal, and international laws and regulations relating to the development, manufacture, use, and sale of LICENSED PRODUCTS and LICENSED PROCESSES.

11.2 Export Control. COMPANY and its AFFILIATES and SUBLICENSEES shall comply with all United States laws and regulations controlling the export of certain commodities and technical data, including without limitation all Export Administration Regulations of the United States Department of Commerce. Among other things, these laws and regulations prohibit or require a license for the export of certain types of commodities and technical data to specified countries. COMPANY hereby gives written assurance that it will comply with, and will cause its AFFILIATES and SUBLICENSEES to comply with, all United States export control laws and regulations, that it bears sole responsibility for any violation of such laws and regulations by itself or its AFFILIATES or SUBLICENSEES, and that it will indemnify, defend, and hold M.I.T. harmless (in accordance with Section 8.1) for the consequences of any such violation.

11.3 <u>Non-Use of M.I.T. Name</u>. COMPANY and its AFFILIATES and SUBLICENSEES shall not use the name of "Montana Institute of Technology," "Missoula Laboratory" or any variation, adaptation, or abbreviation thereof, or of any of its trustees, officers, faculty, students, employees, or agents, or any trademark owned by M.I.T., or any terms of this Agreement in any promotional material or other public announcement or disclosure without the prior written consent of M.I.T. The foregoing notwithstanding, without the consent of M.I.T., COMPANY may state that it is licensed by M.I.T. under one or more of the patents and/or patent applications comprising the PATENT RIGHTS.

11.4 <u>Marking of LICENSED PRODUCTS</u>. To the extent commercially feasible and consistent with prevailing business practices, COMPANY shall mark, and shall cause its AFFILIATES and SUBLICENSEES to mark, all LICENSED PRODUCTS that are manufactured or sold under this Agreement with the number of each issued patent under the PATENT RIGHTS that applies to such LICENSED PRODUCT.

12. TERMINATION.

12.1 <u>Voluntary Termination by COMPANY</u>. COMPANY shall have the right to terminate this Agreement, for any reason, (i) upon at least six (6) months prior written notice to M.I.T., such notice to state the date at least six (6) months in the future upon which termination is to be effective, and (ii) upon payment of all amounts due to M.I.T. through such termination effective date.

12.2 <u>Cessation of Business</u>. If COMPANY ceases to carry on its business related to this Agreement, M.I.T. shall have the right to terminate this Agreement immediately upon written notice to COMPANY.

12.3 <u>Termination for Default</u>.

(a)   <u>Nonpayment</u>. In the event COMPANY fails to pay any amounts due and payable to M.I.T. hereunder, and fails to make such payments within thirty (30) days after receiving written notice of such failure, M.I.T. may terminate this Agreement immediately upon written notice to COMPANY.

(b)   <u>Material Breach</u>. In the event COMPANY commits a material breach of its obligations under this Agreement, except for breach as described in Section 12.3(a), and fails to cure that breach within sixty (60) days after receiving written notice thereof, M.I.T. may terminate this Agreement immediately upon written notice to COMPANY.

12.4 Effect of Termination.

(a) Survival. The following provisions shall survive the expiration or termination of this Agreement: Articles 1, 8, 9, 13 and 14, and Sections 5.2 (obligation to provide final report and payment), 5.4, 11.1, 11.2 and 12.4.

(b) Inventory. Upon the early termination of this Agreement, COMPANY and its AFFILIATES and SUBLICENSEES may complete and sell any work-in-progress and inventory of LICENSED PRODUCTS that exist as of the effective date of termination, provided that (i) COMPANY pays M.I.T. the applicable running royalty or other amounts due on such sales of LICENSED PRODUCTS in accordance with the terms and conditions of this Agreement, and (ii) COMPANY and its AFFILIATES and SUBLICENSEES shall complete and sell all work-in-progress and inventory of LICENSED PRODUCTS within six (6) months after the effective date of termination.

(c) Pre-termination Obligations. In no event shall termination of this Agreement release COMPANY, AFFILIATES, or SUBLICENSEES from the obligation to pay any amounts that became due on or before the effective date of termination.

13. DISPUTE RESOLUTION.

13.1 Mandatory Procedures. The parties agree that any dispute arising out of or relating to this Agreement shall be resolved solely by means of the procedures set forth in this Article, and that such procedures constitute legally binding obligations that are an essential provision of this Agreement. If either party fails to observe the procedures of this Article, as may be modified by their written agreement, the other party may bring an action for specific performance of these procedures in any court of competent jurisdiction.

13.2 Equitable Remedies. Although the procedures specified in this Article are the sole and exclusive procedures for the resolution of disputes arising out of or relating to this Agreement, either party may seek a preliminary injunction or other provisional equitable relief if, in its reasonable judgment, such action is necessary to avoid irreparable harm to itself or to preserve its rights under this Agreement.

13.3 Dispute Resolution Procedures.

(a) Mediation. In the event any dispute arising out of or relating to this Agreement remains unresolved within sixty (60) days from the date the affected party informed the other party of such dispute, either party may initiate mediation upon written notice to the other party ("Notice Date"), whereupon both parties shall be obligated to engage in a mediation proceeding under the then current Center for Public Resources ("CPR") Model Procedure for Mediation of Business Disputes (http://www.cpradr.org), except that specific provisions of this Article shall override inconsistent provisions of the CPR Model Procedure. The mediator will be selected from the CPR Panels of Neutrals. If the parties cannot agree upon the selection of a mediator within fifteen (15) business days after the Notice Date, then upon the request of either party, the CPR shall appoint the mediator. The parties shall attempt to resolve the dispute through mediation until the first of the following occurs: (i) the parties reach a written settlement; (ii) the mediator notifies the parties in writing that they have reached an impasse; (iii) the parties agree in writing that they have reached an impasse; or (iv) the parties have not reached a settlement within sixty (60) days after the Notice Date.

(b)   Trial Without Jury. If the parties fail to resolve the dispute through mediation, or if neither party elects to initiate mediation, each party shall have the right to pursue any other remedies legally available to resolve the dispute, provided, however, that the parties expressly waive any right to a jury trial in any legal proceeding under this Article.

13.4 Performance to Continue. Each party shall continue to perform its undisputed obligations under this Agreement pending final resolution of any dispute arising out of or relating to this Agreement; provided, however, that a party may suspend performance of its undisputed obligations during any period in which the other party fails or refuses to perform its undisputed obligations. Nothing in this Article is intended to relieve COMPANY from its obligation to make undisputed payments pursuant to Articles 4 and 6 of this Agreement.

13.5 Statute of Limitations. The parties agree that all applicable statutes of limitation and time-based defenses (such as estoppel and laches) shall be tolled while the procedures set forth in Sections 13.3(a) are pending. The parties shall cooperate in taking any actions necessary to achieve this result.

14. MISCELLANEOUS.

14.1 Notice. Any notices required or permitted under this Agreement shall be in writing, shall specifically refer to this Agreement, and shall be sent by hand, recognized national overnight courier, confirmed facsimile transmission, confirmed electronic mail, or registered or certified mail, postage prepaid, return receipt requested, to the following addresses or facsimile numbers of the parties:

If to M.I.T.:   Montana Institute of Technology
                Office of Technology Transfer
                101 East Main Street
                Missoula, MT 59802-4458
                Attention: Director
                Tel: 406-253-6966
                Fax: 406-258-6790

If to COMPANY: _____

                     _____

_____

_____

Attention: _____

Tel:_____

Fax: _____

All notices under this Agreement shall be deemed effective upon receipt. A party may change its contact information immediately upon written notice to the other party in the manner provided in this Section.

14.2 <u>Governing Law</u>. This Agreement and all disputes arising out of or related to this Agreement, or the performance, enforcement, breach or termination hereof, and any remedies relating thereto, shall be construed, governed, interpreted and applied in accordance with the laws of the State of Montana, U.S.A., without regard to conflict of laws principles, except that questions affecting the construction and effect of any patent shall be determined by the law of the country in which the patent shall have been granted.

14.3 <u>Force Majeure</u>. Neither party will be responsible for delays resulting from causes beyond the reasonable control of such party, including without limitation fire, explosion, flood, war, strike, or riot, provided that the nonperforming party uses commercially reasonable efforts to avoid or remove such causes of nonperformance and continues performance under this Agreement with reasonable dispatch whenever such causes are removed.

14.4 <u>Amendment and Waiver</u>. This Agreement may be amended, supplemented, or otherwise modified only by means of a written instrument signed by both parties. Any waiver of any rights or failure to act in a specific instance shall relate only to such instance and shall not be construed as an agreement to waive any rights or fail to act in any other instance, whether or not similar.

14.5 <u>Severability</u>. In the event that any provision of this Agreement shall be held invalid or unenforceable for any reason, such invalidity or unenforceability shall not affect any other provision of this Agreement, and the parties shall negotiate in good faith to modify the Agreement to preserve (to the extent possible) their original intent. If the parties fail to reach a modified agreement within thirty (30) days after the relevant provision is held invalid or unenforceable, then the dispute shall be resolved in accordance with the procedures set forth in Article 13. While the dispute is pending resolution, this Agreement shall be construed as if such provision were deleted by agreement of the parties.

14.6 <u>Binding Effect</u>. This Agreement shall be binding upon and inure to the benefit of the parties and their respective permitted successors and assigns.

14.7 <u>Headings</u>. All headings are for convenience only and shall not affect the meaning of any provision of this Agreement.

14.8 <u>Entire Agreement</u>. This Agreement constitutes the entire agreement between the parties with respect to its subject matter and supersedes all prior agreements or understandings between the parties relating to its subject matter.

IN WITNESS WHEREOF, the parties have caused this Agreement to be executed by their duly authorized representatives.

The EFFECTIVE DATE of this Agreement is _____.

MONTANA INSTITUTE OF   TECHLICENSEE, INC.
TECHNOLOGY

By:_____DRAFT_____   By: _____DRAFT_____
Name:_____   Name: _____
Title:_____   Title: _____

APPENDIX A

List of Patent Applications and Patents

I.   United States Patents and Applications

II.   International (non-U.S.) Patents and Applications

APPENDIX B

List of Countries (excluding United States) for which PATENT RIGHTS Applications Will Be Filed, Prosecuted and Maintained

Printed in the USA/Agawam, MA
November 18, 2010

555180.039